SENTENCIN

by Richard Powell

with

Rhian Spink and Alessandro Roveri

em is
intellectual technology

© Richard Powell 2003

Published by
emis professional publishing ltd
31–33 Stonehills House
Welwyn Garden City
Hertfordshire
AL8 6PU

ISBN 1 85811 316 4

Typeset by Jane Conway

Cover design by Jane Conway
Cover photography by Jon Adams

Printed in Great Britain by Lightning Source

CONTENTS

INTRODUCTION

This guide to sentencing is published in two formats and is accompanied by a regular quarterly update bringing developments in sentencing procedure and practice to the attention of the busy criminal practitioner.

The book you are now reading, either on paper or in its electronic form, brings together statutory material dealing with sentencing in both the magistrates' court and the Crown Court. To provide a more coherent picture of the sentencing regime we have decided to remove section numbers and to adapt the wording of statutory provisions so that some of the complicated but necessary cross-referencing between provisions can be avoided. However, the material is unashamedly drawn from statute. It provides the practitioner with all he or she will need to know in order to advise clients and to prepare for the sentencing part of criminal proceedings including breach proceedings and appeals. We have also included a commentary where we feel it would be helpful to state the approach of the higher courts. Whilst this part of the EMIS sentencing service is biased towards statutory materials, we hope to focus more on case law in the regular supplements. This is not to say that we will ignore statutory changes to sentencing, particularly the changes proposed under the Criminal Justice Bill.[1]

Sentencing is seldom out of the headlines. In the first month of 2003 debate has raged in the tabloids and broad sheets over the 'correct' sentencing policy in relation to those who burgle or carry guns. Much of the debate has been ill informed and has demonstrated that public awareness of sentencing policy is poor. Poor awareness leads inevitably to misunderstandings and a lowering in public confidence in the criminal justice system generally.

---

1. In the first chapter of this book, we refer to proposed changes in the sentencing regime set out in the Criminal Justice Bill. We do so to emphasise the dynamics of the sentencing exercise and to provide a hint of what is yet to come. The Bill, however, is not yet law and practitioners should be careful to avoid mistaking the law as it is with the law as the government would like it to be. Our supplements will provide a detailed commentary on the provisions of the Criminal Justice Bill when it is finally enacted.

This publication is not designed to add anything to the public debate. It sets out *for the practitioner* the statutory basis for sentencing in the magistrates' court and the Crown Court supplemented with case law and examples. The publication is intended for use in the court and in the solicitor's office. It will hopefully be of use to all professionals involved in the sentencing process including solicitors, barristers, legal advisers and perhaps even sentencers themselves.

We have endeavoured to produce a practical text and will continue to endeavour to provide practitioners with useful commentaries on the impressive and ambitious changes to the criminal justice system foreshadowed in the Queen's Speech in 2002. Our sister publication, *Magistrates' Courts' Practice* is particularly recommended as a companion purchase dealing as it does with practice and procedure across the wider range of disciplines in the magistrates' court.

We would like to express our thanks to Andrew Griffin at EMIS Professional Publishing for his patience and encouragement during the inception of this publication. We look forward to receiving your comments and views as well. This is intended to be a practical and useful guide to sentencing. If there are improvements to be made, we would be delighted to consider them.

We have tried to state the law as it is on 1 January 2003

Richard Powell
Alessandro Roveri
Rhian Spink

Exeter and Torquay
February 2003

TABLE OF CASES

TABLE OF STATUTES AND CONVENTIONS

Statutes

Conventions

TABLE OF STATUTORY INSTRUMENTS

CHAPTER 1
SENTENCING PRACTICE

Art or Science?

In criminal proceedings, once a defendant has been convicted of, or has pleaded guilty to, the matter or matters charged, the court will pass sentence. One thinks of the sentence as the punishment for the offence and in very general terms this is the aim of the sentencing exercise. However, there are many matters for the court to consider regarding which disposal is the most appropriate. Some sentences are an out-and-out punishment. In addition, the nature and length of certain sentences may seek to warn others of the consequences of certain criminal behaviour, or will seek to protect the public from further harm through the actions of the defendant. Certain court orders will, in addition to imposing a restriction on liberty, aim to provide support to the offender in an effort to prevent him or her from further offending in future.

Which sentence is appropriate depends on a number of factors. The seriousness of the offence will be one such aspect. The court will also consider whether the defendant has, whilst guilty of criminal behaviour, an explanation that makes the offence less serious than would normally be the case. There may also be some aspect of the offender's personal circumstances that shed a different light on the gravity of the offence or how it should be dealt with.

However, whilst it is noted above that sentences are normally imposed by way of punishment, there are disposals that would not be described as such. A defendant may be made the subject of an absolute discharge[1] or a conditional discharge[2] where the court feels that it is inexpedient to inflict punishment. If the defendant appears to the court to be suffering from mental illness, he may be made the subject of a hospital order to treat him for that illness.[3] Where a defendant faces more than one

---

1. Section 12, Powers of Criminal Courts (Sentencing) Act 2000.
2. Section 12, Powers of Criminal courts (Sentencing) Act 2000.
3. Section 37, Mental Health Act 1983.

offence, the court might single out one or more of those for punishment, but order no separate penalty on the remaining matters. Whilst the defendant might look upon it as a punishment, the court might simply order restitution for some loss suffered by an injured party by awarding compensation instead of dealing with him in any other way.[4]

Ancillary orders

When sentence is passed the court may also make certain ancillary orders (and in certain cases will be required to do so). These orders might not be regarded as a sentence, but do form part of the overall exercise of disposing of the case. Orders that fall under this category include matters such as the endorsement of driving licence and disqualification for vehicle related crimes,[5] exclusion from licensed premises,[6] orders for deprivation of property used, or intended to be used, for the purposes of committing a crime,[7] payment of prosecution costs, etc.

Types of sentence

There are a number of sentences available to the courts. The most common are absolute or conditional discharges, fines, community orders[8] and imprisonment. Which sentence will be utilised depends very much on the nature of the offence before the court, and the seriousness of the matter.

Considering the correct sentence

Courts have been reminded that criminal sentences are in almost every case intended to protect the public, whether by punishing the offender or reforming him, or deterring him and others, or all of these things.[9] It has been generally held that there were four principle aims of sentencing: retribution, deterrence, prevention and rehabilitation[10] although not all may be present in any given sentence. A fine is unlikely to offer any rehabilitation, but would reflect retribution. A fine might also act as a warning to others (particularly if it is a large sum).

---

4. Section 130(1), Powers of Criminal Courts (Sentencing) Act 2000.
5. See for example Schedule II, Road Traffic Offenders Act 1988.
6. Section 1, Licensed Premises (Exclusion of Certain Persons) Act 1980.
7. Section 143, Powers of Criminal Courts (Sentencing) Act 2000.
8. For example, community rehabilitation, community punishment and community punishment and rehabilitation orders, curfew orders, drug treatment and testing orders and drug abstinence orders.
9. Per Bingham CJ in *R* v *Howells and others* (1998) 162 JP 731 at page 736.
10. *R* v *Sargeant* [1974] 60 Cr App R 74.

A custodial sentence would be retribution, might act as a deterrent to others, and the defendant might get support from the probation services (especially whilst under licence) so far as rehabilitation is concerned. A community order would reflect a restriction on liberty and, through work with the probation services, be a means of preventing future offending, but might not be viewed as a deterrent to others.

Criminal Justice Act 1991

The Criminal Justice Act 1991 sought to advance a sentencing framework that addressed sentencing on a "just desserts" basis (where the punishment fits the crime and is a proportionate response to the seriousness of the offence). Probation Orders (now Community Rehabilitation Orders) that had traditionally been viewed as an order that afforded an element of social work became an order that was more focussed on restricting liberty. Many sentencing provisions have now been consolidated into

Powers of Criminal Courts (Sentencing) Act 2000

the Powers of Criminal Courts (Sentencing) Act 2000, but "just desserts" remains relevant. The approach requires the court to consider the seriousness of the offence, but the eventual sentence may also have regard to the circumstances of the defendant.

Approaching a sentencing exercise in a structured fashion, the court will have regard to the following factors (where the offence is not one where the sentence is fixed by law):

- Aggravating features of the offence (those matters that make the offence more serious than another offence of its type);

- Mitigating features of the offence (those matters that make the offence less serious than another offence of its type);

- Mitigating features relevant to the offender himself.

Aggravating features of the offence

The following matters are example of features that, if present, may aggravate the seriousness of the offence (this list is not exhaustive):

- Planned or sophisticated offending or professional hallmarks;

- Causing injury to another person;

- Putting people in fear;

- Offending against a vulnerable victim;

- Attempting to evade arrest;

- Use of a weapon;

- Deliberate kicking or biting;

- Offences committed against a person performing a public duty (for example, police officers) or on hospital premises;

- Abusing a position of trust;

- Offending whilst intoxicated;

- Group offending;

- Night time offending (for example, to commit a burglary);

- High value involved;

- Profit making element to the offending;

- Deliberately targeting a victim;

- Being the ringleader in a crime;

- Offending over a long period of time;

- TICs;

The court is also entitled to take into account other offences admitted by the offender but which do not give rise to convictions. The court is not obliged to take other offences into account when imposing sentence and certainly should not do so if the additional offending is more serious than the substantive offence awaiting sentence.

Powers of Criminal Courts (Sentencing) Act 2000

The Powers of Criminal Courts (Sentencing) Act 2000 makes the following provision for factors to be taken into account in sentencing.

Effect of previous convictions and of offending while on bail

In considering the seriousness of any offence, the court may take into account any previous convictions of the offender or any failure of his to respond to previous sentences.

In considering the seriousness of any offence committed while the offender was on bail, the court shall treat the fact that it was committed in those circumstances as an aggravating factor.[11]

---

11.   Section 151, Powers of Criminal Courts (Sentencing) Act 2000.

Increase in sentences for racial aggravation

Section 153,
Powers of Criminal
Courts (Sentencing)
Act 2000
Sections 29 to 32,
Crime and Disorder
Act 1998

Section 153, Powers of Criminal Courts (Sentencing) Act 2000 applies where a court is considering the seriousness of an offence other than one under sections 29 to 32, Crime and Disorder Act 1998 (racially-aggravated assaults, racially-aggravated criminal damage, racially-aggravated public order offences and racially aggravated harassment etc.).

If the offence was racially aggravated, the court:

- shall treat that fact as an aggravating factor (that is to say, a factor that increases the seriousness of the offence); and

- shall state in open court that the offence was so aggravated.

The Criminal Justice Bill will also require the court to consider the offender's culpability in committing the offence and the harm or risk of harm which the offence caused or was intended to cause.

As many offences may now be specifically charged as racially aggravated, with an increase in the maximum sentence, it should be noted that section 153, Powers of Criminal Courts (Sentencing) Act 2000 has a curious effect. It requires the court to aggravate the seriousness of the offence even though the sentence available has already been increased to reflect the aggravating factor in the crime. Similarly the provision requires the court to aggravate the seriousness of a single offence even where it has not been charged in its aggravated form. Arguably, a court doing so, as it is obliged to do by virtue of this provision, will sentence an offender for a more serious offence than that which he has been convicted of.

Mitigating Offence features

The following are examples of matters that may make an offence less serious than another of its type (or may stop the offence from being any more serious):

- Impulsive action;

- Low value;

- Provocation;

- Genuine mistake (where this does not amount to a defence to the offence) or accidental oversight;

- Single blow;

- Cessation of offending once requested to stop;

- No financial gain or commercial motive;

- Unsophisticated offending;

- Good motive that went too far.

Offender mitigation

Having provisionally determined the seriousness of the offence by having regard to any aggravating and then mitigating features present, the court will then look towards any mitigation afforded by the defendants own circumstances and determine whether any adjustment of the sentence is required. Offender mitigation might affect the type of sentence passed, or may affect the length of any sentence. Example of offender mitigation might be:

- A guilty plea entered at an early opportunity;

- Co-operation with the police;

- Previous good character (and especially positive good character, for example voluntary work in the community);[12]

- Evidence of genuine remorse;

- Voluntary restitution to the injured party;

- Age or health (physical or mental) of the defendant;[13]

- The family circumstances of the offender;

- Signs of reform;

- Serious consequences of custody.[14]

12. *R* v *Clark* (Joan) (1999) *The Times* January 27.
13. For example see *R* v *Bernard* (1996) *The Times* July 2 where it was held that a serious medical condition might enable a court to pass a shorter custodial sentence that it might normally impose, but that this was to be regarded as an act of mercy, rather than as a general principle to be applied in all cases, and that fact that an offender has a reduced life expectancy or requires treatment are not in themselves reasons to avoid a custodial sentence.
14. But note that the fact that a defendant may have to be kept away from other prisoners or that he would find it hard to adapt to prison life is not a relevant consideration for the sentencing court (*R* v *Parker (Andrew David)* [1996] 2 Cr App R (S) 275) (cf. *R* v *Holmes* [1979] 1 Cr App R (S) 214 where the appellant was found to be an exceptionally vulnerable offender).

Just desserts?

To summarise just desserts, the punishment should fit the crime. This approach does raise some questions, however. If the court sentences on the seriousness of the offence, how can a deterrent sentence ever be justified?

A further point arises in *R v Oliver* and *R v Little*.[15] In that case it was held that, once an offender qualified for a custodial sentence, the court was not precluded from passing on the same occasion custodial sentences for offences which did not themselves merit custody (albeit to run concurrently to the substantive sentence). This seems a little odd, as if a custodial disposal is not appropriate for the offence, how can the imposition of such a sentence fit the crime? In addition, whilst it may appear to be a technical point, consider this: the fact of a custodial disposal will appear on the defendant's record in future. This may have a serious impact if, for example, the offence which received such a "tidying up" sentence was one of failing to surrender to bail. Even if the failure to answer bail was a minor offence (such as a genuine mistake), the defendant may find the point hard to argue at any future bail application where a fear of failing to surrender is advanced by the prosecution.

Just Deserts and the Youth

As a matter of law, the statutory framework of determining offence seriousness that applies to adults applies equally to the youth court[16] and children and young persons.[17] However, the Judicial Studies Board has published guidelines for magistrates dealing with sentences in the Youth Court that seem to be at variance with the statutory approach in so far as the court is also required to have regard to the level of intervention required to prevent the defendant from re-offending. It is this approach, with suggested seriousness entry points provided by the Judicial Studies Board that creates the problem. Whilst one of the stated aims of the Youth Justice System is to prevent re-offending,[18] the need for intervention and the best order to address this, does not necessarily, in the published guidance, take into account whether the offence is serious enough to merit a community order, or so serious that only a custodial sentence may be imposed.

---

15. [1993] 2 All ER 9.
16. The youth court deals with defendants who are aged between ten and seventeen years inclusive. See the section on sentencing in the youth court below at page XX.
17. Any defendant aged ten to fourteen years is described as a child, and those aged fifteen to seventeen as young persons.
18. Section 37, Crime and Disorder Act 1998.

The traditional philosophy of sentencing

Since the Criminal Justice Act 1991 the main philosophy underpinning sentencing practice in the United Kingdom has been one of punishing an offender for what he has done. In this work, the principle is referred to as just desserts. It introduces a direct relationship between the offender's conduct and the punishment for it. It is based on proportionality.

However, whilst the focus of practice has been directed to just desserts, other principles continue to affect the sentencer's thoughts. Practitioners should consider the following principles which may be uppermost in the sentencer's mind.

Retribution

It is appropriate to visit society's condemnation and abhorrence of criminal behaviour by imposing a sentence which is a punishment in the sense that it is vindictive or retributive. Arguably minimum sentences do not withstand scrutiny by proportionality but may be justified by reference to retribution.

Deterrence

Similarly, minimum sentences are designed to deter others from following certain conduct. A sentence of deterrence is most likely to be effective if it sets an example for others. Again a deterrent sentence may not be proportionate as far as the offender or even his crime is concerned, however, it is justifiable because it will make others think twice. At the time of writing, deterrent sentences were confirmed in the case of those involved in the smuggling of illegal immigrants.[19]

Rehabilitation

Sentences may also rehabilitate. The just dessert's idealogue allows rehabilitative sentences by permitting a sentencer to reduce what would otherwise be a punitive sentence of custody to a community penalty such as a rehabilitation order. In such a case, there is a proportionate relationship between the crime and the punishment even allowing for the concept of seriousness.

---

19.   *The Times,* February 3 2003.

Restoration

Restorative justice characterises the menu of sentences available in the youth court for offenders under the age of 18 years. So far restorative justice has made little impact on sentencing practice for adults. The benefits of restorative justice are well documented but appropriate orders are simply not available in the adult court generally.

Prevention and Intervention

Sentencing practice in the youth court is moving away from sentences based on seriousness and moving towards sentences which will prevent re-offending. A similar process is beginning to be seen in interventionist orders in the adult court such as drug treatment and testing orders and drug abstinence orders.

So what?

Experience suggests that the principles of sentence play a less well defined role in the sentencing exercise than they deserve. The Criminal Justice Bill 2003 will place a greater emphasis on these principles without detracting from the overreaching concept that the punishment should fit the crime. Clause 126 of the Bill provides for the purpose of sentencing and requires that courts dealing with an offender to have regard to the following purposes of sentencing:

- The punishment of offenders

- The reduction of crime by deterrence, reform and rehabilitation

- The protection of the public

- The making of reparation.

The importance of the sentencing purpose is reinforced by the duty, under Clause 157, of sentencers to explain why they have chosen to impose a particular sentence. Although at present, we speculate, it seems to us that a court will be required to link the chosen sentence to one or more of the purposes of sentence and to state that it has done so with relevant, if brief, reasons for doing so.

Guidelines for sentencers

In the magistrates' court, the Magistrates' Court Sentencing Guidelines have been published to provide for some parity in sentencing. The sentencing court and practitioners should also consider decisions of the Court of Appeal in relation to sentencing. However, it should be borne in mind that those Court of Appeal decisions do not form part of the principle of binding precedent. They are guideline authorities to assist with sentencing. Any court that passes sentence must always remember that at the end of the day each case must be considered on its own particular facts.[20]

The Criminal Justice Bill introduces changes to this traditional approach. Clauses 151 to 156 establish the Sentencing Guidelines Council and amends to current functions of the Sentencing Advisory Panel. It is anticipated that the SGC will issue sentencing guidelines. Unlike the current arrangement whereby recommendations are made to the Court of Appeal for translation into guideline cases, the guidelines issued by the SGC will have to be taken into account by sentencers. The guidelines are certain to cause controversy; especially as they may effectively fetter a sentencer's discretion and are generated by a non-judicial agency. However, the aim of the SGC is to improve consistency across the country. Experience with the Magistrates' Courts' sentencing guidelines suggest that this is a positive development.

The totality principle

If an offender faces more than one offence, and the court imposes a sentence in respect of more than one, or all, of the matters before the court, it must consider the outcome and determine whether the total sentence is proper. To illustrate the point, D faces five matters of unsophisticated theft of low value items from shops. The court considers imposing a fine of £200 on each, a total of £1,000. The court considers that in light of the low value of the items the overall figure is too large and reduces it to a sum that can be paid within twelve months.

If the defendant is serving a sentence of imprisonment, and a court is passing a further custodial sentence on a subsequent occasion to the sentence already in force then, if the court is considering whether to make the new sentence consecutive or

---

20.   *R v De Havilland* 5 Cr App R (S) 109.

concurrent to the existing sentence, it must again have regard to the totality of the combined sentence.[21]

If the court is of the opinion that a sentence imposed on one offence sufficiently reflects the totality of the offending, it might elect to impose "no separate penalty" on the other matters.

General Principles

The sentencer and practitioner should be aware of certain authorities that are of general application when deciding on the most appropriate sentence.[22]

The effect on custodial sentences of aggravating and mitigating factors, and offender mitigation

R v Howells[23] provided the test for considering whether an offence was so serious that only a custodial sentence was appropriate. In that case, the former test ("would right-thinking members of the public, knowing all the facts, feel that justice had not been done by the passing of any sentence other than a custodial one?") was disapproved. This is because the sentencing court is bound to give effect to its own subjective judgment of what justice requires on the peculiar facts of the case before it. Instead in approaching cases that are at or near the custody threshold the court will usually find it helpful to begin by considering the following:

- the nature and extent of the defendant's criminal intention and the nature and extent of any injury or damage;

- other things being equal, an offence which is deliberate and premeditated will usually be more serious than one which is spontaneous and unpremeditated or which involves an excessive response to provocation;

- an offence which inflicts personal injury or mental trauma, particularly if permanent, will usually be more serious than one which inflicts financial loss only;

---

21. *R v Jones* [1996] 1 Cr App R (S) 153.
22. Much guidance can, of course, also be found in decisions of the Court of Appeal. Generally, decisions regarding the level of sentence are of persuasive authority only. However, the Court of Appeal may from time to time issue guidelines setting the range of sentences appropriate for classes of offences, highlighting the potential impact of aggravating and mitigating factors. Over time, the electronic supplements to this work will describe key guideline cases.
23   (1998) 162 JP 731.

Section 151(1)
and (2), Powers
of Criminal Courts
(Sentencing) Act
2000

- in accordance with section 151(1) and (2), Powers of Criminal Courts (Sentencing) Act 2000 when considering the seriousness of any offence the court may take into account any previous convictions of the offender or any failure to respond to previous sentences and shall treat as an aggravating factor any offence committed whilst on bail.

In deciding whether to impose a custodial sentence in borderline cases the sentencing court will ordinarily take account of matters relating to the offender:

- the court will have regard to an offender's admission of responsibility for the offence, particularly if reflected in a plea of guilty tendered at the earliest opportunity and accompanied by hard evidence of genuine remorse, as shown (for example) by an expression of regret to the victim and an offer of compensation;

- where offending has been fuelled by addiction to drink or drugs, the court will be inclined to look more favourably on an offender who has already demonstrated (by taking practical steps to that end) a genuine, self-motivated determination to address his addiction;

- youth and immaturity, while affording no defence, will often justify a less rigorous penalty than would be appropriate far an adult;

- Some measure of leniency will ordinarily be extended to offenders of previous good character, the more so if there is evidence of positive good character (such as a solid employment record or faithful discharge of family duties) as opposed to mere absence of previous convictions. It will sometimes be appropriate to take account of family responsibilities, or physical or mental disability;

- While the court will never impose a custodial sentence unless satisfied that it is necessary to do so, there will be an even greater reluctance to impose a custodial sentence on an offender who has never before served such a sentence.

In *R* v *Kefford*[24] the Court of Appeal raised the issue of prison overcrowding, and how this might affect the approach to be taken by sentencing courts. The decision (much like *R* v *Mills*[25] is not authority for suggesting that non-violent offenders (especially single parents) should never be imprisoned, as

---

24.   (2002) *The Times* March 7.
25.   (2002) January 30.

appears to be a common misconception. In *Kefford* it was held that only those who need to be sent to prison should go there, and that they should not be sent there than for any longer than is necessary. Nothing in that authority is intended to deter courts from sending to prison for the appropriate period those who commit offences involving violence or intimidation or other grave crimes. In the case of economic crimes, prison is not necessarily the only appropriate form of punishment, particularly for those of previous good character (for which appearance in court of itself was a form of punishment). The latter point is, in any event, one of the considerations in *Howells* (above) and therefore the decision in *Kefford* is something far short of groundbreaking. The judgment did, however, seek to reiterate a long standing principle which appears to be often forgotten, namely that having carefully decided upon a custodial disposal, the sentence should be as short as possible, consistent only with the duty to protect the interests of the public and to punish and deter the criminal.[26]

In contrast, *R* v *McMaster* and *R* v *Case*,[27] which involved offences of serious violence, prompted the Court of Appeal to voice its concerns that matters of this nature appeared to be on the rise and thus exemplary sentence were called for in such cases. It should also be noted that for short custodial sentences are not normally appropriate for assaults on police officers.[28]

Credit for timely guilty pleas

Section 152, Powers of Criminal Courts (Sentencing) Act 2000

Section 152, Powers of Criminal Courts (Sentencing) Act 2000 provides:

(a) In determining what sentence to pass on an offender who has pleaded guilty to an offence in proceedings before that or another court, a court shall take into account;

(b) the stage in the proceedings for the offence at which the offender indicated his intention to plead guilty; and

(c) the circumstances in which this indication was given.

(2) If, as a result of taking into account any matter referred above, the court imposes a punishment on the offender which is less severe than the punishment it would otherwise have imposed, it shall state in open court that it has done so.

---

26. For further comments regarding custodial sentences being no longer than is necessary, see *R* v *Bibi* [1980] 1 WLR 1193, *R* v *Ollerenshaw* (1998) *The Times* May 6, *R* v *Howells* (1998) 162 JP 731.

27. (1998) *The Times* February 20.

28. *R* v *Crimes* [1983] 5 Cr App R (S) 358.

The section reminds the court to allow a reduction in sentence for a guilty plea. Such credit may be applied in the case of a fine, community sentence or custodial sentence. In fact, the principle of credit for a guilty plea derives from case law. It will be noted from the wording of the section that a court is not obliged to give any credit for a guilty plea, and that no limit is imposed on just how much or how little credit may be afforded where there is an admission of guilt. Historically, an early guilty plea has attracted credit of up to one third.[29] In addition, those who have entered an indication of a guilty plea at a magistrates' court[30] and are committed to the Crown Court for sentence[31] are entitled to greater credit than those who enter a guilty plea to the indictment at the Crown Court[32] (indeed up to one quarter might be appropriate in such cases).[33]

In the past a number of authorities suggested no credit should be afforded where the defendant has no option but to plead guilty, for example, due to being caught red handed.[34] In our opinion it is unhelpful to take this approach. Whilst the evidence may be overwhelming, it is not unknown for technical defences to be argued by a defendant. If he is aware that there is a strong likelihood that he will receive no credit in any event, why should he not "play the system" and cause inconvenience to the courts and witnesses at public expense? If a defendant is aware that he may receive some credit, no matter how small this may be, should he not receive that? It would appear that support for this view can be found in *R v Fearon*[35] where it was held that courts should afford some discount no matter how strong the case against the defendant, but that credit in such cases might be slight. Consider also *R v Hussain*[36] – in that case a guilty plea was entered by the defendant on the day of trial.

---

29.   For example *R v Buffrey* [1993] 14 Cr App R (S) 511.
30.   In accordance with sections 17A to 17C, Magistrates' Courts Act 1980.
31.   See sections 3 and 4, Powers of Criminal Courts (Sentencing) Act 2000 (and in relation to summary offences and offences under section 6(1) or (2), Bail Act 1976 see section 6, Powers of Criminal Courts (Sentencing) Act 2000 and section 6(6), Bail Act 1976 respectively).
32.   *R v Rafferty* (1998) *The Times* April 9 (in addition, where the defendant is on bail, this case is also useful for any defence practitioner required to make representations as to the continuation of bail pending sentence at the Crown Court, as it disapproves *R v Coe* [1968] 53 Cr App R 66).
33.   *R v Barber* (reference unavailable).
34.   For example *R v Hastings* [1996] 1 Cr App R (S) 167.
35.   [1996] Crim LR 212.
36.   [2002] Crim LR 327.

On appeal against a refusal by the judge to allow any credit for the plea, the Court of Appeal made the following points:

Section 152,
Powers of Criminal
Courts (Sentencing)
Act 2000

(a) Section 152, Powers of Criminal Courts (Sentencing) Act 2000 does not oblige the courts to reduce any sentence, but instead places an obligation upon the court to consider whether any credit should be given for the plea;

(b) Whilst there were circumstances when it might be appropriate to reduce or disallow any credit for a guilty plea (for example, where the defendant is caught-red handed) it is the practice of the courts to encourage guilty pleas.

Accordingly, in *Hussain*, it was held that the guilty plea, even though entered on the day of the trial, was admitted in circumstances where the prosecution case could not be described as "overwhelming" and had the effect of saving witnesses from the strain of having to give evidence. In those circumstances the Court of Appeal held that the defendant should have received some credit for his plea.

In *R* v *March*[37] the Court of Appeal held:

(a) The giving of credit for guilty pleas could not be described as "mandatory";

(b) Advocates should be cautious about assuring their clients that they would receive credit for guilty pleas, and build into their advice a warning that credit for a guilty plea cannot necessarily be expected as there were exceptional circumstances where the court could decline to give any credit;

(c) To "take account" of a guilty plea meant just that – there is no rule of general application as to what credit may be afforded;

(d) Despite this, giving credit for guilty pleas was an important incentive to those charged with offences to enter such pleas and save the criminal justice system time and money – it is in the public interest not to undermine such a beneficial practice.

Credit for a guilty plea may be of relevance to the question of committal for sentence from a magistrates' court to the Crown Court where the offence is triable on indictment. In *R* v *Warley Magistrates' Court, ex parte the Director of Public Prosecutions and others*[38] magistrates were encouraged to utilise their full powers of

---

37.   [2002] Crim LR 509.
38.   (1998) 162 JP 559.

imprisonment to reflect credit for a guilty plea where they were able (i.e. by passing a six month sentence of imprisonment[39] for an offence which would normally merit a nine months at the Crown Court). In such circumstances, the court should indicate that it has only been able to retain jurisdiction to sentence because of the plea.

The principle applies equally to a reduction from eighteen months to twelve.[40]

However, in using the latter approach, the twelve-month period must reflect the totality of the offending. It is not permissible to use this approach as a device. By way of an example, D faces an allegation contrary to section 47, Offences Against the Person Act 1861 of assault occasioning actual bodily harm (ABH). He also faces an allegation of theft contrary to section 1, Theft Act 1968 committed on the same occasion. He pleads guilty to both matters. On the facts, the theft merits two month's imprisonment and the ABH eighteen months (before credits for the pleas are applied). The magistrates must not pass consecutive sentences of six months per offence to reach twelve months (reduced from eighteen), even in R v Wheatley[41] applies.[42] Had both offences merited nine months each and had been committed, say, on separate occasions, a sentence of twelve months would be permissible so long as the totality has been reflected.

At this stage, it is appropriate to mention that the basis upon which the court is to sentence must be clear. If there is any disagreement between the prosecution and defence as to the circumstances of the offence or offences, and the difference between them would materially affect the type, or length, of any sentence that may be passed, the court may order that evidence should be called. The court, having heard the evidence, would then indicate the basis on which it is to sentence. The hearing at which the facts would be decided is known as a Newton hearing,

(Margin note:) Section 47, Offences Against the Person Act 1861 Section 1, Theft Act 1968

---

39. Six months imprisonment is the maximum period available to a magistrates court for a single offence committed by an adult (section 78, Magistrates' Courts Act 1980).

40. Twelve months imprisonment is available to a magistrates' court where it has before it two or more offences triable either way (section 133(2), Magistrates' Courts Act 1980) but see the restrictions in the case of an offence triable either way where the value is below £5000 and the special provisions of section 22, Magistrates' Courts Act 1980 apply.

41. (1983) 5 Cr App R (S) 417.

42. Where it was held that consecutive sentence of imprisonment may be imposed for offences committed on the same occasion if there are exceptional circumstances which justify departure from the usual practice not to do so (said usual practice having been confirmed in, e.g., R v Jones [1980] 2 Cr App R (S) 152).

after the case of *R v Newton*.[43] The impact this procedure may have on magistrates allowing credit for a guilty plea and deciding whether to commit for sentence is as follows:

- If the case can be sentenced by the magistrates, they will conduct the Newton hearing;

- If it is obvious that, no matter what the outcome of the Newton hearing, the Crown Court will be required to pass sentence, the facts should be left for the Crown Court to decide;

- If the question of whether to commit depends on the result of the Newton hearing, the magistrates will determine the facts. If after such a hearing the justices determine their powers of sentence are insufficient, they may commit to the Crown Court (and should record their findings for the judge).[44]

One other aspect of allowing credit for a guilty plea – much of the above relates to a reduction in the sentence that is imposed. In *R v Howells* (above) it was held that a timely guilty plea, as an expression of remorse, might be a factor that, in a borderline custody case, has the effect of convincing the court that a non-custodial disposal is appropriate.

The relevance of previous convictions

After an offender has been convicted (whether after trial or by reason of his plea) the court must be provided with a statement of the defendant's record for the purposes of sentence. The record supplied should contain all previous convictions.[45] Those that are spent should, so far as practicable, be marked as such.[46] On a procedural point, no one should refer in open court to a spent conviction without the leave of the court, and this leave will not be granted unless it is in the interests of justice to do so.[47] When passing sentence, the court should make no reference to a spent conviction unless it is necessary for the purpose of explaining the sentence to be passed.[48]

A court considering the seriousness of any offence may take into account the previous convictions of the offender or any failure of

---

43. (1982) 4 Cr App R (S) 388.
44. *R v Warley Magistrates' Court, ex parte the Director of Public Prosecutions and others (supra)*.
45. Paragraph 6.5, Practice Direction of 8 July 2002 [2002] 3 All ER 904.
46. Paragraph 6.5, Practice Direction of 8 July 2002.
47. Paragraph 6.6, Practice Direction of 8 July 2002.
48. Paragraph 6.7, Practice Direction of 8 July 2002.

his to respond to previous sentences.[49] The first and most fundamental matter to arise in relation to the relevance of previous convictions is that the offender should be sentenced on the seriousness of the offence before the court, rather than for his previous record, as he has previously been punished for those matters.[50] Those who are called upon to sentence need to be circumspect in how they use previous convictions when deciding on the most appropriate sentence. Consider two examples, in each case where the defendant faces an offence of driving whilst disqualified. In the first, the defendant has a large number of previous convictions for unrelated matters. Apart from ascertaining whether, for example, he has previously complied with non-custodial disposals, the record may be of little value to the court. In the second example, the record shows that defendant has previously committed an identical offence within the same period of disqualification. It would seem odd if this could not be regarded as an aggravating feature.

From a defence point of view, perhaps one of the most significant aspects in relation to previous convictions is where there are relatively few, or none, previously recorded. In *R v Howells* (above), the fact that a defendant had never previously served a custodial sentence might provide strong offender mitigation in the case of an offence on the threshold of custody.

Practice Direction of 8 July 2002

The Practice Direction of 8 July 2002[51] provides the following guidance concerning a defendant's antecedents: In the Crown Court the police will provide brief details of the circumstances of the last three similar convictions and/or of convictions likely to be of interest to the court, the latter being judged on a case by case basis. This information should be provided separately and attached to the antecedents.[52] Where the current alleged offence could constitute a breach of an existing community order, e.g. community rehabilitation order, and it is known that that order is still in force then, to enable the court to consider the possibility of revoking that order, details of the circumstances of the offence leading to the community order should be included in the antecedents.[53]

The Criminal Justice Bill introduces further restrictions on the use of previous convictions in the sentencing exercise. Clause 127 requires the court to treat each previous conviction, if any, as an aggravating factor if the court considers that it can

---

49. Section 151(1), Powers of Criminal Courts (Sentencing) Act 2000.
50. *R v Queen* [1982] Crim LR 56.
51. [2002] 3 All ER.
52. Paragraph 27.1, Practice Direction of 8 July 2002 [2002] 3 All ER 904.
53. Paragraph 27.2, Practice Direction of 8 July 2002 [2002] 3 All ER 904.

reasonably be so treated having regard to the nature of the older offence and its relevance to the current offence and the time elapsed since that conviction.

Personal statements of victims

On 1 October 2001 a new scheme was introduced to give the victims of crime the opportunity to inform sentencers how they had been affected by crime, and for the court to take that information into account when deciding upon sentence. When the police take a statement from an injured party, they will inform that person of the scheme, and that person will then have an opportunity to make a victim personal statement.

Where there is a victim personal statement, the following points apply:

(a) The victim personal statement and any evidence in support should be considered and taken into account by the court prior to passing sentence.

(b) Evidence of the effects of an offence on the victim contained in the victim in the victim personal statement or other statement, must be in proper form, that is a witness statement made under section 9, Criminal Justice Act 1967 or an expert's report, and served upon the defendant's solicitor or the defendant, if he is not represented, prior to sentence. Except where inferences can properly be drawn from the nature of or circumstances surrounding the offence, a sentencer must not make assumptions unsupported by evidence about the effects of an offence on the victim.

Section 9, Criminal Justice Act 1967

(c) The court must pass what it judges to be the appropriate sentence having regard to the circumstances of the offence and of the offender, taking into account, so far as the court considers it appropriate, the consequences to the victim. The opinions of the victim's close relatives as to what the sentence should be are therefore not relevant, unlike the consequence of the offence on them. Victims should be advised of this. If, despite the advice, opinions as to sentence are included in the statement, the court should pay no attention to them.

(d) The court should consider whether it is desirable in its sentencing remarks to refer to the evidence provided on behalf of the victim.[54]

---

54.   Paragraph 28.2, Practice Direction of 8 July 2002 [2002] 3 All ER 904.

How much reliance the court should place on any such statement will depend greatly on its contents and the circumstances of the offence. It is probably the case that many victims may, understandably, be less than objective in their views. This is understandable, and may provide a graphic illustration as to how they have been affected by a crime. Alternatively, the court might consider the response to be an overreaction. On the reverse side of the argument, a defence advocate may wish the court to be fully aware of the contents of a victim personal statement where the maker expresses forgiveness towards the defendant. This, again, has its down side as the court may wish to disregard the comments when deciding on the sentence.

The Criminal Justice Bill 2003

At the time of final preparation of this book, Parliament was wrestling with the Criminal Justice Bill 2003. If the Bill is enacted in 2003, it will be the seventeenth statute since 1987 to introduce changes to criminal procedure. We do not wish to dismiss the public's concern over the criminal justice system but wonder whether there will ever come a time again when the courts are allowed to 'get on with the job' and are given time to do so without having to manage yet further change.

The Criminal Justice Bill proposes changes to the whole criminal justice system. Some of its provisions fall outside the scope of this work but will be dealt with in our sister publication, *Magistrates' Courts' Practice*. As far as sentencing is concerned, the Bill introduces philosophical changes, procedural changes and new orders and sentences. We will deal with these in due course when the Bill is enacted. Practitioners may find the following summary of changes to sentencing useful.

The Criminal Justice Bill

- Introduces a statutory purpose to sentencing

- Restates the test for assessing the seriousness of an offence by reference to the offender's culpability, requiring previous convictions to be treated as an aggravating factor as are offences committed on bail or which are religiously or racially motivated

- Replaces the current community orders menu of sentences with two orders only called a community order for adults or a youth community order for youths

- Introduces a power to impose a community order on an offender who has been convicted and fined on at least three occasions even where the offence is not otherwise serious enough for a community order

- Increases the maximum sentence of the magistrates' court to twelve months (65 weeks in respect of consecutive sentences)

- Allows Parliament to increase this maximum to 18 months (24 months in respect of consecutive sentences) by way of statutory instrument

- Establishes the Sentencing Guidelines Council and requires courts to have regard to any guidelines given by the SGC

- Imposes a duty on the court to explain why it has decided to impose a particular sentence

- Introduces a single community order which may include one or more of seventeen different requirements which may be of different durations. The requirements include an unpaid work requirement of between 40 and 300 hours, an activity requirement, a programme requirement, a curfew requirement, an exclusion requirement etc

- Provides for Rules to be made which will allow the courts to periodically review community orders

- Requires all sentences of custody of less than 12 months to be expressed in one of two ways

  - *A custody plus order*

    An order of between 28 and 51 weeks, of which at least 2 weeks but not more than 13 weeks is served in prison. The remainder is served in the community subject to one or more of a restricted number of the requirements which could be included in a community order; or

  - *An intermittent custody order*

    An order of between 28 and 51 weeks, of which at least 14 days but not more than 90 days is served in prison on days specified in the order. The remainder is served in the community subject to one or more of a restricted number of the requirements which could be included in a community order. The offender will be subject to the requirements on the days when he is not in custody

- Allows the court to set the period of licence and to attach a restricted number of the requirements which could be included in a community order

- Allows the court to impose a suspended sentence order which commits an offender to custody suspended subject to his compliance with a restricted number of the requirements which could be included in a community order

- Allows an offender who has indicated a not guilty plea or made no plea during the plea before venue procedure to request a binding indication from the magistrates dealing with mode of trial as to whether, if he pleaded guilty, they would be minded to impose either a custodial or an non-custodial sentence

- Increases the maximum sentences for the vast majority of summary only offences to reflect the changes in the maximum sentencing powers in the magistrates' court

Sentencing: An Overview

Having glimpsed the future of sentencing under the Criminal Justice Bill, practitioners may find the following summary of the current position to be a useful reminder

The court has a number of questions to ask itself during the sentencing stage:

- What are the facts in the case?

  The facts will either be those set out by the prosecution, established at trial or after a Newton hearing where the defence and prosecution version of events was irreconcilable and was likely to make a material difference to sentence, or in an agreed basis of plea

- What are the aggravating features of the offence?

- Is the offence racially or religiously motivated?

- Is the offence one committed whilst on bail?

- Does the defendant have any relevant previous convictions?

- What are the mitigating features of the offence?

- How serious is the offence?

- What offender mitigation bears on the likely sentence?

- Has the defendant pleaded guilty and if so, at what stage?

- Does the magistrates' court have sufficient power to sentence this defendant (in the case of either-way offences only)?

- Is the proposed sentence commensurate with the seriousness of the offence (and the offender's culpability)?

- Does the proposed sentence reflect the totality principle?

- Does the proposed sentence reflect credit for the defendant's previous good character, if any?

- Does the proposed sentence appropriately reflect credit for the defendant's early plea or cooperation?

- Looking at the maximum sentence available for this offence in this court, is the offender's culpability sufficient to justify the level of the proposed sentence (steer by the maximum; if there is a worse case to be imagined, then the defendant should not be given the maximum)?

- Does the offence attract any ancillary orders including disqualification and costs?

The Sentencing Matrix in the Magistrates' Court

	Orders of Discharge	Financial Penalty	Community Penalty Available	Commital for Sentence
Inexpedient to punish	x			
Appropriate to punish	x	x		Where a fine is appropriate but the level commensurate with the seriousness of the offence exceeds the statutory maximum of the magistrates' cout
Serious enough	x	x	x	Where a sentence of confinement is in excess of the magistrates' court's maximum would otherwise be appropriate
So serious	x	x	x	Where the length of custodial sentence, taking into account any credit for an early guilty plea, exceeds the maximum available in the magistrates' court.

These notes apply only to offences which are triable either-way.

Youth Court Sentencing Grid

Sentence and Relevant Statute	Age Range	Representation Order Essential?	Reports?
Fine, ss 135–138*	Any	No	No
Absolute Discharge	Any	No	No
Conditional Discharge	Any	No	No
Reparation Order, ss 73–75	Any	No	Yes – not PSR
"Serious Enough Threshold"			
Attendance Centre, ss 60–62	Any	No	No
Action Plan Order, ss 69–72	Any	No	Yes – not PSR
Supervision Order, ss 63–68	Any	No	PSR if add. req., medical if treatment imposed
Community Rehabilitation Order, ss 41–45	16–17	No	PSR if conditions imposed, medical if treatment imposed
Community Punishment Order, ss 46–50	16–17	No	PSR
Community Punishment and Rehabilitation Order, s 51	16–17	No	PSR and medical as for CRO
Curfew Order, ss 37–40	Any	No	Yes – re premises (and family if D under 16)
Drug Treatment and Testing Order, ss 52–58	16–17	No	PSR

* Statutory references are to the Powers of Criminal Courts (Sentencing) Act 2000.

Sentence and Relevant Statute	Age Range	Representation order Essential?	Reports?
"So Serious Threshold"			
Detention and Training Order, ss 100–107	12–17	Yes	PSR

Range	Not With Other Sentences?	Statutory Criteria?	Procedural Points
Up to £1,000 for 14–17 Up to £250 for 10–13	N/A	Means or means of parent/guardian	Parent/guardian may be made liable for payment
N/A	N/A	No	
Up to three years	N/A	No	Not available within 2 years of final warning
24 hrs work within three months	DTO, CPO, CPRO, SO with Sched 6 requirements, APO	No	
"Serious Enough Threshold"			
12 hrs min unless D is under 14 and 12 hrs excessive. 24 max (10–15) 36 max (16–17)	N/A	No	Centre must be available within reasonable distance of D's home. Imprisonable only.
Three mths – standard	DTO, CRO, CPO, CPRO, Attendance Centre, SO	Order must be desirable to ensure D's rehab or prevent further offending	Cannot be made if APO already in force. Imprisonable only if attendance centre included.
Up to three years	RO, APO	No	Requirements can be attached under Sched 6.

Range	Not With Other Sentences?	Statutory Criteria?	Procedural Points
Six months to three years	APO	Order must be desirable to secure D's rehab or protect the public from harm from him or prevent further offending	
40–240 hours all within twelve months	RO, APO	No	Imprisonable only
As for CRO and CPO above – but max 100 hours	RO, APO	Order must be desirable to secure D's rehab or protecting public from harm from him or prevent further offending	Imprisonable only
2–12 hours in any day. Max duration six mths (three if under 16)	N/A	No	May be electronically monitored by contractors.
Six months to three years	N/A	D is drug dependant or misuser and susceptible to treatment.	Offence must have been committed after 29 September 1998.
"So Serious Threshold"			
Fixed term – 4, 6, 8, 10, 12, 18, 24 months	RO, APO	D aged 12–14 must be persistent offender	Imprisonable only. Half served in secure accom, half in community.

CHAPTER 2
ORDERS BEFORE SENTENCE

Introduction

The magistrates' court and the Crown Court have similar sentencing powers. The main difference is in the maximum length of a custodial sentence which each type of court is able to pass. Broadly, magistrates' courts are limited to a maximum of 6 months in respect of one or more summary only offences and 12 months in respect of two or more either-way offences. The restrictions on the court's power to impose a custodial sentence is dealt with later in this chapter.

The procedure governing sentence is also broadly the same in the magistrate's court and Crown Court.

Powers exercisable before sentence

Deferment of sentence

The Crown Court or a magistrates' court may defer passing sentence on an offender for the purpose of enabling the court to have regard in dealing with him to his conduct after conviction or any change in his circumstances.[1] The same applies to any other court to which it falls to deal with him. The maximum period of deferment is 6 months.

The power to defer sentence is exercisable only if the offender consents and the court is satisfied, having regard to the nature of the offence and the character and circumstances of the offender, that it would be in the interests of justice to exercise the power.

Any deferment under this section shall be until such date as may be specified by the court, not being more than six months after the date on which the deferment is announced by the court

---

1.   Section 1(1), Powers of Criminal Courts (Sentencing) Act 2000.

and, subject to the passing of sentence being deferred under section 2(7), it shall not be further deferred.

At the end of the period of deferment the court has power to deal with the offender, in respect of the offence for which passing of sentence has been deferred, in any way in which it could have dealt with him if it had not deferred passing sentence. This may, in the case of a magistrates' court, include the power to commit him to the Crown Court for sentence.

It is usual to attach conditions to a deferment of sentence. The court imposing such conditions should have regard to the need to set clear achievable goals, the attainment of which is likely to reduce the sentence which but for the successful completion of the deferment the court would otherwise be minded to impose.

Commission of further offence during the period of deferment

A court which has deferred passing sentence on an offender may deal with him before the end of the period of deferment if during that period he is convicted in Great Britain of any offence.[2] This provision empowers the deferring court to deal with an offender who commits a later offence in circumstances where the court dealing with the later offence does not sentence the offender for the earlier offences.

Usually the court which passes sentence on him for the later offence will deal with him for the offence or offences for which passing of sentence has been deferred. However, this power may not be exercised by a magistrates' court if the court which deferred passing sentence was the Crown Court. The Crown Court, in exercising this power in a case in which the court which deferred passing sentence was a magistrates' court, may not pass any sentence which could not have been passed by a magistrates' court.

Non-appearance at court at the end of the period of deferment

When a court defers sentence, there is no power to remand an offender either in custody or on bail. If the offender does not appear on the date he is required to appear at the end of the period of deferment the court may issue a summons requiring him to appear before the court, or may issue a warrant for his

---

2.   Section 2, Powers of Criminal Courts (Sentencing) Act 2000.

arrest. As far as the magistrates' court is concerned, in deferring the passing of sentence a magistrates' court shall be regarded as exercising the power of adjourning the trial conferred by section 10(1), Magistrates' Courts Act 1980, and accordingly sections 11(1), 13(1) to (3A) and (5) of that Act (non-appearance of the accused) apply if the offender does not appear on the date specified.

Section 10(1), Magistrates' Courts Act 1980 Sections 11(1), 13(1) to (3A) and (5)

Further deferment in the Crown Court

Where a magistrates' court deals with an offender at the end of a period of deferment and commits him for sentence at the Crown Court, that court has power to defer passing sentence on him as if he had just been convicted of the offence or offences on indictment before the Crown Court.

Ancillary orders

When sentence is deferred, the court effectively postpones consideration of the whole sentencing exercise. Accordingly the court may not make orders ancillary to sentence including orders for costs, endorsement or compensation. However, the court has power to make orders for interim disqualification from the holding of a driving licence by the offender and power to make interim restraining orders under, for example, the Protection from Harassment Act 1997 or interim sex offender orders.

Committal to Crown Court for sentence

Magistrates' courts have power to deal with either-way offences. Where an accused indicates that he intends to plead not guilty to an offence of this kind, or enters no plea, the court will determine whether the offence should be tried in the magistrates' court or the Crown Court. The purpose of this process is to ensure that the more serious either-way offences are tried in the Crown Court. Where, however, an accused indicates his intention to plead guilty to such an offence at the plea before venue stage of proceedings, the magistrates have power to sentence the offender. Where the offences are serious, and, had the offender not indicated a guilty plea, the justices would have committed him for trial, it would be usual for the magistrates at this sentencing stage to commit the offender to the Crown Court for sentence.

Committal for sentence after trial in the magistrates' court

Where, at the initial stage of proceedings, the justices accept jurisdiction of an offence and go on to hold a trial, there remains power after conviction to commit the offender to the Crown Court for sentence. The mode of trial stage of proceedings in which the justices accept jurisdiction to try an offence is an entirely different stage in proceedings from the sentencing stage. Accordingly, there is nothing inconsistent in magistrates accepting jurisdiction to try but declining jurisdiction to sentence an offence. However, where magistrates adjourn proceedings after conviction in order to obtain pre-sentence reports about the offender, they may raise a legitimate expectation that he will be sentenced in the magistrates' court. Good practice suggests that it is appropriate to indicate on such an adjournment that the possibility of a committal for sentence has not been ruled out. Failure to frame an adjournment in such terms may prevent the sentencing court from committing the offender to the Crown Court.[3]

The power arises on the summary trial of an offence triable either way a person aged 18 or over is convicted of an either-way offence.[4] If the court is of the opinion that the offence, or the combination of the offence and one or more offences associated with it, was so serious that greater punishment should be inflicted for the offence than the court has power to impose, or in the case of a violent or sexual offence, that a custodial sentence for a term longer than the court has power to impose is necessary to protect the public from serious harm from the offender, the court may commit the offender who is in custody or is on bail to the Crown Court for sentence.

This section does not apply in relation to an offence of criminal damage where the value is less than £5,000. A similar restriction applies to offences of aggravated vehicle taking where the aggravating factor is damage to property of less than £5,000 in value.

The power to commit an offender for sentence to the Crown Court may be exercised in relation to a corporation.

---

3.   *R v Norwich Magistrates' Court ex parte Elliott* 2000 1 Cr App Rep (S) 152.
4.   Section 3, Powers of Criminal Courts (Sentencing) Act 2000.

Committal for sentence on indication of guilty plea to offence triable either way

- The procedure for committing the more serious either-way offences to the Crown Court after the offender has indicated a plea of guilty in the magistrates' court is set out in *R v Warley Magistrates' Court ex parte DPP*.[5] Briefly the guidance can be summarised as follows.

- Factors for determining whether an offence to which a not guilty plea or no plea has been indicated should be tried in the Crown Court are relevant to determining whether the sentencing court should be the Crown Court or the magistrates' court. The National Mode of Trial Guidelines are likely to be of assistance.

- The magistrates' court must have regard to the discount to be granted on a plea of guilty. Offenders should only be committed to the Crown court for sentence where, having taken account of the usual discount for an early guilty plea, the justices are of the opinion that only a sentence in excess of their maximum powers is appropriate. Where the justices retain power as a result of taking account of the discount, it is appropriate to indicate this in open court.

- Where the justices are of the opinion that the offence is of such gravity that the Crown Court ought to be the appropriate venue for sentence, the justices need not seek pre-sentence reports or listen to a full plea in mitigation. The justices should indicate that they are minded to commit the offender to the Crown Court and hear brief submissions from the defence. If, as a result of those representations, the justices are minded to change their decision and retain jurisdiction, the prosecution should then be invited to address them.

- All aspects of character and antecedents can be taken into account before the justices decide whether or not to commit for sentence.

- In cases where the defendant pleads guilty but disputes the prosecution's version of events, the justices should consider whether to conduct a Newton hearing if the differences between the alleged and accepted facts are likely to materially affect sentence. Where the justices are of the view that they would retain jurisdiction no matter which

5.   [1998] 2 Cr App Rep 307.

version of events was proved, the court should simply proceed to hold a Newton hearing. Where it is plain that the appropriate venue for sentence is the Crown Court, the justices should proceed to commit the offender for sentence. The Newton hearing can then be conducted in the Crown Court. In cases where the decision as to committal for sentence depends on the version of facts proved to the justices, the court should hold a Newton hearing. If the facts found at the Newton hearing are such that the justices decide to commit for sentence, the offender will not usually be permitted to challenge the findings at the Crown Court subject to any material changes coming to light since the Newton hearing in the magistrates' court. It is of course the duty of the magistrates' to record the facts found and transmit them to the Crown Court.

- The power to commit an offender to the Crown court arises only where the magistrates' powers of sentence are insufficient to deal with the offence or offences concerned. The justices may not commit an offender to the Crown Court for sentence merely because the type of offence is one usually dealt with by that level of court.[6]

- If justices decide to seek presentence reports, they should give an indication that the possibility of committal to the Crown Court for sentence has not been ruled out even if the court receives a favourable report. If a court fails to specifically include the power to commit for sentence in the course of an adjournment, the defendant may have a reasonable expectation that he is to be sentenced by the magistrates. Committal for sentence after such a legitimate expectation has been raised, even unwittingly, will be quashed by the High Court on judicial review.[7]

---

6. Although *Warley* does not refer to the practice in particular, it is likely that it would be wrong to commit an offender to the Crown Court for administrative expediency for example where the offender has separate proceedings before both courts.
7. Where the court has given an indication that committal for sentence has been ruled out but the offender fails to attend the Probation Service for interview, the justices do not have power to change their minds. The offender is to be punished for his offending and not for his attitude towards the Probation Service; *R v Norwich Magistrates' Court ex parte Elliott* 2000 1 Cr App Rep (S) 152.

Committal ruled out where the court deals with breach of a community penalty

Where the justices have previously imposed a community penalty in respect of an either way offence after either trial or guilty plea, there is no power to commit the offender to the Crown Court if he subsequently breaches the terms of the order. The same rule seems likely to apply to community orders made by the Crown Court on appeal from a decision of the magistrates' sentence as such an order is treated as if it had been made in the magistrates' court.

Power to commit for sentence offences of which the offender has been convicted where other offences are to be committed for trial

The magistrates' court may commit an offender to the Crown Court for sentence where it commits the same offender for trial in respect of offences related[8] to those to which the offender has indicated a guilty plea.[9] Where the offender indicates a guilty plea to such offences related to the offences which the court proposes to commit for trial, the court must postpone its decision in respect of the offences to which guilty pleas have been indicated until the court decides to commit the related offences for trial.

Where the court commits the offender to the Crown Court for sentence to be dealt with in respect of the offence, and does not state that, in its opinion, it also has power so to commit him because the offence merits a sentence in excess of the magistrates' powers, section 5(1) of the Powers of Criminal Courts (Sentencing) Act 2000 shall not apply unless he is convicted before the Crown Court of one or more of the related offences.

Section 5(1), Powers of Criminal Courts (Sentencing) Act 2000

Section 5(1)

Where section 5(1) does not apply, the Crown Court may deal with the offender in respect of the offence in any way in which the magistrates' court could deal with him if it had just convicted him of the offence.

Where an offender has been committed to the Crown Court for sentence on the back of related offences committed for trial and the offender is not convicted by the Crown Court of those related offences, the Crown Court's sentencing powers are restricted to those available to the magistrates' court so long as

---

8. For the purposes of this section one offence is related to another if, were they both to be prosecuted on indictment, the charges for them could be joined in the same indictment.

9. Section 4, Powers of Criminal Courts (Sentencing) Act 2000.

the justices have indicated that they would not have committed the offender for sentence in any event.

Power of Crown Court on committal for sentence under sections 3 and 4 of the Powers of Criminal Courts (Sentencing) Act 2000

Section 5(1), Powers of Criminal Courts (Sentencing) Act 2000

The Crown Court has power to deal with an offender committed for sentence by virtue of section 5(1), Powers of Criminal Courts (Sentencing) Act 2000 which provides that the Crown Court shall inquire into the circumstances of the case and may deal with the offender in any way in which it could deal with him if he had just been convicted of the offence on indictment before the court.

Committal for sentence in certain cases where offender committed in respect of another offence

The Crown Court may also sentence offenders committed to it by the magistrates' court under a variety of legislative measures.[10]

This section applies where a magistrates' court ("the committing court") commits a person in custody or on bail to the Crown Court under any enactment mentioned below to be sentenced or otherwise dealt with in respect of an offence ("the relevant offence").

Where this section applies and the relevant offence is an indictable offence, the committing court may also commit the offender, in custody or on bail as the case may require, to the Crown Court to be dealt with in respect of any other offence whatsoever in respect of which the committing court has power to deal with him (being an offence of which he has been convicted by that or any other court).

- Where this section applies and the relevant offence is a summary offence, the committing court may commit the offender, in custody or on bail as the case may require, to the Crown Court to be dealt with in respect of any other offence of which the committing court has convicted him, being either–

    - an offence punishable with imprisonment; or

    - an offence in respect of which the committing court has a power or duty to order him to be disqualified

---

10.   Section 6(1), Powers of Criminal Courts (Sentencing) Act 2000.

Section 34, 35 or
36, Road Traffic
Offenders Act 1988

under section 34, 35 or 36, Road Traffic Offenders Act 1988 (disqualification for certain motoring offences); or

- any suspended sentence in respect of which the committing court has power to deal with him.

The enactments referred to above are –

Vagrancy Act 1824

- the Vagrancy Act 1824 (incorrigible rogues);

Sections 3 and 4,
Powers of Criminal
Courts (Sentencing)
Act 2000

- sections 3 and 4, Powers of Criminal Courts (Sentencing) Act 2000 above (committal for sentence for offences triable either way);

Section 13(5),
Powers of Criminal
Courts (Sentencing)
Act 2000

- section 13(5), Powers of Criminal Courts (Sentencing) Act 2000 (conditionally discharged person convicted of further offence);

Section 116(3)(b),
Powers of Criminal
Courts (Sentencing)
Act 2000

- section 116(3)(b), Powers of Criminal Courts (Sentencing) Act 2000 (offender convicted of offence committed during currency of original sentence); and

Section 120(2),
Powers of Criminal
Courts (Sentencing)
Act 2000

- section 120(2), Powers of Criminal Courts (Sentencing) Act 2000 (offender convicted during operational period of suspended sentence).

Power of Crown Court on committal for sentence under section 6

Where a magistrates' court commits a person to be dealt with by the Crown Court in respect of an offence, the Crown Court may after inquiring into the circumstances of the case deal with him in any way in which the magistrates' court could deal with him if it had just convicted him of the offence.

This does not apply where under section 6 above a magistrates' court commits a person to be dealt with by the Crown Court in respect of a suspended sentence, but in such a case the powers under section 119 below (power of court to deal with suspended sentence) shall be exercisable by the Crown Court.[11]

---

11. See section XX below dealing with suspended sentences of imprisonment.

Where under a magistrates' court commits a person to be dealt with by the Crown Court under section 6, Powers of Criminal Courts (Sentencing) Act 2000, any duty or power which, apart from this subsection, would fall to be discharged or exercised by the magistrates' court shall not be discharged or exercised by that court but shall instead be discharged or may instead be exercised by the Crown Court.

Section 6, Powers of Criminal Courts (Sentencing) Act 2000

Where under section 6 a magistrates' court commits a person to be dealt with by the Crown Court in respect of an offence triable only on indictment in the case of an adult (being an offence which was tried summarily because of the offender's being under 18 years of age), the Crown Court's powers under subsection (1) above in respect of the offender after he attains the age of 18 shall be powers to do either or both of the following –

- to impose a fine not exceeding £5,000;

- to deal with the offender in respect of the offence in any way in which the magistrates' court could deal with him if it had just convicted him of an offence punishable with imprisonment for a term not exceeding six months.

Remittal of Cases

Power and duty to remit young offenders to youth courts for sentence

Where a child or young person (that is to say, any person aged under 18) is convicted by or before any court of an offence other than homicide, the court may and, if it is not a youth court, shall unless satisfied that it would be undesirable to do so, remit the case –

- if the offender was committed for trial or sent to the Crown Court for trial under section 51, Crime and Disorder Act 1998, to a youth court acting for the place where he was committed for trial or sent to the Crown Court for trial;

Section 51, Crime and Disorder Act 1998

- in any other case, to a youth court acting either for the same place as the remitting court or for the place where the offender habitually resides;

but in relation to a magistrates' court other than a youth court
this power has effect subject to section 8(6), Powers of Criminal
Courts (Sentencing) Act 2000. This provides that where such a
magistrates' court convicts a child or young person of an offence
it must exercise that power unless:

Section 8(6),
Powers of Criminal
Courts (Sentencing)
Act 2000

- the court would, were it not so to remit the case, be required
  by section 16(2) below to refer the offender to a youth
  offender panel (in which event the court may, but need not,
  so remit the case);

Section 16(2)

- In circumstances where the court is not required to refer the
  offender to a youth offending panel, the court is of the
  opinion that the case is one which can properly be dealt
  with by means of –

  - an order discharging the offender absolutely or
    conditionally, or

  - an order for the payment of a fine, or

Section 150

  - an order (under section 150 below) requiring the
    offender's parent or guardian to enter into a
    recognizance to take proper care of him and exercise
    proper control over him,

  - with or without any other order that the court has
    power to make when absolutely or conditionally
    discharging an offender.

Where a case is remitted under this provision the offender shall
be brought before a youth court accordingly, and that court may
deal with him in any way in which it might have dealt with him
if he had been tried and convicted by that court.[12]

Power of youth court to remit offender who attains age of 18 to magistrates' court other than youth court for sentence

Where a person who appears or is brought before a youth court
charged with an offence subsequently attains the age of 18, the
youth court may, at any time after conviction and before
sentence, remit him for sentence to a magistrates' court (other
than a youth court) acting for the same petty sessions area as the
youth court.[13]

The court to which the offender is remitted ("the other court")
may deal with the case in any way in which it would have power

---

12. See section XX below on the sentencing of youths for a fuller description of
the youth court's powers.
13. Section 9, Powers of Criminal Courts (Sentencing) Act 2000.

to deal with it if all proceedings relating to the offence which took place before the youth court had taken place before the other court.

Where an offender is remitted under this provision he shall have no right of appeal against the order of remission (but without prejudice to any right of appeal against an order made in respect of the offence by the court to which he is remitted).

Power of magistrates' court to remit case to another magistrates' court for sentence

There exists power to remit an adult offender to another magistrates' court for sentence.[14] The power arises where a person aged 18 or over ("the offender") has been convicted by a magistrates' court ("the convicting court") of an offence and it appears to the convicting court that some other magistrates' court ("the other court") has convicted him of another such offence in respect of which the other court has neither passed sentence on him nor committed him to the Crown Court for sentence nor dealt with him in any other way.

Provided the other court consents to the offender being remitted under this section to the other court, the convicting court may remit him to the other court to be dealt with in respect of the instant offence by the other court instead of by the convicting court.

The power only applies to:

• any offence punishable with imprisonment; and

Section 34, 35 or 36, Road Traffic Offenders Act 1988

• any offence in respect of which the convicting court has a power or duty to order the offender to be disqualified under section 34, 35 or 36, Road Traffic Offenders Act 1988 (disqualification for certain motoring offences).

An offender may be remitted on bail or in custody from the convicting court to the other court.

The other court may deal with the case in any way in which it would have power to deal with it if all proceedings relating to the instant offence which took place before the convicting court had taken place before the other court. This includes, where applicable, the power to remit the offender under this section to another magistrates' court in respect of the instant offence.

---

14.   Section 10, Powers of Criminal Courts (Sentencing) Act 2000.

Where the convicting court has remitted the offender under this section to the other court, the other court may remit him back to the convicting court.

There is no right of appeal against the order of remission (but without prejudice to any right of appeal against any other order made in respect of the instant offence by the court to which he is remitted).

Section 148, Powers of Criminal Courts (Sentencing) Act 2000

Nothing in this section, however, precludes the convicting court from making any order which it has power to make under section 148, Powers of Criminal Courts (Sentencing) Act 2000 (restitution orders) by virtue of the offender's conviction of the instant offence.

Pre-sentence drug testing

Where a person aged 18 or over is convicted of an offence and the court is considering passing a community sentence, it may make an order for the offender to provide samples for the purpose of ascertaining whether the offender has any specified Class A drug in his body.[15]

If it is proved to the satisfaction of the court that the offender has, without reasonable excuse, failed to comply with the order it may impose on him a fine of an amount not exceeding level 4 on the standard scale.[16]

The power to make a pre-sentence drug test order is only available if the court has been notified by the Secretary of State that the power to make such orders is exercisable by the court.

Reports

Upon conviction magistrates may be able to sentence on the day subject to hearing a plea in mitigation by or on behalf of the offender. This is usually appropriate where the court is minded to impose a financial penalty or either an absolute or conditional discharge. In other circumstances where the court is

---

15.   Section 36A, Powers of Criminal Courts (Sentencing) Act 2000.
16.   The standard of proof is expressed to be to the satisfaction of the court. Given that the section clearly creates a criminal offence, it is reasonable to interpret this as meaning to the criminal standard. It is unclear whether the offence must be prosecuted by the court (and if so, how bearing in mind article 6 of the European Convention and the Human Rights Act 1998) or by the Crown or Probation Service.

considering either a community penalty or a custodial sentence it will be usual to obtain reports on the offender.[17]

Reports usually take the form of either a Specific Sentence Report or a Pre-sentence Report prepared by the Probation Service either on the day or after an adjournment.

A Specific Sentence Report is generally not suitable where the court is considering a custodial sentence or where the court is considering certain complicated community penalties. Such sentencing options usually require investigation away from the court precincts. In all other ways a Specific Sentence Report is a pre-sentence report completed to national standards.

Disclosure of presentence reports

Where a court obtains a pre-sentence report, the court shall give a copy of the report to the offender or his counsel or solicitor and to the prosecutor, that is to say, the person having the conduct of the proceedings in respect of the offence.[18]

If the offender is aged under 17 and is not represented by counsel or a solicitor, a copy of the report need not be given to him but shall be given to his parent or guardian if present in court.

If the prosecutor is not of a description prescribed by order made by the Secretary of State, a copy of the report need not be given to the prosecutor if the court considers that it would be inappropriate for him to be given it.

No information obtained by disclosure shall be used or disclosed otherwise than for the purpose of determining whether representations as to matters contained in the report need to be made to the court or making such representations to the court.

Other reports of probation officers and members of youth offending teams

Where a report by a probation officer or a member of a youth offending team is made to any court (other than a youth court) with a view to assisting the court in determining the most suitable method of dealing with any person in respect of an offence and the report is not a pre-sentence report, the court shall give a copy of the report to the offender or his counsel or solicitor.[19]

---

17.   See section XX below dealing with information for sentencing.
18.   Section 156, Powers of Criminal Courts (Sentencing) Act 2000.
19.   Section 157, Powers of Criminal Courts (Sentencing) Act 2000.

If the offender is aged under 17 and is not represented by counsel or a solicitor, a copy of the report need not be given to him but shall be given to his parent or guardian if present in court.

The court also has power to obtain medical reports about the offender.

Remand by magistrates' court for medical examination

If, on the trial by a magistrates' court of an offence punishable on summary conviction with imprisonment, the court –

- is satisfied that the accused did the act or made the omission charged, but

- is of the opinion that an inquiry ought to be made into his physical or mental condition before the method of dealing with him is determined,

the court shall adjourn the case to enable a medical examination and report to be made, and shall remand him.[20]

An adjournment under this provision shall not be for more than three weeks at a time where the court remands the accused in custody, nor for more than four weeks at a time where it remands him on bail.

Section 3(6), Bail Act 1976

Where on an adjournment the accused is remanded on bail, the court shall impose conditions under paragraph (d) of section 3(6), Bail Act 1976 and the requirements imposed as conditions under that paragraph shall be or shall include requirements that the accused –

- undergo medical examination by a registered medical practitioner or, where the inquiry is into his mental condition and the court so directs, two such practitioners; and

- for that purpose attend such an institution or place, or on such practitioner, as the court directs and, where the inquiry is into his mental condition, comply with any other directions which may be given to him for that purpose by any person specified by the court or by a person of any class so specified.

---

20.   Section 11, Powers of Criminal Courts (Sentencing) Act 2000.

CHAPTER 3
AVAILABLE SENTENCES
FOR ADULT OFFENDERS

Introduction

There are four sentencing categories. The orders and sentences
in each category reflect the seriousness of the offence or offences
falling to be sentenced. The first task for the sentencing court
is to make an assessment of the seriousness of the offence or
offences.

- If an offence is so serious that only a custodial sentence can
  be imposed, the court may pass a custodial sentence but is
  not required to do so. There may be relevant and compelling
  reasons to impose a lesser sentence. The importance of
  deciding that an offence is so serious is that it allows the
  court to consider all sentencing options.

- If an offence is serious enough for a community penalty, the
  court has ruled out the possibility of a custodial sentence.
  The court must move on to pass either a community penalty
  or a lesser penalty such as a fine or discharge.

- If the offence is neither so serious nor serious enough, the
  court is precluded from passing either a custodial sentence
  or a community penalty. The sentencing options for the
  court in respect of such offences is effectively limited to a
  fine. It is correct to say that in this category, it is appropriate
  to punish.

- If it is not appropriate to punish an offender, the court may
  impose either an absolute or conditional discharge. In this
  category the court has decided it is inexpedient to punish
  the offender.[1]

---

1. This may affect the making of certain ancillary orders.

Against this background[2] the following sentences described in this and the following chapters are available to both the magistrates' court and Crown Court.

No Separate Penalty

Strictly, an order of no separate penalty is not a sentence. It has no statutory basis in either the magistrates' court or the Crown Court. Its use has developed[3] largely in relation to offenders convicted of a large number of minor offences, such as road traffic offences. Rather than imposing separate penalties the practice has developed for the court to impose a penalty in respect of one offence and then to make no separate penalty in respect of the others. There is no reason why no separate penalty cannot be employed in respect of more serious offences in appropriate circumstances.

Absolute and conditional discharge

Where a court by or before which a person is convicted of an offence (not being an offence the sentence for which is fixed by law) is of the opinion, having regard to the circumstances including the nature of the offence and the character of the offender, that it is inexpedient to inflict punishment, the court may make an order either:

- Discharging him absolutely; or

- If the court thinks fit, discharging him subject to the condition that he commits no offence during such period, not exceeding three years from the date of the order, as may be specified in the order.[4]

Before making an order for conditional discharge, the court shall explain to the offender in ordinary language that if he commits another offence during the period of conditional discharge he will be liable to be sentenced for the original offence.

The order remains in force for the period specified in the order unless it is brought to an end by the offender being sentenced for the original offence having committed a further offence during the period of the discharge.

---

2.   See section XX below on seriousness for further commentary.
3.   The practice is entrenched and has received judicial approval in countless cases.
4.   Section 12, Powers of Criminal Courts (Sentencing) Act 2000.

Rarely used today is the power to take a recognisance in respect of a discharge. However section 12(6), Powers of Criminal Courts (Sentencing) Act 2000 provides that on making an order for conditional discharge, the court may, if it thinks it expedient for the purpose of the offender's reformation, allow any person who consents to do so to give security for the good behaviour of the offender.

Section 12(6), Powers of Criminal Courts (Sentencing) Act 2000

On discharging an offender absolutely or conditionally in respect of any offence the court is not prevented from making an order for costs against the offender or imposing any disqualification on him or from making in respect of the offence compensation orders, deprivation orders and restitution orders.

Commission of further offence by person conditionally discharged

If an offender who has been conditionally discharged commits an offence during the period of the discharge, he may be sentenced in respect of both the new offence and any offence which gave rise to the discharge.[5]

The power to deal with the discharge depends on the court before which the offender is convicted of the new offence.

- If the offender was discharged by the same magistrates' court before which he is convicted of the new offence, that court may deal with him for the original offence.

- If the offender was discharged by a different magistrates' court before he is convicted of the new offence, the new court may seek the consent of the original court to its dealing with the original offence, or may notify the original court that the offender has been convicted of a new offence during the period of its discharge.

- If the offender was discharged by the Crown Court, the magistrates' court before which he is convicted of the new offence may commit the offender to the Crown Court to be dealt with for the breach of the conditional discharge (and, where the new offence is either-way, commit him for sentence in respect of the new offence), or notify the Crown Court that the offender has been convicted of a new offence during the period of its discharge.

5.   Section 13, Powers of Criminal Courts (Sentencing) Act 2000.

If it appears to the Crown Court, or to a justice of the peace having jurisdiction to deal with the breach, that a person in whose case an order for conditional discharge has been made –

- has been convicted by a court in Great Britain of an offence committed during the period of conditional discharge, and

- has been dealt with in respect of that offence,

that court or justice may issue a summons requiring that person to appear at the place and time specified in it or a warrant for his arrest.

A justice of the peace shall not issue a summons under this section except on information and shall not issue a warrant under this section except on information in writing and on oath.

A summons or warrant issued under this section shall direct the person to whom it relates to appear or to be brought before the court by which the order for conditional discharge was made.

Where it is proved to the satisfaction of the court by which an order for conditional discharge was made that the person in whose case the order was made has been convicted of an offence committed during the period of conditional discharge, the court may deal with him, for the offence for which the order was made, in any way in which it could deal with him if he had just been convicted by or before that court of that offence.

If a person in whose case an order for conditional discharge has been made by a magistrates' court:

- is convicted before the Crown Court of an offence committed during the period of conditional discharge, or

- is dealt with by the Crown Court for any such offence in respect of which he was committed for sentence to the Crown Court,

the Crown Court may deal with him, for the offence for which the order was made, in any way in which the magistrates' court could deal with him if it had just convicted him of that offence.

Effect of discharge

A conviction of an offence for which an order is made discharging the offender absolutely or conditionally shall be deemed not to be a conviction for any purpose other than the purposes of the proceedings in which the order is made and of any subsequent proceedings which may be taken against the offender under section 13 above.

Section 13

Where the offender was aged 18 or over at the time of his conviction of the offence in question and is subsequently sentenced (under section 13 above) for that offence, the above shall cease to apply to the conviction.

Without prejudice to the foregoing, the conviction of an offender who is discharged absolutely or conditionally shall in any event be disregarded for the purposes of any enactment or instrument which:

• imposes any disqualification or disability upon convicted persons; or

• authorises or requires the imposition of any such disqualification or disability.

This power does not however permit a court to avoid imposing orders for the endorsement of an offender's driving licence or his disqualification from holding or obtaining a driving licence under the road traffic legislation. A recommendation for deportation may also be made in addition to a discharge whether absolute or conditional.

The statutory scheme dealing with the effect of a discharge does not affect:

• an offender from relying on his conviction in bar of any subsequent proceedings for the same offence;

• the restoration of any property in consequence of the conviction of any such offender;

• the operation, in relation to any such offender, of any enactment or instrument in force on 1st July 1974 which is expressed to extend to persons dealt with under section 1(1), Probation of Offenders Act 1907 as well as to convicted persons.

Section 1(1)
Probation of
Offenders Act 1907

Section 13, Powers of Criminal Courts (Sentencing) Act 2000

Where an order for conditional discharge has been made on appeal, for the purposes of section 13 above it shall be deemed:

- if it was made on an appeal brought from a magistrates' court, to have been made by that magistrates' court;

- if it was made on an appeal brought from the Crown Court or from the criminal division of the Court of Appeal, to have been made by the Crown Court.

Section 13, Powers of Criminal Courts (Sentencing) Act 2000

In proceedings before the Crown Court under section 13, Powers of Criminal Courts (Sentencing) Act 2000, any question whether any person in whose case an order for conditional discharge has been made has been convicted of an offence committed during the period of conditional discharge shall be determined by the court and not by the verdict of a jury.

CHAPTER 4
FINANCIAL PENALTIES
AND ORDERS

Financial circumstances orders

Before imposing a fine the court is under a duty to take into account the offender's financial circumstances. To this end, where an individual has been convicted of an offence, the court may, before sentencing him, make a financial circumstances order with respect to him.[1] The power to make such an order also arises under the written plea of guilty procedures under section 12 of the Magistrates' Courts Act 1980.

Section 12,
Magistrates' Courts
Act 1980

A financial circumstances order means, in relation to any individual, an order requiring him to give to the court, within such period as may be specified in the order, such a statement of his financial circumstances as the court may require.

An individual who without reasonable excuse fails to comply with a financial circumstances order shall be liable on summary conviction to a fine not exceeding level 3 on the standard scale.

If an individual, in furnishing any statement in pursuance of a financial circumstances order:

- makes a statement which he knows to be false in a material particular,

- recklessly furnishes a statement which is false in a material particular, or

- knowingly fails to disclose any material fact,

he shall be liable on summary conviction to imprisonment for a term not exceeding three months or a fine not exceeding level 4 on the standard scale or both.

---

1. Section 126, Powers of Criminal Courts (Sentencing).

Section 127(1)
Magistrates'
Courts Act 1980

Proceedings in respect of this offence may, notwithstanding anything in section 127(1), Magistrates' Courts Act 1980 (limitation of time), be commenced at any time within two years from the date of the commission of the offence or within six months from its first discovery by the prosecutor, whichever period expires the earlier.

Fines in general

Every criminal offence has a maximum fine fixed by either primary or secondary legislation. Generally the maximum fine is set by reference to a standard scale which may change from time to time according to statutory instrument. In addition to fines set by reference to the standard scale, certain offences may be punishable by reference to the prescribed sum set out in the relevant legislation and usually larger than the standard scale. The standard scale and the prescribed sum generally apply to proceedings in the magistrates' court. The Crown Court may have additional powers to impose an unlimited fine but any restriction on the sentencing powers of the Crown Court will be set out in the relevant legislation.

The Standard Scale

The standard scale is as follows[2]

Level 1   £200

Level 2   £500

Level 3   £1,000

Level 4   £2,500

Level 5   £5,000

The statutory maximum fine on summary conviction for an offence triable either way, where this is referred to in legislation, is £5,000.[3]

The maximum fine on summary conviction where the legislation does not express a power to fine is at level 3 of the standard scale.[4]

---

2.   Section 37, Criminal Justice Act 1982.
3.   Sections 24(3), (4) and 36(1) and (2), Magistrates' Courts Act 1980.
4.   Section 34(3), Magistrate's Courts Act 1980.

General power of Crown Court to fine offender convicted on indictment

Where a person is convicted on indictment of any offence, other than an offence for which the sentence is fixed by law, the court, if not precluded from sentencing the offender by its exercise of some other power, may impose a fine instead of or in addition to dealing with him in any other way in which the court has power to deal with him.

Fixing of fines

Before fixing the amount of any fine to be imposed on an offender who is an individual, a court shall inquire into his financial circumstances.

The amount of any fine fixed by a court shall be such as, in the opinion of the court, reflects the seriousness of the offence.

In fixing the amount of any fine to be imposed on an offender (whether an individual or other person), a court shall take into account the circumstances of the case including, among other things, the financial circumstances of the offender so far as they are known, or appear, to the court.

This applies whether taking into account the financial circumstances of the offender has the effect of increasing or reducing the amount of the fine.

Section 11 or 12, Magistrates' Courts Act 1980

Where an offender has been convicted in his absence in pursuance of section 11 or 12, Magistrates' Courts Act 1980 (non-appearance of accused), or an offender has failed to comply with a financial circumstances order or has otherwise failed to co-operate with the court in its inquiry into his financial circumstances, and the court considers that it has insufficient information to make a proper determination of the financial circumstances of the offender, it may make such determination as it thinks fit.

Remission of fines

Section 129, Powers of Criminal Courts (Sentencing) Act 2000

The court has specific power to remit fines imposed in circumstances where the court did not have sufficient information to make a proper determination of the offender's means. Section 129, Powers of Criminal Courts (Sentencing) Act 2000 provides that if, on subsequently inquiring into the offender's financial circumstances, the court is satisfied that had it had the results of that inquiry when sentencing the offender it would:

- have fixed a smaller amount, or

- not have fined him,

it may remit the whole or any part of the fine.

Section 139,
Powers of Criminal
Courts (Sentencing)
Act 2000
Section 82(5),
Magistrates' Courts
Act 1980
Where under this section the court remits the whole or part of a fine after a term of imprisonment has been fixed under section 139, Powers of Criminal Courts (Sentencing) Act 2000 (powers of Crown Court in relation to fines) or section 82(5), Magistrates' Courts Act 1980 (magistrates' powers in relation to default), it shall reduce the term by the corresponding proportion. In calculating any reduction required, any fraction of a day shall be ignored.

The enforcement of fines

The successful enforcement of fines begins with the appropriate imposition of a sum which reflects the seriousness of the offence concerned and is within the reasonable ability of the offender to pay. Enforcement of fines is dealt with in fuller detail later in this work at page XX.

Compensation orders against convicted persons

Powers of Criminal
Courts (Sentencing)
Act 2000
The Powers of Criminal Courts (Sentencing) Act 2000 sets out the statutory scheme for the making of orders to compensate the victims of crime.[5] A court by or before which a person is convicted of an offence, instead of or in addition to dealing with him in any other way, may, on application or otherwise, make an order requiring him:

- to pay compensation for any personal injury, loss or damage resulting from that offence or any other offence which is taken into consideration by the court in determining sentence; or

- to make payments for funeral expenses or bereavement in respect of a death resulting from any such offence, other than a death due to an accident arising out of the presence of a motor vehicle on a road.

---

5.   Section 130, Powers of Criminal Courts (Sentencing) Act 2000.

A court shall give reasons, on passing sentence, if it does not make a compensation order in a case where this section empowers it to do so.

Compensation shall be of such amount as the court considers appropriate, having regard to any evidence and to any representations that are made by or on behalf of the accused or the prosecutor. The amount must be specified together with any order for payments by instalments.[6] The purpose of a compensation order is to give effect to the victim's civil right to sue for damages. It does not stand in the place of his right to take civil proceedings.

Theft Act 1968 In the case of an offence under the Theft Act 1968, where the property in question is recovered, any damage to the property occurring while it was out of the owner's possession shall be treated for the purposes of this provision as having resulted from the offence, however and by whomever the damage was caused.

A compensation order may only be made in respect of injury, loss or damage (other than loss suffered by a person's dependants in consequence of his death) which was due to an accident arising out of the presence of a motor vehicle on a road, if:

- it is in respect of damage which is treated above as resulting from an offence under the Theft Act 1968; or

- it is in respect of injury, loss or damage as respects which:

  - the offender is uninsured in relation to the use of the vehicle; and

  - compensation is not payable under any arrangements to which the Secretary of State is a party.[7]

Where a compensation order is made in respect of injury, loss or damage due to an accident arising out of the presence of a motor vehicle on a road, the amount to be paid may include an amount representing the whole or part of any loss of or reduction in preferential rates of insurance attributable to the accident.

---

6. *R v Scott* 1986 150 JP 286.
7. There exists a scheme for claiming damages against an uninsured driver operated by the Motor Insurer's Bureau (see *Road Traffic Accident Claims* EMIS Professional Publishing). The arrangements do not provide for the first £300 of a claim made under the scheme and accordingly, justices are limited to making an order to a maximum of £300 in respect of loss, damage or injuries caused by an uninsured driver. Compensation should not generally be ordered in respect of an insured driver as the insurance policy exists to compensate those suffering injury or damage.

A compensation order in respect of funeral expenses may be made for the benefit of anyone who incurred the expenses.

A compensation order in respect of bereavement may be made only for the benefit of a person for whose benefit a claim for damages for bereavement could be made under section 1A, Fatal Accidents Act 1976; and the amount of compensation in respect of bereavement shall not exceed the amount for the time being specified in section 1A(3) of that Act.

Section 1A, Fatal Accidents Act 1976

Section 1A(3), Fatal Accidents Act 1976

In determining whether to make a compensation order against any person, and in determining the amount to be paid by any person under such an order, the court shall have regard to his means so far as they appear or are known to the court.

Where the court considers that it would be appropriate both to impose a fine and to make a compensation order, but the offender has insufficient means to pay both an appropriate fine and appropriate compensation, the court shall give preference to compensation (though it may impose a fine as well).

In *R* v *Inwood*,[8] Scarman LJ said that compensation orders were not introduced to enable the convicted to buy themselves out of the usual penalties but as a convenient and rapid means of avoiding the expense of civil litigation.

In the case of joint offenders, each party is wholly and severally responsible. However, a single order against one of joint offenders should generally be avoided and the amount of compensation should usually be divided between the joint offenders.[9] This principle may be distinguished where one of the offenders has the ability to pay a compensation order but another does not.[10]

Limit on amount payable under compensation order of magistrates' court

The compensation to be paid under a compensation order made by a magistrates' court in respect of any offence of which the court has convicted the offender shall not exceed £5,000.

The compensation or total compensation to be paid under a compensation order or compensation orders made by a magistrates' court in respect of any offence or offences taken

---

8.   [1974] 60 Cr App Rep 70.
9.   *R* v *Schofield* 1978 2 All ER 705.
10. *R* v *Grundy* 1974 1 All ER 292.

into consideration in determining sentence shall not exceed the difference (if any) between:

- the amount or total amount which under subsection (1) above is the maximum for the offence or offences of which the offender has been convicted; and

- the amount or total amounts (if any) which are in fact ordered to be paid in respect of that offence or those offences.

Compensation orders and appeals

A person in whose favour a compensation order is made shall not be entitled to receive the amount due to him until (disregarding any power of a court to grant leave to appeal out of time) there is no further possibility of an appeal on which the order could be varied or set aside. This restriction does not prevent the court from taking enforcement action before the last date of appeal.

Compensation and offences taken into consideration

Where a compensation order has been made against any person in respect of an offence taken into consideration in determining his sentence, the order shall cease to have effect if he successfully appeals against his conviction of the offence or, if more than one, all the offences, of which he was convicted in the proceedings in which the order was made. The offender may appeal against the order as if it were part of the sentence imposed in respect of the offence or, if more than one, any of the offences, of which he was so convicted.

Review of compensation orders

The magistrates' court for the time being having functions in relation to the enforcement of a compensation order (in this section referred to as "the appropriate court") may, on the application of the person against whom the compensation order was made, discharge the order or reduce the amount which remains to be paid.

The appropriate court may exercise the power of review only:

- at a time when (disregarding any power of a court to grant leave to appeal out of time) there is no further possibility of an appeal on which the compensation order could be varied or set aside; and

- at a time before the person against whom the compensation order was made has paid into court the whole of the compensation which the order requires him to pay.

The appropriate court may exercise the review power only if it appears to the court:

- that the injury, loss or damage in respect of which the compensation order was made has been held in civil proceedings to be less than it was taken to be for the purposes of the order; or

- in the case of a compensation order in respect of the loss of any property, that the property has been recovered by the person in whose favour the order was made; or

Part VI, Criminal
Justice Act 1988

- that the means of the person against whom the compensation order was made are insufficient to satisfy in full both the order and a confiscation order under Part VI, Criminal Justice Act 1988 made against him in the same proceedings; or

- that the person against whom the compensation order was made has suffered a substantial reduction in his means which was unexpected at the time when the order was made, and that his means seem unlikely to increase for a considerable period.

Where the compensation order was made by the Crown Court, the appropriate court shall not exercise any power to review the compensation order unless it has first obtained the consent of the Crown Court.

Where a compensation order has been made on appeal, for the purposes of determining which court is to be deemed to have made the order, it shall be deemed:

- if it was made on an appeal brought from a magistrates' court, to have been made by that magistrates' court;

- if it was made on an appeal brought from the Crown Court or from the criminal division of the Court of Appeal, to have been made by the Crown Court.

Effect of compensation order on subsequent award of damages in civil proceedings

Where a compensation order, or a service compensation order or award, has been made in favour of any person in respect of any injury, loss or damage and a claim by him in civil proceedings for damages in respect of the injury, loss or damage subsequently falls to be determined, the damages in the civil proceedings shall be assessed without regard to the order or award, but the plaintiff may only recover an amount equal to the aggregate of the following:

- any amount by which they exceed the compensation; and

- a sum equal to any portion of the compensation which he fails to recover,

and may not enforce the judgment, so far as it relates to the sum of the compensation order, without the leave of the court.

Best practice would be for the court to draw also the attention of a victim to the Criminal Injuries Compensation Scheme. The Scheme is unlikely to meet claims in respect of moderate injuries where the amount of any award is likely to be less than £1,000 and courts and practitioners should be aware of this limitation to the victim's ability to obtain damages outwith the criminal proceedings.[11]

The duties of Crown Court in relation to fines

Powers and duties of Crown Court in relation to fines and forfeited recognizances

If the Crown Court imposes a fine on any person or forfeits his recognizance, the court may make an order:

- allowing time for the payment of the amount of the fine or the amount due under the recognizance;

- directing payment of that amount by instalments of such amounts and on such dates as may be specified in the order;

- in the case of a recognizance, discharging the recognizance or reducing the amount due under it.

---

11. *The Tariff Scheme* Issue 2 (4/94).

If the Crown Court imposes a fine on any person or forfeits his recognizance, the court shall make an order fixing a term of imprisonment or of detention which he is to undergo if any sum which he is liable to pay is not duly paid or recovered.

No person shall on the occasion when a fine is imposed on him or his recognizance is forfeited by the Crown Court be committed to prison or detained unless:

- in the case of an offence punishable with imprisonment, he appears to the court to have sufficient means to pay the sum forthwith;

- it appears to the court that he is unlikely to remain long enough at a place of abode in the United Kingdom to enable payment of the sum to be enforced by other methods; or

- on the occasion when the order is made the court sentences him to immediate imprisonment, custody for life or detention in a young offender institution for that or another offence, or so sentences him for an offence in addition to forfeiting his recognizance, or he is already serving a sentence of custody for life or a term:

    - of imprisonment;

    - of detention in a young offender institution; or

Section 108, Powers of Criminal Courts (Sentencing) Act 2000

- of detention under section 108, Powers of Criminal Courts (Sentencing) Act 2000.

The periods set out in the second column of the following Table shall be the maximum relevant periods of imprisonment or detention above applicable respectively to the amounts set out opposite them.

Table 1	Period
An amount not exceeding £200	7 days
An amount exceeding £200 but not exceeding £500	14 days
An amount exceeding £500 but not exceeding £1,000	28 days
An amount exceeding £1,000 but not exceeding £2,500	45 days
An amount exceeding £2,500 but not exceeding £5,000	3 months
An amount exceeding £5,000 but not exceeding £10,000	6 months
An amount exceeding £10,000 but not exceeding £20,000	12 months
An amount exceeding £20,000 but not exceeding £50,000	18 months
An amount exceeding £50,000 but not exceeding £100,000	2 years
An amount exceeding £100,000 but not exceeding £250,000	3 years
An amount exceeding £250,000 but not exceeding £1 million	5 years
An amount exceeding £1 million	10 years

Where any person liable for the payment of a fine or a sum due under a recognizance to which this section applies is sentenced by the court to, or is serving or otherwise liable to serve, a term of imprisonment or detention in a young offender institution or a term of detention, the court may order that any term of imprisonment or detention fixed under this part above shall not begin to run until after the end of the first-mentioned term.

Section 139, Powers of Criminal Courts (Sentencing) Act 2000

The power conferred by section 139, Powers of Criminal Courts (Sentencing) Act 2000 to discharge a recognizance or reduce the amount due under it shall be in addition to the powers conferred by any other Act relating to the discharge, cancellation, mitigation or reduction of recognizances or sums forfeited under recognizances.

The powers conferred by this section shall not be taken as restricted by any enactment which authorises the Crown Court to deal with an offender in any way in which a magistrates' court might have dealt with him or could deal with him.

Section 139(2)
Powers of Criminal
Courts (Sentencing)
Act 2000

Section 149(1)
Customs and Excise
Management Act
1979

Any term fixed under section 139(2), Powers of Criminal Courts (Sentencing) Act 2000 above as respects a fine imposed in pursuance of such an enactment, that is to say a fine which the magistrates' court could have imposed, shall not exceed the period applicable to that fine (if imposed by the magistrates' court) under section 149(1), Customs and Excise Management Act 1979 (maximum periods of imprisonment in default of payment of certain fines).

These provisions do not apply to a fine imposed by the Crown Court on appeal against a decision of a magistrates' court.

Any references in this section, to the term of imprisonment or other detention to which a person has been sentenced or which, or part of which, he has served, consecutive terms and terms which are wholly or partly concurrent shall, unless the context otherwise requires, be treated as a single term.

Enforcement of fines imposed and recognizances forfeited by Crown Court

A fine imposed or a recognizance forfeited by the Crown Court shall be treated for the purposes of collection, enforcement and remission of the fine or other sum as having been imposed or forfeited by a magistrates' court specified in an order made by the Crown Court. If no such order is made, treated as imposed by the magistrates' court by which the offender was committed to the Crown Court to be tried or dealt with or by which he was sent to the Crown Court for trial under section 51, Crime and Disorder Act 1998, and, in the case of a fine, as having been so imposed on conviction by the magistrates' court in question.

Section 51, Crime
and Disorder Act
1998

Where the offender fails to pay as ordered, the magistrates' court is required to take measures to enforce the fine against him. If the magistrates court proceeds to issue a warrant of commitment on a default in the payment of the sum due, the term of imprisonment due to be served will be the period set by the Crown Court, less any proportionate reduction for part payment, and is not limited to the maximum periods of detention in default applicable to the magistrates' court.

Section 85(1) or
120, Magistrates'
Courts Act 1980

A magistrates' court shall not, under section 85(1) or 120, Magistrates' Courts Act 1980, remit the whole or any part of a fine imposed by, or sum due under a recognizance forfeited by the Crown Court, the criminal division of the Court of Appeal, or the House of Lords on appeal from that division, without the consent of the Crown Court.

Power of Crown Court to allow time for payment, or payment by instalments, of costs and compensation

Where the Crown Court makes any such orders against accused for the payment of costs or compensation, the court may allow time for the payment of the sum due under the order and direct payment of that sum by instalments of such amounts and on such dates as the court may specify.

Power of Crown Court to order search of persons before it

The Crown Court may order any person before it to be searched. Any money found on a person in a search under this section may be applied, unless the court otherwise directs, towards payment of the fine or other sum payable by him; and the balance, if any, shall be returned to him.

Enforcement in the magistrates' court

When a sum to be paid is imposed, both the magistrates' court and the Crown Court have the power to dispense with immediate payment, and may order the sum be paid by a certain date, or be paid in instalments.[12] The same is true of compensation and costs.[13] This course of action should, however, be avoided if the sum can be satisfied forthwith.

It is possible for imprisonment in lieu of payment of fines to be imposed by a magistrates' court on the occasion of conviction. This may occur in the following circumstances:

(a) In the case of an offence punishable with imprisonment, the defendant appears to have sufficient means to pay the sum forthwith;

(b) It appears to the court to the court that the defendant is unlikely to remain long enough at a place of abode in the

---

12. In the magistrates' court this power is found in section 75(1) and (2), Magistrates' Courts Act 1980. For the Crown Court see section 139(1), Powers of Criminal Courts (Sentencing) Act 2000.
13. For example, see section 141, Powers of Criminal Courts (Sentencing) Act 2000.

United Kingdom to enable payment of the sum to be enforced by other methods; or

(c) On the occasion of conviction the court sentences him to immediate imprisonment, detention in a young offender institution for that or another offence or he is already serving a sentence of custody for life, or a term of imprisonment, detention in a young offender institution, or detention in such an institution for life.[14]

In addition magistrates can order detention until 8 o'clock in the evening on the occasion of conviction in lieu of payment of a financial penalty.[15] They also have the power to issue a warrant of arrest that operates in a similar fashion (although in the case of such a warrant, the period of detention is until 8 o'clock in the morning of the day following arrest or, if the defendant is arrested between midnight and eight o'clock in the morning, until 8 o'clock on the day he was arrested.[16]

Where the Crown Court imposes a financial penalty, and circumstances similar to those matters listed at (a) to (c) above apply, it is required to consider whether a period of imprisonment should be imposed, suspended until such time that there is any default of any payment terms set.[17]

It is also worth noting another "enforcement" step that can be taken on the occasion of conviction and that is the power of both the Crown and magistrates' courts to order a defendant to be searched and to apply the monies to the sum imposed.[18] In addition, the magistrates are empowered to order such a search at a later hearing where the defendant is said to be in default of payments (a "means inquiry" hearing).[19] In either court, the money may be applied to the sum imposed or outstanding.

Notification of penalties

Where a magistrates' court:

(a) is tasked to collect a financial penalty imposed by a Crown Court, or

(b) has allowed time to pay a sum adjudged to be paid by summary conviction, or

---

14. Section 82(1), Magistrates' Courts Act 1980.
15. Section 135(1), Magistrates' Courts Act 1980.
16. Section 136, Magistrates' Courts Act 1980.
17. Section 139, Powers of Criminal Courts (Sentencing) Act 2000.
18. Section 80(1), Magistrates' Courts Act 1980 and section 142, Powers of Criminal Courts (Sentencing) Act 2000.
19. Section 80(1), Magistrates' Courts Act 1980.

(c) has allowed payments by instalments, or

(d) where a fine has been imposed in the absence of a defendant

that court must serve written notice on the defendant, stating the amount of the sum and, if applicable, the amount of any instalments, and the date on which any payment or instalments are to be paid. Such notice must be served on the defendant last known or usual place of abode, and if this is not done, a distress warrant cannot be issued.[20]

Enforcement powers

The powers available in the magistrates' court to enforce financial penalties are dealt with in the section on enforcement later in this book at pages XX.

---

20.   Rule 46(1) and (2), Magistrates' Courts Rules 1981.

CHAPTER 5
COMMUNITY PENALTIES

Introduction

Community penalties represent the middle band of sentencing, lying between fines and discharges at the lower end and custody at the upper end of the sentencing matrix.

Powers of Criminal Courts (Sentencing) Act 2000

The Powers of Criminal Courts (Sentencing) Act 2000[1] provides that a "community order" means, as far as adult offender are concerned, any of the following orders

- a curfew order;

- a community rehabilitation order (a probation order);

- a community punishment order (a community service order);

- a community rehabilitation and punishment order (a combination order);

- a drug treatment and testing order;

- an attendance centre order;

- a supervision order.

A "community sentence" means a sentence which consists of or includes one or more community orders.

A community sentence is not available where the sentence for an offence is fixed by law or attracts a minimum sentence of imprisonment by operation of statute.

---

1.   Section 33, Powers of Criminal Courts (Sentencing) Act 2000.

Restrictions on imposing community sentences

A court shall not pass a community sentence on an offender unless it is of the opinion that the offence, or the combination of the offence and one or more offences associated with it, was serious enough to warrant such a sentence.

Where a court passes a community sentence the particular order or orders comprising or forming part of the sentence shall be such as in the opinion of the court is, or taken together are, the most suitable for the offender; and the restrictions on liberty imposed by the order or orders shall be such as in the opinion of the court are commensurate with the seriousness of the offence, or the combination of the offence and one or more offences associated with it.

Procedural requirements for community sentences: pre-sentence reports etc

In forming any opinion as to the suitability of a community order a court shall take into account all such information as is available to it about the circumstances of the offence or (as the case may be) of the offence and the offence or offences associated with it, including any aggravating or mitigating factors. Usually such information will be provided to the court by way of the offender's plea in mitigation and the pre-sentence reports produced by the National Probation Service.

In forming any such opinion a court may take into account any information about the offender which is before it.

Where the court is considering the following types of community orders, the court shall obtain and consider a pre-sentence report before forming an opinion as to the suitability for the offender of one or more of the orders. However, this requirement does not apply if, in the circumstances of the case, the court is of the opinion that it is unnecessary to obtain a pre-sentence report.

No community sentence which consists of or includes an order from the following list shall be invalidated by the failure of a court to obtain and consider a pre-sentence report before forming an opinion as to the suitability of the order for the offender. However, any court on an appeal against such a sentence shall obtain and consider a report unless the appeal court is of the opinion that the court below was justified in forming an opinion that it was unnecessary to obtain a pre-sentence report; or that, although the court below was not justified in forming that opinion, in the circumstances of the case at the time it is before the court, it is unnecessary to obtain a pre-sentence report.

The community orders to which this provision applies are:

- a rehabilitation order which includes additional requirements;

- a community punishment order;

- a community rehabilitation and punishment order;

- a drug treatment and testing order.

Community Orders are available only where the offender is aged over 16 years of age.

Rehabilitation orders

Powers of Criminal Courts (Sentencing) Act 2000

Rehabilitation orders are referred to in the Powers of Criminal Courts (Sentencing) Act 2000 as probation orders.[2]

Where a person aged 16 or over is convicted of an offence and the court by or before which he is convicted is of the opinion that his supervision is desirable in the interests of:

- securing his rehabilitation, or

- protecting the public from harm from him or preventing the commission by him of further offences,

the court may make an order requiring him to be under supervision for a period specified in the order of not less than six months nor more than three years.

A probation order shall specify the petty sessions area in which the offender resides or will reside. If the offender is aged 18 or over at the time when the probation order is made, he shall be required to be under the supervision of a probation officer appointed for or assigned to the petty sessions area specified in the order.

---

2. Section 41(2), Powers of Criminal Courts (Sentencing) Act 2000.

Before making a probation order, the court shall explain to the offender in ordinary language:

- the effect of the order (including any additional requirements proposed to be included in the order);

- the consequences which may follow if he fails to comply with any of the requirements of the order; and

- that the court has power to review the order on the application either of the offender or of the responsible officer.

On making a probation order, the court may, if it thinks it expedient for the purpose of the offender's reformation, allow any person who consents to do so to give security for the good behaviour of the offender. This is a power rarely employed.

Additional requirements which may be included in probation orders

A probation order may in addition require the offender to comply during the whole or any part of the probation period with such requirements as the court, having regard to the circumstances of the case, considers desirable in the interests of:

- securing the rehabilitation of the offender; or

- protecting the public from harm from him or preventing the commission by him of further offences.

Without prejudice to the power of the court to make a compensation order, the payment of sums by way of damages for injury or compensation for loss shall not be included among the additional requirements of a probation order.

Schedule 2, Powers of Criminal Courts (Sentencing) Act 2000

The additional requirements which may be included in a probation order are set out in Schedule 2, Powers of Criminal Courts (Sentencing) Act 2000 as follows.

Requirements as to residence

A probation order may include requirements as to the residence of the offender. Before making a probation order containing any such requirement, the court shall consider the home surroundings of the offender.

Where a probation order requires the offender to reside in an approved hostel or any other institution, the period for which he is required to reside there shall be specified in the order.

Requirements as to activities etc.

A probation order may require the offender:

- to present himself to a person or persons specified in the order at a place or places so specified;

- to participate or refrain from participating in activities specified in the order

  - on a day or days so specified; or

  - during the probation period or such portion of it as may be so specified.

The court shall not include in a probation order such a requirement unless:

- it has consulted in the case of an offender aged 18 or over, a probation officer; or in the case of an offender aged under 18, either a probation officer or a member of a youth offending team; and

- it is satisfied that it is feasible to secure compliance with the requirement.

A court shall not include such a requirement or a requirement to participate in activities if it would involve the co-operation of a person other than the offender and the offender's responsible officer, unless that other person consents to its inclusion.

Such a requirement operates to require the offender:

- in accordance with instructions given by his responsible officer, to present himself at a place or places for not more than 60 days in the aggregate; and

- while at any place, to comply with instructions given by, or under the authority of, the person in charge of that place.

A requirement to participate in activities shall operate to require the offender:

- in accordance with instructions given by his responsible officer, to participate in activities for not more than 60 days in the aggregate; and

- while participating, to comply with instructions given by, or under the authority of, the person in charge of the activities.

Instructions given by the offender's responsible officer shall, as far as practicable, be such as to avoid any conflict with the offender's religious beliefs or with the requirements of any other community order to which he may be subject; and any interference with the times, if any, at which he normally works or attends school or any other educational establishment.

Requirements as to attendance at probation centre

A probation order may require the offender during the probation period to attend at a probation centre specified in the order.

A court shall not include in a probation order such a requirement unless it has consulted in the case of an offender aged 18 or over, a probation officer, or in the case of an offender aged under 18, either a probation officer or a member of a youth offending team.

A court shall not include such a requirement in a probation order unless it is satisfied

- that arrangements can be made for the offender's attendance at a centre; and

- that the person in charge of the centre consents to the inclusion of the requirement.

A requirement of this kind shall operate to require the offender:

- in accordance with instructions given by his responsible officer, to attend on not more than 60 days at the centre specified in the order; and

- while attending there to comply with instructions given by, or under the authority of, the person in charge of the centre.

Instructions given by the offender's responsible officer shall, as far as practicable, be such as to avoid any conflict with the offender's religious beliefs or with the requirements of any other community order to which he may be subject; and any interference with the times, if any, at which he normally works or attends school or any other educational establishment.

References to attendance at a probation centre include references to attendance elsewhere than at the centre for the purpose of participating in activities in accordance with instructions given by, or under the authority of, the person in charge of the centre. The Secretary of State may make rules for regulating the provision and carrying on of probation centres and the attendance at such centres of persons subject to probation orders; and such rules may in particular include provision with respect to hours of attendance, the reckoning of days of attendance and the keeping of attendance records.

Extension of requirements for sexual offenders

If the court so directs in the case of an offender who has been convicted of a sexual offence the requirements to attend and participate in specified activities or to attend at a probation centre shall each have effect as if for the reference to 60 days there were substituted a reference to such greater number of days as may be specified in the direction.

Requirements as to treatment for mental condition etc.

The probation order may include a requirement that the offender shall submit, during the whole of the probation period or during such part or parts of that period as may be specified in the order, to treatment by or under the direction of a registered medical practitioner or a chartered psychologist (or both, for different parts) with a view to the improvement of the offender's mental condition.

Section 12, Mental Health Act 1983

The power to include such a requirement arises only where the court is satisfied, on the evidence of a registered medical practitioner approved for the purposes of section 12, Mental Health Act 1983, that the mental condition of the offender:

- is such as requires and may be susceptible to treatment; but

- is not such as to warrant the making of a hospital order or guardianship order within the meaning of that Act.

The treatment required by any such order shall be such one of the following kinds of treatment as may be specified in the order:

- treatment as a resident patient in a hospital or mental nursing home within the meaning of the Mental Health Act 1983, but not hospital premises at which high security psychiatric services within the meaning of that Act are provided;

- treatment as a non-resident patient at such institution or place as may be specified in the order;

- treatment by or under the direction of such registered medical practitioner or chartered psychologist (or both) as may be so specified;

but the nature of the treatment shall not be otherwise specified in the order.

A court shall not include in a probation order a requirement that the offender shall submit to treatment for his mental condition unless:

- it is satisfied that arrangements have been or can be made for the treatment intended to be specified in the order (including arrangements for the reception of the offender where he is to be required to submit to treatment as a resident patient); and

- the offender has expressed his willingness to comply with such a requirement.

While the offender is under treatment as a resident patient in pursuance of a requirement of the probation order, his responsible officer shall carry out the supervision of the offender to such extent only as may be necessary for the purpose of the revocation or amendment of the order.

Where the medical practitioner or chartered psychologist by whom or under whose direction an offender is being treated for his mental condition in pursuance of a probation order is of the opinion that part of the treatment can be better or more conveniently given in or at an institution or place which:

- is not specified in the order, and

- is one in or at which the treatment of the offender will be given by or under the direction of a registered medical practitioner or chartered psychologist,

he may, with the consent of the offender, make arrangements for him to be treated accordingly.

Such alternative arrangements may provide for the offender to receive part of his treatment as a resident patient in an institution or place notwithstanding that the institution or place is not one which could have been specified for that purpose in the probation order.

Where any such arrangements are made for the treatment of an offender:

- the medical practitioner or chartered psychologist by whom the arrangements are made shall give notice in writing to the offender's responsible officer, specifying the institution or place in or at which the treatment is to be carried out; and

- the treatment provided for by the arrangements shall be deemed to be treatment to which he is required to submit in pursuance of the probation order.

Requirements as to treatment for drug or alcohol dependency

The probation order may include a requirement that the offender shall submit, during the whole of the probation period or during such part of that period as may be specified in the order, to treatment by or under the direction of a person having the necessary qualifications or experience with a view to the reduction or elimination of the offender's dependency on drugs or alcohol.

The power to include such a requirement arises only where the court proposing is satisfied:

- that the offender is dependent on drugs or alcohol;

- that his dependency caused or contributed to the offence in respect of which the order is proposed to be made; and

- that his dependency is such as requires and may be susceptible to treatment.

The treatment required by any such order shall be such one of the following kinds of treatment as may be specified in the order:

- treatment as a resident in such institution or place as may be specified in the order;

- treatment as a non-resident in or at such institution or place as may be so specified;

- treatment by or under the direction of such person having the necessary qualifications or experience as may be so specified;

but the nature of the treatment shall not be otherwise than that specified in the order.

A court shall not include in a probation order a requirement that the offender shall submit to treatment for his dependency on drugs or alcohol unless:

- it is satisfied that arrangements have been or can be made for the treatment intended to be specified in the order (including arrangements for the reception of the offender where he is to be required to submit to treatment as a resident); and

- the offender has expressed his willingness to comply with such a requirement.

While the offender is under treatment as a resident in pursuance of a requirement of the probation order, his responsible officer shall carry out the offender's supervision to such extent only as may be necessary for the purpose of the revocation or amendment of the order.

Where the person by whom or under whose direction an offender is being treated for dependency on drugs or alcohol in pursuance of a probation order is of the opinion that part of the treatment can be better or more conveniently given in or at an institution or place which:

- is not specified in the order, and

- is one in or at which the treatment of the offender will be given by or under the direction of a person having the necessary qualifications or experience, he may, with the consent of the offender, make arrangements for him to be treated accordingly.

The reference to the offender being dependent on drugs or alcohol includes a reference to his having a propensity towards the misuse of drugs or alcohol; and references to his dependency on drugs or alcohol shall be construed accordingly.

However, where the court has received notification that that arrangements for implementing drug treatment and testing orders are available in the area proposed to be specified in the probation order, the power to make requirements of this kind arises only in respect of alcohol.

Breach, revocation and amendment of probation orders

Schedule 3, Powers of Criminal Courts (Sentencing) Act 2000

Schedule 3, Powers of Criminal Courts (Sentencing) Act 2000 deals with the breach, revocation and amendment of probation orders.[3]

Community service orders

Community Punishment Orders are referred to in the Powers of Criminal Courts (Sentencing) Act 2000 as community service orders.[4]

Where a person aged 16 or over is convicted of an offence punishable with imprisonment, the court by or before which he is convicted may make an order requiring him to perform unpaid work.[5]

The number of hours which a person may be required to work under a community service order shall be specified in the order and shall be in the aggregate:

• not less than 40; and

• not more than 240.

A court shall not make a community service order in respect of an offender unless, after hearing (if the court thinks it necessary) an appropriate officer, the court is satisfied that the offender is a suitable person to perform work under such an order.

---

3. See the section dealing with breach, revocation and amendment.
4. Section 46(2), Powers of Criminal Courts (Sentencing) Act 2000.
5. The performance of community service or the community service element of a combination order is governed by the Community Service and Combination Order Rules 1992.

An appropriate officer means:

- in the case of an offender aged 18 or over, a probation officer or social worker of a local authority social services department; and

- in the case of an offender aged under 18, a probation officer, a social worker of a local authority social services department or a member of a youth offending team.

Where a court makes community service orders in respect of two or more offences of which the offender has been convicted by or before the court, the court may direct that the hours of work specified in any of those orders shall be concurrent with or additional to those specified in any other of those orders, but so that the total number of hours which are not concurrent shall not exceed the maximum of 240 hours.[6]

Before making a community service order, the court shall explain to the offender in ordinary language:

- the purpose and effect of the order;

- the consequences which may follow if he fails to comply with any of those requirements; and

- that the court has power to review the order on the application either of the offender or of the responsible officer.

Obligations of person subject to community service order

An offender in respect of whom a community service order is in force shall:[7]

- keep in touch with the responsible officer in accordance with such instructions as he may from time to time be given by that officer and notify him of any change of address; and

- perform for the number of hours specified in the order such work at such times as he may be instructed by the responsible officer.

The instructions given by the responsible officer shall, as far as practicable, be such as to avoid any conflict with the offender's religious beliefs or with the requirements of any other community order to which he may be subject and any

6.   Consecutive orders may be imposed at different times; however, they should not total more than 240 hours. The question is whether the total number of hours exceeds 240 hours and not whether there remains 240 hours to be served *R v Anderson* 1989 11 Cr App Rep (S) 417.

7.   Section 47, Powers of Criminal Courts (Sentencing) Act 2000.

interference with the times, if any, at which he normally works or attends school or any other educational establishment.

Subject to the power to extend an order, the work required to be performed under a community service order shall be performed during the period of twelve months beginning with the date of the order; but, unless revoked, the order shall remain in force until the offender has worked under it for the number of hours specified in it.

The responsible officer will usually be a member of the Probation Service or the Youth Offending Team depending on the age of the offender.

Breach, revocation and amendment of community service orders

Schedule 3, Powers of Criminal Courts (Sentencing) Act 2000

Schedule 3, Powers of Criminal Courts (Sentencing) Act 2000 provides for the power to deal with breaches, revocation and amendment of community service orders.[8]

Combination orders

Community Rehabilitation and Punishment Orders are referred to in the Powers of Criminal Courts (Sentencing) Act 2000 as combination orders.

Probation and community service may only be imposed in respect of the same offence by the making of a combination order.[9]

Where a person aged 16 or over is convicted of an offence punishable with imprisonment the court may make an order requiring him both:

- to be under supervision for a period specified in the order, being not less than twelve months nor more than three years; and

- to perform unpaid work for a number of hours so specified, being in the aggregate not less than 40 nor more than 100.[10]

---

8. See below.
9. It would appear to follow that it would be unwise if not unlawful to make a probation order in respect of one offence and a community service order in respect of another where an offender has been convicted of two or more offences.
10. Section 51, Powers of Criminal Courts (Sentencing) Act 2000.

The power to make a combination order arises only where the court is of the opinion that the making of a combination order is desirable in the interests of

- securing the rehabilitation of the offender; or

- protecting the public from harm from him or preventing the commission by him of further offences.

The probation part of a combination order may include any of the additional requirements available for inclusion in a dedicated probation order.

Breach, amendment and revocation

Schedule 3, Powers of Criminal Courts (Sentencing) Act 2000

Schedule 3, Powers of Criminal Courts (Sentencing) Act 2000 which makes provision for dealing with failures to comply with the requirements of certain community orders, for revoking such orders with or without the substitution of other sentences and for amending such orders applies to combination orders.[11]

Drug treatment and testing orders

Where a person aged 16 or over is convicted of an offence, the court by or before which he is convicted may make an order which has effect for a period specified in the order of not less than six months nor more than three years ("the treatment and testing period") and includes requirements for treatment and testing.[12]

The order may not be made in relation to an offence committed before 30th September 1998.

A court shall not make a drug treatment and testing order in respect of an offender unless it is satisfied:

- that he is dependent on or has a propensity to misuse drugs; and

- that his dependency or propensity is such as requires and may be susceptible to treatment.

For the purpose of ascertaining whether the offender has any drug in his body, the court may by order require him to provide samples of such description as it may specify; but the court shall not make such an order unless the offender expresses his willingness to comply with its requirements.

---

11.   See below.
12.   Section 52, Powers of Criminal Courts (Sentencing) Act 2000.

Before making a drug treatment and testing order, the court shall explain to the offender in ordinary language:

- the effect of the order and of the requirements proposed to be included in it;

- the consequences which may follow if he fails to comply with any of those requirements;

- that the order will be periodically reviewed at intervals as provided for in the order; and

- that the order may be reviewed on the application either of the offender or of the responsible officer.

A court shall not make a drug treatment and testing order unless the offender expresses his willingness to comply with its requirements. Practice has also developed of reserving drug treatment and testing orders for offenders who are at high risk of receiving a custodial sentence and have expressed a willingness to undergo an intensive supervised programme of drug treatment. Given the financial implications of such an order for the treatment providers, drug treatment and testing orders are not likely to be made without heavy thought by the court, the practitioner and offender.

The treatment and testing requirements

A drug treatment and testing order shall include a requirement ("the treatment requirement") that the offender shall submit, during the whole of the treatment and testing period, to treatment by or under the direction of a specified person having the necessary qualifications or experience ("the treatment provider") with a view to the reduction or elimination of the offender's dependency on or propensity to misuse drugs.

The required treatment for any particular period shall be:

- treatment as a resident in such institution or place as may be specified in the order; or

- treatment as a non-resident in or at such institution or place, and at such intervals, as may be so specified;

but the nature of the treatment shall not be otherwise specified in the order.

A court shall not make a drug treatment and testing order unless it is satisfied that arrangements have been or can be made for the treatment intended to be specified in the order (including arrangements for the reception of the offender where he is to be required to submit to treatment as a resident).

A drug treatment and testing order shall include a requirement ("the testing requirement") that, for the purpose of ascertaining whether he has any drug in his body during the treatment and testing period, the offender shall during that period, at such times or in such circumstances as may (subject to the provisions of the order) be determined by the treatment provider, provide samples of such description as may be so determined.

The testing requirement shall specify for each month the minimum number of occasions on which samples are to be provided.

Provisions of order as to supervision and periodic review

An offender made the subject of a drug treatment and testing order will be placed under the supervision of a responsible officer from either the Probation Service or the youth offending team depending on the offender's age.

A drug treatment and testing order shall also:

- require the offender to keep in touch with the responsible officer in accordance with such instructions as he may from time to time be given by that officer, and to notify him of any change of address; and

- provide that the results of the tests carried out on the samples provided by the offender in pursuance of the testing requirement shall be communicated to the responsible officer.

Supervision by the responsible officer shall be carried out to such extent only as may be necessary for the purpose of enabling him

- to report on the offender's progress to the court responsible for the order;

- to report to that court any failure by the offender to comply with the requirements of the order; and

- to determine whether the circumstances are such that he should apply to that court for the revocation or amendment of the order.

A drug treatment and testing order shall:

- provide for the order to be reviewed periodically at intervals of not less than one month;

- provide for each review of the order to be made at a hearing held for the purpose by the court responsible for the order (a "review hearing");

- require the offender to attend each review hearing;

- provide for the responsible officer to make to the court responsible for the order, before each review, a report in writing on the offender's progress under the order; and

- provide for each such report to include the test results communicated to the responsible officer and the views of the treatment provider as to the treatment and testing of the offender.

Periodic reviews

At a review hearing the court may, after considering the responsible officer's report, amend any requirement or provision of the drug treatment and testing order.

The court:

- shall not amend the treatment or testing requirement unless the offender expresses his willingness to comply with the requirement as amended;

- shall not amend any provision of the order so as to reduce the treatment and testing period below the minimum period, or to increase it above the maximum period; and

- except with the consent of the offender, shall not amend any requirement or provision of the order while an appeal against the order is pending.

If the offender fails to express his willingness to comply with the treatment or testing requirement as proposed to be amended by the court, the court may revoke the order and deal with him, for the offence in respect of which the order was made, in any way in which it could deal with him if he had just been convicted by the court of the offence.

In dealing with the offender under this provision the court shall take into account the extent to which the offender has complied with the requirements of the order; and may impose a custodial sentence (where the order was made in respect of an offence punishable with such a sentence).

If at a review hearing the court, after considering the responsible officer's report, is of the opinion that the offender's progress under the order is satisfactory, the court may so amend the order as to provide for each subsequent review to be made by the court without a hearing.

If at a review without a hearing the court, after considering the responsible officer's report, is of the opinion that the offender's progress under the order is no longer satisfactory, the court may require the offender to attend a hearing of the court at a specified time and place.

At that hearing the court, after considering that report, may exercise its powers as if the hearing were a review hearing and amend the order as to provide for each subsequent review to be made at a review hearing.

Any reference to the court, in relation to a review without a hearing, shall be construed in the case of the Crown Court, as a reference to a judge of the court and in the case of a magistrates' court, as a reference to a justice of the peace acting for the commission area for which the court acts.

Breach, revocation and amendment of drug treatment and testing orders

Schedule 3, Powers of Criminal Courts (Sentencing) Act 2000

Schedule 3, Powers of Criminal Courts (Sentencing) Act 2000 which makes provision for dealing with failures to comply with the requirements of certain community orders, for revoking such orders with or without the substitution of other sentences and for amending such orders applies to drug treatment and testing orders.[13]

---

13.   See below.

Community orders available for offenders of any age

Curfew orders

Where a person is convicted of an offence, the court by or before which he is convicted may make an order requiring him to remain, for periods specified in the order, at a place so specified.[14]

An order of this kind is referred to as a "curfew order".

A curfew order may specify different places or different periods for different days, but shall not specify:

- periods which fall outside the period of six months beginning with the day on which it is made; or

- periods which amount to less than two hours or more than twelve hours in any one day.

The requirements in a curfew order shall, as far as practicable, be such as to avoid any conflict with the offender's religious beliefs or with the requirements of any other community order to which he may be subject and any interference with the times, if any, at which he normally works or attends school or any other educational establishment.

A curfew order shall include provision for making a person responsible for monitoring the offender's whereabouts during the curfew periods specified in the order; and a person who is made so responsible shall be of a description specified in an order made by the Secretary of State.

Before making a curfew order, the court shall obtain and consider information about the place proposed to be specified in the order (including information as to the attitude of persons likely to be affected by the enforced presence there of the offender).

Before making a curfew order, the court shall explain to the offender in ordinary language:

- the effect of the order (including any additional requirements proposed to be included in the order in accordance with section 38 of the Act dealing with electronic monitoring);

---

14. Section 37, Powers of Criminal Courts (Sentencing) Act 2000.

- the consequences which may follow if he fails to comply with any of the requirements of the order; and

- that the court has power to review the order on the application either of the offender or of the responsible officer.

Electronic monitoring of curfew orders

A curfew order may in addition include requirements for securing the electronic monitoring of the offender's whereabouts during the curfew periods specified in the order. Electronic monitoring arrangements made by the Secretary of State under this section may include entering into contracts with other persons for the electronic monitoring by them of offenders' whereabouts.

Breach, revocation and amendment of curfew orders

Schedule 3,
Powers of Criminal
Courts (Sentencing)
Act 2000

Schedule 3, Powers of Criminal Courts (Sentencing) Act 2000 which makes provision for dealing with failures to comply with the requirements of certain community orders, for revoking such orders with or without the substitution of other sentences and for amending such orders applies to curfew orders.

Attendance centre orders; offenders aged under 21 years

Attendance centre orders

Where:

- a person aged under 21 is convicted by or before a court of an offence punishable with imprisonment; or

- a court would have power, but for the restrictions on imprisonment of young offenders and defaulters, to commit a person aged under 21 to prison in default of payment of any sum of money or for failing to do or abstain from doing anything required to be done or left undone; or

- a court has power to commit a person aged at least 21 but under 25 to prison in default of payment of any sum of money, the court may, if it has been notified by the Secretary of State that an attendance centre is available for the reception of persons of his description, order him to attend at such a centre, to be specified in the order, for such number of hours as may be so specified.[15]

An order of this kind is referred to as an "attendance centre order".

The aggregate number of hours for which an attendance centre order may require a person to attend at an attendance centre shall not be less than 12 except where:

- he is aged under 14; and

- the court is of the opinion that 12 hours would be excessive, having regard to his age or any other circumstances.

The aggregate number of hours shall not exceed 12 except where the court is of the opinion, having regard to all the circumstances, that 12 hours would be inadequate, and in that case:

- shall not exceed 24 where the person is aged under 16; and

- shall not exceed 36 where the person is aged 16 or over but under 21 or under 25.

A court may make an attendance centre order in respect of a person before a previous attendance centre order made in respect of him has ceased to have effect, and may determine the number of hours to be specified in the order without regard:

- to the number specified in the previous order; or

- to the fact that that order is still in effect.

An attendance centre order shall not be made unless the court is satisfied that the attendance centre to be specified in it is reasonably accessible to the person concerned, having regard to his age, the means of access available to him and any other circumstances.

The times at which a person is required to attend at an attendance centre shall, as far as practicable, be such as to avoid any conflict with his religious beliefs or with the requirements of any other community order to which he may be subject and

---

15. Section 60, Powers of Criminal Courts (Sentencing) Act 2000. For fuller details of the provisions as they apply in the youth court see the section of the sentencing of youths below at page XX.

any interference with the times, if any, at which he normally works or attends school or any other educational establishment.

The first time at which the person is required to attend at an attendance centre shall be a time at which the centre is available for his attendance in accordance with the notification of the Secretary of State and shall be specified in the order. Subsequent times are fixed by the manager of the attendance centre in accordance with the Attendance Centre Rules 1995.

Attendance Centre Rules 1995

A person shall not be required under this section to attend at an attendance centre on more than one occasion on any day, or for more than three hours on any occasion.

Where a person ("the defaulter") has been ordered to attend at an attendance centre in default of the payment of any sum of money:

- on payment of the whole sum to any person authorised to receive it, the attendance centre order shall cease to have effect;

- on payment of a part of the sum to any such person, the total number of hours for which the defaulter is required to attend at the centre shall be reduced proportionately, that is to say by such number of complete hours as bears to the total number the proportion most nearly approximating to, without exceeding, the proportion which the part bears to the whole sum.

Breach, revocation and amendment of attendance centre orders

Schedule 5, Powers of Criminal Courts (Sentencing) Act 2000

Schedule 5, Powers of Criminal Courts (Sentencing) Act 2000 (which makes provision for dealing with failures to comply with attendance centre orders, for revoking such orders with or without the substitution of other sentences and for amending such orders) applies to attendance centre orders.

Breach of order or attendance centre rules

Where an attendance centre order is in force and it appears on information to a justice acting for a relevant petty sessions area that the offender:

- has failed to attend in accordance with the order; or

- while attending has committed a breach of rules which cannot be adequately dealt with under those rules,

the justice may issue a summons requiring the offender to appear at the place and time specified in the summons before a magistrates' court acting for the area or, if the information is in writing and on oath, may issue a warrant for the offender's arrest requiring him to be brought before such a court.

If it is proved to the satisfaction of the magistrates' court before which an offender appears or is brought that he has failed without reasonable excuse to attend or has committed such a breach of rules, that court may deal with him in any one of the following ways:

- it may impose on him a fine not exceeding £1,000;

- where the attendance centre order was made by a magistrates' court, it may deal with him, for the offence in respect of which the order was made, in any way in which he could have been dealt with for that offence by the court which made the order if the order had not been made; or

- where the order was made by the Crown Court, it may commit him to custody or release him on bail until he can be brought or appear before the Crown Court.

Where the court decides to impose a fine, this is without prejudice to the continuation of the order itself.

Where a magistrates' court deals with an offender in any way in which he could have been dealt with for that offence by the court which made the order if the order had not been made, it shall revoke the attendance centre order if it is still in force.

In dealing with an offender a magistrates' court:

- shall take into account the extent to which the offender has complied with the requirements of the attendance centre order; and

- in the case of an offender who has wilfully and persistently failed to comply with those requirements, may impose a custodial sentence.

A person sentenced in this way for an offence may appeal to the Crown Court against the sentence.

Where the offender is brought or appears before the Crown Court and it is proved to the satisfaction of the court:

- that he has failed without reasonable excuse to attend; or

- that he has committed a breach of rules which cannot be dealt with under those rules;

that court may deal with him, for the offence in respect of which the order was made, in any way in which it could have dealt with him for that offence if it had not made the order.

Where the Crown Court deals with an offender in this way, it shall revoke the attendance centre order if it is still in force.

In dealing with an offender, the Crown Court:

- shall take into account the extent to which the offender has complied with the requirements of the attendance centre order; and

- in the case of an offender who has wilfully and persistently failed to comply with those requirements, may impose a custodial sentence.

In proceedings before the Crown Court any question whether there has been a failure to attend or a breach of the rules shall be determined by the court and not by the verdict of a jury.

Revocation of order with or without re-sentencing

Where an attendance centre order is in force in respect of an offender, an appropriate court may, on an application made by the offender or by the officer in charge of the relevant attendance centre, revoke the order.

The appropriate court means:

- the Crown Court where the court which made the order was the Crown Court and there is included in the order a direction that the power to revoke the order is reserved to that court;

- in any other case, either of the following:

  - 'a magistrates' court acting for the petty sessions area in which the relevant attendance centre is situated;

- the court which made the order.

Any power conferred on a magistrates' court to revoke an attendance centre order made by such a court, or on the Crown Court to revoke an attendance centre order made by the Crown Court, includes power to deal with the offender, for the offence in respect of which the order was made, in any way in which he could have been dealt with for that offence by the court which made the order if the order had not been made.

A person sentenced by a magistrates' court under as part of the revocation process above for an offence may appeal to the Crown Court against the sentence.

Amendment of order

Where an attendance centre order is in force in respect of an offender, an appropriate magistrates' court may, on an application made by the offender or by the officer in charge of the relevant attendance centre, by order:

- vary the day or hour specified in the order for the offender's first attendance at the relevant attendance centre; or

- substitute for the relevant attendance centre an attendance centre which the court is satisfied is reasonably accessible to the offender, having regard to his age, the means of access available to him and any other circumstances.

The appropriate magistrates' court means a magistrates' court acting for the petty sessions area in which the relevant attendance centre is situated or (except where the attendance centre order was made by the Crown Court) the magistrates' court which made the order.

Orders made on appeal

Schedule 5, Powers
of Criminal Courts
(Sentencing) Act
2000

Where an attendance centre order has been made on appeal, for the purposes of Schedule 5, Powers of Criminal Courts (Sentencing) Act 2000 it shall be deemed:

- if it was made on an appeal brought from a magistrates' court, to have been made by that magistrates' court;

- if it was made on an appeal brought from the Crown Court or from the criminal division of the Court of Appeal, to have been made by the Crown Court.

Orders for defaulters

Schedule 5

The provisions of Schedule 5 are amended to deal with breach, revocation and amendment where the order was made in respect of defaulters. These amendments are not reproduced here.

CHAPTER 6
BREACH, REVOCATION AND AMENDMENT OF COMMUNITY ORDERS

Schedule 3 of the Powers of Criminal Courts (Sentencing) Act 2000

Schedule 3

Schedule 3 applies to the following community orders:

- a curfew order;

- a probation order;

- a community service order;

- a combination order;

- a drug treatment and testing order.

The court with jurisdiction to deal with breach proceedings, revocation or amendment of such orders is initially the magistrates' court unless a community penalty made in the Crown Court on indictment has been reserved to the judge who made the order. In such a case the role of the magistrates' court is limited to the issue of a summons or warrant to secure the attendance of the offender before the relevant Crown Court. In all other cases, whether the magistrates' court retain jurisdiction depends on which court made the order in question and whether or not it is intended to revoke that order and re-sentence the offender in respect of the original offences.

In relation to a curfew order, the term "the petty sessions area concerned" means the petty sessions area in which the place for the time being specified in the order is situated. In relation to a probation, community service, combination or drug treatment and testing order, the petty sessions area for the time being specified in the order.

Orders made on appeal

Schedule 3
Powers of Criminal
Courts (Sentencing)
Act 2000
Where a curfew, probation, community service or combination order has been made on appeal, for the purposes of Schedule 3 it shall be deemed if it was made on an appeal brought from a magistrates' court, to have been made by a magistrates' court and if it was made on an appeal brought from the Crown Court or from the criminal division of the Court of Appeal, to have been made by the Crown Court.

An offender subject to a community order against whom it is alleged that he has failed to comply with the requirements of the relevant order may be brought before the magistrates' court (or Crown Court, if the breach of the order has been reserved to the judge who made the order) by either summons or warrant issued by a justice of the peace.[1]

Powers of magistrates' court

If it is proved to the satisfaction of a magistrates' court before which an offender appears or is brought that he has failed without reasonable excuse to comply with any of the requirements of the relevant order, the court may deal with him in respect of the failure in any one of the following ways:

- it may impose on him a fine not exceeding £1,000;

- where the offender is aged 16 or over it may make a community service order in respect of him;

- where

    - the relevant order is a curfew order and the offender is aged under 16, or

    - the relevant order is a probation order or combination order and the offender is aged under 21,

    it may make an attendance centre order in respect of him; or

---

1. Paragraph 3, Schedule 3, Powers of Criminal Courts (Sentencing) Act 2000.

- where the relevant order was made by a magistrates' court, it may deal with him for the offence in respect of which the order was made, in any way in which it could deal with him if he had just been convicted by the court of the offence.

In dealing with an offender for the original offences, a magistrates' court:

- shall take into account the extent to which the offender has complied with the requirements of the relevant order; and

- in the case of an offender who has wilfully and persistently failed to comply with those requirements, may impose a custodial sentence

If the magistrates' court deals with the offender for the original offences in any way it shall revoke the relevant order if it is still in force.

Where a relevant order was made by the Crown Court the magistrates' courts' powers are limited to:

- where the offender is aged 16 or over it may make a community service order in respect of him;

- where

  - the relevant order is a curfew order and the offender is aged under 16, or

  - the relevant order is a probation order or combination order and the offender is aged under 21,

  it may, subject to paragraph 8 below, make an attendance centre order in respect of him; or

  - If the magistrates' court forms the opinion that neither of these methods of disposal are suitable, and the discretion is unfettered, it may instead commit him to custody or release him on bail until he can be brought or appear before the Crown Court.

Powers of Crown Court

Where an offender is brought or appears before the Crown Court and it is proved to the satisfaction of that court that he has failed without reasonable excuse to comply with any of the requirements of the relevant order, the Crown Court may deal with him in respect of the failure in any one of the following ways:

- it may impose on him a fine not exceeding £1,000;

- where the offender is aged 16 or over it may make a community service order in respect of him;

- where

    - the relevant order is a curfew order and the offender is aged under 16, or

    - the relevant order is a probation order or combination order and the offender is aged under 21,

    it may make an attendance centre order in respect of him; or

- it may deal with him, for the offence in respect of which the order was made, in any way in which it could deal with him if he had just been convicted by the court of the offence.

In dealing with an offender for the original offences, the Crown Court:

- shall take into account the extent to which the offender has complied with the requirements of the relevant order; and

- in the case of an offender who has wilfully and persistently failed to comply with those requirements, may impose a custodial sentence.

Where the Crown Court deals with an offender for the original offences, it shall revoke the relevant order if it is still in force.

In proceedings before the Crown Court under this paragraph any question whether the offender has failed to comply with the requirements of the relevant order shall be determined by the court and not by the verdict of a jury.

Community Orders – Non-breaches

Further offences

An offender who is convicted of a further offence while a relevant order is in force in respect of him shall not on that account be liable to be dealt with as if in respect of a failure to comply with any requirement of the order.

Refusal to undertake certain treatments

An offender who is required by a probation order or combination order to submit to treatment for his mental condition, or his dependency on or propensity to misuse drugs or alcohol or is required by a drug treatment and testing order to submit to treatment for his dependency on or propensity to misuse drugs, shall not be treated as having failed to comply with that requirement on the ground only that he has refused to undergo any surgical, electrical or other treatment if, in the opinion of the court, his refusal was reasonable having regard to all the circumstances.

Secondary Orders

Community service orders imposed for breach of relevant order

The normal duties, powers and obligations relevant to a community service order shall apply equally to a community service order made for breach of a relevant order. This type of community service order is known as a secondary order.

The number of hours which an offender may be required to work under a secondary order shall be specified in the order and shall not exceed 60 in the aggregate and:

- where the relevant order is a community service order, the number of hours which the offender may be required to work under the secondary order shall not be such that the total number of hours under both orders exceeds the maximum of 240 hours; and

- where the relevant order is a combination order, the number of hours which the offender may be required to work under the secondary order shall not be such that the total number of hours under the secondary order and the community service element of the combination order, exceeds 100 hours.

Sections 35 and 36, Powers of Criminal Courts (Sentencing) Act 2000 The restrictions and procedural requirements for community sentences set out in sections 35 and 36, Powers of Criminal Courts (Sentencing) Act 2000 do not apply in relation to a secondary order.

Breach of secondary order

- The power conferred on the court to deal with the offender for the offence in respect of which the order was made shall be construed as a power to deal with the offender, for his failure to comply with the original order, in any way in which the court could deal with him if that failure had just been proved to the satisfaction of the court;

- References to the offence in respect of which the order was made shall be construed as references to the failure to comply in respect of which the order was made; and

- The power conferred on the Crown Court to deal with the offender for the offence in respect of which the order was made shall be construed as a power to deal with the offender, for his failure to comply with the original order, in any way in which a magistrates' court (if the original order was made by a magistrates' court) or the Crown Court (if the original order was made by the Crown Court) could deal with him if that failure had just been proved to its satisfaction;

and in this context "the original order" means the relevant order the failure to comply with which led to the making of the secondary order.[2]

Similar provisions apply in respect of an attendance centre order made for breach of a community order.

What happens to the original order?

The original community order remains in force until such time as it is revoked by the court on re-sentence or application to revoke or its terms are fully complied with.[3]

---

2.   Paragraph 7, Schedule 3, Powers of Criminal Courts (Sentencing) Act 2000.
3.   Paragraph 9, Schedule 3, Powers of Criminal Courts (Sentencing) Act 2000.

Breach of a relevant order by a child or young person

Where a relevant order was made by a magistrates' court in the case of an offender under 18 years of age in respect of an offence triable only on indictment in the case of an adult, any powers exercisable in respect of the breach in respect of the offender after he attains the age of 18 shall be powers to do either or both of the following:

- to impose a fine not exceeding £5,000 for the offence in respect of which the order was made;

- to deal with the offender for that offence in any way in which a magistrates' court could deal with him if it had just convicted him of an offence punishable with imprisonment for a term not exceeding six months.

Revocation of order

With or without re-sentencing: powers of magistrates' court

Paragraph 10, schedule 3, Powers of Criminal Courts (Sentencing) Act 2000

The court has power to revoke a community order. The power arises under paragraph 10 of Schedule 3, Powers of Criminal Courts (Sentencing) Act 2000 where a relevant order made by a magistrates' court is in force in respect of any offender and on the application of the offender or the responsible officer it appears to the appropriate magistrates' court that, having regard to circumstances which have arisen since the order was made, it would be in the interests of justice for the order to be revoked or for the offender to be dealt with in some other way for the offence in respect of which the order was made.

"The appropriate magistrates court" means in the case of a drug treatment and testing order, the magistrates' court responsible for the order and in the case of any other relevant order, a magistrates' court acting for the petty sessions area concerned.

The appropriate magistrates' court may revoke the order or both revoke the order and deal with the offender, for the offence in respect of which the order was made, in any way in which it could deal with him if he had just been convicted by the court of the offence.

The circumstances in which a probation, combination or drug treatment and testing order may be revoked without re-sentence shall include the offender's making good progress or his responding satisfactorily to supervision or, as the case may be, treatment.

In dealing with an offender by re-sentencing him, a magistrates' court shall take into account the extent to which the offender has complied with the requirements of the relevant order.

Where a magistrates' court proposes to exercise its powers under this paragraph otherwise than on the application of the offender, it shall summon him to appear before the court and, if he does not appear in answer to the summons, may issue a warrant for his arrest.

No application may be made by the offender for revocation while an appeal against the relevant order is pending. Once a court has dealt with the revocation an offender may appeal against any re-sentence to the Crown Court.

With or without re-sentencing: powers of Crown Court on conviction etc.

The Crown Court is also empowered to deal with revocation where a relevant order made by the Crown Court is in force in respect of an offender and the offender or the responsible officer applies to the Crown Court for the order to be revoked or for the offender to be dealt with in some other way for the offence in respect of which the order was made. The same is true for an offender in respect of whom a relevant order is in force is convicted of an offence before the Crown Court or, having been committed by a magistrates' court to the Crown Court for sentence, is brought or appears before the Crown Court.

If it appears to the Crown Court to be in the interests of justice to do so, having regard to circumstances which have arisen since the order was made, the Crown Court may revoke the order or both revoke the order and deal with the offender, for the offence in respect of which the order was made, in any way in which the court which made the order could deal with him if he had just been convicted of that offence by or before the court which made the order.

The circumstances in which a probation, combination or drug treatment and testing order may be revoked without re-sentence shall include the offender's making good progress or his responding satisfactorily to supervision or, as the case may be, treatment.

In dealing with an offender by way of re-sentence, the Crown Court shall take into account the extent to which the offender has complied with the requirements of the relevant order.

Substitution of conditional discharge for probation or combination order

The appropriate court may revoke the probation or combination order and make an order discharging the offender in respect of the offence for which the probation or combination order was made, subject to the condition that he commits no offence during the period specified in the order. The period specified in the order shall be the period beginning with the making of that order and ending with the date when the probation period specified in the probation or combination order would have ended.

This power may be exercised where a probation order or combination order is in force in respect of any offender and where on the application of the offender or the responsible officer to the appropriate court it appears to the court that, having regard to circumstances which have arisen since the order was made, it would be in the interests of justice for the order to be revoked and for an order to be made discharging the offender conditionally for the offence for which the probation or combination order was made.

The appropriate court means:

- where the probation or combination order was made by a magistrates' court, a magistrates' court acting for the petty sessions area concerned; or

- where the probation or combination order was made by the Crown Court, the Crown Court.

An application under this provision may be heard in the offender's absence if the application is made by the responsible officer and that officer produces to the court a statement by the offender that he understands the effect of an order for conditional discharge and consents to the making of the application.

No application may be made under this paragraph while an appeal against the probation or combination order is pending.

Sections 1(11), 2(9) and 66(4) Crime and Disorder Act 1998

Practitioners should be careful to note that in respect of children and young offenders sections 1(11), 2(9) and 66(4), Crime and Disorder Act 1998 (which prevent a court from making an order for conditional discharge in certain cases) shall have effect as if the reference to the court by or before which a person is convicted of an offence there mentioned included a reference to a court dealing with an application under this power in respect of the offence.

Revocation following custodial sentence by magistrates' court unconnected with order

Where:

- an offender in respect of whom a relevant order is in force is convicted of an offence by a magistrates' court unconnected with the order;

- the court imposes a custodial sentence on the offender; and

- it appears to the court, on the application of the offender or the responsible officer, that it would be in the interests of justice to exercise its powers under this paragraph, having regard to circumstances which have arisen since the order was made;

the court may

- if the order was made by a magistrates' court, revoke it;

- if the order was made by the Crown Court, commit the offender in custody or release him on bail until he can be brought or appear before the Crown Court.

Where an offender is brought or appears before the Crown Court and it appears to the Crown Court to be in the interests of justice to do so, having regard to circumstances which have arisen since the relevant order was made, the Crown Court may revoke the order.

Amendment of order

Amendment by reason of change of residence

A court has power to amend community orders from time to time. The most usual amendment is made when an offender moves from one petty sessions area to another and the order is amended accordingly.

Where, at any time while a relevant order (other than a drug treatment and testing order) is in force in respect of an offender, a magistrates' court acting for the petty sessions area concerned is satisfied that the offender proposes to change, or has changed, his residence from that petty sessions area to another petty sessions area. The court may, and on the application of the responsible officer shall, amend the relevant order by substituting the other petty sessions area for the area specified in the order or, in the case of a curfew order, a place in that other area for the place so specified.

The court shall not amend under this power a probation or curfew order which contains requirements which, in the opinion of the court, cannot be complied with unless the offender continues to reside in the petty sessions area concerned unless it either cancels those requirements or substitutes for those requirements other requirements which can be complied with if the offender ceases to reside in that area.

The court shall not amend a community service order or combination order under this power unless it appears to the court that provision can be made for the offender to perform work under the order under the arrangements which exist for persons who reside in the other petty sessions area to perform work under such orders.

Amendment of requirements of probation, combination or curfew order

A magistrates' court acting for the petty sessions area concerned may, on the application of the offender or the responsible officer, by order amend a probation or curfew order or the probation element of a combination order:

- by cancelling any of the requirements of the probation or curfew order or of the probation element of the combination order; or

- by inserting in the probation or curfew order or probation element of the combination order (either in addition to or in substitution for any of its requirements) any requirement which the court could include if it were then making the order.

A magistrates' court shall not amend a probation order or the probation element of a combination order:

- by reducing the probation period, or by extending that period beyond the end of three years from the date of the original order; or

- by inserting in it a requirement that the offender shall submit to treatment for his mental condition, or his dependency on or propensity to misuse drugs or alcohol, unless the offender has expressed his willingness to comply with such a requirement andthe amending order is made within three months after the date of the original order.

A magistrates' court shall not amend a curfew order by extending the curfew periods beyond the end of six months from the date of the original order.

Amendment of treatment requirements of probation or combination order on report of practitioner

Where the medical practitioner or other person by whom or under whose direction an offender is of the opinion, in pursuance of any requirement of a probation or combination order, being treated for his mental condition or his dependency on or propensity to misuse drugs or alcohol:

- that the treatment of the offender should be continued beyond the period specified in that behalf in the order;

- that the offender needs different treatment;

- that the offender is not susceptible to treatment; or

- that the offender does not require further treatment, or

- is for any reason unwilling to continue to treat or direct the treatment of the offender,

he shall make a report in writing to that effect to the responsible officer and that officer shall apply to a magistrates' court acting for the petty sessions area concerned for the variation or cancellation of the requirement.

Amendment of drug treatment and testing order

The court responsible for a drug treatment and testing order may by order vary, cancel or amend any of the requirements or provisions of the order on an application by the responsible officer.

Where the treatment provider is of the opinion that the treatment or testing requirement of the order should be varied or cancelled he shall make a report in writing to that effect to the responsible officer and that officer shall apply to the court for the variation or cancellation of the requirement.

Where the responsible officer is of the opinion:

- that the treatment or testing requirement of the order should be so varied as to specify a different treatment provider,

- that any other requirement of the order, or a provision of the order, should be varied or cancelled, or

- that the order should be so amended as to provide for each subsequent periodic review to be made without a hearing instead of at a review hearing, or *vice versa*,

he shall apply to the court for the variation or cancellation of the requirement or provision or the amendment of the order.

Section 52(1), Powers of Criminal Courts (Sentencing) Act 2000

The court shall not amend the treatment or testing requirement unless the offender expresses his willingness to comply with the requirement as amended and shall not amend any provision of the order so as to reduce the treatment and testing period below the minimum specified in section 52(1), Powers of Criminal Courts (Sentencing) Act 2000, or to increase it above the maximum so specified.

If the offender fails to express his willingness to comply with the treatment or testing requirement as proposed to be amended by the court, the court may revoke the order and deal with him, for the offence in respect of which the order was made, in any way in which it could deal with him if he had just been convicted by or before the court of the offence.

In dealing with the offender in this way, the court shall take into account the extent to which the offender has complied with the requirements of the order and may impose a custodial sentence (where the order was made in respect of an offence punishable with such a sentence).

Extension of community service or combination order

Where a community service order or combination order is in force in respect of any offender, and on the application of the offender or the responsible officer, it appears to a magistrates' court acting for the petty sessions area concerned that it would be in the interests of justice to do so having regard to circumstances which have arisen since the order was made, the court may, in relation to the order, extend the period of twelve months in which the order is to be usually completed.

Where a court proposes to exercise its powers under this part of Schedule 3, otherwise than on the application of the offender, the court shall summon him to appear before the court and if he does not appear in answer to the summons, may issue a warrant for his arrest. This does not apply to an order cancelling a requirement of a relevant order or reducing the period of any requirement, or substituting a new petty sessions area or a new place for the one specified in a relevant order.

CHAPTER 7
CUSTODIAL SENTENCES

Introduction

This part deals with the statutory scheme for custodial sentences in both the magistrates' court and Crown Court. Custodial sentences represent the most severe penalty a court can impose and accordingly should be reserved for the most serious of offences. If a court is able to consider a custodial sentence, all other sentences including community penalties, fines and discharges are theoretically available.

Custodial sentences in the magistrates' court

Meaning of "custodial sentence"[1]

A custodial sentence in the magistrates' court means:

- a sentence of imprisonment;

- a sentence of detention in a young offender institution; or

- a detention and training order.[2]

General limit on magistrates' court's power to impose imprisonment or detention in a young offender institution

A magistrates' court shall not have power to impose imprisonment, or detention in a young offender institution, for more than six months in respect of any one offence.[3]

Unless expressly excluded, this restriction applies even if the offence in question is one for which a person would otherwise be liable on summary conviction to imprisonment or detention in a young offender institution for more than six months.

---

1. Section 76, Powers of Criminal Courts (Sentencing) Act 2000.
2. See the section on the sentencing of youths at page XX.
3. Section 78, Powers of Criminal Courts (Sentencing) Act 2000.

Any power of a magistrates' court to impose a term of imprisonment for non-payment of a fine, or for want of sufficient distress to satisfy a fine, shall not be limited by these restrictions.

The term "impose imprisonment" means pass a sentence of imprisonment or fix a term of imprisonment for failure to pay any sum of money, or for want of sufficient distress to satisfy any sum of money, or for failure to do or abstain from doing anything required to be done or left undone. This is an important qualification as sentences which have been imposed on a previous occasion may be activated on a subsequent date and made consecutive to the term imposed at the same time.[4]

Section 133, Magistrates' Courts Act 1980

Section 133, Magistrates' Courts Act 1980 provides that a magistrates' court imposing imprisonment or detention on any person may order that the term of imprisonment or detention shall commence on the expiration of any other term of imprisonment or detention imposed by that or any other court; but where a magistrates' court imposes two or more terms of imprisonment or detention to run consecutively the aggregate of such terms shall not exceed 6 months.

If two or more terms imposed by the court are imposed in respect of an offence triable either way which was tried summarily, the aggregate of the terms so imposed and any other terms imposed by the court may exceed 6 months but shall not exceed 12 months.

The effect of these provisions can be usefully summarised as follows:

Summary only offence	6 months maximum
Summary + summary offences	6 months maximum
Either way offence	6 months maximum
Either way + either way offences	12 months maximum
Either way + summary only offence	12 months maximum

---

4.   For example, a suspended sentence may be activated at the same time as imprisonment is imposed and made consecutive to the instant term without offending the general restriction. *R v Chamberlain* 1991 156 JP 440.

Any of the above periods may be ordered to begin at the expiration of a sentence of imprisonment or detention currently being served by the offender.

Imprisonment not imposed on the same occasion such as a suspended sentence may be activated either concurrently or consecutively to any of the above periods.

Where the court returns an offender to serve the balance of his remaining custodial sentence following his conviction for a further offence whilst subject to recall after early release, any of the above periods may be ordered to run concurrently or consecutively with the period of recall.[5]

The minimum period of imprisonment which a magistrates' court may impose is 5 days.[6]

General restrictions on imposing discretionary custodial sentences

The court shall not pass a custodial sentence on an offender unless it is of the opinion:

- that the offence, or the combination of the offence and one or more offences associated with it, was so serious that only such a sentence can be justified for the offence; or

- where the offence is a violent or sexual offence, that only such a sentence would be adequate to protect the public from serious harm from him.

This does not, however, prevent the court from passing a custodial sentence on the offender if he fails to express his willingness to comply with:

- a requirement which is proposed by the court to be included in a probation order or supervision order and which requires an expression of such willingness; or

- a requirement which is proposed by the court to be included in a drug treatment and testing order or an order to provide samples.

Where a court passes a custodial sentence, it shall state in open court that it is of the opinion that the offence is either so serious that only a custodial sentence can be justified or that only such

---

5.   See recall to prison below. *R v Worthing Justices ex parte Varley* 1998 1 WLR 819.
6.   Section 132, Magistrates' Courts Act 1980.

a sentence is adequate to protect the public from serious harm, as appropriate and state why it is of that opinion.

In any case explain to the offender in open court and in ordinary language why it is passing a custodial sentence on him. A magistrates' court shall cause a reason stated by it to be specified in the warrant of commitment and to be entered in the register.[7]

Length of custodial sentences in the magistrates' court

Subject to the above statutory restrictions the custodial sentence shall be:

* for such term (not exceeding the permitted maximum) as in the opinion of the court is commensurate with the seriousness of the offence, or the combination of the offence and one or more offences associated with it; or

* where the offence is a violent or sexual offence, for such longer term (not exceeding that maximum) as in the opinion of the court is necessary to protect the public from serious harm from the offender.

Where the court passes a custodial sentence for a term longer than is commensurate with the seriousness of the offence, or the combination of the offence and one or more offences associated with it, the court shall state in open court why it is of that opinion and explain to the offender in ordinary language why the sentence is for such a term.

Procedural requirements for imposing discretionary custodial sentences

Pre-sentence reports and other requirements

A court shall obtain and consider a pre-sentence report before forming any of the opinions it is required to form before imposing a custodial sentence. This rule does not apply if, in the circumstances of the case, the court is of the opinion that it is unnecessary to obtain a pre-sentence report.

No custodial sentence shall be invalidated by the failure of a court to obtain and consider a pre-sentence report before forming its opinion but any court on an appeal against such a sentence shall obtain and consider a pre-sentence report if none was obtained

---

7.   Section 79, Powers of Criminal Courts (Sentencing) Act 2000.

by the court below unless the appeal court is of the opinion that the court below was justified in forming an opinion that it was unnecessary to obtain a pre-sentence report or that, although the court below was not justified in forming that opinion, in the circumstances of the case at the time it is before the court, it is unnecessary to obtain a pre-sentence report.

In forming its opinion whether an offence is so serious or that the public need to be protected from the offender, a court

- shall take into account all such information as is available to it about the circumstances of the offence or (as the case may be) of the offence and the offence or offences associated with it, including any aggravating or mitigating factors; and

- in the case of an opinion that the public need to be protected from the offender, may take into account any information about the offender which is before it.

Additional requirements in case of mentally disordered offender

In any case where the offender is or appears to be mentally disordered, the court shall obtain and consider a medical report before passing a custodial sentence. This does not apply if, in the circumstances of the case, the court is of the opinion that it is unnecessary to obtain a medical report. Before passing a custodial sentence on an offender who is or appears to be mentally disordered, a court shall consider any information before it which relates to his mental condition (whether given in a medical report, a pre-sentence report or otherwise) and the likely effect of such a sentence on that condition and on any treatment which may be available for it.

No custodial sentence which is passed shall be invalidated by the failure of a court to obtain a report, but any court on an appeal against such a sentence shall obtain and consider a medical report if none was obtained by the court below.

The term "mentally disordered", in relation to any person, means suffering from a mental disorder within the meaning of the Mental Health 1983 and a "medical report" means a report as to an offender's mental condition made or submitted orally or in writing by a registered medical practitioner who is approved for the purposes of section 12, Mental Health Act 1983 by the Secretary of State as having special experience in the diagnosis or treatment of mental disorder.

Restriction on imposing custodial sentences on persons not legally represented

A magistrates' court on summary conviction shall not pass a sentence of imprisonment or detention on a person who:

- is not legally represented in that court, and

- has not been previously sentenced to that punishment by a court in any part of the United Kingdom,

unless he was granted a right to representation funded by the Legal Services Commission as part of the Criminal Defence Service but the right was withdrawn because of his conduct;[8] or having been informed of his right to apply for such representation and having had the opportunity to do so, he refused or failed to apply.[9]

For the purposes of this provision a person is to be treated as legally represented in a court if, but only if, he has the assistance of counsel or a solicitor to represent him in the proceedings in that court at some time after he is found guilty and before he is sentenced.

Restriction on consecutive sentences for released prisoners

A court sentencing a person to a term of imprisonment shall not order or direct that the term shall commence on the expiry of any other sentence of imprisonment from which he has been released. This does not prevent the court from ordering an offender to be recalled to serve the remainder of his term where he has been convicted of a further offence during the at-risk period between his actual release from a custodial sentence and the date of the expiry of that sentence.

---

8. A defendant remains unrepresented if he has been granted a representation order but dismisses his advocate before sentence until such time as the representation order is withdrawn. *R v Wilson* 1995 16 Cr App Rep (S) 997.

9. Section 83, Powers of Criminal Courts (Sentencing) Act 2000. A sentence passed in breach of this provision is not authorised by law. *R v Birmingham Justices ex parte Wyatt* 1975 3 All ER 897.

Detention of Young Offenders

Restriction on imposing imprisonment on persons under 21

Detention in a young offender institution

A young offender is a person aged at least 18 but under 21[10] is convicted of an offence which is punishable with imprisonment in the case of a person aged 21 or over, and the court is of the opinion that either the offence (or offences) is so serious that only a custodial sentence can be justified or that the public need to be protected from him, the sentence that the court is to pass is a sentence of detention in a young offender institution.[11]

Term of detention in a young offender institution, and consecutive sentences

The maximum term of detention in a young offender institution that a court may impose for an offence is the same as the maximum term of imprisonment that it may impose for that offence. A court shall not pass a sentence for an offender's detention in a young offender institution for less than 21 days.[12] This is subject to one exception. A court may pass a sentence of detention in a young offender institution for less than 21 days for an offence under section 65(6), Criminal Justice Act 1991 (breach of requirement imposed on young offender on his release from detention).

Section 65(6), Criminal Justice Act 1991

Where:

- an offender is convicted of more than one offence for which he is liable to a sentence of detention in a young offender institution, or

- an offender who is serving a sentence of detention in a young offender institution is convicted of one or more further offences for which he is liable to such a sentence,

the court shall have the same power to pass consecutive sentences of detention in a young offender institution as if they were sentences of imprisonment.

Where an offender who is serving a sentence of detention in a young offender institution and is aged 21 or over, is convicted of one or more further offences for which he is liable to imprisonment, the court shall have the power to pass one or

---

10. For sentences of detention on youths aged under 18 see the section of youth sentences.
11. Section 96, Powers of Criminal Courts (Sentencing) Act 2000.
12. Section 97, Powers of Criminal Courts (Sentencing) Act 2000.

more sentences of imprisonment to run consecutively upon the sentence of detention in a young offender institution.

Return to prison[13] where offence committed during original sentence

The power to order an offender's return to prison[14] arises where

- the offender has been serving a determinate sentence of imprisonment which he began serving on or after 1st October 1992;

Part II, Criminal Justice Act 1991

- he is released under Part II, Criminal Justice Act 1991 (early release of prisoners);

- before the date on which he would (but for his release) have served his sentence in full, he commits an offence punishable with imprisonment ("the new offence"); and

- whether before or after that date, he is convicted of the new offence.

The court by or before which a person to whom this provision applies is convicted of the new offence may, whether or not it passes any other sentence on him, order him to be returned to prison for the whole or any part of the period which:

- begins with the date of the order; and

- is equal in length to the period between the date on which the new offence was committed and the date on which his sentence would have expired but for his early release.

A magistrates' court shall not have power to order a person to whom this provision applies to be returned to prison for a period of more than six months but where the period for which he might otherwise be returned to prison exceeds this period, the court may commit him in custody or on bail to the Crown Court.

Where a person is committed to the Crown Court, it may order him to be returned to prison for the whole or any part of the period.

The power to commit the offender to the Crown Court for the purposes of determining his recall to prison is not be taken to

---

13.   In this context, an offender aged 18 to 21 years is a rule of return to a young offender institution. references to prior should be so construed.
14.   Section 116, Powers of Criminal Courts (Sentencing) Act 2000.

confer on the magistrates' court a power to commit the person to the Crown Court for sentence for the new offence, but this is without prejudice to any such power conferred on the magistrates' court by any other provision of this Act. Accordingly a new summary offence may be committed to the Crown Court under section 6, Powers of Criminal Courts (Sentencing) Act 2000 and an either way offence under section 3 of the same Act

Section 6, Powers of Criminal Courts (Sentencing) Act 2000
Section 3

The period of return is not imposed at the time of sentencing for the new offence and thus does not restrict the length of sentence which a magistrates' court can otherwise impose under section 133, Magistrates' Courts Act 1980. Nevertheless, the period shall be taken to be a sentence of imprisonment for the purposes of Part II, Criminal Justice Act 1991 shall, as the court may direct, either be served before and be followed by, or be served concurrently with, the sentence imposed for the new offence and in either case, shall be disregarded in determining the appropriate length of that sentence.

Section 133, Magistrates' Courts Act 1980
Part II, Criminal Justice Act 1991

The period of recall should be determined first and any custodial sentence (if any) in respect of the new offence should be ordered to run either concurrently or consecutively to the period of return. A sentence expressed otherwise is unlawful.[15] It is important to note that the court is not obliged to return an offender to serve part of all of the remainder of his original sentence, nor is the court required to consider the new offence to be so serious that only custody can be justified in order to activate the period of recall even if it then decides not to impose a custodial sentence for the new offence.

A further practical difficulty is found in the calculation of the period of recall. The date of the expiry of a sentence may include an allowance for time spent on remand or in the police station. It may also include punishment days under the prison's discipline regime, added to the sentence but not forming part of that sentence. Practitioners should ensure that the calculation of the period of recall takes account of the actual date of expiry of the original court sentence. It would be imprudent to rely on the Police National Computer record of sentences or even on certified extracts from the court's register as neither will necessarily record accurately the date of expiry of the sentence.

Where the new offence is found to have been committed over a period of two or more days, or at some time during a period of

---

15.   *R* v *Jones* 1996 Crim LR 524.

two or more days, it shall be taken for the purposes of this section to have been committed on the last of those days.

Treatment for purposes of section 116(1) of person serving two or more sentences or extended sentence

Section 116(1)
Power of Criminal
Courts (Sentencing)
Act 2000

For the purposes of any reference in section 116(1) to the term of imprisonment to which a person has been sentenced, consecutive terms and terms which are wholly or partly concurrent shall be treated as a single term if:

- the sentences were passed on the same occasion; or

Part II, Criminal
Justice Act 1991

- where the sentences were passed on different occasions, the person has not been released under Part II, Criminal Justice Act 1991 at any time during the period beginning with the first and ending with the last of those occasions.

Section 51(2),
Criminal Justice
Act 1991

But this applies only where one or more of the sentences concerned were passed on or after 30th September 1998; but where, by virtue of section 51(2), Criminal Justice Act 1991 as enacted, the terms of two or more sentences passed before 30th September 1998 have been treated as a single term for the purposes of Part II of that Act, they shall be treated as a single term for the purposes of section 116(1).

Section 116(1)
Power of Criminal
Courts (Sentencing)
Act 2000

Where a suspended sentence of imprisonment is ordered to take effect, with or without any variation of the original term, the occasion on which that order is made shall be treated for the purposes of section 116 (1) as the occasion on which the sentence is passed.

Where a person has been sentenced to two or more terms of imprisonment which are wholly or partly concurrent and do not fall to be treated as a single term, the date of expiry of the sentence shall be taken to be that on which he would (but for his release) have served each of the sentences in full.

Suspended sentences in the magistrates' court

Suspended sentences of imprisonment

A court which passes a sentence of imprisonment for a term of not more than two years for an offence may order that the sentence shall not take effect unless, during a period specified in the order, the offender commits in Great Britain another offence punishable with imprisonment and thereafter a court having power to do so orders that the original sentence shall take effect.[16]

The period specified in an order must be a period of not less than one year nor more than two years beginning with the date of the order.

A court shall not deal with an offender by means of a suspended sentence unless it is of the opinion that the case is one in which a sentence of imprisonment would have been appropriate even without the power to suspend the sentence and that the exercise of that power can be justified by the exceptional circumstances of the case.

A suspended sentence is only available in respect of a sentence of imprisonment. As offenders under the age of 21 cannot be sentenced to imprisonment,[17] a suspended sentence may only be made in respect of an offender aged 21 or over.

A court which passes a suspended sentence on any person for an offence shall consider whether the circumstances of the case are such as to warrant in addition the imposition of a fine or the making of a compensation order.

A court which passes a suspended sentence on any person for an offence shall not impose a community sentence in his case in respect of that offence or any other offence of which he is convicted by or before the court or for which he is dealt with by the court.

On passing a suspended sentence the court shall explain to the offender in ordinary language his liability to be imprisoned if during the operational period he commits an offence punishable with imprisonment.

Section 119, Powers of Criminal Courts (Sentencing) Act 2000

A suspended sentence which has not taken effect under section 119, Powers of Criminal Courts (Sentencing) Act 2000 shall be treated as a sentence of imprisonment for the purposes of all enactments and instruments made under enactments except any enactment or instrument which provides for disqualification for or loss of office, or forfeiture of pensions, of persons sentenced to imprisonment.

---

16. Section 118, Powers of Criminal Courts (Sentencing) Act 2000.
17. Such an offender is sentenced instead to detention in a young offenders institution, or, in the case of a youth to a detention and training order.

Power of court on conviction of further offence to deal with suspended sentence

Where an offender is convicted of an offence punishable with imprisonment committed during the operational period of a suspended sentence and either he is so convicted by or before a court having power under section 120, Powers of Criminal Courts (Sentencing) Act 2000 to deal with him in respect of the suspended sentence or he subsequently appears or is brought before such a court, then, unless the sentence has already taken effect, that court shall consider his case and deal with him by one of the following methods:

Section 120,
Powers of Criminal
Courts (Sentencing)
Act 2000

- the court may order that the suspended sentence shall take effect with the original term unaltered;

- the court may order that the sentence shall take effect with the substitution of a lesser term for the original term;

Section 118(1)
Powers of Criminal
Courts (Sentencing)
Act 2000

- the court may by order vary the original order under section 118(1) of the Act by substituting for the period specified in that order a period ending not later than two years from the date of the variation; or

- the court may make no order with respect to the suspended sentence.

The court shall make an order putting into effect the term of imprisonment unless it is of the opinion that it would be unjust to do so in view of all the circumstances, including the facts of the subsequent offence; and where it is of that opinion the court shall state its reasons.

Where a court orders that a suspended sentence shall take effect, with or without any variation of the original term, the court may order that that sentence shall take effect immediately or that the term of that sentence shall commence on the expiry of another term of imprisonment passed on the offender by that or another court.

For the purposes of any enactment conferring rights of appeal in criminal cases, any order made by a court with respect to a suspended sentence shall be treated as a sentence passed on the offender by that court for the offence for which the suspended sentence was passed.

Court by which suspended sentence may be dealt with

An offender may be dealt with in respect of a suspended sentence by the Crown Court or, where the sentence was passed by a magistrates' court, by any magistrates' court before which he appears or is brought.[18]

Where an offender is convicted by a magistrates' court of an offence punishable with imprisonment and the court is satisfied that the offence was committed during the operational period of a suspended sentence passed by the Crown Court, the court may, if it thinks fit, commit him in custody or on bail to the Crown Court and if it does not, shall give written notice of the conviction to the appropriate officer of the Crown Court.

For the purposes of deciding which court has power to deal with such a sentence made on appeal, a suspended sentence passed on an offender on appeal shall be treated as having been passed by the court by which he was originally sentenced.

Procedure where court convicting of further offence does not deal with suspended sentence

If it appears to the Crown Court, where that court has jurisdiction or to a justice of the peace having jurisdiction, that an offender has been convicted in Great Britain of an offence punishable with imprisonment committed during the operational period of a suspended sentence and that he has not been dealt with in respect of the suspended sentence, that court or justice may, subject to the following provisions of this section, issue a summons requiring the offender to appear at the place and time specified in it, or a warrant for his arrest.

Jurisdiction is dependent on the court which made the original order. If the suspended sentence was passed by the Crown Court, that court has jurisdiction and if it was passed by a magistrates' court, by a justice acting for the area for which that court acted.

Unless he is acting in consequence of a notice issued in respect of an offender convicted in Scotland, a justice of the peace shall not issue a summons under this section except on information and shall not issue a warrant under this section except on information in writing and on oath.

---

18.   Section 120, Powers of Criminal Courts (Sentencing) Act 2000.

A summons or warrant issued under this section shall direct the offender to appear or to be brought before the court by which the suspended sentence was passed.

Custodial sentences in the Crown Court

This part sets out the statutory scheme for custodial sentences in the Crown Court. To avoid unnecessary cross-referencing, the relevant materials from the section dealing with custodial sentences in the magistrates' court are reproduced.

Meaning of "custodial sentence"

The term "custodial sentence" means:[19]

- a sentence of imprisonment;

Section 90 or 91, Powers of Criminal Courts (Sentencing) Act 2000

- a sentence of detention under section 90 or 91, Powers of Criminal Courts (Sentencing) Act 2000;

- a sentence of custody for life;

- a sentence of detention in a young offender institution; or

- a detention and training order

The phrase "sentence of imprisonment" does not include a committal for contempt of court or any kindred offence.

Liability to imprisonment on conviction on indictment

Where a person is convicted on indictment of an offence against any enactment and is for that offence liable to be sentenced to imprisonment, but the sentence is not by any enactment either limited to a specified term or expressed to extend to imprisonment for life, the person so convicted shall be liable to imprisonment for not more than two years.

In all other cases, the maximum period of imprisonment is set by statute save for certain common law offences. The Crown Court is subject to the same restrictions as a magistrates' court as regards the imposition of either community or custodial sentences. A community penalty may only be imposed if the offence is serious enough to merit such a sentence.

---

19.   Section 76, Powers of Criminal Courts (Sentencing) Act 2000.

General restrictions on imposing discretionary custodial sentences

Where a person is convicted of an offence punishable with a custodial sentence other than one:

- fixed by law; or

Section 109(2), 110(2) or 111(2),

- falling to be imposed under section 109(2), 110(2) or 111(2), Powers of Criminal Courts (Sentencing) Act 2000

the court shall not pass a custodial sentence on the offender unless it is of the opinion:

- that the offence, or the combination of the offence and one or more offences associated with it, was so serious that only such a sentence can be justified for the offence; or

- where the offence is a violent or sexual offence, that only such a sentence would be adequate to protect the public from serious harm from the offender.[20]

However, this general restriction does not prevent the court from passing a custodial sentence on the offender if he fails to express his willingness to comply with:

- a requirement which is proposed by the court to be included in a probation order or supervision order and which requires an expression of such willingness; or

- a requirement which is proposed by the court to be included in a drug treatment and testing order or an order to provide samples.

Where a court passes a custodial sentence, it shall state in open court that it is of the opinion that it is of the opinion that either the offence if so serious or that the public need to be protected from serious harm and why it is of that opinion and explain to the offender in open court and in ordinary language why it is passing a custodial sentence on him.

---

20.   Section 79, Powers of Criminal Courts (Sentencing) Act 2000.

Length of discretionary custodial sentences

Section 109(2)
Powers of Criminal
Courts (Sentencing)
Act 2000

Save where the sentence is one fixed by law or falling to be imposed under section 109(2), Powers of Criminal Courts (Sentencing) Act 2000, the sentence shall be:

- for such term (not exceeding the permitted maximum) as in the opinion of the court is commensurate with the seriousness of the offence, or the combination of the offence and one or more offences associated with it; or

- where the offence is a violent or sexual offence, for such longer term (not exceeding that maximum) as in the opinion of the court is necessary to protect the public from serious harm from the offender.

Where the court passes a custodial sentence for a term longer than is commensurate with the seriousness of the offence, or the combination of the offence and one or more offences associated with it, the court shall:

- state in open court that it is of the opinion that a longer sentence than is commensurate with the seriousness of the offence is necessary to protect the public and why it is of that opinion; and

- explain to the offender in open court and in ordinary language why the sentence is for such a term.

A custodial sentence for an indeterminate period shall be regarded for these purposes as a custodial sentence for a term longer than any actual term.

Pre-sentence reports and other requirements

A court shall obtain and consider a pre-sentence report before forming any the opinion that a custodial sentence is appropriate unless in the circumstances of the case, the court is of the opinion that it is unnecessary to obtain a pre-sentence report.[21]

The court is also required to take into account all such information as is available to it about the circumstances of the offence or (as the case may be) of the offence together with any offence or offences associated with it, including any aggravating or mitigating factors and may take into account any

---

21.   Section 81, Powers of Criminal Courts (Sentencing) Act 2000.

information which is before it to determine whether the public need to be protected from the offender.

No custodial sentence shall be invalidated by the failure of a court to obtain and consider a pre-sentence report before forming an opinion that custody is appropriate but any court on an appeal against such a sentence shall obtain and consider a pre-sentence report if none was obtained by the court below unless the appeal court is of the opinion that the court below was justified in forming an opinion that it was unnecessary to obtain a pre-sentence report or that, although the court below was not justified in forming that opinion, in the circumstances of the case at the time it is before the court, it is unnecessary to obtain a pre-sentence report.

Additional requirements in case of mentally disordered offender

In any case where the offender is or appears to be mentally disordered, the court shall obtain and consider a medical report before passing a custodial sentence. This does not apply if, in the circumstances of the case, the court is of the opinion that it is unnecessary to obtain a medical report. Before passing a custodial sentence on an offender who is or appears to be mentally disordered, a court shall consider any information before it which relates to his mental condition (whether given in a medical report, a pre-sentence report or otherwise) and the likely effect of such a sentence on that condition and on any treatment which may be available for it.

No custodial sentence which is passed shall be invalidated by the failure of a court to comply with that subsection, but any court on an appeal against such a sentence shall obtain and consider a medical report if none was obtained by the court below.

Section 12, Mental Health Act 1983

The term "mentally disordered", in relation to any person, means suffering from a mental disorder within the meaning of the Mental Health 83 and a "medical report" means a report as to an offender's mental condition made or submitted orally or in writing by a registered medical practitioner who is approved for the purposes of section 12, Mental Health Act 1983 by the Secretary of State as having special experience in the diagnosis or treatment of mental disorder.

Restriction on imposing custodial sentences on persons not legally represented

A Crown Court on committal for sentence or on conviction on indictment shall not pass a sentence of imprisonment or detention on a person who:

- is not legally represented in that court, and

- has not been previously sentenced to that punishment by a court in any part of the United Kingdom,

unless he was granted a right to representation funded by the Legal Services Commission as part of the Criminal Defence Service but the right was withdrawn because of his conduct;[22] or having been informed of his right to apply for such representation and having had the opportunity to do so, he refused or failed to apply.[23]

For the purposes of this provision a person is to be treated as legally represented in a court if, but only if, he has the assistance of counsel or a solicitor to represent him in the proceedings in that court at some time after he is found guilty and before he is sentenced.

Restriction on consecutive sentences for released prisoners

A court sentencing a person to a term of imprisonment shall not order or direct that the term shall commence on the expiry of any other sentence of imprisonment from which he has been released. This does not prevent the court from ordering an offender to be recalled to serve the remainder of his term where he has been convicted of a further offence during the at-risk period between his actual release from a custodial sentence and the date of the expiry of that sentence.[24]

---

22. A defendant remains unrepresented if he has been granted a representation order but dismisses his advocate before sentence until such time as the representation order is withdrawn. *R v Wilson* 1995 16 Cr App Rep (S) 997.
23. Section 83, Powers of Criminal Courts (Sentencing) Act 2000. A sentence passed in breach of this provision is not authorised by law. *R v Birmingham Justices ex parte Wyatt* 1975 3 All ER 897.
24. Section 84, Powers of Criminal Courts (Sentencing) Act 2000.

Sexual or violent offences: extension of certain custodial sentences for licence purposes

The court may pass on the offender an extended sentence, that is to say, a custodial sentence the term of which is equal to the aggregate of:

- the term of the custodial sentence that the court would have imposed if it had passed a custodial sentence otherwise than under this section ("the custodial term"); and

- a further period ("the extension period") for which the offender is to be subject to a licence and which is of such length as the court considers necessary.[25]

The power may be exercised where a court:

- proposes to impose a custodial sentence for a sexual or violent offence committed on or after 30th September 1998; and

- considers that the period (if any) for which the offender would, apart from this section, be subject to a licence would not be adequate for the purpose of preventing the commission by him of further offences and securing his rehabilitation.

Where the offence is a violent offence, the court shall not pass an extended sentence the custodial term of which is less than four years.

The extension period shall not exceed:

- 10 years in the case of a sexual offence; and

- five years in the case of a violent offence.

The term of an extended sentence passed in respect of an offence shall not exceed the maximum term permitted for that offence.

In determining the length of discretionary custodial sentences the term of an extended sentence imposed to protect the public is not to be treated as including the extension period.

---

25. Section 85, Powers of Criminal Courts (Sentencing) Act 2000. This power is theoretically available in the magistrates' court but the circumstances where it would apply are very rare. The majority of cases where the powers should be properly exercised are likely to be either-way offences committed to the Crown Court for sentence or trial, or indictable only offences.

Custody and young offenders in the Crown Court

Youth offenders are effectively defined as children or young persons aged under 18 years. Such offenders are more likely to be sentenced in the youth court unless they have committed an offence of homicide or, having been charged with certain grave crimes, have been committed to the Crown Court for trial.[26]

Offenders who commit murder when under 18: duty to detain at Her Majesty's pleasure

Where a person convicted of murder appears to the court to have been aged under 18 at the time the offence was committed, the court shall sentence him to be detained during Her Majesty's pleasure.[27]

Offenders under 18 convicted of certain serious offences: power to detain for specified period

Section 91, Powers of Criminal Courts (Sentencing) Act 2000

Where a youth court has determined that an offence is a grave crime, a youth may be committed to the Crown Court for trial and, if convicted on indictment, for sentence under section 91, Powers of Criminal Courts (Sentencing) Act 2000. Only certain offences are legally capable of being considered to be grave crimes. Whether the instant offence is actually a grave crime depends on the seriousness of the offence and whether the youth court is of the opinion that there is a real prospect that the offender could receive a custodial sentence in excess of two years. The offences are:

- an offence punishable in the case of a person aged 21 or over with imprisonment for 14 years or more, not being an offence the sentence for which is fixed by law; or

Section 14, Sexual Offences Act 1956

- an offence under section 14, Sexual Offences Act 1956 (indecent assault on a woman); or

Section 15, Sexual Offences Act 1956

- an offence under section 15 of that Act (indecent assault on a man) committed after 30th September 1997;

and, where a person aged at least 14 but under 18 is convicted of an offence under:

Section 1, Road Traffic Act 1988

- section 1, Road Traffic Act 1988 (causing death by dangerous driving); or

---

26. For a fuller commentary see the section on the sentencing of youths at page XX.
27. Section 90, Powers of Criminal Courts (Sentencing) Act 2000.

Section 3A, Road
Traffic Act 1988

- section 3A of that Act (causing death by careless driving while under influence of drink or drugs).

If the court is of the opinion that none of the other methods in which the case may legally be dealt with is suitable, the court may sentence the offender to be detained for such period, not exceeding the maximum term of imprisonment with which the offence is punishable in the case of a person aged 21 or over, as may be specified in the sentence.

Detention under sections 90 and 91: place of detention etc

A person sentenced to be detained under section 90 or 91 Powers of Criminal Courts (Sentencing) Act 2000 shall be liable to be detained in such place and under such conditions:

- as the Secretary of State may direct; or

- as the Secretary of State may arrange with any person.

Duty to impose custody for life in certain cases where offender under 21

Where a person aged under 21 is convicted of murder or any other offence the sentence for which is fixed by law as imprisonment for life, the court shall sentence him to custody for life unless he is liable to be detained at Her Majesty's pleasure.

Power to impose custody for life in certain other cases where offender at least 18 but under 21

Where a person aged at least 18 but under 21 is convicted of an offence for which the sentence is not fixed by law, but for which a person aged 21 or over would be liable to imprisonment for life, the court shall, if it considers that a sentence for life would be appropriate, sentence him to custody for life.

Custody for life: place of detention

An offender of this age sentenced to custody for life shall be detained in a young offender institution unless the Secretary of State directs that an offender sentenced to custody for life shall be detained in a prison or remand centre instead of a young offender institution.

Custody for life: adult offenders aged over 21

An adult offender convicted of an offence for which punishment is fixed by law shall be detained in a prison.

Determination of tariffs

If a court passes a life sentence in circumstances where the sentence is not fixed by law or the offender was aged under 18 when he committed the offence, the court shall order that the early release provisions shall apply to the offender as soon as he has served the part of his sentence which is specified in the order.[28] This minimum period is referred to as the tariff period.

This part of the sentence shall be such as the court considers appropriate taking into account:

- the seriousness of the offence, or the combination of the offence and one or more offences associated with it;

- the effect of any direction crediting periods of remand in custody (when in force); and

- the early release provisions.

if the court is of the opinion that, because of the seriousness of the offence or of the combination of the offence and one or more offences associated with it, no order should be made, the court shall order that the early release provisions shall not apply to the offender.

Where the court makes such an order that the early release provisions shall not apply to an offender who was aged under 18 at the time he committed the offence, the Secretary of State may direct that the early release provisions shall apply to the offender at any time it appears appropriate to do so.

In the case of offenders sentenced to custody for life where the sentence was fixed by law, traditionally the Secretary of State has set the tariff period of the offender's sentence to be served before he is eligible to apply for parole. Usually the Secretary of State acted on the recommendation of the trial judge but was not bound to do so.

In a series of successful challenges in the Court of Human Rights it was established in 2002 that the Secretary of State's power to set a tariff administratively was in violation of article 6 of the

---

28. Section 82A, Powers of Criminal Courts (Sentencing) Act 2000.

Section 1, Murder
(Abolition of Death
Penalty) Act 1965
Section 29, Crime
(Sentences) Act
1997

European Convention on Human Rights. In *R (Anderson)* v *Secretary of State*,[29] the House of Lords held that the Home Secretary acted incompatibly with article 6(1) of the Convention in fixing the tariff term to be served for punitive purposes by a defendant sentenced to life imprisonment under section 1, Murder (Abolition of Death Penalty) Act 1965 and accordingly made a declaration of incompatibility in respect of section 29, Crime (Sentences) Act 1997. At the time of writing, detailed changes to the procedure by which the tariff period for a sentence fixed by law would be set by a senior judge were anticipated to bring the system within the rules of the Convention.

Detention in a young offender institution for other cases where offender at least 18 but under 21

Where a person aged at least 18 but under 21 is convicted of an offence which is punishable with imprisonment in the case of a person aged 21 or over and the court is of the opinion that either the offence is so serious or that the public need to be protected from the offender, the sentence that the court is to pass is a sentence of detention in a young offender institution.[30]

Term of detention in a young offender institution, and consecutive sentences

The maximum term of detention in a young offender institution that a court may impose for an offence is the same as the maximum term of imprisonment that it may impose for that offence.

A court shall not pass a sentence for an offender's detention in a young offender institution for less than 21 days unless dealing with the offender for breach of requirement imposed on young offender on his release from detention.

Where:

- an offender is convicted of more than one offence for which he is liable to a sentence of detention in a young offender institution, or

- an offender who is serving a sentence of detention in a young offender institution is convicted of one or more further offences for which he is liable to such a sentence,

---

29. (2002) *The Times* 26 November.
30. Section 96, Powers of Criminal Courts (Sentencing) Act 2000.

the court shall have the same power to pass consecutive sentences of detention in a young offender institution as if they were sentences of imprisonment.

Where an offender who is serving a sentence of detention in a young offender institution and is aged 21 or over, is convicted of one or more further offences for which he is liable to imprisonment, the court shall have the power to pass one or more sentences of imprisonment to run consecutively upon the sentence of detention in a young offender institution.[31]

Detention in a young offender institution: place of detention

An offender sentenced to detention in a young offender institution shall be detained in such an institution unless the Secretary of State directs that an offender sentenced to detention in a young offender institution shall be detained in a prison or remand centre instead of a young offender institution.

Conversion of sentence of detention or custody to sentence of imprisonment

Generally, where an offender has been sentenced to a term of detention in a young offender institution and either:

- he has attained the age of 21, or

- he has attained the age of 18 and has been reported to the Secretary of State by the board of visitors of the institution in which he is detained as exercising a bad influence on the other inmates of the institution or as behaving in a disruptive manner to the detriment of those inmates,

the Secretary of State may direct that he shall be treated as if he had been sentenced to imprisonment for the same term.

Where the Secretary of State gives a such directions in relation to an offender, the portion of the term of detention in a young offender institution imposed by the sentence of detention in a young offender institution which he has already served shall be deemed to have been a portion of a term of imprisonment.

Section 90 or 91   This provision applies to a person who is detained under section 90 or 91 above, or who is serving a sentence of custody for life,

---

31.   Section 97, Powers of Criminal Courts (Sentencing) Act 2000.

as it applies to a person serving a sentence of detention in a young offender institution.[32]

Offenders under 18: detention and training orders

Detention and training orders are dealt with at length in the section on the sentencing of youths at page XX below.

Required custodial sentences for certain offences

Life sentence for second serious offence

In respect of certain offences and offenders the court shall impose a life sentence unless the court is of the opinion that there are exceptional circumstances relating to either of the offences or to the offender which justify its not doing so.[33]

The statutory duty to impose a life sentence arises where a person is convicted of a serious offence committed after 30th September 1997 and at the time when that offence was committed, he was 18 or over and had been convicted in any part of the United Kingdom of another serious offence.

An offence committed in England and Wales is a serious offence for the purposes of this provision if it is any of the following, namely:

- an attempt to commit murder, a conspiracy to commit murder or an incitement to murder;

Section 4, Offences Against the Person Act 1861

- an offence under section 4, Offences Against the Person Act 1861 (soliciting murder);

- manslaughter;

Section 18, Offences Against the Person Act 1861

- an offence under section 18, Offences Against the Person Act 1861 (wounding, or causing grievous bodily harm, with intent);

- rape or an attempt to commit rape;

Section 5, Sexual Offences Act 1956

- an offence under section 5, Sexual Offences Act 1956 (intercourse with a girl under 13);

---

32.   Section 98, Powers of Criminal Courts (Sentencing) Act 2000.
33.   Section 109, Powers of Criminal Courts (Sentencing) Act 2000.

Section 16
Section 17
Section 18
Firearms Act 1968

- an offence under section 16 (possession of a firearm with intent to injure), section 17 (use of a firearm to resist arrest) or section 18 (carrying a firearm with criminal intent) of the Firearms Act 1968; and

- robbery where, at some time during the commission of the offence, the offender had in his possession a firearm or imitation firearm within the meaning of that Act.

An offence committed in Scotland is a serious offence for the purposes of this section if the conviction for it was obtained on indictment in the High Court of Justiciary and it is any of the following, namely:

- culpable homicide;

- attempted murder, incitement to commit murder or conspiracy to commit murder;

- rape or attempted rape;

- clandestine injury to women or an attempt to cause such injury;

- sodomy, or an attempt to commit sodomy, where the complainer, that is to say, the person against whom the offence was committed, did not consent;

- assault where the assault is aggravated because it was carried out to the victim's severe injury or the danger of the victim's life or was carried out with an intention to rape or to ravish the victim;

Firearms Act 1968

- robbery where, at some time during the commission of the offence, the offender had in his possession a firearm or imitation firearm within the meaning of the Firearms Act 1968;

Section 16
Section 17
Section 18

- an offence under section 16 (possession of a firearm with intent to injure), section 17 (use of a firearm to resist arrest) or section 18 (carrying a firearm with criminal intent) of that Act;

- lewd, libidinous or indecent behaviour or practices; and

Section 5(1),
Criminal Law
(Consolidation)
(Scotland) Act
1995

- an offence under section 5(1), Criminal Law (Consolidation) (Scotland) Act 1995 (unlawful intercourse with a girl under 13).

An offence committed in Northern Ireland is a serious offence for the purposes of this section if it is any of the following, namely:

- an attempt to commit murder, a conspiracy to commit murder or an incitement to murder;

Section 4, Offences
Against the Person
Act 1861

- an offence under section 4, Offences Against the Person Act 1861 (soliciting murder);

- manslaughter;

Section 18

- an offence under section 18, Offences Against the Person Act 1861 (wounding, or causing grievous bodily harm, with intent);

- rape or an attempt to commit rape;

Section 4, Criminal
Law Amendment
Act 1885
Article 17
Article 18(1)
Article 19
Firearms (Northern
Ireland) Order 1981

- an offence under section 4, Criminal Law Amendment Act 1885 (intercourse with a girl under 14);

- an offence under Article 17 (possession of a firearm with intent to injure), Article 18(1) (use of a firearm to resist arrest) or Article 19 (carrying a firearm with criminal intent) of the Firearms (Northern Ireland) Order 1981; and

- robbery where, at some time during the commission of the offence, the offender had in his possession a firearm or imitation firearm within the meaning of that Order.

An offence the sentence for which is imposed by virtue of these provisions is not to be regarded as an offence the sentence for which is fixed by law.

Where the court does not impose a life sentence, it shall state in open court that it is of that opinion and what the exceptional circumstances are.

The impact of the requirement to impose a life sentence upon repeat conviction for a serious offence was considered at length in *R* v *Offen*[34] in light of the Human Rights Act 1998. Broadly speaking, the Court of Appeal held that the purpose of the legislation was to protect the public from a person who

---

34.   [2001] 1 WLR 253.

committed serious offences. This was the norm envisaged by the legislative provision. If, therefore, the facts showed that the public did not need to be so protected in the future, this was a deviation from the norm and amounted to exceptional circumstances to justify not passing such a mandatory sentence.

In deciding whether there was a significant risk to the public in the future the sentencing court should have regard to a number of factors including:

- The time elapsed between the two serious offences concerned;

- The nature of the serious offences particularly if they were different in nature;

- The age of the offender;

In *R v Kelly (Number 2)*[35] the Court of Appeal went on to say that the statutory presumption remained until such time as it was displaced by the offender through evidence such as positive psychiatric or other evidence. The offender has to establish that there is no need to protect the public in the future or, expressed slightly differently, that he presents no significant risk to the public in the future.

Minimum of seven years for third class A drug trafficking offence

Where:

- a person is convicted of a class A drug trafficking offence committed after 30th September 1997;

- at the time when that offence was committed, he was 18 or over and had been convicted in any part of the United Kingdom of two other class A drug trafficking offences; and

- one of those other offences was committed after he had been convicted of the other,

the court shall impose an appropriate custodial sentence for a term of at least seven years except where the court is of the opinion that there are particular circumstances which relate to any of the offences or to the offender and would make it unjust to do so in all the circumstances.

---

35.   [2002] 1 Cr App Rep (S) 127.

Where the court does not impose such a sentence, it shall state in open court that it is of that opinion and what the particular circumstances are.

Section 110(4), Powers of Criminal Courts (Sentencing) Act 2000
Section 51, Crime and Disorder Act 1998

Such an offence which is otherwise triable either way is converted by section 110(4), Powers of Criminal Courts (Sentencing) Act 2000 into an offence triable only on indictment. Accordingly the magistrates' court must transfer the case to the Crown Court under section 51, Crime and Disorder Act 1998 on its first appearance and may not conduct either the plea before venue or mode of trial procedure in respect of the offence.

Minimum of three years for third domestic burglary

Similar provisions apply in relation to offences of domestic burglary.[36]

Where:

- a person is convicted of a domestic burglary committed after 30th November 1999;

- at the time when that burglary was committed, he was 18 or over and had been convicted in England and Wales of two other domestic burglaries; and

- one of those other burglaries was committed after he had been convicted of the other, and both of them were committed after 30th November 1999.

the court shall impose an appropriate custodial sentence for a term of at least three years except where the court is of the opinion that there are particular circumstances which relate to any of the offences or to the offender and would make it unjust to do so in all the circumstances.

Where the court does not impose such a sentence, it shall state in open court that it is of that opinion and what the particular circumstances are.

Section 111(4), Powers of Criminal Courts (Sentencing) Act 2000
Section 51, Crime and Disorder Act 1998

Such an offence which is otherwise triable either way is converted by section 111(4), Powers of Criminal Courts (Sentencing) Act 2000 into an offence triable only on indictment. Accordingly the magistrates' court must transfer the case to the Crown Court under section 51, Crime and Disorder Act 1998 on its first appearance and may not conduct either the plea before venue or mode of trial procedure in respect of the offence.

36. Section 111, Powers of Criminal Courts (Sentencing) Act 2000. It was reported on BBC News on 2 January 2003 that since the power to impose such a minimum sentence in 1999, the courts had made use of it in 6 cases only.

Certificates of convictions for purposes of minimum sentences

Where:

- on any date after 30th September 1997 a person is convicted in England and Wales of a serious offence or a class A drug trafficking offence, or on any date after 30th November 1999 a person is convicted in England and Wales of a domestic burglary, and

- the court by or before which he is so convicted states in open court that he has been convicted of such an offence on that date, and

- that court subsequently certifies that fact,

the certificate shall be evidence that he was convicted of such an offence on that date.

Where:

- after 30th September 1997 a person is convicted in England and Wales of a class A drug trafficking offence or after 30th November 1999 a person is convicted in England and Wales of a domestic burglary, and

- the court by or before which he is so convicted states in open court that the offence was committed on a particular day or over, or at some time during, a particular period, and

- that court subsequently certifies that fact,

the certificate shall be evidence that the offence was committed on that day or over, or at some time during, that period.

It is the certification of the conviction and not the conviction itself which operates to trigger the changes to the type of offence and the duty of the Crown Court to impose a minimum sentence. Practitioners should therefore ensure that an accurate note is made of whether the court certifies that a given offence is a qualifying offence for this purpose

Offences under service law

Section 114, Powers of Criminal Courts (Sentencing) Act 2000

Section 70, Army Act 1955

Section 70, Air Force Act 1955

Section 42, Naval Discipline Act 1957

Section 114, Powers of Criminal Courts (Sentencing) Act 2000 provides that certain offences under service law are capable of activating the minimum sentencing provisions. These offences are convictions of an offence under section 70, Army Act 1955, section 70, Air Force Act 1955 or section 42, Naval Discipline Act 1957, and where the corresponding civil offence (within the meaning of that Act) was a serious offence, a class A drug trafficking offence or a domestic burglary.

Return to prison[37] where offence committed during original sentence

The power to order an offender's return to prison[38] arises where:

- the offender has been serving a determinate sentence of imprisonment which he began serving on or after 1st October 1992;

Part II, Criminal Justice Act 1991

- he is released under Part II, Criminal Justice Act 1991 (early release of prisoners);

- before the date on which he would (but for his release) have served his sentence in full, he commits an offence punishable with imprisonment ("the new offence"); and

- whether before or after that date, he is convicted of the new offence.

The court by or before which a person to whom this provision applies is convicted of the new offence may, whether or not it passes any other sentence on him, order him to be returned to prison for the whole or any part of the period which:

- begins with the date of the order; and

- is equal in length to the period between the date on which the new offence was committed and the date on which his sentence would have expired but for his early release.

A magistrates' court shall not have power to order a person to whom this provision applies to be returned to prison for a period of more than six months but where the period for which

---

37. In this context, we refer to adults aged 21 years or over. The priorities are similar to those discussed previously for young offenders but we repeated here for ease of use.
38. Section 116, Powers of Criminal Courts (Sentencing) Act 2000.

he might otherwise be returned to prison exceeds this period, the court may commit him in custody or on bail to the Crown Court.

Where a person is committed to the Crown Court, it may order him to be returned to prison for the whole or any part of the period.

The power to commit the offender to the Crown Court for the purposes of determining his recall to prison is not be taken to confer on the magistrates' court a power to commit the person to the Crown Court for sentence for the new offence, but this is without prejudice to any such power conferred on the magistrates' court by any other provision of this Act. Accordingly a new summary offence may be committed to the Crown Court under section 6, Powers of Criminal Courts (Sentencing) Act 2000 and an either way offence under section 3 of the same Act.

Section 6, Powers
of Criminal Courts
(Sentencing) Act
2000; section 3

Part II, Criminal
Justice Act 1991

The period of return shall be taken to be a sentence of imprisonment for the purposes of Part II, Criminal Justice Act 1991 shall, as the court may direct, either be served before and be followed by, or be served concurrently with, the sentence imposed for the new offence and in either case, shall be disregarded in determining the appropriate length of that sentence.

The period of recall should be determined first and any custodial sentence (if any) in respect of the new offence should be ordered to run either concurrently or consecutively to the period of return. A sentence expressed otherwise is unlawful.[39] It is important to note that the court is not obliged to return an offender to serve part of all of the remainder of his original sentence, nor is the court required to consider the new offence to be so serious that only custody can be justified in order to activate the period of recall even if it then decides not to impose a custodial sentence for the new offence.

A further practical difficulty is found in the calculation of the period of recall. The date of the expiry of a sentence may include an allowance for time spent on remand or in the police station. It may also include punishment days under the prison's discipline regime, added to the sentence but not forming part of that sentence. Practitioners should ensure that the calculation of the period of recall takes account of the actual date of expiry of the original court sentence. It would be imprudent to rely on the

---

39.   *R* v *Jones* 1996 Crim LR 524.

Police National Computer record of sentences or even on certified extracts from the court's register as neither will necessarily record accurately the date of expiry of the sentence.

Where the new offence is found to have been committed over a period of two or more days, or at some time during a period of two or more days, it shall be taken for the purposes of this section to have been committed on the last of those days.

Treatment for purposes of section 116(1) of person serving two or more sentences or extended sentence

Section 116(1)

For the purposes of any reference in section 116(1) to the term of imprisonment to which a person has been sentenced, consecutive terms and terms which are wholly or partly concurrent shall be treated as a single term if:

- the sentences were passed on the same occasion; or

Part II, Criminal
Justice Act 1991

- where they were passed on different occasions, the person has not been released under Part II, Criminal Justice Act 1991 at any time during the period beginning with the first and ending with the last of those occasions.

Section 51(2),
Criminal Justice
Act 1991
Part II
Section 116(1)

But this applies only where one or more of the sentences concerned were passed on or after 30th September 1998; but where, by virtue of section 51(2), Criminal Justice Act 1991 as enacted, the terms of two or more sentences passed before 30th September 1998 have been treated as a single term for the purposes of Part II of that Act, they shall be treated as a single term for the purposes of section 116(1) above.

Section 116(1)

Where a suspended sentence of imprisonment is ordered to take effect, with or without any variation of the original term, the occasion on which that order is made shall be treated for the purposes of section 116 (1) as the occasion on which the sentence is passed.

Where a person has been sentenced to two or more terms of imprisonment which are wholly or partly concurrent and do not fall to be treated as a single term, the date of expiry of the sentence shall be taken to be that on which he would (but for his release) have served each of the sentences in full.

Suspended sentences in the Crown Court

Suspended sentences of imprisonment

A court which passes a sentence of imprisonment for a term of not more than two years for an offence may order that the sentence shall not take effect unless, during a period specified in the order, the offender commits in Great Britain another offence punishable with imprisonment and thereafter a court having power to do so orders that the original sentence shall take effect.[40]

A suspended sentence is only available in respect of a sentence of imprisonment. As offenders under the age of 21 cannot be sentenced to imprisonment,[41] a suspended sentence may only be made in respect of an offender aged 21 or over.

The period specified in an order must be a period of not less than one year nor more than two years beginning with the date of the order.

A court shall not deal with an offender by means of a suspended sentence unless it is of the opinion that the case is one in which a sentence of imprisonment would have been appropriate even without the power to suspend the sentence and that the exercise of that power can be justified by the exceptional circumstances of the case.

A court which passes a suspended sentence on any person for an offence shall consider whether the circumstances of the case are such as to warrant in addition the imposition of a fine or the making of a compensation order.

A court which passes a suspended sentence on any person for an offence shall not impose a community sentence in his case in respect of that offence or any other offence of which he is convicted by or before the court or for which he is dealt with by the court.

On passing a suspended sentence the court shall explain to the offender in ordinary language his liability to be imprisoned if during the operational period he commits an offence punishable with imprisonment.

A suspended sentence which has not taken effect under section 119 below shall be treated as a sentence of imprisonment for the purposes of all enactments and instruments made under

---

40.   Section 118, Powers of Criminal Courts (Sentencing) Act 2000.
41.   Such an offender is sentenced instead to detention in a young offenders institution, or, in the case of a youth to a detention and training order.

enactments except any enactment or instrument which provides for disqualification for or loss of office, or forfeiture of pensions, of persons sentenced to imprisonment.

Power of court on conviction of further offence to deal with suspended sentence

Section 120,
Powers of Criminal
Courts (Sentencing)
Act 2000

Where an offender is convicted of an offence punishable with imprisonment committed during the operational period of a suspended sentence and either he is so convicted by or before a court having power under section 120, Powers of Criminal Courts (Sentencing) Act 2000 to deal with him in respect of the suspended sentence or he subsequently appears or is brought before such a court, then, unless the sentence has already taken effect, that court shall consider his case and deal with him by one of the following methods:

- the court may order that the suspended sentence shall take effect with the original term unaltered;

- the court may order that the sentence shall take effect with the substitution of a lesser term for the original term;

Section 118(1)

- the court may by order vary the original order under section 118(1) of the Act by substituting for the period specified in that order a period ending not later than two years from the date of the variation; or

- the court may make no order with respect to the suspended sentence.

The court shall make an order putting into effect the term of imprisonment unless it is of the opinion that it would be unjust to do so in view of all the circumstances, including the facts of the subsequent offence; and where it is of that opinion the court shall state its reasons.

Where a court orders that a suspended sentence shall take effect, with or without any variation of the original term, the court may order that that sentence shall take effect immediately or that the term of that sentence shall commence on the expiry of another term of imprisonment passed on the offender by that or another court.

For the purposes of any enactment conferring rights of appeal in criminal cases, any order made by a court with respect to a suspended sentence shall be treated as a sentence passed on the offender by that court for the offence for which the suspended sentence was passed.

Court by which suspended sentence may be dealt with

An offender may be dealt with in respect of a suspended sentence by the Crown Court or, where the sentence was passed by a magistrates' court, by any magistrates' court before which he appears or is brought.[42]

Where an offender is convicted by a magistrates' court of an offence punishable with imprisonment and the court is satisfied that the offence was committed during the operational period of a suspended sentence passed by the Crown Court, the court may, if it thinks fit, commit him in custody or on bail to the Crown Court and if it does not, shall give written notice of the conviction to the appropriate officer of the Crown Court.

For the purposes of deciding which court has power to deal with such a sentence made on appeal, a suspended sentence passed on an offender on appeal shall be treated as having been passed by the court by which he was originally sentenced.

Procedure where court convicting of further offence does not deal with suspended sentence

If it appears to the Crown Court, where that court has jurisdiction or to a justice of the peace having jurisdiction that an offender has been convicted in Great Britain of an offence punishable with imprisonment committed during the operational period of a suspended sentence and that he has not been dealt with in respect of the suspended sentence, that court or justice may, subject to the following provisions of this section, issue a summons requiring the offender to appear at the place and time specified in it, or a warrant for his arrest.

Jurisdiction is dependent on the court which made the original order. If the suspended sentence was passed by the Crown Court, that court has jurisdiction and if it was passed by a magistrates' court, by a justice acting for the area for which that court acted.

Unless he is acting in consequence of a notice issued in respect of an offender convicted in Scotland, a justice of the peace shall not issue a summons under this section except on information

---

42.   Section 120, Powers of Criminal Courts (Sentencing) Act 2000.

and shall not issue a warrant under this section except on information in writing and on oath.

A summons or warrant issued under this section shall direct the offender to appear or to be brought before the court by which the suspended sentence was passed.

In proceedings for dealing with an offender in respect of a suspended sentence which take place before the Crown Court, any question whether the offender has been convicted of an offence punishable with imprisonment committed during the operational period of the suspended sentence shall be determined by the court and not by the verdict of a jury.

Suspended sentence supervision orders

Where a court passes on an offender a suspended sentence for a term of more than six months for a single offence, the court may make a suspended sentence supervision order, that is to say, an order placing the offender under the supervision of a supervising officer for a period which is specified in the order and does not exceed the operational period of the suspended sentence.

A suspended sentence supervision order shall specify the petty sessions area in which the offender resides or will reside; and the supervising officer shall be a probation officer appointed for or assigned to the area for the time being specified in the order.

An offender in respect of whom a suspended sentence supervision order is in force shall keep in touch with the supervising officer in accordance with such instructions as he may from time to time be given by that officer and shall notify him of any change of address.

On making a suspended sentence supervision order, the court shall explain its effect to the offender in ordinary language.

Where a court deals with an offender in respect of a suspended sentence by varying the operational period of the sentence or by making no order with respect to the sentence, the court may make a suspended sentence supervision order in respect of the offender:

• in place of any such order made when the suspended sentence was passed; or

• if the court which passed the sentence could have made such an order but did not do so.

Breach of requirement of suspended sentence supervision order

If, at any time while a suspended sentence supervision order is in force in respect of an offender, it appears on information to a justice of the peace acting for the petty sessions area for the time being specified in the order that the offender has failed to comply with any of the requirements of the order, the justice may issue a summons requiring the offender to appear at the place and time specified in it or if the information is in writing and on oath, issue a warrant for his arrest.

Any summons or warrant issued under this section shall direct the offender to appear or be brought before a magistrates' court acting for the petty sessions area for the time being specified in the suspended sentence supervision order.

If it is proved to the satisfaction of the court before which an offender appears or is brought under this section that he has failed without reasonable cause to comply with any of the requirements of the order, the court may, without prejudice to the continuance of the order, impose on him a fine not exceeding £1000.

Suspended sentence supervision orders: revocation, amendment and cessation

A suspended sentence supervision order may be revoked on the application of the supervising officer or the offender:

- if it was made by the Crown Court and includes a direction reserving the power of revoking it to that court, by the Crown Court;

- in any other case, by a magistrates' court acting for the petty sessions area for the time being specified in the order.

Where a suspended sentence supervision order has been made on appeal, for these purposes it shall be deemed if it was made on an appeal brought from a magistrates' court, to have been made by that magistrates' court and if it was made on an appeal brought from the Crown Court or from the criminal division of the Court of Appeal, to have been made by the Crown Court.

If a magistrates' court acting for the petty sessions area for the time being specified in a suspended sentence supervision order is satisfied that the offender proposes to change, or has changed, his residence from that petty sessions area to another petty sessions area, the court may, and on the application of the supervising officer shall, amend the order by substituting the other petty sessions area for the area specified in the order.

A suspended sentence supervision order shall cease to have effect if before the end of the period specified in it a court orders that a suspended sentence passed in the proceedings in which the order was made shall have effect or the order is revoked.

Other forms of detention

Detention of offender for one day in court-house or police station

A magistrates' court may order a person convicted of an offence punishable with imprisonment[43] to be detained within the precincts of the court-house, or at any police station until such hour, not later than 8.00 o'clock in the evening of the day on which the order is made, as the court may direct.[44]

A court may not make such an order as will deprive the offender of a reasonable opportunity of returning to his abode on the day of the order.

A court making such an order may not impose imprisonment at the same time for the offence and it would probably be wrong to impose any other form of penalty. An offender aged 18 or older may be made the subject of the order. It would not seem that this power is available to a youth court. The power may be exercised in respect of the non-payment of financial penalties without requiring the court to take enforcement measures, including financial penalties imposed on the day the order for detention is made.

---

43. This is a particularly useful power which practitioners should always consider where the offender is in custody for a relatively minor offence and is not able to or likely to be able to complete a community order or pay a fine but the court is unlikely to be persuaded to discharge him.
44. Section 135, Magistrates' Courts Act 1980.

Committal to custody overnight at police station for non-payment of sum adjudged by conviction

Where an offender is liable to pay fines, costs or compensation, the court may, instead of taking formal enforcement procedures against him,[45] commit him to detention at a police station.[46]

There is no requirement that the offender be present in order that he may be committed to detention but the rules of natural justice would doubtless require that he be given notice of the court's consideration of such an order.

The order authorises any person employed by an authority prescribed by the Secretary of State[47] and authorised to execute warrants of this kind, acting within the area of his employer, to detain a defaulter and take him to a police station.

The offender must then be detained until 8.00 am of the day following the date on which he is arrested or, if he is arrested between midnight and 8.00 am, until 8.00 am on the day on which he is arrested.

The police officer responsible for his detention may release the defaulter at any time within 4 hours before 8.00 am if he thinks it expedient to do so in order to enable him to go to his work or for any other reason appearing to the officer to be sufficient.

Again, the power extends to include offenders in default aged between 18 and 21 years as well as adults.

---

45.   See the section on enforcement of fines at page XX below.
46.   Section 136, Magistrates' Courts Act 1980.
47.   Magistrates' Courts Committees, local authorities and the police.

CHAPTER 8
ANCILLARY ORDERS

In addition to its substantive powers to impose sentence, the courts have a wide range of ancillary orders which may be imposed on an offender after conviction. This part sets out the most important and regularly used powers. This part is not intended to be comprehensive or exclusive and practitioners are advised to pay particular attention to less common criminal legislation which may give rise to orders of disqualification and disability not described here.

The following orders may be regarded as ancillary:

• Bind overs

• Confiscation orders

• Costs[1]

• Deprivation orders

• Destruction orders (property)

• Orders in respect of dogs

• Disqualification from holding or obtaining a driving licence[2]

• Disqualification from being a company director

• Disqualification from having custody of animals

• Disqualification from working with children

• Exclusion from licensed premises

• Football banning orders

• Recommendations for deportation

---

1.   See the section on costs in this work at page XX below.
2.   See the section on road traffic in this work at page XX below.

- Restitution orders

- Restraining orders

- Sex offender orders

- Travel restriction orders

Bind overs

Justice of the
Peace Act 1361
Human Rights
Act 1998

The magistrates' court has power by virtue of the Justice of the Peace Act 1361 to impose a bind over to keep the peace (but not to be of good behaviour, since the Human Rights Act 1998) on any person appearing before the court. A bind over may be conditioned by accepting a recognisance in an appropriate amount subject to the individual's means. A bind over may not be imposed as a sentence in its own right but may be imposed in addition to any other substantive sentence. A judge in the Crown Court is, by his office, also a justice of the peace and can therefore impose a bind over in the same circumstances.

Confiscation orders

The power to make a confiscation order arises in the Crown Court in the circumstances prescribed in the Drug Trafficking Act 1994. The procedure is described briefly in the following passages of this work.[3]

The Crown Court has to take steps towards the making of a confiscation order where:

- an offender has been convicted on indictment of one or more drug trafficking offences;[4] or

- an offender has been convicted in a magistrates' court of one or more drug trafficking offences and committed for sentence to the Crown Court; and

- the prosecution requests the court to do so; or

- the court considers it is appropriate to do so.

---

3.   This work does not provide detailed commentary on the power of the Crown Court to make confiscation orders under the Drug Trafficking Act 1994 and practitioners are advised to seek specialist guidance before advising on the arrangements for, and consequences of, confiscation orders.

4.   Section 1, Drug Trafficking Act 1994 sets out the offences which are included within the definition of a drug trafficking offence.

Where the court embarks on such an investigation it must first decide whether the offender has benefited from drug trafficking.[5]

A person has benefited from drug trafficking if he has at any time (whether before or after the commencement of the Act) received any payment or other reward in connection with drug trafficking carried on by him or another person.

Section 4 of the Drug Trafficking Act 1994 requires the court to make certain assumptions unless those assumptions are shown to be incorrect or the court is satisfied that there would be a serious risk of injustice in the defendant's case if the assumption were to be made.

The required assumptions are:

- that any property appearing to the court to have been held by the defendant at any time since his conviction or to have been transferred to him at any time since the beginning of the period of 6 years ending when the proceedings were instituted against him, was received by him, at the earliest time at which he appears to the court to have held it, as a payment or reward in connection with drug trafficking carried on by him;

- that any expenditure of his since the beginning of that period was met out of payments received by him in connection with drug trafficking carried on by him; and

- that, for the purposes of valuing any property received or assumed to have been received by him at any time as such a reward, he received the property free of any other interests in it.

The prosecution is required to submit a prosecutor's statement setting out any matters relevant to the decision as to whether the offender has benefited from drug trafficking. If the defendant has made admissions as to any of the allegations in the prosecutor's statement, the court may treat the admissions as conclusive. If the defendant has not made any admissions, the court may require him to indicate any matters he proposes to rely on. If he does not do so, the court is entitled to deem that he has accepted the allegation. This does not apply to an allegation that he has benefited from drug trafficking or that any payment or other reward has been received by him in connection with drug trafficking.[6] The court is also able to direct

---

5.   Section 2(2), Drug Trafficking Act 1994.
6.   Section 11, Drug Trafficking Act 1994.

that the defendant provide such information as it requires within a specified period. If the defendant fails to comply with such an order, the court may draw such inferences from that failure as it considers appropriate.

Once the court has determined that the defendant has benefited from drug trafficking, the court must next decide the amount to be recovered. This is a two stage process:[7]

- The court must determine the value of the defendant's proceeds of drug trafficking. This is the aggregate value of all payments and other rewards made to him at any time in connection with drug trafficking carried on by himself or another;

- Once the court has determined the value of the offender's proceeds from drug trafficking, it must make a confiscation order in that sum unless it is satisfied that the amount that might be realised is less than that total amount.

Section 6, Drug Trafficking Act 1994 provides a detailed scheme for determining the amount that might be realised. Once the court has determined the amount that might be realised, it will have before it two amounts of money. The confiscation order must be made in the lesser of those two sums.

A confiscation order is enforceable in the magistrates' court as any other fine or financial penalty imposed by the Crown Court. The Crown Court is obliged to fix a term of detention in default in accordance with section 139(4), Powers of Criminal Courts (Sentencing) Act 2000. The court may order payments by instalments or allow time to pay.

The Drug Trafficking Act 1994 also provides for enforcement of a confiscation order through the High Court.[8]

The power to make confiscation orders under the Drug Trafficking Act 1994 is replaced by powers under the Proceeds of Crime Act 2002[9] as follows:

Powers to confiscate from convicted defendants their benefit from crime were first introduced in England & Wales by the Drug Trafficking Offences Act 1986. A similar regime was introduced in Scotland by the Criminal Justice (Scotland) Act 1987. Although confiscation was initially available only in drug

Section 6, Drug Trafficking Act 1994

Section 139(4), Powers of Criminal Courts (Sentencing) Act 2000

Proceeds of Crime Act 2002

---

7. Section 6, Drug Trafficking Act 1994.
8. Section 29, Drug Trafficking Act 1994.
9. Provisions of which were subject to commencement orders at the time of writing.

trafficking cases, it was extended by the Criminal Justice Act 1988 and the Criminal Justice (Scotland) Act 1995 to cover non-drug indictable offences and specified summary offences. Most of this legislation has been amended since its introduction and, while some has been consolidated (in, for example, the Drug Trafficking Act 1994, the Proceeds of Crime (Scotland) Act 1995 and the Proceeds of Crime (Northern Ireland) Order 1996), much has not.

Confiscation orders are available following a conviction. The purpose of confiscation proceedings is to recover the financial benefit that the offender has obtained from his criminal conduct. The court calculates the value of that benefit and orders the offender to pay an equivalent sum (or less where a lower sum is available for confiscation). Proceedings are conducted according to the civil standard of proof, i.e. on the balance of probabilities. In certain circumstances the court is empowered to assume that the defendant's assets, and his income and expenditure during the period of six years before proceedings were brought, have been derived from criminal conduct and to calculate the confiscation order accordingly. In England, Wales and Northern Ireland the court is required to make this assumption following a conviction for drug trafficking, unless to do so would give rise to a serious risk of injustice.

Existing legislation was replaced by the Proceeds of Crime Act 2002. The Act creates the Assets Recovery Agency and makes arrangements for the civil recovery of the proceeds of crime in addition to certain powers arising in the criminal jurisdiction. This guide provides a summary of the powers to make confiscation orders after conviction.

Making of order

Section 6, Proceeds of Crime Act 2002

Section 6, Proceeds of Crime Act 2002 sets out the circumstances in which confiscation orders under Part 2 of the Act can be made. Confiscation orders may only be made in the Crown Court; the limited power of the magistrates' court under earlier confiscation legislation to make a confiscation order is abolished. Under the Act, a confiscation order may be made following any conviction in the Crown Court or the magistrates' court. Where the conviction takes place in the magistrates' court, a confiscation order can only be made if the defendant is either committed to the Crown Court for sentence or committed to the Crown Court for sentence and confiscation under the new power created in the Act.[10] The confiscation procedures are mandatory: the Crown Court must go through them where asked to do so by the prosecutor or the Director of the new Agency.

A confiscation order is an order to a convicted defendant to pay a sum of money representing the defendant's benefit from crime. The approach of the Act to confiscation therefore reflects that adopted by previous legislation. This Part of the Act provides for confiscation of the defendant's benefit from either his "general criminal conduct" or his "particular criminal conduct". General criminal conduct means any criminal conduct of the defendant's, whenever the conduct occurred and whether or not it has ever formed the subject of any criminal prosecution. Particular criminal conduct means the offences of which the defendant has been convicted in the current proceedings, together with any taken into consideration by the court in passing sentence.

Confiscation is by reference to the defendant's benefit from his general criminal conduct where he is identified by the court on conviction as having a criminal lifestyle. This is determined by reference to the nature of the offence or offences of which he has been convicted in the current proceedings or certain previous proceedings. The offences in question are specified in section 75, read in conjunction with Schedule 2. If the court decides that the defendant does not have a criminal lifestyle, confiscation is by reference to his benefit from his particular criminal conduct.

Recoverable amount

Section 7 specifies how the amount recoverable under a confiscation order is to be calculated. The method of calculation is much the same as in the previous confiscation statutes. The amount is the amount of the defendant's benefit from either his general criminal conduct or his particular criminal conduct (as the case may be), unless the amount available for confiscation is considered by the court and found to be less than the benefit in question, in which case the order must be made in that lesser amount. The amount available for confiscation is described as the available amount (equivalent to the term "the amount that might be realised" in the earlier confiscation legislation) and the amount actually ordered to be confiscated as the recoverable amount (equivalent to "the amount to be recovered" in the

---

10.   Section 70, Proceeds of Crime Act 2002.

earlier confiscation legislation). The legislation affirms a line of case law to the effect that the burden is on the defendant to show that the available amount is less than the benefit and to show the extent of the available amount. Where the court decides the available amount (and it will only do so at the defendant's request), section 6(5) requires it to include a statement of its calculations in the confiscation order. This is intended to assist enforcement by alerting the enforcing authorities to the property available for confiscation.

Defendant's benefit

Section 8 describes how the court must work out whether the defendant has benefited from criminal conduct and what the value of that benefit is. The court must regard the defendant as having benefited by the value of any property obtained by him from criminal conduct up to the time the court makes its decision.

Available amount

The available amount is calculated in the same way as "the amount that might be realised" in the earlier confiscation legislation. The available amount is the value of all the defendant's property, *minus* certain prior obligations of the defendant's such as earlier fines, *plus* the value of all tainted gifts[11] made by the defendant.

Assumptions to be made in case of criminal lifestyle

Section 10 applies where the court has decided that the defendant has a criminal lifestyle and it is, accordingly, considering the defendant's benefit from general criminal conduct. The section requires the court to make certain specified assumptions to establish whether the defendant has benefited from general criminal conduct, and, if so, by how much. The court is not, however, permitted to make an assumption in relation to particular property or expenditure if it is shown to be incorrect or there would be a serious risk of injustice if it were made. Where for any reason the court does not make any of the assumptions specified in the legislation, it must nevertheless continue to decide whether the defendant has benefited from general criminal conduct and decide the recoverable amount, albeit without the assistance of the assumptions.

---

11. Section 77, Proceeds of Crime Act 2002.

The earlier confiscation legislation provides for similar assumptions to be made. They are mandatory in confiscation proceedings following a conviction for a drug trafficking offence, but discretionary in all other confiscation cases (and, in the latter case, other criteria must be satisfied before they can be made). Section 11 creates a single scheme under which the assumptions are mandatory in all cases where a person has a criminal lifestyle as defined in section 75.

Time for payment

Section 11 indicates how long the court may allow the defendant to pay the amount due under the confiscation order. Under earlier legislation, there was no limit on the time that may be allowed. Section 11 provides that the amount is to be paid immediately, unless the defendant can demonstrate to the court that he needs more time to pay. The prosecutor and Director will have the right to be heard at any application by the defendant for time to pay, or an extension of time to pay. If the court is satisfied that time to pay is required, it may allow up to six months to pay, and up to a further six months on a later occasion if there are exceptional reasons justifying the extension. In no case, however, will more than 12 months be granted from the day on which the confiscation order is made.

Interest

Section 12 makes it clear that the defendant must pay interest on a confiscation order that is not paid in full by the time allowed. It leaves no room for doubt that the payment of interest is mandatory in all cases (the existing legislation is framed in terms of a "liability" to pay interest and it has been suggested occasionally that this implies a discretion as to whether or not interest is added to a particular unpaid order).

Effect of order on court's other powers

Section 13 requires the court to have regard to the confiscation order before imposing a fine or other order involving payment on the defendant, except for a compensation order, but otherwise to leave the confiscation order out of account in sentencing the defendant. It reproduces the effect of existing legislation.

Postponement

Section 14 enables the court to postpone the confiscation proceedings on one or more occasions for up to a total of two years from the defendant's conviction, or three months from the date on which any appeal against conviction is disposed of, if the three months ends more than two years after the date of conviction. There is no limit to the period of postponement where there are exceptional circumstances. The provision extends the period of postponement permitted under the earlier confiscation legislation, which is normally only up to six months. Where the court does *not* postpone confiscation proceedings, it must make a confiscation order before it sentences the defendant.

Proceedings may be postponed for any reason. This enables a postponement to be made if it is required, for example, because a judge is ill. Under earlier confiscation legislation, a postponement can only be made so that the court can obtain further information about the defendant's benefit or the realisable property.

Effect of postponement

Section 15 makes it clear that, as under earlier confiscation legislation, the court may sentence the defendant at any time during the period of postponement. The purpose of the provision is to avoid the sentence being delayed while confiscation is considered. The court is not allowed to impose a fine or ancillary order (such as a forfeiture order) when it sentences the defendant in the postponement period because it needs to know the amount of the confiscation order before it does this. However, it may vary the sentence within 28 days of the end of the postponement period by making one or more of these disposals, by which time any confiscation order will have been made. This will, in particular, enable the forfeiture and destruction of drugs to be ordered in a drug trafficking case.

Statement of information

Where the prosecutor or the Director of the Agency requires the court to hold a confiscation hearing, the prosecutor (or the Director, as the case may be) is required to give the court a statement detailing the defendant's benefit from criminal conduct. The nature of the information in the statement will depend on whether the prosecutor or the Director believes the defendant has a criminal lifestyle.[12] If the prosecutor or Director does believe that the defendant has a criminal lifestyle, under sub-section (4) the statement must include information relevant to the making of the assumptions and for the purpose of enabling the court to decide if it should not make an assumption. The statement will therefore include information about matters known to the prosecutor or Director which could cause the court to decide that making an assumption would give rise to a serious risk of injustice.

Subsection (2) provides that, where the court holds a confiscation hearing of its own volition, it may require the prosecutor (but not the Director) to present a statement. The provision is based on the assumption that the court will never hold a confiscation hearing of its own volition in a case in which the Director is involved.

Section 17: Defendant's response to statement of information

The statement of information procedure is designed to provide a quick and effective method of identifying the extent of the defendant's benefit, where there is agreement between defendant and prosecutor or Director, and of identifying areas of dispute, where there is not. Where the prosecutor or the Director serves a statement of information on the defendant (as will normally happen), the court may require the defendant to respond separately to every allegation in the statement, and to indicate to what extent each allegation is accepted. Where an allegation is accepted by the defendant, the court may treat the acceptance as conclusive as far as any matters to which it relates are concerned.

Where an allegation is disputed, the defendant must provide particulars (i.e. full details) of any matters relied on. The purpose of the procedure is to identify areas of dispute for the confiscation hearing, where evidence may be brought in relation to the disputed points by the prosecutor or Director (as the case may be), or the defendant. If the defendant fails to respond to an allegation, the defendant may be treated as having accepted it. Thus, if the defendant fails to respond to a statement of fact, the fact may be deemed to be true. If, for example, the fact in question is that the defendant spent x sum on y date, and the defendant fails to respond to that, that fact is deemed to be true. However, the defendant is not to be treated as accepting any allegation that he has benefited from general or

---

12.   Section 16, Proceeds of Crime Act 2002.

particular criminal conduct because it is not thought appropriate that the defendant's silence should be conclusive of these matters.

However, where the defendant accepts an allegation that he has benefited from criminal conduct, the acceptance is not admissible in any proceedings for an offence. The exemption is intended to encourage defendants to be more forthcoming by preventing the admissions made from being used in a future prosecution against them or anybody else. Defendants might otherwise be reluctant to admit benefit from criminal conduct which has not been the subject of a prosecution.

Provision of information by defendant

Section 18 empowers the court, at any stage in the confiscation procedures, to order the defendant to provide any information it needs to enable it to carry out its confiscation functions. The court might use the provision where, for example, the defendant has proposed to rely on certain matters in responding to the statement of information, and the court considers that it requires more information from the defendant in deciding the point at issue.

Where the defendant fails to comply with the court's order without reasonable excuse, the court may draw any inference it believes appropriate. Section 18 (9) contains provision protecting the defendant from incriminating himself and others by making an admission under section 18. However, it does not prevent the authorities from prosecuting the defendant or another person using other evidence which may come to light following such an admission.

Reconsideration

Sections 19 and 20 enable a confiscation order to be made where none was made in the original proceedings. Section 21 enables a confiscation order which has already been made to be increased. In all cases, application must be made to the Crown Court within six years of the original conviction. Section 19 applies where no confiscation hearing was held after the original conviction. Section 20 applies where a hearing was held, the court decided that the defendant had a criminal lifestyle but had not benefited from his general criminal conduct or that he did not have a criminal lifestyle and had not benefited from his particular criminal conduct. Section 21 applies where a confiscation order has already been made. It may be used to increase the amount payable under a confiscation order on one or more occasions.

The principle underlying these sections is that a reconsideration should only be applied for where new evidence comes to light. It is not appropriate for an authority to have evidence at the time of the earlier proceedings, not to apply for a confiscation order on that occasion but to apply for a reconsideration at a later date. Provision is included to reflect this principle.

Order made: reconsideration of available amount

Section 22 applies where the court made a confiscation order in an amount lower than the defendant's assessed benefit because there was insufficient realisable property to satisfy an order in the full amount. The prosecutor, the Director, or a receiver appointed in the case may apply to the Crown Court for the court to recalculate the available amount. This is an example of a function exercised by the Crown Court under the Act that has previously been exercised by the High Court.

Any number of applications may be made and there is no limitation to the time when an application may be made (in contrast to sections 19 to 21, under which application must be made within six years of the defendant's conviction). If the court calculates that the available amount has increased, it may vary the amount payable under the confiscation order but may not increase it beyond the defendant's assessed benefit (meaning either the benefit assessed when the confiscation order was originally made or when it was increased on a revaluation under section 21). Subsection (5) requires the court to have regard to any fine, ancillary order or compensation order imposed on the defendant following the original conviction because these may affect the amount the offender is able to pay. However, subsection (6) contains similar technical provision to section 21(10) to prevent allowance being made twice in the defendant's favour for the same compensation order.

Inadequacy of available amount: variation of order

Where a confiscation order has been made, there is a procedure in the earlier confiscation legislation for the defendant or a receiver appointed in the case to apply to the High Court for a "certificate of inadequacy" on demonstrating that the realisable property is insufficient to satisfy the confiscation order. Where the High Court issues a certificate of inadequacy, the certificate may be presented to the Crown Court or magistrates' court and the amount of the confiscation order must then be reduced.

This certificate of inadequacy procedure is cumbersome and expensive. Section 23 provides instead for application to be made directly to the Crown Court by the defendant or a receiver appointed in the case.

Inadequacy of available amount: discharge of order

Under earlier confiscation legislation, there is no provision for writing off a confiscation order. In principle it should not be necessary, as an order cannot be made in a sum greater than the value of the property available to satisfy it and the certificate of inadequacy procedure, as now implemented by section 23, is available to defendants. The absence of any provision for write-offs has, however, led on occasion to unnecessary practical difficulties, for example, where a court makes a confiscation order based on an assessment of realisable property in the form of foreign currency seized at an airport, and a shortfall in payment of the order arises later due entirely to a change in the value of the currency concerned in the period between the order being made and payment.

Section 24 therefore provides that, where a justices' chief executive in the magistrates' court is enforcing a confiscation order, the justices' chief executive may apply to the Crown Court and the Crown Court may write the order off if the outstanding sum is under £1,000 and the reason for the shortfall is a fluctuation in exchange rates or some other factor specified in secondary legislation, or some combination of the two. The sum of £1,000 is variable by order. No similar provision is either available or necessary where the Director is enforcing a confiscation order because enforcement by the Director will always involve the appointment of a receiver, who will be able to apply to the Crown Court under section 23.

Small amount outstanding: discharge of order

Section 25 also applies only where a justices' chief executive is enforcing a confiscation order. It deals with the situation where a confiscation order has been satisfied almost in its entirety, but a sum of £50 or less is outstanding. Under these circumstances, the justices' chief executive may apply to the Crown Court for the confiscation order to be written off. Like section 24, this section introduces an exception to the general principle that a confiscation order may not be written off, but this is made subject to judicial oversight, and applies only where a small amount is outstanding. In such circumstances, the recovery of the sum in question would not justify the expense required to recover it. The sum of £50 is variable by secondary legislation.

Orders made in Absence

Sections 26 to 30, Proceeds of Crime Act 2002

Sections 26 to 30, Proceeds of Crime Act 2002 make provision for the making of confiscation orders in the absence of an offender when he has absconded

Enforcement authority

Section 34

Section 34 sets out the criteria that determine whether the confiscation order is to be enforced by the Director or by a magistrates' court. Under the earlier confiscation legislation, all confiscation orders are enforced by magistrates' courts, with the assistance of the prosecutor. Section 34 provides that the Director is to be responsible for the enforcement of a confiscation order either where the Director applied for the order (including applications under the reconsideration and absconder provisions), where the Director appealed against a decision in respect of a confiscation order or where the Director applied to the court before the order was made to be appointed to enforce it. In all other cases, the confiscation order will be enforced by the magistrates' court and prosecutor, much as at present.

Thus, if the Director is to enforce a confiscation order applied for by a prosecutor, this will have to be arranged when the confiscation order is about to be made, and no later.

Enforcement as fines etc

Section 35

Section 35 explains how confiscation orders are to be enforced where the magistrates' court is the enforcement authority. The order will be treated as a Crown Court fine and enforced, as is a Crown Court fine, by the use of the magistrates' court's fine enforcement powers, as set out in Part 3 of the Magistrates' Courts Act 1980 but subject to some modifications. One of the main features of treating the order as a Crown Court fine is that the Crown Court, where it makes a confiscation order, is required to set a term of imprisonment in default of payment. The maximum default term that may be imposed is determined by the amount payable under the confiscation order. The maximum default term applicable to a particular confiscation order varies from 7 days, for an amount not exceeding £200 to, at the other end of the scale, ten years for an amount exceeding £1 million.

Provisions about imprisonment or detention

Section 38

Section 38 contains general provision on imprisonment in default of payment of a sum due under a confiscation order, applicable whether the default term is imposed by a magistrates' court or by the Crown Court in response to an application by the Director. The provision reflects that in existing legislation and provides, in particular, that a term of imprisonment in default must be served consecutively to the substantive term imposed for the offence(s), and that the service of a default term does not prevent the sum due under the confiscation order from being collected subsequently by other means.

Section 39

Section 12

Where the confiscation order is reconsidered or varied, and the effect of the variation is to *decrease* the amount due under the order so that the new amount falls into a lower band, section 39 requires the court to *reduce* the default term to one lower than the maximum applicable to the band in question. In other cases the court is given a discretion to amend the term of imprisonment in default, i.e. the court has power to *increase* it. In addition, where the amount due under the confiscation order is increased by interest payable under section 12, the Director or the prosecutor may apply to the court to increase the term of imprisonment in default.

Sums received by justices' chief executive

Section 55

Section 50

Section 55 sets out how an enforcing justices' chief executive must dispose of any monies received in satisfaction of a confiscation order, whether from a receiver appointed under section 50 or otherwise (for example, voluntary payments by a defendant or the proceeds of the chief executive's own enforcement activities). The provision is similar to the earlier confiscation legislation, with certain exceptions.

Firstly, an earlier obligation of the justices' chief executive to reimburse the prosecutor out of confiscated monies for sums the prosecutor has paid to a receiver in advance has been abolished as unnecessary, as prosecutors do not make advance payments to receivers. Secondly, under the earlier legislation, victims who receive confiscated monies in satisfaction of a compensation order made in their favour in the same proceedings have to pay a share of the costs of enforcement. This obligation has also been abolished. Thirdly, where the confiscation order takes precedence over parallel bankruptcy proceedings and monies are left over in the receiver's hands after the confiscation order has been satisfied, they go into the bankrupt's estate, rather than being entrusted to the confiscation court to dispose of.

Seized money

Section 67

Section 67 provides the magistrates' court with a new power to order any realisable property in the form of money in a bank or building society account to be paid to the justices' chief executive in satisfaction of a confiscation order. The power is only available where a confiscation order has been made, time to pay has expired, the confiscation order is being enforced by a justices' chief executive (i.e. not by the Director) and the money is subject to a restraint order.

The new power provides an alternative to garnishee proceedings to enable justices' chief executives to seize money held by the defendant in a bank or building society account. A garnishee order is an order to a person who owes a debt to one person (the defendant) to pay it to another (the justices' chief executive). It is usually used to seize money of the defendant's in a bank account. A garnishee order can only be made by the civil courts (the High Court or a county court). Unlike garnishee orders, the new order will be made by the magistrates' court.

Section 67

Section 67(6)

Section 67 also enables justices' chief executives to confiscate money in the form of cash which has been seized from defendants as evidence and subsequently paid into a bank account. Under earlier legislation, the only legal means of getting at the money without the defendant's consent is by having a receiver appointed. Section 67(6) enables the magistrates' court to order a bank or building society which fails to comply with one of the new orders to pay a sum of up to £5,000. It also provides that this sum is to be treated as if it were adjudged to be paid by a conviction of the court. The effect of this is that the fine enforcement powers in Part 3 of the Magistrates' Courts Act 1980 are available to enforce payment of this sum.

Committal by magistrates' court

Section 70,
Proceeds of
Crime Act 2002
Section 6(2)(c)

Section 70, Proceeds of Crime Act 2002 needs to be read in conjunction with section 6(2)(c). Its effect is that a person may be committed to the Crown Court for confiscation proceedings following a conviction of any offence, indictable or summary, in the magistrates' court. Where the prosecutor asks the magistrates' court to do so, the court *must* commit the defendant to the Crown Court under this section. The power to have a person committed is granted only to the prosecutor, not to the Director of the Agency. However the Director can assume responsibility for the subsequent confiscation proceedings in the Crown Court.

Section 71

Where the defendant is convicted of an either way offence, section 70(5) requires the magistrates' court to state whether it would have committed the defendant to the Crown Court for sentence anyway. This subsection is required because, under section 71, the Crown Court's sentencing powers following a committal for confiscation are normally limited to the sentencing powers the magistrates' court would have had in the same case.

Sentencing by Crown Court

Section 71

Section 71 provides that, where a person is committed to the Crown Court for confiscation proceedings, the Crown Court will also assume responsibility for the sentencing process.

Interpretation: Criminal lifestyle

Section 75, 6
Schedule 2

Section 75 is to be read in conjunction with section 6 and Schedule 2. The question of whether a person has a criminal lifestyle is central to the operation of Part 2 of the Act, because it determines whether the defendant is subject to the confiscation of benefit from his particular criminal conduct or his general criminal conduct. Section 75 set out in detail the criteria that govern whether or not a person has a criminal lifestyle.

Section 75

The criminal lifestyle regime is based on the principle that an offender who gives reasonable grounds to believe that he is living off crime should be required to account for his assets, and should have them confiscated to the extent that he is unable to account for their lawful origin. The criminal lifestyle tests, therefore, are designed to identify offenders who may be regarded as normally living off crime. Under section 75, a person has a criminal lifestyle if he satisfies one or more of the tests set out in that section:

- The first test is that he is convicted of an offence specified in Schedule 2;

- The second test is that the defendant is convicted of an offence of any description, provided it was committed over a period of at least six months and he obtained not less than £5,000 from that offence and/or any others taken into consideration by the court on the same occasion;

- The third test is that the defendant is convicted of a combination of offences amounting to "a course of criminal activity".

The third test is more complicated than the other two. The defendant satisfies it if he has (a) been convicted in the current proceedings of four or more offences of any description from which he has benefited, or (b) he has been convicted in the current proceedings of any one such offence and has other convictions for any such offences on at least two separate occasions in the last six years. In addition, the total benefit from the offences and/or any others taken into consideration by the court on the same occasion (or, in the case of (b), occasions) must be not less than £5,000.

The first test is based on the earlier drug confiscation legislation, where conviction of a drug trafficking offence is always regarded as indicative of a criminal lifestyle (although the term itself is not used in the earlier legislation). The second test is new. The third test is similar to that in the earlier non-drug legislation, where an enquiry may be launched into benefit from a person's entire past criminal conduct (other than drug trafficking) where the person is convicted in the current proceedings of two or more offences from which he has benefited, or of one offence in the current proceedings and another one in the last six years. However, the number of triggering offences is greater in the Act because, under section 10, the application of the assumptions is mandatory where a criminal lifestyle is identified, whereas it is discretionary in the earlier non-drug legislation.

Interpretation: Conduct and benefit

Section 76

Section 76 defines criminal conduct as any conduct constituting an offence in England and Wales or which (if it took place elsewhere in the United Kingdom or abroad) would constitute an offence there. The restriction of the scope of confiscation under earlier confiscation legislation to the proceeds of drug trafficking, other indictable offences and specified summary offences is thus abolished. Under the Act, the Crown Court that makes a confiscation order will only need to consider whether the defendant has benefited from any conduct which is, or would be contrary to the criminal law of England and Wales. Section 76 also defines "general criminal conduct" and "particular criminal conduct".

Section 76 also provides that a person benefits from criminal conduct if he obtains property as a result of or in connection with the conduct. This unites in one new provision two similar but not identical definitions in the earlier confiscation legislation relating to drug trafficking, and that relating to other offences. Under the earlier drug trafficking legislation a person benefits from drug trafficking if he receives any payment or reward in connection with drug trafficking carried on by him or another person. Under the earlier legislation relating to other offences, a person benefits from an offence if he obtains any property as a result of or in connection with its commission.

Interpretation: Tainted gifts; Gifts and their recipients

Section 77

Section 77 is another section which aligns two similar but slightly different provisions in the earlier drug and non-drug confiscation legislation (where a tainted gift is referred to as a "gift caught by this Act"). Like the Act, the earlier legislation enables gifts made by the defendant to other persons to be recovered in satisfaction of the confiscation order, and makes ancillary provision (for example, to enable assets of the recipient of a gift to be placed under restraint).

The new scheme provides that, where the court has decided that the defendant has a criminal lifestyle, any gift made by the defendant to any person in the period beginning six years before the commencement of proceedings is caught, together with any gift made at any time out of the proceeds of crime. This is relevant both at the confiscation hearing and for the purposes of enforcement. If the court decides that the defendant does not have a criminal lifestyle, only gifts made since the beginning of the earliest of the offences committed are caught. Again, this is relevant at the confiscation hearing and for the purposes of enforcement.

However, in relation to a time before the court has decided whether the defendant has a criminal lifestyle, for example, at a pre-trial restraint hearing, the wider definition of tainted gifts applies. When making a restraint order, the court must exercise its discretion as to how much property to restrain by reference to the size of the confiscation order that may eventually be made. So, although a court can technically apply the wider definition of tainted gifts at the restraint stage, if it is clear at that time that the defendant does not have a criminal lifestyle and that therefore the narrower definition will apply at the confiscation hearing, the court will have to take this into account when making the restraint order.

Section 78

Section 78 makes it clear that a gift includes a transaction for a consideration which is significantly less than the value of the gift at the time of the transfer; for example, if the defendant sells a car worth £10,000 at the time of the transfer for £2,000. This is a departure from the earlier legislation, where an undervalue transaction is defined as the difference between the value of the property when the defendant received it and its value at the time of the transfer. The old definition could cause injustice when the property transferred at an undervalue has depreciated in value between its receipt by the defendant and its transfer.

Interpretation: Value: the basic rule; Value of property obtained from conduct; Value of tainted gifts

Sections 79–81

Sections 79–81 set out how the court is to work out the value of property held by a person, the value of property obtained from criminal conduct and the value of a tainted gift. These sections broadly reproduce the property valuation principles set out in the earlier legislation and are not reproduced in this work.

Interpretation: Lifestyle offences: England and Wales

Schedule 2

Schedule 2 lists offences which are always criminal lifestyle offences. An offender convicted of one instance of any of these offences has a criminal lifestyle under the Act.

The first group of offences listed are drug trafficking offences. Under the earlier drug confiscation legislation, drug trafficking offences are criminal lifestyle offences (although the term itself is not used in the earlier legislation). Under the Drug Trafficking Act 1994, appearance in the Crown Court for sentence following a conviction of any listed drug trafficking offence can trigger an examination of all the defendant's past drug trafficking and the mandatory application of the assumptions.

Drug Trafficking
Act 1994
Section 8, Misuse
of Drugs Act 1971

The drug trafficking offences listed in paragraph 1 are slightly different from those listed in section 1 of the Drug Trafficking Act 1994. Firstly, the offence of allowing premises to be used for drug related activities (section 8 of the Misuse of Drugs Act 1971) is regarded as having the characteristics of a criminal lifestyle offence and so has been added to the list. Secondly, drug money laundering offences have been removed from the list, because the Act abolishes the separate drug money laundering offences found in the earlier proceeds of crime legislation. It replaces them with a single set of money laundering offences applicable to the proceeds of all criminal conduct.

Some of these new money laundering offences have also been listed in Schedule 2. Other criminal lifestyle offences listed in Schedule 2 also address areas of criminal conduct associated with professional criminals, organised crime and racketeering (for example, counterfeiting, intellectual property offences) and which in some cases are also of major public concern (for example, arms trafficking, trafficking for the purposes of sexual exploitation).[13]

Costs

The power to award costs is dealt with in detail in the section dealing with costs elsewhere in this work.[14]

Deprivation orders

Powers to deprive offender of property used etc. for purposes of crime

Where a person is convicted of an offence and the court by or before which he is convicted is satisfied that any property which has been lawfully seized from him, or which was in his possession or under his control at the time when he was

---

13. Reproduced from Explanatory Notes subject to licence from Crown Copyright. The full text including notes on civil proceedings is available on line [INSERT WEBLINK].

14. See the section on costs in this work at page XX below.

apprehended for the offence or when a summons in respect of it was issued:

- has been used for the purpose of committing, or facilitating the commission of, any offence, or

- was intended by him to be used for that purpose,

the court may make an order under section 143, Powers of Criminal Courts (Sentencing) Act 2000 in respect of that property.

Where a person is convicted of an offence and the offence, or an offence which the court has taken into consideration in determining his sentence, consists of unlawful possession of property which:

- has been lawfully seized from him, or

- was in his possession or under his control at the time when he was apprehended for the offence of which he has been convicted or when a summons in respect of that offence was issued,

the court may make an order under this section in respect of that property.

An order under this section shall operate to deprive the offender of his rights, if any, in the property to which it relates, and the property shall (if not already in their possession) be taken into the possession of the police.

The power may be exercised whether or not the court also deals with the offender in any other way in respect of the offence of which he has been convicted.

In considering whether to make an order under this section in respect of any property, a court shall have regard to the value of the property and to the likely financial and other effects on the offender of the making of the order (taken together with any other order that the court contemplates making).

Where a person commits an offence to which this power applies by:

- driving, attempting to drive, or being in charge of a vehicle, or

Section 7, Road Traffic Act 1988

- failing to comply with a requirement made under section 7, Road Traffic Act 1988 (failure to provide specimen for analysis or laboratory test) in the course of an investigation into whether the offender had committed an offence while driving, attempting to drive or being in charge of a vehicle, or

Section 170(2) or (3) Road Traffic Act 1988

- failing, as the driver of a vehicle, to comply with section 170(2) or (3), Road Traffic Act 1988 (duty to stop and give information or report accident),

Powers of Criminal Courts (Sentencing) Act 2000

the vehicle shall be regarded for the purposes of deprivation orders or for the purposes of imposing driving disqualifications[15] under the Powers of Criminal Courts (Sentencing) Act 2000 as used for the purpose of committing the offence (and for the purpose of committing any offence of aiding, abetting, counselling or procuring the commission of the offence).

The offences in question allowing the court to deprive an offender of a vehicle or disqualify him from driving (when in force) are:

Road Traffic Act 1988

- an offence under the Road Traffic Act 1988 which is punishable with imprisonment;

- an offence of manslaughter; and

Section 35, Offences Against the Person Act 1861

- an offence under section 35, Offences Against the Person Act 1861 (wanton and furious driving).

Facilitating the commission of an offence shall be taken for the purposes of this power to include the taking of any steps after it has been committed for the purpose of disposing of any property to which it relates or of avoiding apprehension or detection.

Application of proceeds of forfeited property

Section 143, Powers of Criminal Courts (Sentencing) Act 2000

Where a court makes a deprivation order under section 143, Powers of Criminal Courts (Sentencing) Act 2000 in a case where the offender has been convicted of an offence which has resulted in a person suffering personal injury, loss or damage or any such offence is taken into consideration by the court in determining sentence, the court may also make an order that any proceeds which arise from the disposal of the property and which do not exceed a sum specified by the court shall be paid to that person.

---

15. Not yet in force.

The court may make an order under this section only if it is satisfied that but for the inadequacy of the offender's means it would have made a compensation order under which the offender would have been required to pay compensation of an amount not less than the specified amount.

Destruction orders (property)

Where an offender is convicted of an offence involving the possession or use of a thing which is either unlawful in itself or in its use, the court may order that the item is forfeited and destroyed by the police. This power is regularly used in respect of drugs, knives, offensive weapons, obscene material and firearms. In each case the power arises as follows:

Section 27, Misuse of Drugs Act 1971

• Section 27, Misuse of Drugs Act 1971 – includes drugs and personal property

Section 1, Prevention of Crime Act 1953

• Section 1, Prevention of Crime Act 1953 – possession of offensive weapons in a public place without lawful authority

Section 1, Obscene Publications Act 1964

• Section 1 Obscene Publications Act 1964

Section 52, Firearms Act 1968

• Section 52 of the Firearms Act 1968

Police Property Act 1897

Powers of Criminal Courts (Sentencing) Act 2000

The police are unable to destroy items otherwise forfeited without an order from the court. Items in police custody are subject to applications under the Police Property Act 1897 as amended by the Powers of Criminal Courts (Sentencing) Act 2000.

Orders in respect of dogs

Dangerous Dogs Act 1991

Section 2, Dogs Act 1871

Under the Dangerous Dogs Act 1991 the court may make an order for a dangerous dog to be destroyed. The court also has power to make an order on complaint that a dog shall be kept under proper control whilst in public under section 2, Dogs Act 1871. Such an order may be made whether or not the dog is shown to have injured any person and may specify the measures to be taken for keeping the dog under proper control, whether

Section 2

Dangerous Dogs Act 1991

by muzzling, keeping on a lead, excluding it from specified places or otherwise. If it appears to a court on a complaint under section 2, Dogs Act 1871 that the dog to which the complaint relates is a male and would be less dangerous if neutered the court may make an order requiring it to be neutered. In some cases, the making of an order that a dog be kept under proper control may be sufficient to meet the mischief envisaged by a prosecution under the Dangerous Dogs Act 1991.[16]

Section 4

Section 1, Dangerous Dogs Act 1991

Section 3(1) or (3)

Under section 4, Dangerous Dogs Act 1991, where a person is convicted of an offence under the Act the court may order the destruction of any dog in respect of which the offence was committed and shall do so in the case of an offence under section 1, Dangerous Dogs Act 1991 or an aggravated offence under section 3(1) or (3) of the Act and may order the offender to be disqualified, for such period as the court thinks fit, for having custody of a dog.

Section 1

Dangerous Dogs (Amendment) Act 1997

The duty to order the destruction of a dog upon conviction under section 1 of the Act or for an aggravated offence (broadly, where a person is injured by the dog) becomes a power if the courts is satisfied that the dog would not constitute a danger to public safety or is the subject of a prohibition set out in the Dangerous Dogs (Amendment) Act 1997.

Where a court makes an order for the destruction of a dog owned by a person other than the offender, the owner may appeal to the Crown Court against the order.

A dog shall not be destroyed pursuant to an order until the end of the period for giving notice of appeal against the conviction or, against the order and if notice of appeal is given within that period, until the appeal is determined or withdrawn, unless the offender and, as appropriate, the owner of the dog give notice to the court that made the order that there is to be no appeal.

Where a court makes an order for the destruction of a dog it may appoint a person to undertake the destruction of the dog and require any person having custody of it to deliver it up for that purpose and order the offender to pay such sum as the court may determine to be the reasonable expenses of destroying the dog and of keeping it pending its destruction. Such a sum is enforceable as a fine.

---

16. The benefit for the owner is that under the Dogs Act 1871 there is no penalty available to the court. Under the Dangerous Dogs Act 1991 the owner (broadly speaking) may face conviction on indictment and imprisonment in addition to an order against the dog.

Any person who is disqualified for having custody of a dog by virtue of an order under the Act may, at any time after the end of the period of one year beginning with the date of the order, apply to the court that made it (or a magistrates' court acting for the same petty sessions area as that court) for a direction terminating the disqualification.

On an application for removal of a disqualification order the court may having regard to the applicant's character, his conduct since the disqualification was imposed and any other circumstances of the case, grant or refuse the application and order the applicant to pay all or any part of the costs of the application. Where an application in respect of an order is refused no further application in respect of that order shall be entertained if made before the end of the period of one year beginning with the date of the refusal.

Disqualification from holding or obtaining a driving licence

Road Traffic
Offenders Act 1988
Powers of Criminal
Courts (Sentencing)
Act 2000

The general power[17] to order that an offender be disqualified for holding or obtaining a driving licence[18] (i.e. disqualified from driving) arises under the Road Traffic Offenders Act 1988. This is dealt with in more detail in the section on road traffic. The Powers of Criminal Courts (Sentencing) Act 2000 provides (when in force) an additional or alternative power to order disqualification.[19]

Driving disqualification for any offence

The court by or before which a person is convicted of an offence committed after 31st December 1997 may, instead of or in addition to dealing with him in any other way, order him to be disqualified, for such period as it thinks fit, for holding or obtaining a driving licence.

A court which makes such an order disqualifying a person for holding or obtaining a driving licence shall require him to produce any such licence held by him together with its counterpart.

17.　See the section on road traffic in this work at page XX.
18.　This unusual grammatical form derives from the legislation.
19.　Section 146, Powers of Criminal Courts (Sentencing) Act 2000.

Driving disqualification where vehicle used for purposes of crime

Section 147,
Powers of Criminal
Courts (Sentencing)
Act 2000

Section 147, Powers of Criminal Courts (Sentencing) Act 2000 applies where a person:

- is convicted before the Crown Court of an offence punishable on indictment with imprisonment for a term of two years or more;

Section 3,
Powers of Criminal
Courts (Sentencing)
Act 2000

- having been convicted by a magistrates' court of such an offence, is committed under section 3, Powers of Criminal Courts (Sentencing) Act 2000 to the Crown Court for sentence; or

- is convicted by or before any court of common assault or of any other offence involving an assault (including an offence of aiding, abetting, counselling or procuring, or inciting to the commission of, an offence).

If the Crown Court is satisfied that a motor vehicle was used (by the person convicted or by anyone else) for the purpose of committing, or facilitating the commission of, the offence in question, the court may order the person convicted to be disqualified, for such period as the court thinks fit, for holding or obtaining a driving licence.

If the court is satisfied that the assault was committed by driving a motor vehicle, the court may order the person convicted to be disqualified, for such period as the court thinks fit, for holding or obtaining a driving licence.

A court which makes an order under this section disqualifying a person for holding or obtaining a driving licence shall require him to produce any such licence held by him together with its counterpart.

Facilitating the commission of an offence shall be taken for the purposes of this section to include the taking of any steps after it has been committed for the purpose of disposing of any property to which it relates or of avoiding apprehension or detection.

Disqualification from being a company director

A disqualification order is an order that a person shall not be a director of a company, act as a receiver of a company's property or in any way, whether directly or indirectly, be concerned or take part in the promotion, formation or management of a company unless he has the leave of the court and he shall not act as an insolvency practitioner.[20]

Such an order may be made by the Crown Court where the subject of the order is convicted of an indictable offence (but not necessarily on indictment) in connection with the promotion, formation, management, liquidation or striking off of a company, or with the receivership or management of a company's property.

The maximum period of a disqualification order made in the Crown Court is 15 years.

A magistrates' court may also make an order for disqualification for a maximum of 5 years provided the following conditions are satisfied:[21]

* the offender has been convicted in consequence of a contravention of, or failure to comply with any provision of the companies legislation requiring a return, account or other document to be filed with, delivered or sent, or notice of any matter to be given, to the registrar of companies; and

* that during the 5 years ending with the date of conviction, the person has had made against him, or has been convicted of, in total not less than 3 default orders and offences dealing with the type of conduct described above. In calculating the number of such orders or convictions, the offences of which he has just been convicted count.

If a person acts in contravention of a disqualification order, he is liable on conviction on indictment, to imprisonment for not more than 2 years or a fine or both and on summary conviction, to imprisonment of not more than 6 months or a fine not exceeding the statutory maximum or both.[22]

---

20.   Section 2, Company Directors Disqualification Act 1986.
21.   Section 5, Company Directors Disqualification Act 1986.
22.   Section 13, Company Directors Disqualification Act 1986.

Disqualification from having custody of animals etc

Destruction of an animal

Section 2, Protection of Animals Act 1911

Section 2, Protection of Animals Act 1911 provides that where the owner of an animal is convicted of an offence of cruelty, it shall be lawful for the court, if the court is satisfied that it would be cruel to keep the animal alive, to direct that the animal be destroyed. The court may assign the animal to any suitable person to carry out the destruction order, usually a vet and may order that the owner pay the expenses of the destruction. Such costs are recoverable as a civil debt.

Deprivation of ownership

If the owner of an animal is convicted of an offence of cruelty, the court may, in addition to any other punishment, deprive such person of the ownership of the animal and may make such order as it thinks fit for the disposal of the animal. No order shall be made unless it is shown by evidence as to a previous conviction or as to the character of the owner that the animal, if left with the owner, is likely to be exposed to further cruelty.[23]

Disqualification from having custody of animals

Protection of Animals Act 1911

Section 13, Powers of Criminal Courts (Sentencing) Act 2000

Where a person has been convicted of an offence under the Protection of Animals Act 1911 the court may, if it thinks fit, in addition to or in substitution for any other punishment, order him to be disqualified from having custody of any animal or any kind of animal specified in the order. The order may be for any period the court thinks fit.[24] In the absence of specific authority it would seem that an order for disqualification may not be combined with an order for discharge, absolute or conditional by virtue of the restrictions on the effect of a discharge in section 13, Powers of Criminal Courts (Sentencing) Act 2000.

The court may order that the disqualification is suspended for such period as the court thinks necessary for enabling arrangements to be made for the animals concerned or pending appeal. The power to suspend appears to be exercisable only by the court which makes the order.

A person who is disqualified from having the custody of any animal may from time to time apply to the court by which the

---

23. Section 3, Protection of Animals Act 1911.
24. Section 1, Protection of Animals (Amendment) Act 1954.

order was made (i.e. any court of the same jurisdiction as the court which made the order initially) for the disqualification to be removed. The application cannot be made during the first twelve months of the period of disqualification. In determining, the application the court must have regard to the character of the offender, his conduct subsequent to the order, the nature of the original offence and any other circumstances.

The court may direct that the order be removed from such date as may be specified by the court or vary the order as to apply to other specified animals or refuse the application. No further application to remove or vary the disqualification may then be entertained for a further twelve months.

A person having custody of an animal specified in the order in contravention of an order for disqualification is liable on summary conviction to a fine not exceeding level 3 on the standard scale or to imprisonment for a term not exceeding 3 months or to both.

Disqualification from working with children

Criminal Justice and Court Services Act 2000

The Criminal Justice and Court Services Act 2000 introduced an order of disqualification from working with children. The legislation came into effect on 11 January 2001 and applies only in respect of offences committed after that date.[25]

Section 26, Criminal Justice and Court Services Act 2000

Section 26, Criminal Justice and Court Services Act 2000 provides the basis of the power to disqualify a person working with children. For the purposes of disqualification, an individual commits an offence against a child if:

paragraph 1 Schedule 4

- he commits any offence mentioned in paragraph 1 of Schedule 4 to the Act,

paragraph 2

- he commits against a child any offence mentioned in paragraph 2 of that Schedule, or

paragraph 3

- he falls within paragraph 3 of that Schedule,

and references to being convicted of, or charged with, an offence against a child are to be read accordingly.

---

25. This restriction may no longer be correct following *R v Field* (2003) *The Times* January 16 in which the Court of Appeal decided that an order disqualifying an adult from working with children was not a penalty within the lawful punishment provisions of Article 7 of the European Convention on Human Rights and therefore it could apply to offences committed before the Act came into force.

Disqualification from working with children: adults

The court must order an individual to be disqualified from working with children provided that either of the conditions set out below is satisfied in the case of that individual.[26]

The first condition is that:

- the individual is convicted of an offence against a child committed when he was aged 18 or over, and

- a qualifying sentence is imposed by a senior court in respect of the conviction.

The second condition is that:

- the individual is charged with an offence against a child committed when he was aged 18 or over, and

- a relevant order is made by a senior court in respect of the act or omission charged against him as the offence.

An order shall not be made under this section if the court is satisfied, having regard to all the circumstances, that it is unlikely that the individual will commit any further offence against a child. In making this assessment the court should not apply the criminal standard of proof.[27]

If the court does not make an order under this section, it must state its reasons for not doing so and cause those reasons to be included in the record of the proceedings.

Disqualification from working with children: juveniles

The court must order an individual to be disqualified from working with children provided that either of the conditions set out below is satisfied in the case of that individual.[28]

The first condition is that:

- the individual is convicted of an offence against a child committed at a time when the individual was under the age of 18, and

- a qualifying sentence is imposed by a senior court in respect of the conviction.

---

26. Section 28, Criminal Justice and Court Services Act 2000.
27. *R v MG* [2002] 2 Cr App Rep (S) 1.
28. Section 29, Criminal Justice and Court Services Act 2000.

The second condition is that:

- the individual is charged with an offence against a child committed at a time when the individual was under the age of 18, and

- a relevant order is made by a senior court in respect of the act or omission charged against him as the offence.

If the court is satisfied, having regard to all the circumstances, that it is likely that the individual will commit a further offence against a child, it must order the individual to be disqualified from working with children.

If the court makes an order under this section, it must state its reasons for doing so and cause those reasons to be included in the record of the proceedings.

The term "qualifying sentence" means:

- a sentence of imprisonment for a term of 12 months or more;

- a sentence of detention in a young offender institution for a term of 12 months or more;

- a sentence of detention during Her Majesty's pleasure;

Section 91, Powers of Criminal Courts (Sentencing) Act 2000

- a sentence of detention for a period of 12 months or more under section 91, Powers of Criminal Courts (Sentencing) Act 2000 (offenders under 18 convicted of certain serious offences);

- a detention and training order for a term of 12 months or more;

- a sentence of detention for a term of 12 months or more imposed by a court-martial or the Courts-Martial Appeal Court;

Mental Health Act 1983

- a hospital order within the meaning of the Mental Health Act 1983; or

- a guardianship order.

The term "senior court" means the Crown Court, the Court of Appeal, a court-martial or the Courts-Martial Appeal Court.

Section 28 or 29	If, for the purpose of making an order under section 28 or 29, the court determines, after considering any available evidence, that an individual was, or was not, under the age of 18 at the time when the offence in question was committed, his age at that time shall be taken, for the purposes of that sections (and in particular for the purpose of determining any question as to the validity of the order), to be that which the court determined it to be.

Appeals

An individual may appeal against a disqualification order:[29]

Section 28 or 29	• where the first condition mentioned in section 28 or 29 is satisfied in his case, as if the order were a sentence passed on him for the offence of which he has been convicted;
Section 28 or 29	• where the second condition mentioned in section 28 or 29 is satisfied in his case, as if he had been convicted of an offence on indictment and the order were a sentence passed on him for the offence.

Effect of disqualification from working with children

Persons disqualified from working with children: offences

An individual who is disqualified from working with children is guilty of an offence if he knowingly applies for, offers to do, accepts or does any work in a regulated position.

An individual is guilty of an offence if he knowingly:

• offers work in a regulated position to, or procures work in a regulated position for, an individual who is disqualified from working with children; or

• fails to remove such an individual from such work.

It is a defence for an individual charged with an offence under the first limb to prove that he did not know, and could not reasonably be expected to know, that he was disqualified from working with children.

---

29. Section 31, Criminal Justice and Court Services Act 2000.

An individual is disqualified from working with children for the purposes of this part of the Act if:

Section 1, Protection
of Children Act 1999

- he is included (otherwise than provisionally) in the list kept under section 1, Protection of Children Act 1999 (individuals considered unsuitable to work with children);

section 218(6),
Education Reform
Act 1988

- he is included, on the grounds of not being a fit person, in the list kept for the purposes of regulations under section 218(6), Education Reform Act 1988 (prohibition or restriction on employment as teacher etc.);

section 470 or 471,
Education Act 1996

- he is included, on the grounds that he is unsuitable to work with children, in any list kept by the Secretary of State or the National Assembly for Wales of persons disqualified under section 470 or 471, Education Act 1996; or

- he is subject to a disqualification order.

An individual who is guilty of an offence under this provision is liable

- on summary conviction, to imprisonment for a term not exceeding six months, or to a fine not exceeding the statutory maximum, or to both,

- on conviction on indictment, to imprisonment for a term not exceeding five years, or to a fine, or to both.

Schedule 4, Criminal
Justice and Court
Services Act 2000

The triggering offences are set out in Schedule 4, Criminal Justice and Court Services Act 2000:

Schedule 4

Meaning of offence against a child

1. The offences mentioned in paragraph (a) of subsection (1) of section 26 of the act are–

    (a) an offence under section 1 of the Children and Young Persons Act 1933 (cruelty to children),

    (b) an offence under section 1 of the Infanticide Act 1938 (infanticide),

    (c) an offence under section 5 of the Sexual Offences Act 1956 (intercourse with a girl under 13),

(d) an offence under section 6 of that Act (intercourse with a girl under 16),

(e) an offence under section 19 or 20 of that Act (abduction of girl under 18 or 16),

(f) an offence under section 25 or 26 of that Act (permitting girl under 13, or between 13 and 16, to use premises for intercourse),

(g) an offence under section 28 of that Act (causing or encouraging prostitution of, intercourse with or indecent assault on, girl under 16),

(h) an offence under section 1 of the Indecency with Children Act 1960 (indecent conduct towards young child),

(i) an offence under section 54 of the Criminal Law Act 1977 (inciting girl under sixteen to incest),

(j) an offence under section 1 of the Protection of Children Act 1978 (indecent photographs of children),

(k) an offence under section 1 of the Child Abduction Act 1984 (abduction of child by parent),

(l) an offence under section 160 of the Criminal Justice Act 1988 (possession of indecent photograph of child),

(m) an offence under section 3 of the Sexual Offences (Amendment) Act 2000 (abuse of trust).

2. The offences mentioned in paragraph (b) of that subsection are–

(a) murder,

(b) manslaughter,

(c) kidnapping,

(d) false imprisonment,

(e) an offence under section 18 or 20 of the Offences against the Person Act 1861 (wounding and causing grievous bodily harm),

(f) an offence under section 47 of that Act (assault occasioning actual bodily harm),

(g) an offence under section 1 of the Sexual Offences Act 1956 (rape),

(h) an offence under section 2 or 3 of that Act (procurement of woman by threats or false pretences),

(i) an offence under section 4 of that Act (administering drugs to obtain or facilitate intercourse),

(j) an offence under section 14 or 15 of that Act (indecent assault),

(k) an offence under section 16 of that Act (assault with intent to commit buggery),

(l) an offence under section 17 of that Act (abduction of woman by force or for the sake of her property),

(m) an offence under section 24 of that Act (detention of woman in brothel or other premises).

3. A person falls within this paragraph if–

(a) he commits an offence under section 16 of the Offences against the Person Act 1861 (threats to kill) by making a threat to kill a child,

(b) he commits an offence under section 7 of the Sexual Offences Act 1956 (intercourse with defective) by having sexual intercourse with a child,

(c) he commits an offence under section 9 of that Act (procurement of defective) by procuring a child to have sexual intercourse,

(d) he commits an offence under section 10 of that Act (incest by a man) by having sexual intercourse with a child,

(e) she commits an offence under section 11 of that Act (incest by a woman) by allowing a child to have sexual intercourse with her,

(f) he commits an offence under section 12 of that Act by committing buggery with a child under the age of 16,

(g) he commits an offence under section 13 of that Act by committing an act of gross indecency with a child,

(h) he commits an offence under section 21 of that Act (abduction of defective from parent or guardian) by taking a child out of the possession of her parent or guardian,

(i) he commits an offence under section 22 of that Act (causing prostitution of women) in relation to a child,

(j) he commits an offence under section 23 of that Act (procuration of girl under 21) by procuring a child to have sexual intercourse with a third person,

(k) he commits an offence under section 27 of that Act (permitting defective to use premises for intercourse) by inducing or suffering a child to resort to or be on premises for the purpose of having sexual intercourse,

(l) he commits an offence under section 29 of that Act (causing or encouraging prostitution of defective) by causing or encouraging the prostitution of a child,

(m) he commits an offence under section 30 of that Act (man living on earnings of prostitution) in a case where the prostitute is a child,

(n) she commits an offence under section 31 of that Act (woman exercising control over prostitute) in a case where the prostitute is a child,

(o) he commits an offence under section 128 of the Mental Health Act 1959 (sexual intercourse with patients) by having sexual intercourse with a child,

(p) he commits an offence under section 4 of the
     Sexual Offences Act 1967 (procuring others to
     commit homosexual acts) by–

     (i)   procuring a child to commit an act of buggery
           with any person, or

     (ii) procuring any person to commit an act of
           buggery with a child,

(q) he commits an offence under section 5 of that Act
     (living on earnings of male prostitution) by living
     wholly or in part on the earnings of prostitution of
     a child,

(r) he commits an offence under section 9(1)(a) of the
     Theft Act 1968 (burglary), by entering a building or
     part of a building with intent to rape a child,

(s) he commits an offence under section 4(3) of the
     Misuse of Drugs Act 1971 by–

     (i)   supplying or offering to supply a Class A drug
           to a child,

     (ii) being concerned in the supplying of such a
           drug to a child, or

     (iii) being concerned in the making to a child of an
           offer to supply such a drug,

(t) he commits an offence of–

     (i)   aiding, abetting, counselling, procuring or
           inciting the commission of an offence against
           a child, or

     (ii) conspiring or attempting to commit such an
           offence.

Exclusion from licensed premises

Where a court by or before which a person is convicted of an
offence committed on licensed premises is satisfied that in
committing the offence he resorted to violence or offered or
threatened to resort to violence, the court may make an order

prohibiting him from entering those premises, or any other premises, without the express consent of the licensee of the premises, his servant or agent.

An exclusion order may be made in addition to any sentence imposed in respect of the offence of which the person is convicted. This includes an order discharging the offender either absolutely or conditionally.[30]

An exclusion order shall have effect for the period specified in the order but the minimum period is 3 months and the maximum period is 2 years.

A person who enters any premises in breach of an exclusion order shall be guilty of an offence and liable on summary conviction to a fine not exceeding level 3 on the standard scale or to imprisonment for a term not exceeding 1 month or both. The conviction of a person does not affect the exclusion order unless the court decides to terminate the order or to vary it by deleting the name of any of the specified premises. The court is under a duty to consider these powers on conviction.[31]

There is no procedure to allow a court to entertain an application to remove or vary an exclusion order.

Football banning orders

There are two types of football banning orders: civil and criminal. Civil orders may be made by a court on complaint and are not directly related to the sentencing process. Accordingly, this work does not deal with them.

Football banning orders may be made on conviction for certain offences. The following guide deals with football banning orders as they might be made in criminal proceedings.

A football banning order prohibits the subject of an order from entering a football ground to attend a regulated football match and may require him to report to a police station to ensure that he does not travel to a regulated match played abroad.[32]

Football Spectators (Prescription) Order 2000

A regulated football match is defined in the Football Spectators (Prescription) Order 2000 as an associated football match played in England and Wales or a match played outside England and Wales in which one or both teams represent a club which is a

30. Section 1(2)(b), Licensed Premises (Exclusion of Certain Persons) Act 1980.
31. Presumably, this is to deal with an offender who enters licensed premises without consent but whose presence is not opposed in the future.
32. Section 14(4), Football Supporters Act 1989.

member of the Football League, the Football Association Premier League or the Football Conference.[33]

A football banning order may be made in either the Crown Court, the magistrates' court or the youth court in respect of a person who has been convicted of a football-related offence committed in connection with a regulated football match. The relevant offences are set out in Schedule 1, Football Spectators Act 1989.

Schedule 1,
Football Spectators
Act 1989

Banning orders made on conviction of an offence

Where a person (the "offender") is convicted of a relevant offence, if the court is satisfied that there are reasonable grounds to believe that making a banning order would help to prevent violence or disorder at or in connection with any regulated football matches, it must make such an order in respect of the offender.

If the court is not so satisfied, it must in open court state that fact and give its reasons.

Declaration of relevance

If the offence was committed away from the football ground or in connection with a journey to or from a designated football match, the court must make a declaration of relevance.[34]

Unless the defence waive notice and concede that the offence in question is football related, the court may not make a declaration of relevance unless the court is satisfied that the prosecution have given notice that it proposes to establish that the offence is football related, in writing at least 5 days before the first date of trial.

Sentence generally

A banning order may only be made:

- in addition to a sentence imposed in respect of the relevant offence; or

- in addition to an order discharging him conditionally.

---

33.   It has been suggested that a football match in the LDV Trophy does not fall within the definition of an associated football match and that consequently a person subject to a football banning order is able to attend such a fixture.
34.   Section 23(1), Football Spectators Act 1989.

Sections 12 and 14, Powers of the Criminal Courts (Sentencing) Act 2000

A banning order may be made in spite of anything in sections 12 and 14, Powers of the Criminal Courts (Sentencing) Act 2000 (which relate to orders discharging a person absolutely or conditionally and their effect).

The term "the court" in relation to an offender means:

- the court by or before which he is convicted of the relevant offence, or

- if he is committed to the Crown Court to be dealt with for that offence, the Crown Court.

Football Spectators Act 1989

The amended Football Spectators Act 1989 also provides certain key definitions:

"violence" means violence against persons or property and includes threatening violence and doing anything which endangers the life of any person.

"disorder" includes

(a) stirring up hatred against a group of persons defined by reference to colour, race, nationality (including citizenship) or ethnic or national origins, or against an individual as a member of such a group,

(b) using threatening, abusive or insulting words or behaviour or disorderly behaviour,

(c) displaying any writing or other thing which is threatening, abusive or insulting.

"violence" and "disorder" are not limited to violence or disorder in connection with football.

Banning orders: general

On making a banning order, a court must in ordinary language explain its effect to the person subject to the order.

A banning order must require the person subject to the order to report initially at a police station in England and Wales specified in the order within the period of five days beginning with the day on which the order is made.

A banning order must, unless it appears to the court that there are exceptional circumstances, impose a requirement as to the surrender in accordance with this Part, in connection with regulated football matches outside the United Kingdom, of the passport of the person subject to the order.

If it appears to the court that there are such circumstances, it must in open court state what they are.

In the case of a person detained in legal custody the requirement under this section to report at a police station is suspended until his release from custody.

If he is released from custody more than five days before the expiry of the period for which the order has effect, and he was precluded by his being in custody from reporting initially, the order is to have effect as if it required him to report initially at the police station specified in the order within the period of five days beginning with the date of his release.

Period of banning orders

A banning order has effect for a period beginning with the day on which the order is made. Where the order is made on conviction in addition to a sentence of imprisonment taking immediate effect, the maximum is ten years and the minimum is six years; and in this subsection "imprisonment" includes any form of detention.

In any other case where the order is made on conviction, the maximum is five years and the minimum is three years.[35]

Additional requirements of orders

A banning order may, if the court making the order thinks fit, impose additional requirements on the person subject to the order in relation to any regulated football matches.

The court by which a banning order was made may, on an application made by:

- the person subject to the order, or

- the person who applied for the order or who was the prosecutor in relation to the order,

---

35.   Section 14F, Football Spectators Act 1989.

vary the order so as to impose, replace or omit any such requirements.

Termination of orders

If a banning order has had effect for at least two-thirds of its period the person subject to the order may apply to the court by which it was made to terminate it.

On the application, the court may by order terminate the banning order as from a specified date or refuse the application.

In exercising its powers to consider terminating a banning order, the court must have regard to the person's character, his conduct since the banning order was made, the nature of the offence or conduct which led to it and any other circumstances which appear to it to be relevant.

Where an application to terminate a banning order is refused, no further application in respect of the order may be made within the period of six months beginning with the day of the refusal.

Offences

A person subject to a banning order who fails to comply with the order is guilty of an offence.

A person guilty of an offence under this section is liable on summary conviction to imprisonment for a term not exceeding six months, or a fine not exceeding level 5 on the standard scale, or both.

Function of enforcement authorities

If, in connection with any regulated football match outside England and Wales, the enforcing authority is of the opinion that requiring any person subject to a banning order to report is necessary or expedient in order to reduce the likelihood of violence or disorder at or in connection with the match, the authority must give him a notice in writing.

The notice must require that person:

- to report at a police station specified in the notice at the time, or between the times, specified in the notice,

- if the match is outside the United Kingdom and the order imposes a requirement as to the surrender by him of his passport, to surrender his passport at a police station specified in the notice at the time, or between the times, specified in the notice,

and may require him to comply with any additional requirements of the order in the manner specified in the notice.

In the case of any regulated football match, the enforcing authority may by notice in writing require any person subject to a banning order to comply with any additional requirements of the order in the manner specified in the notice.

A notice under this section:

- may not require the person subject to the order to report except in the control period in relation to a regulated football match outside England and Wales or an external tournament;

- may not require him to surrender his passport except in the control period in relation to a regulated football match outside the United Kingdom or an external tournament which includes such matches.

Where a notice under this section requires the person subject to the order to surrender his passport, the passport must be returned to him as soon as reasonably practicable after the end of the control period in question.

The relevant offences

The triggering offences for a football banning order are as follows:[36]

Schedule 1

OFFENCES

1. This Schedule applies to the following offences:

    (a) any offence under section 2(1), 5(7), 14J(1) or 21C(2) of the Football Spectators Act 1989,

    (b) any offence under section 2 or 2A of the Sporting Events (Control of Alcohol etc.) Act 1985 (alcohol,

---

36.   Schedule 1, Football Spectators Act 1989 as amended.

containers and fireworks) committed by the accused at any football match to which this Schedule applies or while entering or trying to enter the ground,

(c) any offence under section 5 of the Public Order Act 1986 (harassment, alarm or distress) or any provision of Part III of that Act (racial hatred) committed during a period relevant to a football match to which this Schedule applies at any premises while the accused was at, or was entering or leaving or trying to enter or leave, the premises,

(d) any offence involving the use or threat of violence by the accused towards another person committed during a period relevant to a football match to which this Schedule applies at any premises while the accused was at, or was entering or leaving or trying to enter or leave, the premises,

(e) any offence involving the use or threat of violence towards property committed during a period relevant to a football match to which this Schedule applies at any premises while the accused was at, or was entering or leaving or trying to enter or leave, the premises,

(f) any offence involving the use, carrying or possession of an offensive weapon or a firearm committed during a period relevant to a football match to which this Schedule applies at any premises while the accused was at, or was entering or leaving or trying to enter or leave, the premises,

(g) any offence under section 12 of the Licensing Act 1872 (persons found drunk in public places, etc.) of being found drunk in a highway or other public place committed while the accused was on a journey to or from a football match to which this Schedule applies being an offence as respects which the court makes a declaration that the offence related to football matches,

(h) any offence under section 91(1) of the Criminal Justice Act 1967 (disorderly behaviour while drunk in a public place) committed in a highway or other

public place while the accused was on a journey to
or from a football match to which this Schedule
applies being an offence as respects which the
court makes a declaration that the offence related
to football matches,

(j)   any offence under section 1 of the Sporting Events
(Control of Alcohol etc.) Act 1985 (alcohol on
coaches or trains to or from sporting events)
committed while the accused was on a journey to
or from a football match to which this Schedule
applies being an offence as respects which the
court makes a declaration that the offence related
to football matches,

(k)   any offence under section 5 of the Public Order Act
1986 (harassment, alarm or distress) or any
provision of Part III of that Act (racial hatred)
committed while the accused was on a journey to
or from a football match to which this Schedule
applies being an offence as respects which the
court makes a declaration that the offence related
to football matches,

(l)   any offence under section 4 or 5 of the Road Traffic
Act 1988 (driving etc. when under the influence of
drink or drugs or with an alcohol concentration
above the prescribed limit) committed while the
accused was on a journey to or from a football match
to which this Schedule applies being an offence as
respects which the court makes a declaration that
the offence related to football matches,

(m) any offence involving the use or threat of violence
by the accused towards another person committed
while one or each of them was on a journey to or
from a football match to which this Schedule
applies being an offence as respects which the
court makes a declaration that the offence related
to football matches,

(n)   any offence involving the use or threat of violence
towards property committed while the accused was
on a journey to or from a football match to which
this Schedule applies being an offence as respects

which the court makes a declaration that the offence related to football matches,

(o) any offence involving the use, carrying or possession of an offensive weapon or a firearm committed while the accused was on a journey to or from a football match to which this Schedule applies being an offence as respects which the court makes a declaration that the offence related to football matches,

(p) any offence under the Football (Offences) Act 1991,

(q) any offence under section 5 of the Public Order Act 1986 (harassment, alarm or distress) or any provision of Part III of that Act (racial hatred)–

    (i) which does not fall within paragraph (c) or (k) above,

    (ii) which was committed during a period relevant to a football match to which this Schedule applies, and

    (iii) as respects which the court makes a declaration that the offence related to that match or to that match and any other football match which took place during that period,

(r) any offence involving the use or threat of violence by the accused towards another person–

    (i) which does not fall within paragraph (d) or (m) above,

    (ii) which was committed during a period relevant to a football match to which this Schedule applies, and

    (iii) as respects which the court makes a declaration that the offence related to that match or to that match and any other football match which took place during that period,

(s) any offence involving the use or threat of violence towards property–

    (i)   which does not fall within paragraph (e) or (n) above,

    (ii) which was committed during a period relevant to a football match to which this Schedule applies, and

    (iii) as respects which the court makes a declaration that the offence related to that match or to that match and any other football match which took place during that period,

(t) any offence involving the use, carrying or possession of an offensive weapon or a firearm–

    (i)   which does not fall within paragraph (f) or (o) above,

    (ii) which was committed during a period relevant to a football match to which this Schedule applies, and

    (iii) as respects which the court makes a declaration that the offence related to that match or to that match and any other football match which took place during that period.

(u) any offence under section 166 of the Criminal Justice and Public Order Act 1994 (sale of tickets by unauthorised persons) which relates to tickets for a football match.

2. Any reference to an offence in paragraph 1 above includes–

(a) a reference to any attempt, conspiracy or incitement to commit that offence, and

(b) a reference to aiding and abetting, counselling or procuring the commission of that offence.

3. For the purposes of paragraphs 1(g) to (o) above–

(a) a person may be regarded as having been on a journey to or from a football match to which this

Schedule applies whether or not he attended or intended to attend the match, and

(b) a person's journey includes breaks (including overnight breaks).

4. In this Schedule, "football match" means a match which is a regulated football match for the purposes of Part II of this Act.

Recommendations for deportation

A person who is not a British citizen may be deported from the United Kingdom if he is convicted of an offence which is punishable with imprisonment, and on his conviction he is recommended for deportation by a court empowered to do so.[37]

The Crown Court, the magistrates' court and, in the case of an offender aged 17 years, a youth court, are empowered to make recommendations for deportation. If the court imposes an order for the absolute or conditional discharge of the offender it is not prohibited from making a recommendation for deportation.

A court may not make a recommendation for deportation unless the offender has been given not less than seven clear days' notice. It is the duty of the police to serve the notice and the duty of the prosecution to bring the offender's potential liability for deportation to the court's attention. Proceedings may be adjourned to await the service of the required notice.

An offender liable for deportation will not be deported simply because the court has recommended it. The decision to deport is not a judicial act; it is an administrative act performed by the Secretary of State for the Home Department.

A distinction must be drawn between citizens of Member States of the European Union and citizens of states who are not part of the European Union. The following table sets out the key questions to be asked in either case.

---

37.   Section 3(6), Immigration Act 1971.

Nationals of non-member States	Nationals of Member States
Full inquiry to be held	Full inquiry to be held
Legal aid to be granted	Legal aid to be granted
Reasons to be given	Reasons to be given
Nazari[38] criteria	Nazari/Bouchereau[39] criteria
Is the accused's continued presence in the UK to its detriment?	Is the accused's continued presence in the UK to its detriment?
	Is there a genuine and sufficiently serious threat to the requirements of public order affecting one of the fundamental interests of society to justify the order?
	Is the measure reasonable and not disproportionate to the gravity of the offender's conduct?
The court is not concerned with the political system of the country of return	The court is not concerned with the political system of the country of return
What is the effect of the order on innocent parties?	What is the effect of the order on innocent parties?
Does the detrimental effect of the offender remaining in the UK outweigh the effect on innocent parties?	Does the detrimental effect of the offender remaining in the UK outweigh the effect on innocent parties?
Is there evidence of mental instability connected with or resulting in the commission of a serious criminal offence?	Is there evidence of mental instability connected with or resulting in the commission of a serious criminal offence?
Note the impact of article 8 of the human rights convention under the Human Rights Act 1998	Note the impact of article 8 of the human rights convention under the Human Rights Act 1998

38.   *R v Nazari* [1988] 3 All ER 880.
39.   *R v Bouchereau* [1981] 2 All ER 924.

Where an offender is recommended for deportation he may be remanded on bail or detained in custody pending deportation.[40]

Restitution orders

Where goods have been stolen, and either:

- a person is convicted of any offence with reference to the theft (whether or not the stealing is the gist of his offence); or

- a person is convicted of any other offence, but an offence with reference to the theft of that property is taken into consideration in determining his sentence,

the court by or before which the offender is convicted may on the conviction (whether or not the passing of sentence is in other respects deferred) exercise any of the following powers.

- The court may order anyone having possession or control of the stolen goods to restore them to any person entitled to recover them from him; or

- on the application of a person entitled to recover from the person convicted any other goods directly or indirectly representing the stolen goods (as being the proceeds of any disposal or realisation of the whole or part of them or of goods so representing them), the court may order those other goods to be delivered or transferred to the applicant; or

- the court may order that a sum not exceeding the value of the stolen goods shall be paid, out of any money of the person convicted which was taken out of his possession on his apprehension, to any person who, if those goods were in the possession of the person convicted, would be entitled to recover them from him.

Where the court has power on a person's conviction to make an order against him with reference to the stealing of the same goods, the court may make such orders provided that the person in whose favour the orders are made does not thereby recover more than the value of those goods.

Where the court on a person's conviction makes an order for the restoration of any goods, and it appears to the court that the

40.   Paragraph 2, Schedule 3 Immigration Act 1971.

person convicted has sold the goods to a person acting in good faith or has borrowed money on the security of them from a person so acting, the court may order that there shall be paid to the purchaser or lender, out of any money of the person convicted which was taken out of his possession on his apprehension, a sum not exceeding the amount paid for the purchase by the purchaser or, as the case may be, the amount owed to the lender in respect of the loan.

The court shall not exercise the powers to make an order for restitution unless in the opinion of the court the relevant facts sufficiently appear from evidence given at the trial or the available documents, together with admissions made by or on behalf of any person in connection with any proposed exercise of the powers.

The term "the available documents" means:

- any written statements or admissions which were made for use, and would have been admissible, as evidence at the trial; and

- such written statements, depositions and other documents as were tendered by or on behalf of the prosecutor at any committal proceedings.

Theft Act 1968

The term "goods", except in so far as the context otherwise requires, includes money and every other description of property (within the meaning of the Theft Act 1968) except land, and includes things severed from the land by stealing.

Where a restitution order is made against any person in respect of an offence taken into consideration in determining his sentence:

- the order shall cease to have effect if he successfully appeals against his conviction of the offence or, if more than one, all the offences, of which he was convicted in the proceedings in which the order was made;

- he may appeal against the order as if it were part of the sentence imposed in respect of the offence or, if more than one, any of the offences, of which he was so convicted.

Any such order made by a magistrates' court shall be suspended:

- in any case until the end of the period for the time being prescribed by law for the giving of notice of appeal against a decision of a magistrates' court;

- where notice of appeal is given within the period so prescribed, until the determination of the appeal;

but this subsection shall not apply where the order is made under section 148(2)(a) or (b), Powers of Criminal Courts (Sentencing) Act 2000 and the court so directs, being of the opinion that the title to the goods to be restored or, as the case may be, delivered or transferred under the order is not in dispute.[41]

Section 148(2)(a) or (b), Powers of Criminal Courts (Sentencing) Act 2000

Restraining orders

Section 2 or 4, Protection from Harassment Act 1997

Where a person is convicted of an offence under section 2 or 4, Protection from Harassment Act 1997 the court may (as well as sentencing him or dealing with him in any other way) make a restraining order.

The order may, for the purpose of protecting the victim of the offence, or any other person mentioned in the order, from further conduct which amounts to harassment, or will cause a fear of violence, prohibit the defendant from doing anything described in the order.

The order may have effect for a specified period or until further order.

The prosecutor, the defendant or any other person mentioned in the order may apply to the court which made the order for it to be varied or discharged by a further order.

If without reasonable excuse the defendant does anything which he is prohibited from doing by an order under this section, he is guilty of an offence. A person guilty of an offence under this section is liable:

- on conviction on indictment, to imprisonment for a term not exceeding five years, or a fine, or both, or

- on summary conviction, to imprisonment for a term not exceeding six months, or a fine not exceeding the statutory maximum, or both.

---

41.   Section 148, Powers of Criminal Courts (Sentencing) Act 2000.

Sex offender orders

The Sex Offenders Act 1997 introduced the requirement for offenders convicted of certain offences to register certain details in a notification procedure with the police. Strictly, a sex offender order is a specific civil order made on complaint. This section deals with the requirement to register with the police as a consequence of certain convictions.

A person becomes subject to the notification requirements if:

- he is convicted of a sexual offence to which the legislation applies;

- he is found not guilty of such an offence by reason of insanity, or to be under a disability and to have done the act charged against him in respect of such an offence; or

- in England and Wales or Northern Ireland, he is cautioned by a constable in respect of such an offence which, at the time when the caution is given, he has admitted. This also applies to children and young persons given either a warning or reprimand.

A person also becomes subject to these requirements if:

- he has been convicted of a sexual offence to which this Part applies but has not been dealt with in respect of the offence; or

- he has been found not guilty of such an offence by reason of insanity, or to be under a disability and to have done the act charged against him in respect of such an offence, but has not been dealt with in respect of the finding.

A person also becomes subject to these requirements if:

- he is serving a sentence of imprisonment or a term of service detention, or is subject to a community order, in respect of a relevant sexual offence;

- he is subject to supervision, having been released from prison after serving the whole or part of a sentence of imprisonment in respect of such an offence;

- he is detained in a hospital, or is subject to a guardianship order, having been convicted of such an offence; or

- he is detained in a hospital, having been found not guilty of such an offence by reason of insanity, or to be under a disability and to have done the act charged against him in respect of such an offence.

A person required to comply with the notification procedure shall continue to be subject to those requirements for the period set out opposite a person of his description in the second column of the following table.

Description of person	Applicable period
A person who, in respect of the offence, is or has been sentenced to imprisonment for life or for a term of 30 months or more	An indefinite period
A person who, in respect of the offence or finding, is or has been admitted to a hospital subject to a restriction order	An indefinite period
A person who, in respect of the offence, is or has been sentenced to imprisonment for a term of more than 6 months but less than 30 months	A period of 10 years beginning with the relevant date
A person who, in respect of the offence, is or has been sentenced to imprisonment for a term of 6 months or less	A period of 7 years beginning with that date
A person who, in respect of the offence or finding, is or has been admitted to a hospital without being subject to a restriction order	A period of 7 years beginning with that date
A person of any other description	A period of 5 years beginning with that date

In the case of a person who is under 18 on the relevant date the periods shall have effect as if for any reference to a period of 10 years, 7 years or 5 years there were substituted a reference to one-half of that period.

Where a relevant person is or has been sentenced, in respect of two or more relevant sexual offences to consecutive terms of imprisonment or to terms of imprisonment which are partly concurrent, the periods set out in the table shall have effect as if the person were or had been sentenced, in respect of each of the offences, to a term of imprisonment which:

- in the case of consecutive terms, is equal to the aggregate of those terms;

- in the case of concurrent terms, is equal to the aggregate of those terms after making such deduction as may be necessary to secure that no period of time is counted more than once.

Discharges

It is the accepted case that an offender made the subject of a discharge[42] is not required to comply with the notification requirements.[43] However, he may be subject to an interim order pending sentence. Practitioners should ensure in such cases where the offender is discharged, that the police are notified that the requirement to ??? no longer applies.

Effect of notification requirements

A person who is subject to the notification requirements shall, before the end of the period of 14 days beginning with the date of the finding of guilt, sentence or caution notify to the police the following information, namely:

- his name and, where he also uses one or more other names, each of those names; and

- his home address.

A person who is subject to these requirements shall also, before the end of the period of 14 days beginning with:

- his using a name which has not been notified to the police under this section;

- any change of his home address; or

---

42. *R v Oliver & Others* 2002. See Magistrate Courts Practice Volume 7 Issue 2.
43. Given that the legislation requires compliance with the notification requirements in respect of a caution, warning and reprimand which are meant to represent diversion from court proceedings, this may appear to be an oversight?

- his having resided or stayed, for a qualifying period, at any premises in the United Kingdom the address of which has not been notified to the police under this section,

notify that name, the effect of that change or, as the case may be, the address of those premises to the police.

A notification given to the police by any person shall not be regarded as complying with the legislation unless it also states:

- his date of birth;

- his name on the relevant date and, where he used one or more other names on that date, each of those names; and

- his home address on that date.

For the purpose of determining any period for the purposes notification to the police, there shall be disregarded any time when the person in question:

- is remanded in or committed to custody by an order of a court;

- is serving a sentence of imprisonment or a term of service detention;

- is detained in a hospital; or

- is outside the United Kingdom.

A person may give a notification under this section by attending at any police station in his local police area and giving an oral notification to any police officer, or to any person authorised for the purpose by the officer in charge of the station or by sending a written notification to any such police station.

The term "home address", in relation to any person, means the address of his home, that is to say, his sole or main residence in the United Kingdom or, where he has no such residence, premises in the United Kingdom which he regularly visits.

Offences

If a person fails, without reasonable excuse, to comply the requirements or notifies to the police any information which he knows to be false, he shall be liable on summary conviction to a fine not exceeding level 5 on the standard scale, or to imprisonment for a term not exceeding six months, or to both.

Proceedings for an offence under this section may be commenced in any court having jurisdiction in any place where the person charged with the offence resides or is found.

In the case of a child or young person under the age of 18 (16 in Scotland) at the time of either the finding of guilt or sentence, the court may direct that, until he attains that age, the notification requirements shall have effect as if an individual having parental responsibility for him:

- were authorised to comply on his behalf with the provisions of section 2 of the Act; and

- were liable in his stead for any failure to comply with those provisions.

Schedule 1, Sex
Offenders Act 1997

The offences to which the notification requirements apply are set out in Schedule 1 of the Sex Offenders Act 1997 reproduced here in full.[44]

Schedule 1

SEXUAL OFFENCES TO WHICH PART I APPLIES

Offences in England and Wales

1. – (1) This Part of this Act applies to the following sexual offences under the law of England and Wales, namely–

    (a) offences under the following provisions of the Sexual Offences Act 1956–

    (i) section 1 (rape);

    (ii) section 5 (intercourse with a girl under 13);

    (iii) section 6 (intercourse with a girl between 13 and 16);

    (iv) section 10 (incest by a man);

    (v) section 12 (buggery);

---

44. Practitioners should ensure familiarity with the qualifications as they apply from time to time to the basic descriptions of the offences triggering a requirement to comply with the sex offender register requirements.

(vi) section 13 (indecency between men);

(vii) section 14 (indecent assault on a woman);

(viii) section 15 (indecent assault on a man);

(ix) section 16 (assault with intent to commit buggery);

(x) section 28 (causing or encouraging prostitution of, intercourse with, or indecent assault on, girl under 16);

(b) an offence under section 1(1) of the Indecency with Children Act 1960 (indecent conduct towards young child);

(c) an offence under section 54 of the Criminal Law Act 1977 (inciting girl under 16 to have incestuous sexual intercourse);

(d) an offence under section 1 of the Protection of Children Act 1978 (indecent photographs of children);

(e) an offence under section 170 of the Customs and Excise Management Act 1979 (penalty for fraudulent evasion of duty etc) in relation to goods prohibited to be imported under section 42 of the Customs Consolidation Act 1876 (prohibitions and restrictions); and

(f) an offence under section 160 of the Criminal Justice Act 1988 (possession of indecent photographs of children).

(2) In sub-paragraph (1) above–

(a) paragraph (a)(iii), (v) and (vi) does not apply where the offender was under 20;

(b) subject to sub-paragraph (3) below, paragraph (a)(iv) to (ix) does not apply where the victim of or, as the case may be, the other party to the offence was 18 or over; and

(c) paragraph (e) does not apply where the prohibited goods did not include indecent photographs of persons who were under the age of 16.

(3) Sub-paragraph (2)(b) above does not prevent the application of sub-paragraph (1)(a)(vii) or (viii) above in any case where, in respect of the offence or finding, the offender–

(a) is or has been sentenced to imprisonment for a term of 30 months or more; or

(b) is or has been admitted to a hospital subject to a restriction order.

(4) For the purposes of sub-paragraph (2)(c) above–

(a) section 7 of the Protection of Children Act 1978 (interpretation) shall apply as it applies for the purposes of that Act; and

(b) a person shall be taken to have been under the age of 16 at any time if it appears from the evidence as a whole that he was under that age at that time.

OFFENCES IN SCOTLAND

2. – (1) This Part of this Act applies to the following sexual offences under the law of Scotland, namely–

(a) the following offences–

(i) rape;

(ii) clandestine injury to women;

(iii) abduction of a woman or girl with intent to rape;

(iv) assault with intent to rape or ravish;

(v) indecent assault;

(vi) lewd, indecent or libidinous behaviour or practices;

(vii) shameless indecency; and

(viii) sodomy;

(b) an offence under section 170 of the Customs and Excise Management Act 1979 (penalty for fraudulent evasion of duty etc) in relation to goods prohibited to be imported under section 42 of the Customs Consolidation Act 1876 (prohibitions and restrictions);

(c) offences under–

(i) section 52 of the Civic Government (Scotland) Act 1982 (taking and distribution of indecent images of children); and

(ii) section 52A of that Act (possession of indecent images of children);

(d) offences under the following provisions of the Criminal Law (Consolidation) (Scotland) Act 1995–

(i) section 1 (incest);

(ii) section 2 (intercourse with a step-child);

(iii) section 3 (intercourse with child under 16 by person in position of trust);

(iv) section 5 (unlawful intercourse with girl under 16);

(v) section 6 (indecent behaviour towards girl between 12 and 16);

(vi) section 8 (abduction of girl under 18 for purposes of unlawful intercourse);

(vii) section 10 (person having parental responsibilities causing or encouraging sexual activity in relation to a girl under 16); and

(viii) subsection (5) of section 13 (homosexual offences).

(2) In sub-paragraph (1) above–

(a) subject to sub-paragraph (3) below, paragraphs (a)(iii) to (v) and (vii) and (d)(i) and (ii) do not apply where every person involved in the offence other than the offender was 18 or over;

(b) paragraphs (a)(viii) and (d)(viii) above do not apply where every person involved in the offence, other than the offender, was 18 or over and was a willing participant;

(c) paragraph (b) does not apply where the prohibited goods did not include indecent photographs of persons who were under the age of 16;

(d) paragraph (a)(viii) does not apply where the offender was under 20 and every other person involved in the offence was a willing participant;

(e) paragraph (d)(iv) does not apply in the case of an offence in contravention of subsection (3) of section 5 (unlawful sexual intercourse with a girl over 13 but under 16) where the offender was under 20; and

(f) paragraph (d)(viii) does not apply where the offender was under 20 and–

(i) where the offence involved an act of sodomy contrary to subsection (5) of section 13, every other person involved in the offence was a willing participant; or

(ii) the offence involved an act of gross indecency or shameless indecency contrary to the said subsection (5).

(3) Sub-paragraph (2)(a) above does not prevent the application of sub-paragraph (1)(a)(iii) to (v) above in any case where, in respect of the offence or finding, the offender–

(a) is or has been sentenced to imprisonment for a term of 30 months or more; or

(b) is or has been admitted to a hospital subject to a restriction order.

(4) For the purposes of sub-paragraph (2)(c) above–

(a) subsections (2) to (2C) and (8) of section 52 of the Civic Government (Scotland) Act 1982 shall apply as they apply for the purposes of that section; and

(b) a person shall be taken to have been under the age of 16 at any time if it appears from the evidence as a whole that he was under that age at that time.

OFFENCES IN NORTHERN IRELAND

3. – (1) This Part of this Act applies to the following sexual offences under the law of Northern Ireland, namely–

(a) an offence of rape;

(b) offences under–

(i) section 52 of the Offences against the Person Act 1861 (indecent assault upon a female person);

(ii) section 61 of that Act (buggery); and

(iii) section 62 of that Act (assault with intent to commit buggery or indecent assault upon a male person);

(c) offences under–

(i) section 4 of the Criminal Law Amendment Act 1885 of unlawful carnal knowledge of a girl under 14; and

(ii) section 5 of that Act of unlawful carnal knowledge of a girl under 17;

(d) an offence under section 11 of that Act (committing, or being party to the commission of, or procuring or attempting to procure the commission of, any act of gross indecency with another male);

(e) an offence under section 1 of the Punishment of Incest Act 1908 (incest by males);

(f) offences under–

   (i)   section 21 of the Children and Young Persons Act (Northern Ireland) 1968 (causing or encouraging seduction or prostitution of a girl under 17); and

   (ii) section 22 of that Act (indecent conduct towards a child);

(g) an offence under Article 3 of the Protection of Children (Northern Ireland) Order 1978 (indecent photographs of children);

(h) an offence under section 170 of the Customs and Excise Management Act 1979 (penalty for fraudulent evasion of duty etc) in relation to goods prohibited to be imported under section 42 of the Customs Consolidation Act 1876 (prohibitions and restrictions);

(i) an offence under Article 9 of the Criminal Justice (Northern Ireland) Order 1980 (inciting girl under 16 to have incestuous sexual intercourse); and

(j) an offence under Article 15 of the Criminal Justice (Evidence, etc.) (Northern Ireland) Order 1988 (possession of indecent photographs of children).

(2) In sub-paragraph (1) above–

(a) paragraphs (b)(ii), (c)(ii) and (d) do not apply where the offender was under 20;

(b) subject to sub-paragraph (3) below, paragraphs (b), (d) and (e) do not apply where the victim of or, as the case may be, the other party to the offence was 18 or over; and

(c) paragraph (h) does not apply where the prohibited goods did not include indecent photographs of persons who were under the age of 16.

(3) Sub-paragraph (2)(b) above does not prevent the application of sub-paragraph (1)(b)(i), or sub-paragraph (b)(iii) above so far as relating to indecent assault on a male person, in any case where, in respect of the offence or finding, the offender–

(a) is or has been sentenced to imprisonment for a term of 30 months or more; or

(b) is or has been admitted to a hospital subject to a restriction order.

(4) For the purposes of sub-paragraph (2)(c) above–

(a) Article 2(2) and (3)(b) of the Protection of Children (Northern Ireland) Order 1978 (interpretation) shall apply as it applies for the purposes of that Act; and

(b) a person shall be taken to have been under the age of 16 at any time if it appears from the evidence as a whole that he was under that age at that time.

OFFENCES UNDER SERVICE LAW

4. This Part of this Act applies to an offence under–

(a) section 70 of the Army Act 1955;

(b) section 70 of the Air Force Act 1955; or

(c) section 42 of the Naval Discipline Act 1957,

of which the corresponding civil offence (within the meaning of that Act) is a sexual offence to which this Part of this Act applies by virtue of paragraph 1 above.

General

5. – (1) Any reference in paragraph 1(1), 2(1), 3(1) or 4 above to an offence includes–

  (a) a reference to any attempt, conspiracy or incitement to commit that offence; and

  (b) except in the case of a reference in paragraph 2(1)(a) above, a reference to aiding and abetting, counselling or procuring the commission of that offence.

  (2) Any reference in paragraph 1(2), 2(2) or 3(2) above to a person's age is a reference to his age at the time of the offence.

Travel restriction orders

Criminal Justice and Police Act 2001

Under the Criminal Justice and Police Act 2001 the court has power to make a travel restriction order.[45]

The power applies where:

• a person ("the offender") has been convicted by any court of a post-commencement drug trafficking offence;

• the court has determined that it would be appropriate to impose a sentence of imprisonment for that offence; and

• the term of imprisonment which the court considers appropriate is a term of four years or more.[46]

In such circumstances, it shall be the duty of the court, on sentencing the offender:

• to consider whether it would be appropriate for the sentence for the offence to include the making of a travel restriction order in relation to the offender;

• if the court determines that it is so appropriate, to make such a travel restriction order in relation to the offender as the court thinks suitable in all the circumstances (including any other convictions of the offender for post-commencement drug trafficking offences in respect of which the court is also passing sentence); or

---

45. Sections 33–37 Criminal Justice and Police Act 2001.

46. The power is therefore limited to the Crown Court although an offender need not be convicted on indictment and the Crown Court may exercise its powers in respect of an offender committed for sentence by the magistrates' court.

- if the court determines that it is not so appropriate, to state its reasons for not making a travel restriction order.

A travel restriction order is an order that prohibits the offender from leaving the United Kingdom at any time in the period which begins with the offender's release from custody and continues after that time for such period of not less than two years as may be specified in the order.

A travel restriction order may contain a direction to the offender to deliver up, or cause to be delivered up, to the court any UK passport held by him; and where such a direction is given, the court shall send any passport delivered up in pursuance of the direction to the Secretary of State at such address as the Secretary of State may determine.

Where the offender's passport is held by the Secretary of State by reason of the making of any direction contained in a travel restriction order, the Secretary of State (without prejudice to any other power or duty of his to retain the passport) may retain it for so long as the prohibition imposed by the order applies to the offender, and is not for the time being suspended and shall not return the passport after the prohibition has ceased to apply, or when it is suspended, except where the passport has not expired and an application for its return is made to him by the offender.

References in this section to the offender's release from custody are references to his first release from custody after the imposition of the travel restriction order which is neither a release on bail nor a temporary release for a fixed period.

Meaning of "drug trafficking offence"

Section 33

In section 33 of the Act "drug trafficking offence" means any of the following offences (including one committed by aiding, abetting, counselling or procuring):

Section 4(2) or (3), Misuse of Drugs Act 1971

- an offence under section 4(2) or (3) of the Misuse of Drugs Act 1971 (production and supply of controlled drugs);

Section 20

- an offence under section 20 of that Act (assisting in or inducing commission outside United Kingdom of an offence punishable under a corresponding law);

- any such other offence under that Act as may be designated by order made by the Secretary of State;

- an offence under–

Section 50(2) or (3),
Customs and Excise
Management Act 1979

- section 50(2) or (3), Customs and Excise Management Act 1979 (improper importation),

Section 68(2)

- section 68(2) of that Act (exportation), or

Section 170

- section 170 of that Act (fraudulent evasion),

Section 3, Misuse
of Drugs Act 1971

- in connection with a prohibition or restriction on importation or exportation having effect by virtue of section 3, Misuse of Drugs Act 1971;

Section 1, Criminal
Law Act 1977
Article 9, Criminal
Attempts and
Conspiracy (Northern
Ireland) Order 1983

- an offence under section 1, Criminal Law Act 1977 or Article 9 of the Criminal Attempts and Conspiracy (Northern Ireland) Order 1983, or in Scotland at common law, of conspiracy to commit any of the offences in paragraphs (a) to (d) above;

Section 1, Criminal
Attempts Act 1981
Article 3, Criminal
Attempts and
Conspiracy (Northern
Ireland) Order 1983

- an offence under section 1, Criminal Attempts Act 1981 or Article 3, Criminal Attempts and Conspiracy (Northern Ireland) Order 1983, or in Scotland at common law, of attempting to commit any of those offences; and

Section 19, Misuse
of Drugs Act 1971

- an offence under section 19, Misuse of Drugs Act 1971 or at common law of inciting another person to commit any of those offences.

Revocation and suspension of a travel restriction order

Section 33

The court by which a travel restriction order has been made in relation to any person under section 33 of the Act may:

- on an application made by that person at any time which is after the end of the minimum period, and is not within three months after the making of any previous application for the revocation of the prohibition, revoke the prohibition imposed by the order with effect from such date as the court may determine; or on an application made by that person at any time after the making of the order, suspend the prohibition imposed by the order for such period as the court may determine.

A court to which an application for the revocation of the prohibition imposed on any person by a travel restriction order is made shall not revoke that prohibition unless it considers that it is appropriate to do so in all the circumstances of the case and having regard, in particular, to:

- that person's character;

- his conduct since the making of the order; and

- the offences of which he was convicted on the occasion on which the order was made.

A court shall not suspend the prohibition imposed on any person by a travel restriction order for any period unless it is satisfied that there are exceptional circumstances, in that person's case, that justify the suspension on compassionate grounds of that prohibition for that period.

In making any determination on an application for the suspension of the prohibition imposed on any person by a travel restriction order, a court shall also have regard to:

- that person's character;

- his conduct since the making of the order;

- the offences of which he was convicted on the occasion on which the order was made; and

- any other circumstances of the case that the court considers relevant.

Section 33(4)

Where the prohibition imposed on any person by a travel restriction order is suspended, it shall be the duty of that person to be in the United Kingdom when the period of the suspension ends and if the order contains a direction under section 33(4), to surrender, before the end of that period, any passport returned or issued to that person, in respect of the suspension, by the Secretary of State and a passport that is required to be surrendered under the order shall be surrendered to the Secretary of State in such manner or by being sent to such address as the Secretary of State may direct at the time when he returns or issues it.

"The minimum period"

- in the case of a travel restriction order imposing a prohibition for a period of four years or less, means the period of two years beginning at the time when the period of the prohibition began;

- in the case of a travel restriction order imposing a prohibition of more than four years but less than ten years, means the period of four years beginning at that time; and

- in any other case, means the period of five years beginning at that time.

Offences of contravening orders

A person who leaves the United Kingdom at a time when he is prohibited from leaving it by a travel restriction order is guilty of an offence and liable:

- on summary conviction to imprisonment for a term not exceeding six months or to a fine not exceeding the statutory maximum, or to both;

- on conviction on indictment, to imprisonment for a term not exceeding five years or to a fine, or to both.

A person who is not in the United Kingdom at the end of a period during which a prohibition imposed on him by a travel restriction order has been suspended shall be guilty of an offence and liable:

- on summary conviction, to imprisonment for a term not exceeding six months or to a fine not exceeding the statutory maximum, or to both;

- on conviction on indictment, to imprisonment for a term not exceeding five years or to a fine, or to both.

A person who fails to comply with:

- a direction contained in a travel restriction order to deliver up a passport to a court, or to cause such a passport to be delivered up, or

- any duty imposed on him to surrender a passport to the Secretary of State,

shall be guilty of an offence and liable, on summary conviction, to imprisonment for a term not exceeding six months or to a fine not exceeding level 5 on the standard scale, or to both.

Saving for powers to remove a person from the United Kingdom

A travel restriction order made in relation to any person shall not prevent the exercise in relation to that person of any prescribed removal power under the immigration legislation.[47]

---

47. Section 37, Criminal Justice and Police Act 2001.

CHAPTER 9
SENTENCING YOUTH OFFENDERS

Introduction

The sentencing of a child or young person usually takes place in the youth court. The youth court is a special kind of magistrates' court having jurisdiction to deal with children and young persons.

Children and Young Persons Act 1933 Youth Court (Constitution) Rules 1954

The composition and operation of the youth court are prescribed by statute. The relevant statutory provisions may be found in the Children and Young Persons Act 1933 Youth Court (Constitution) Rules 1954.

Powers of Criminal Courts (Sentencing) Act 2000

Sentencing in the youth court is mainly conducted under the provisions of the Powers of Criminal Courts (Sentencing) Act 2000.

Definitions

There is confusion over the use of the terms youth, child, juvenile and young person. The youth court exercises jurisdiction over children and young persons who may conveniently be described as youths or juveniles. The terms juveniles has largely become redundant in recent times although it remains extant in certain legislation.

Section 107, Children and Young Persons Act 1933

A child is defined in section 107, Children and Young Persons Act 1933 as meaning a person under the age of 14 years. In other legislation the term is used generically to describe any person under 18 years of age.

A young person is also defined in the same provision as meaning a person who has attained the age of 14 years and is under the age of 18 years.

The Determination of Age

Legislation provides a simple procedure for determining the age of a child or young person. The court is under a duty to make due inquiry as to the age of an offender. Having made due inquiry and taken into account such matters as may be forthcoming the offender shall be deemed to be that which it appears to be to the court. Where it later transpires after the proceedings have been completed, that the defendant is of a different age than that which the court has declared him to be, this has no effect on the validity of any judgments or orders made.[1]

Powers of Criminal Courts (Sentencing) Act 2000

The Powers of Criminal Courts (Sentencing) Act 2000 also provides that an offender's age shall be deemed to be the age it appears to the court.[2]

Section 46, Children and Young Persons Act 1933

Where an offender's true age is discovered during the course of proceedings the statutory presumption is displaced and the court must amend its procedure where necessary to account for the new information. However, section 46, Children and Young Persons Act 1933 effectively gives the court (whether adult or youth) discretion to remit to the appropriate jurisdiction, as discussed below.

Age and Mode of Trial

Section 51, Crime and Disorder Act 1998

Detailed commentary of mode of trial falls outside the scope of this commentary. As a general rule the right to elect trial in the Crown Court, or to be dealt with on indictment under section 51, Crime and Disorder Act 1998 arises only where the accused is aged 18 years or older. A child or young person may only be proceeded against on indictment:

Section 24, Magistrates Courts Act 1980
Section 91, Powers of Criminal Courts (Sentencing) Act 2000

• where the provisions of section 24, Magistrates Courts Act 1980 apply and the court has made a decision relating to the punishment of certain grave crimes under section 91, Powers of Criminal Courts (Sentencing) Act 2000;[3]

• where the child or young person is jointly charged with an adult and the court considers it necessary in the interests of justice to commit them both for trial; or

Section 51, Crime and Disorder Act 1998

• where the child or young person is charged jointly with an adult with offences to which section 51, Crime and Disorder Act 1998 apply

1. Section 99, Children and Young Persons Act 1933 and Section 150(4), Magistrates' Courts Act 1980; *R* v *Brown* [1989] Crim LR 750.
2. Section 164, Powers of Criminal Courts (Sentencing) Act 2000.
3. Discussed below at page XX.

As far as the determination of age is concerned the relevant date is the apparent age of the child or young person on the date on which mode of trial is to be determined.[4]

Age and Sentence

Where a child or young person attains the age of 18 after conviction but before sentence the court has discretion to either sentence him in the youth court or to remit him to the adult court for sentence.[5] However there also exists power for the youth court to sentence a young offender who attains 18 years before sentence as if he had not attained that age.[6]

As far as the determination of age is concerned the relevant date is the apparent age of the child or young person on the date of finding of guilt or conviction.[7]

Where a defendant is no longer a child or young person the adult and youth court retain concurrent jurisdiction to deal with any breach of conditional discharge.[8] Proceedings for breach of a supervision order where the child or young person has attained 18 years of age are matters within the jurisdiction of the adult court[9] whereas breach of an action plan order falls to be dealt with by the youth court.

Criminal Responsibility

There is an irrebuttable presumption in law that a child under the age of 10 years is incapable of being convicted[10] of a criminal offence.[11] Prior to the Crime and Disorder Act 1998 there also existed a rebuttable presumption that a child aged between 10 and 14 years was incapable of committing an offence in law. This was known as the principle of *doli incapax* and it was necessary for the prosecution to show that the child of such an age knew that what he did was seriously wrong in addition to

Crime and
Disorder Act 1998

---

4.   *R v Islington North Juvenile Court, ex parte Daley* [1983] 1 AC 347.
5.   Section 9, Powers of Criminal Courts (Sentencing) Act 2000.
6.   Section 29, Children and Young Persons Act 1963.
7.   *R v Danga* [1991] 13 Cr App Rep (S) 408.
8.   Section 48(2), Children and Young Persons Act 1933.
9.   Schedule 7, Para 1, Powers of Criminal Courts (Sentencing) Act 2000.
10. In this text, unless the context requires otherwise, the phrases 'convicted' and 'conviction' are used as convenient shorthand for 'findings of guilt' and 'found guilty' notwithstanding section 59, Children and Young Persons Act 1933. Similarly, the word 'sentence' is used notwithstanding the statutory disuse of such words and phrases.
11. Where there are allegations arising out of the behaviour of a child under the age of 10 years, application may be made to a Family Proceedings Court for a Child Safety Order under section 11, Crime and Disorder Act 1998.

the elements of the specific offence. This requirement has now been repealed.

The Youth Justice System

Crime and Disorder Act 1998

The Crime and Disorder Act 1998 introduced a number of important changes to the administration of the youth justice system. The changes introduced the concept of aims and objectives to the youth justice system, the national co-ordination of youth justice policy and the local delivery of services aimed at supporting the delivery of the system's objectives.

For the practitioner, a knowledge of these changes might assist the preparation of mitigation as the system, whilst ostensibly similar to that which exists in the case of adults, is based on a different perceptions, values and expectations.

Persistent Young Offenders

For the purposes of the administration of the youth justice system, all agencies are required to distinguish between youth offenders and persistent young offenders. The objective of these classifications is generally to focus attention, support and services on those classes of children and young offenders regarded at most risk of re-offending.

There is no statutory definition of a persistent young offender. However the term is defined in a joint Home Office/Lord Chancellor's Department circular[12] as follows:

> 'A child or young person sentenced by any court on three or more separate occasions for one or more recordable offences, and within three years of the last sentencing occasion is subsequently arrested or has an information laid against him for a further recordable offence'

Where a child or young person falls within the definition of a persistent young offender the court and all other agencies in the youth justice system are subject to certain targets to complete the case, from arrest to sentence within a specified time period. The targets are simply targets and no sanction exists to enforce these measures.[13]

---

12. *Measuring Performance to Reduce Delays in the Youth Justice System.*
13. However, in certain areas there exists a pilot scheme where strict time limits have been imposed for the listing of cases from charge through to sentence. The scheme operating in the 27 specified petty sessions area may, if successful be extended to cover the country in due course and arises out of the Prosecution of Offences (Youth Court Time Limits) Regulations 1999.

The definition of a persistent young offender should not be confused with the term persistent offender. This term arises in determining whether a child or young person under 15 years of age is at risk of receiving a detention and training order as a sentence in the youth court. In *R v Charlton*[14] the Court of Appeal held that the non-statutory definition in the circular did not apply to help define the term persistent offender for this purpose.[15]

A youth offender is an offender who is either a child or young person and the category includes those juveniles who are neither persistent young offenders nor spree offenders.

The Aim of the Youth Justice System

Section 37(1), Crime and Disorder Act 1998

Section 37(1), Crime and Disorder Act 1998 provides that it shall be the principal aim of the youth justice system to prevent offending by children and young persons.

One of the aims of sentencing a child or young person is to eliminate the risk of further offending behaviour. The prevention of juvenile crime is placed at the centre of the youth justice system unlike in the adult sentencing scheme where the primary focus for the court is the seriousness of the offence. In the adult court the prevention of further offending is but one of a number of competing principles. In the youth justice system it has greater priority.

The Welfare Principle

Section 44, Children and Young Persons Act 1933

In addition to the aim of the youth justice system, every court shall, in accordance with section 44, Children and Young Persons Act 1933, have regard to the welfare of the child or young person, and shall in a proper case take steps for removing him from undesirable surroundings and for securing that proper provision is made for his education and training.

The welfare principle in the youth court has not attracted the same status as the welfare principle in the family proceedings court. It is however a principle of general application in the youth court and should be considered at the sentencing stage of proceedings as well as during the remand stages of proceedings where its injunction might appear to be more relevant.

---

14.   [2002] All ER (D) 1254.
15.   See below at page XX.

The Youth Justice Board

Section 41,
Crime and
Disorder Act 1998

The Youth Justice Board has responsibility for the national coordination of youth justice policy. The composition and functions of the Youth Justice Board are set out in section 41, Crime and Disorder Act 1998. The Board has strategic responsibility for monitoring the operation of the youth justice system and an advisory role to the Secretary of State on matters including how the principal aim of the system might be most effectively pursued and what steps might be taken to prevent offending by children and young persons.

The Youth Justice board has undertaken a number of important initiatives since its creation. Training materials for justices in the youth court together with a handbook for use in court have been prepared in conjunction with the Judicial Studies Board. Practitioners should also be aware of statistics and press releases prepared for and issued by the Board from time to time providing information and guidance upon a range of issues relating to the youth justice system as a whole and to sentencing in particular.

Youth Offending Teams

Sections 38 to 40,

The provision of youth justice system services at local level is the responsibility of the relevant local authority. Sections 38 to 40, Crime and Disorder Act 1998 set out the functions and responsibilities of the local authority including the establishment of an annual youth justice plan and the creation and operation of youth offending teams.

This part of the Crime and Disorder Act 1998 does not focus upon the court setting alone and practitioners should see the provision of local services as a part of the local authority's overall responsibility to take measures to encourage children and young offenders not to commit offences.

The Youth Offending Teams are multi-disciplinary teams of professionals[16] engaged specifically to coordinate the provision of youth justice services and to carry out such functions as are assigned to the team under the youth justice plan.

The role of the Youth Offending Team extends to include the provision of pre-sentence reports, the management and enforcement of community based penalties, support services in

---

16. Including at least one of each of the following, a probation officer, a social worker, a police officer, an officer of the health authority and an officer of the local education authority.

relation to custodial remands and sentences and to the establishment and operation of Youth Offending Panels.

The Investigation of Offences

Police and
Criminal Evidence
Act 1984

The investigation of offences committed by juveniles falls outside the scope of this work. However, practitioners should be aware of the general powers of search, seizure, arrest, detention and interview of children and young persons. The Police and Criminal Evidence Act 1984 and the Codes of Practice apply also to juveniles with appropriate amendments.

For the purposes of the Police and Criminal Evidence Act 1984 the amended provisions giving additional protection to the young offender apply to persons aged under 17 years of age. Accordingly a young person aged 17 will be subject to the adult regime as far as his detention, treatment and questioning are concerned but subject to the youth court regime as far as any criminal proceedings are concerned.[17]

Diversion from Court Proceedings

Crime and
Disorder Act 1998

Prior to the Crime and Disorder Act 1998 there existed a non statutory process permitting youths to be cautioned by the police for admitted offences rather than formal criminal proceedings being instigated against the child or young person.

Sections 65 and
66, Crime and
Disorder Act 1998

Sections 65 and 66, Crime and Disorder Act 1998 replaced the former procedure with a formal scheme of reprimands and warnings. The scheme operates to divert children and young persons from the court process but allows intervention by the Youth Offending Teams in certain situations where the risk of re-offending may be regarded as high.

The diversion scheme, by its nature, does not arise once an offender has been found guilty or convicted of an offence in court. There is however scope to employ the scheme after charge where the prosecution (and the police) might be persuaded that, in all the circumstances of the case it is more appropriate to divert than to prosecute. The use of a reprimand or warning is regulated by statute and has an important impact on the sentencing powers subsequently available to the youth court in relation to later offences.

---

17. For the purposes of the Bail Act 1976 a young person aged 17 is treated as if he were an adult.

Reprimands and Warnings

The power to impose either a reprimand or warning arises where:[18]

- a constable has evidence that a child or young person has committed an offence;

- the constable considers that the evidence is such that if the offender were prosecuted for the offence, there would be a realistic prospect of his being convicted;

- the offender admits to the constable that he committed the offence;

- the offender has not previously been convicted of an offence; and

- the constable is satisfied that it would not be in the public interest for the offender to be prosecuted.[19]

Where these criteria are met the constable may either reprimand or warn the offender.

A reprimand is available where the offender has not previously been reprimanded or warned.[20]

The constable may warn the offender if:

- the offender has not previously been warned; or

- where the offender has previously been warned, the offence was committed more than two years after the date of the previous warning and the constable considers the offence to be not so serious as to require a charge to be brought.[21]

In any event, no person may be warned more than once.[22]

If the constable considers that the offence is so serious as to require a warning, he may do so even where the offender has not previously been reprimanded.[23]

---

18. Section 65(1), Crime and Disorder Act 1998.
19. The Association of Chief Police Officers has produced notes of guidance on the identification of the public interest cross-referencing certain offences against factors of gravity.
20. Section 65(2), Crime and Disorder Act 1998.
21. Section 65(3), Crime and Disorder Act 1998.
22. Section 65(3), Crime and Disorder Act 1998.
23. Section 65(4), Crime and Disorder Act 1998.

The Effect of a Reprimand

There are two main implications where a warning has been given to a child or young person so far as sentencing is concerned.

(1) Any reprimand may be cited in criminal proceedings in the same circumstances as a conviction may be cited.

(2) A child or young person may only be reprimanded once.

The Effect of a Warning

There are three main implications where a warning has been given to a child or young person so far as sentencing is concerned.

(1) As soon as practicable after a warning has been given the constable shall refer the youth to a Youth Offending Team for assessment and inclusion in a rehabilitation programme. The programme will be in accordance with guidance published by the Secretary of State and will be aimed at rehabilitation and the prevention of further offending.[24]

(2) Any warning or failure to participate in a rehabilitation programme may be cited in criminal proceedings in the same circumstances as a conviction may be cited.[25]

(3) Where a child or young person is convicted by a court of an offence within two years of the warning, the court may not conditionally discharge the offender unless it is of the opinion that there are exceptional circumstances relating to the offence or the offender which justify its doing so. The opinion has to be stated in open court.[26]

Criminal Proceedings

Where a child or young person is believed to have committed an offence so serious that it is appropriate to prosecute, or where the offender is barred from statutory diversion by way of reprimand or warning, the offender will usually be charged or summonsed to the youth court.

A child or young person's attendance at court can be secured in the same way as an adult through the issue of a summons or a warrant following the laying of an information or the making of

---

24. Section 66(1), Crime and Disorder Act 1998.
25. Section 66(5), Crime and Disorder Act 1998.
26. Section 66(4), Crime and Disorder Act 1998.

a charge.[27] Save in specific situations, a child or young person will appear in the youth court.[28]

Circumstances where a Child or Young Person may Appear in the Adult Court

Where the child or young person is jointly charged with an offence with an adult[29] the trial of the joint offence must take place in the adult court unless section 29, Magistrates Courts Act 1980 applies.

Section 29, Magistrates Courts Act 1980

For the purposes of a remand hearing, either an adult or youth court may deal with a child or young person.[30] In the following situations the adult court retains a discretion, rarely exercised for practical reasons, to remit to the youth court but may otherwise hear cases involving children and young persons:

- Where an adult offender is charged with aiding, abetting, causing, procuring, allowing or permitting the offence charged against the child or young person;[31]

- Where the court has embarked on proceedings in the belief that the offender is an adult but it transpires during the proceedings that he is a child or young person;[32]

- Where the child or young person is charged with aiding, abetting, causing, procuring, allowing or permitting the offence charged against an adult at the same time;[33]

- Where the child or young person is charged with an offence arising out of circumstances which are the same as or connected with those giving rise to an offence with which the adult is charged;[34]

- Where a child or young person has appeared before the youth court and subsequently attains the age of 18 years, the youth court may remit him for sentence to an adult court at any time after conviction and before sentence;[35]

---

27. See, generally, the Magistrates' Courts Act 1980.
28. Section 46(1), Children and Young Persons Act 1933.
29. *Ibid.*
30. Section 46(2), Children and Young Persons Act 1933.
31. Section 46(1), Children and Young Persons act 1933.
32. *Ibid.*
33. Section 18(1)(a), Children and Young Persons Act 1963.
34. Section 18(1)(b), Children and Young Persons Act 1963.
35. Section 9(1), Powers of Criminal Courts (Sentencing) Act 2000.

Section 12

- Where the court has received a notice of intention to plead guilty by post under section 12, Magistrates' Courts Act 1980 and the court has no reason to be aware that the defendant is in fact a child or young person.[36]

Circumstances where a Child or Young Person Appearing in the Adult Court may be Remitted to Appear in the Youth Court

The court may become aware in the course of proceedings that the offender is in fact a child or young person and decline to continue with the trial.[37]

Remittal to youth court

Where the child or young person is jointly charged with an adult and

- The adult pleads guilty but the child or young person pleads not guilty; or

- The adult is committed for trial or discharged after committal and, having proceeded to summary trial the child or young person pleads not guilty

the adult court may remit him to the youth court for trial.[38]

There is no appeal against the decision to remit to the youth court for trial.[39]

Section 24,
Magistrates
Courts Act 1980

In proceedings conducted in respect of the adult as examining justices the adult court may only commit a child or young person where it has declined to accept jurisdiction under section 24, Magistrates Courts Act 1980.

No remittal to youth court

Where a child or young person has been convicted or found guilty of any offence other than homicide by any court, the young offender shall be remitted to a youth court for sentence unless one of the following apply:[40]

Section 51,
Crime and Disorder

- Where the offender was either sent to the Crown Court under section 51, Crime and Disorder Act 1998 or committed for trial, the offender shall be remitted to a

---

36. Section 46(1A), Children and Young Persons Act 1933.
37. Section 46(1)(c), Children and Young Persons Act 1933.
38. Section 29(2), Magistrates' Courts Act 1980.
39. Section 29(3), Magistrates' Courts Act 1980.
40. Section 8(1), Powers of Criminal Courts (Sentencing) Act 2000.

Act 1998

youth court for sentence unless the court is satisfied that it would be undesirable to do so.[41]

- Where the case is such that the court would be required to make a referral order to the Youth Offending Panel. In such a situation there is no duty to remit to the youth court for sentence and the adult court, having convicted or found the child or young person guilty may impose a referral order;[42]

- Where the court is of the opinion that the case is one which can properly be dealt with by means of either:

  - an absolute or conditional discharge;

  - a fine; or

  - a parental bind-over

  with or without other ancillary orders.

The youth court to which a child or young person is remitted will be the youth court acting for the place where he was committed or sent for trial in the case of a remittal from the Crown Court, or acting same place as the remitting court or for the place where the offender habitually resides.[43]

Habitual residence has not been defined. Difficulties may exist with this provision where a child or young person is subject to a care order to a local authority but is housed in another area where he commits offences. Generally, the child or young person would be remitted to the area where he is resident. However, this area may only accommodate him temporarily and his connection might be entirely transitory. In the absence of specific authority, it would seem appropriate to regard his habitual residence as being in the compass of the local authority in whose care he has been placed.

Proceedings before the Crown Court

The youth court has exclusive jurisdiction to deal with children and young persons save in the following circumstances:

- where the magistrates' court is dealing with a child or young person jointly charged with an adult or for an offence connected with an offence charged against an adult;

---

41. Section 8(2), Powers of Criminal Courts (Sentencing) Act 2000.
42. Section 8(6), Powers of Criminal Courts (Sentencing) Act 2000.
43. Section 8(2), Powers of Criminal Courts (Sentencing) Act 2000.

- where the magistrates' having convicted the child or young person does not remit him to be sentenced to the youth court;

Section 51,
Crime and
Disorder Act 1951

- where the child or young person has been sent to the Crown Court for an indictable only offence under section 51, Crime and Disorder Act 1951;

- where the child or young person has been committed for trial to the Crown Court where it is in the interests of justice for him to be dealt with on indictment in relation to a joint offence with an adult;

- where the youth court has determined that the child or young person should be punished for a grave crime.[44]

The Crown Court has jurisdiction to deal with a child or young person where:

- the child or young person has been convicted on indictment of an offence of homicide;[45]

Section 51,
Crime and
Disorder Act 1951

- the child or young person has been sent to the Crown Court for an indictable only offence under section 51, Crime and Disorder Act 1951;

- the child or young person has been committed for trial to the Crown Court where it is in the interests of justice for him to be dealt with on indictment in relation to a joint offence with an adult;

- the youth court has determined that the child or young person should be punished for a grave crime.

Where a child or young person is found guilty or convicted on indictment the Crown Court has the full range of sentences

---

44. The phrase 'grave crime' is used as convenient shorthand for the power previously available to the court under section 53(2), Children and Young Persons Act 1933. It should more properly be regarded as the power available to the Crown Court to impose detention in respect of persons convicted of certain serious offences.

45. Homicide includes any offence of unlawful killing. It has been argued by the editors of *Stone's Justices Manual* without authority that the offence of causing death by dangerous driving is an offence of homicide which must be tried on indictment. An offence of causing death through careless driving whilst under the influence of drink or drugs may similarly be an offence of homicide. However, section 91(2), Powers of Criminal Courts (Sentencing) Act 2000 may resolve the point by implying that such offences are not offences of homicide but are capable of being determined to be grave crimes instead. Driving without due care and attention where death results is not an offence of homicide.

Section 8(1), Powers of Criminal Courts (Sentencing) Act 2000

available in the youth court open to it. However, section 8(1), Powers of Criminal Courts (Sentencing) Act 2000 applies to direct the court to consider remitting the child or young person to the youth court for sentence unless satisfied that it would be undesirable to do so.

In *R* v *Lewis*[46] the Court of Appeal effectively gave the Crown Court an unfettered discretion in the exercise of this power and it is relatively rare to find cases where such cases are remitted to the youth court. The following reasons for sentencing a child or young person in the Crown Court have been found to be sufficient to avoid remission:

- That the court before which the trial was conducted or guilty plea entered will be in a better informed position to deal properly with the case than the youth court;

- In cases where a child or young person has been convicted jointly with an adult, retaining the case in the Crown Court will help to reduce the risk of sentencing disparity;

- That remitting a case to the youth court would cause delay, duplication and unnecessary extra expense.

Where, however a child or young person is convicted on indictment of an offence of homicide or a grave crime, the Crown Court has exclusive sentencing powers and there is no power to remit the case to the youth court after conviction.

The power of the Crown Court to sentence a child or young person so convicted are considered separately in this text.[47]

Practitioners should note that the power to commit a child or young person to the Crown Court for sentence following a finding of guilt or conviction in the youth court has been repealed.

Grave Crimes

Section 24(1)(a), Magistrates' Courts Act 1980

A child or young person may be committed to the Crown Court in respect of certain indictable offences[48] in accordance with the procedure contained in section 24(1)(a), Magistrates' Courts Act 1980. A child or young person so committed may be sentenced

---

46.   [1984] 79 Cr App R 94.
47.   See the section on Sentencing in the Crown Court at page XX above.
48.   In this context, the word 'indictable' refers to offences which are not capable of being dealt with summarily in the case of an adult and includes all either way offences.

Section 91, Powers
of Criminal Courts
(Sentencing) Act 2000

in the Crown Court under section 91, Powers of Criminal Courts (Sentencing) Act 2000.[49]

The determination of whether a relevant offence is capable of being declared to be a grave crime is the equivalent of determining mode of trial in the case of an adult. However the plea before venue procedure does not apply. The youth court must hear representations from the prosecution and defence[50] on the suitable venue of trial. The procedure is not set out in either statute or rules of court but common practice has developed a similar approach to the traditional procedure employed for determining mode of trial in the adult court.

The timing of the determination is important. The determination should be made before the court begins summary trial of the relevant offence.[51] Commencement of the trial does not, however, preclude the court from considering the position again. It is permissible for a bench of magistrates to re-determine the issue before the commencement of summary trial if there are any new

Section 25(6),
Magistrates
Courts Act 1980

or additional factors to be accounted for.[52] Similarly, section 25(6), Magistrates Courts Act 1980 permits justices to discontinue summary trial and to sit as examining justices where it appears to them before the conclusion of the prosecution case that the offence ought not to be tried summarily.

This does not however permit the court to change its mind without cause nor does it allow the prosecution to invite the court to do so before commencement of summary trial in order to 'correct' an earlier determination.[53]

A youth court hearing committal proceedings having determined the offence to be a grave crime may revert to summary proceedings.[54]

---

49. Although the grave crimes procedure is necessarily conducted before conviction and before sentence, its relevance to sentencing is so crucial that it is right to include the procedure in this text.
50. But the defence version of events will be irrelevant as this is a decision as to mode of trial and the court should take the prosecution case at its highest.
51. *R v Newham Juvenile Court ex parte F (a minor)* [1986] 3 All ER 17, a decision potentially cast into doubt by 49 below.
52. Ibid but note *Devises Youth Court, ex parte A* [2000] 164 JP 330.
53. *R v Fareham Youth Court and Morey ex parte CPS* (1999) 163 JP 812.
54. Section 25(7), Magistrates' Court Act 1980 and *R v Brent Juvenile Court ex parte S* (1991) *The Times* June 18.

Offences Capable of being Declared Grave Crimes

Section 24(1)(a),
Magistrates
Courts Act 1980
Section 91, Powers
of Criminal Courts
(Sentencing) Act 2000

The following offences are capable of being determined grave crimes under section 24(1)(a), Magistrates Courts Act 1980 and therefore may be committed to the Crown Court on indictment for sentence after conviction under section 91, Powers of Criminal Courts (Sentencing) Act 2000

- An offence punishable in the case of a person aged 21 years or over with imprisonment for 14 years or more

Section 14, Sexual
Offences Act 1956

- An offence under section 14, Sexual Offences Act 1956 (indecent assault on a woman)

Section 15, Sexual
Offences Act 1956

- An offence under section 15, Sexual Offences Act 1956 (indecent assault on a man)

- Where a person aged at least 14 years but under 18 years is convicted of an offence of:

  - Causing death by dangerous driving; or

  - Causing death by careless driving while under the influence of drink or drugs.[55]

Determining Grave Crimes

Section 24(1),
Magistrates
Courts Act 1980

Not every offence capable of being determined a grave crime under section 24(1), Magistrates Courts Act 1980 will necessarily be so determined. The powers of the Crown Court to sentence a child or young person are the same as those of the youth court save where the court is dealing with an offender convicted of certain serious offences.

Section 91(3),
Powers of Criminal
Courts (Sentencing)
Act 2000

Section 91(3), Powers of Criminal Courts (Sentencing) Act 2000 provides that if the Crown court is of the opinion that none of the other methods in which the case may legally be dealt with is suitable, the court may sentence the offender to be detained for such period, not exceeding that maximum term of imprisonment with which the offence is punishable in the case of a person aged 21 or over, as may be specified in the sentence.

The test is set out in *R v Inner London Youth Court ex parte DPP*.[56] The justices should ask whether it ought to be possible for the

---

55.   See further footnote 42 above.
56.   [1996] Crim LR 834.

Section 91(3),
Powers of Criminal
Courts (Sentencing)
Act 2000
Section 24(1)(a),
Magistrates
Courts Act 1980

court sentencing the child or young person for the offence to have open to it the possibility of imposing detention under section 91(3), Powers of Criminal Courts (Sentencing) Act 2000.

In *R (on the application of D)* v *Manchester City Youth Court*[57] this came down to the following statement of principle. The effect of section 24(1)(a), Magistrates Courts Act 1980 was that a youth court should not decline jurisdiction unless the offence and the circumstances made it more than a vague or theoretical possibility that a sentence of detention for a long period (i.e. in excess of two years) might be passed.[58]

Section 24(1)(a),
Magistrates
Courts Act 1980

Circumstances where the Youth Court should decline jurisdiction under section 24(1)(a), Magistrates Courts Act 1980:

- where the offence and the circumstances made it more than a vague or theoretical possibility that a sentence of detention for a long period (i.e. in excess of two years) might, on conviction be passed;

- where the child or young person is charged with rape;[59]

- where the charges are of a grave nature such as:

  - robbery or intent to rob;[60]

  - grievous bodily harm with intent;[61]

  - offences of robbery involving mobile phones;[62]

  - armed robbery.[63]

Regard should also be had to the general principles regarding the suitability of the youth court environment commended in the Court of Human Rights in *T* v *UK* and *V* v *UK*[64] although much

---

57. (2002) 166 JP 15.
58. In this case, the High Court considered that it was unreasonable to so conclude where a child aged 13 was charged with indecent assault on another boy aged 8 or 9 in circumstances where the victim was threatened with a knife and prevented from leaving the room before being forced to masturbate the defendant.
59. *R* v *Billam* [1986] 1 All ER 985.
60. *R* v *Learnmouth* (1988) 153 JP 18.
61. *R* v *North Hampshire Youth Court ex parte DPP* (2000) 164 JP 377.
62. *Attorney General's References (No 4 of 2001)* CA January 29, a case involving adults aged 19 but relevant in principle to cases occupying the youth court.
63. *R* v *Weston* [1985] 7 Cr App Rep (S) 420.
64. [2001] Crim LR 187.

of the mischief which may have made youth court trial more favourable has been put right by the Practice Direction (Crown Court: Young Defendants).[65]

Practice Direction (Crown Court: Young Defendants)

Age and Previous Convictions

The Crown Court and youth court have a concurrent and equivalent sentencing jurisdiction as far as it relates to children and young persons with the sole exception of detention for certain serious crimes.

The youth court's only custodial sentence is the Detention and Training Order.[66] Under a Detention and Training Order, which may be passed for a minimum of 4 months and a maximum of 2 years, half the sentence is to be served in the secure estate in detention with the second half of the sentence served in the community under supervision.

A Detention and Training Order may be imposed by the youth court or the Crown Court where the child or young person aged 15 years has been convicted of an offence which is so serious that only custody can be justified. Where the child or young person is aged 14 or less, the order may only be passed in respect of a persistent offender.

A child or young person under the age of 15 may fall into the category of a persistent offender for the purposes of a Detention and Training Order depending on the existence of warnings, reprimands or convictions arising either before or after the commission of the offence falling to be sentenced.

Section 24(1)(a), Magistrates Courts Act 1980

If a child or young person aged under 15 years is charged with an offence to which section 24(1)(a), Magistrates Courts Act 1980 might apply the youth court will be without a crucial piece of information informing their decision as to mode of trial. If the child or young person is not a persistent offender there will be no power to impose upon him a Detention and Training Order. If however, it is known to the court that the child is not within the definition, the court may be able to determine that the offence is a grave crime and commit him to the Crown Court. In the Crown Court, the judge would have open to him, after conviction the power to order detention under section 91(3), Powers of Criminal Courts (Sentencing) Act 2000.

Section 91(3), Powers of Criminal Courts (Sentencing) Act 2000

---

65.   [2000] 1 WLR 659.
66.   See below at page XX.

In *R* v *Hammersmith Juvenile Court ex parte O (a minor)*[67] it was decided that it was wrong in both law and principle to draw the offender's record to the attention of the court determining mode of trial.

The changes to the overall scheme have led some commentators, the Justices' Clerks' Society for example, to conclude that it is now permissible to bring the existence of wrong-doing sufficient to engage the notion of persistent offending to the attention of the youth court at the grave crime determination stage.

Section 91(3)

Little help has so far been provided by the higher courts. In *R* v *Fairhurst*[68] it was held that where an offender was under 15 years of age and so ineligible for a Detention and Training Order, a sentence of detention could properly be passed under section 91(3) even if the period was less than two years.

Doubt on this decision was cast by *R (on the application of D)* v *Manchester City Youth Court* (above) where it was held that a youth court should not decline jurisdiction unless the offence and the circumstances made it more than a vague or theoretical possibility that a sentence of detention for a long period (i.e. in excess of two years) might be passed.

Section 91

The position was clarified in *R (on the application of W)* v *Southampton Youth Court*[69] which confirmed the approach in Manchester City Justices and indicated that section 91 should only be used in exceptional circumstances in relation to children under the age of 15 years.

Sentences in the Youth Court

A child or young person convicted in any court may be sentenced to a wide range of sentences. The adult magistrates' court is limited to imposing either a referral order, where it is required to do so, or a discharge or fine. The Crown Court has jurisdiction to impose any of the available sentencing options and may, where the child or young person has been convicted on indictment of certain serious offences, impose detention under section 91(3), Powers of Criminal Courts (Sentencing) Act 2000.

Section 91(3), Powers of Criminal Courts (Sentencing) Act 2000

Many of the sentences available in respect of children and young persons will be familiar to practitioners from their

67. (1987) 151 JP 740.
68. [1987] 1 All ER 46.
69. (2002) 23 July.

practice in the adult court. There are however a range of orders peculiar to the youth court.

Menu of Sentences Available in the Youth Court

- Referral Order

  This is a mandatory order which must be imposed where a first-time offender pleads guilty before a youth or adult court.

The following orders fall within the lower tier of sentencing options and involve the least interference with an offender or his behaviour:

- Absolute Discharge

- Conditional Discharge

- Fines

- Compensation

- Reparation Order

- Curfew Order

  The curfew order involves a significant level of interference with an offender and his lifestyle. Although it may be imposed as a sentence for any offence, the order should be reserved for those offences and offenders where the restriction of liberty is commensurate with the seriousness of their offending.

The following orders are only available where the offending is serious enough for a community penalty. These orders represent a significant restriction on liberty and are regarded by government as the most effective way of tackling youth crime:

- Action Plan Order

- Supervision Order

- Community Rehabilitation Order

- Attendance Centre Order

- Community Punishment Order

- Community Rehabilitation and Punishment Order

Where the offending is so serious that only custody can be justified, the youth court is empowered to impose a Detention and Training Order

- Detention and Training Order

Part of the government's initiative in tackling youth crime has been to impose responsibilities of the parents of children and young people who offend. In certain circumstances the youth court has either a duty or discretion to impose an order against parents:

- Parental Bind-Over

- Parenting Order

In addition to these substantive sentences and orders, the youth court may impose such ancillary orders as are appropriate including costs, disqualifications, exclusions, forfeitures and endorsements.

Referral Orders

Sections 16 to 32 and Schedule 1, Parts I and II, Powers of Criminal Courts (Sentencing) Act 2000

Sections 16 to 32 and Schedule 1, Parts I and II, Powers of Criminal Courts (Sentencing) Act 2000 deal with referral orders. The order became available nationally after a series of pilot schemes from April 1 2002.

A referral order is available as a sentence in the adult magistrates' court or the youth court after a guilty plea has been entered.[70] The Crown Court has jurisdiction to impose a referral order only where it is sitting in its appellate capacity hearing appeals against sentence from the magistrates' or youth court.

Where a child or young person is convicted in the Crown Court on indictment after pleading guilty, his case must be remitted to the youth court for sentence where a referral order is the correct method of disposal.

The referral order marks the end of judicial discretion in sentencing and establishes a new administrative agency with responsibilities for the operation of a sentence of the court. This new body is called the Youth Offender Panel.

---

70.   A referral order may only be made in the circumstances prescribed by statute and would not be available in respect of an offender convicted after a trial.

Criteria

The sentencing court has a duty or power to refer certain young offenders to the Youth Offender Panel where the offence or any connected offence is not one for which the sentence is fixed by law; and the court is not proposing either:

- to impose a custodial sentence;

- make a hospital order; or

- absolutely discharge the offender in respect of the offence.[71]

Compulsory and Discretionary Referral

The court is required to make a referral order where:

- the child or young person pleads guilty to the offence and to any connected offence;

- the child or young person has not previously been convicted; and

- has not been bound over in criminal proceedings.[72]

The court has discretion to make a referral order where:

- the child or young person is being dealt with by the court for the offence or one or more connected offences;

- although he pleaded guilty to at least one of the offences, he also pleaded not guilty to at least one of them;

- the child or young person has not previously been convicted; and

- has not been bound over in criminal proceedings.[73]

Section 17(3), (4), Powers of Criminal Cases (Sentencing) Act 2000

Section 17(3) and (4), Powers of Criminal Cases (Sentencing) Act 2000 allow the Secretary of State to vary these conditions by regulation.

---

71. Section 16(1), Powers of Criminal Courts (Sentencing) Act 2000.
72. Section 17(1), Powers of Criminal Courts (Sentencing) Act 2000.
73. Section 17(2), Powers of Criminal Courts (Sentencing) Act 2000.

What Does the Referral Order Contain?

Section 18(1),
Powers of Criminal
Courts (Sentencing)
Act 2000

Section 18(1), Powers of Criminal Courts (Sentencing) Act 2000 provides that the order shall:

- specify the youth offending team responsible for implementing the order;

- require the offender to attend each of the meetings of a youth offender panel to be established by the team for the offender; and

- specify the period for which the contract taking effect between the offender and the panel is to have effect between 3 and 12 months.

The court's task is therefore limited to determining the length of the referral order. The period should be commensurate with the seriousness of the offence.

The court has no power to impose any other form of punishment on the offender when it makes a referral order including any order of bind over. However, other ancillary orders such as costs, compensation, endorsement and disqualification may be imposed according to law.[74] The court's power to defer sentence is also removed,[75] although the court retains the power to adjourn the proceedings for further inquiries such as a pre-sentence report where the court is proposing a custodial sentence but may be persuaded otherwise.

On making a referral order shall explain in ordinary language the effect of the order and the consequences which may follow if either the contract does not take effect or if the offender breaches any terms of the contract.[76]

Multiple Offences

Where the court is sentencing a child or young person in respect of a series of connected offences, it may pass a referral order in respect of each offence. The orders may be of different lengths and may be imposed either consecutively or concurrently provided that the minimum period of three months and the maximum period of twelve months are respected. Such orders however act to refer the child or young person to one single youth offender panel.

---

74. Section 19(1), Powers of Criminal Courts (Sentencing) Act 2000.
75. Section 19(7), Powers of Criminal Courts (Sentencing) Act 2000.
76. Section 18(3), Powers of Criminal Courts (Sentencing) Act 2000.

When Does the Order Start?

The order begins to run not from the date of the court proceedings but from the date when the contract with the youth offender panel is agreed.

Referral Orders and Parents

The making of a referral order prevents the court from making an order binding a parent or guardian over or from making a parenting order.[77]

Where the child or young person the subject of the referral order is under 16 the court shall require at least one appropriate adult to attend meetings of the panel unless it is unreasonable to do so.[78] Where the offender is over 16 the court may make such an order.

If the child or young person is looked after by the local authority the court may order a representative of that authority to attend with the child in the same way as it could for an appropriate adult.

The Purpose of a Referral Order

The court's role is limited to determining the length of the order commensurate with the seriousness of the offence. The determination of seriousness requires the court to look at the intrinsic harm involved in the offence, any aggravating or mitigating features of the offence or offender and to make an assessment of the likelihood of re-offending. The overall assessment of seriousness can then be reduced to a level. Where the risk can be categorised as low, medium or high, the court should impose an order of sufficient length to allow the panel to begin and finish interventionist work addressing the risk of

---

77.   Section 19(5), Powers of Criminal Courts (Sentencing) Act 2000.
78.   Section 20, Powers of Criminal Courts (Sentencing) Act 2000.

further offending. Guidance has been issued suggesting the following:[79]

Level of seriousness	Length of referral order	Amount of reparation[80]
Low	3–4 months	3–9 hours
Medium	5–7 months	10–19 hours
High	8–9 months	20–29 hours

The Guidance continues to explain why the ceiling is set at 9 months. This allows:

- orders of 10 – 12 months to be reserved for the most serious of cases;

- orders to be extended by a subsequent court where a further offence comes to light;

- orders of 10–12 months to be made where courts exercise their discretion to make an order following mixed pleas;

- orders of 10–12 months to be made where a plea of guilty is entered at a late stage.

The Guidance also includes a table showing proposed entry points of seriousness for certain common offences. This table is reproduced at Appendix A.

The youth offender panel's role is to determine the level of intervention necessary to address the offender's behaviour and to prevent him from re-offending. The panel operates on the principles of restorative justice. The key features of restorative justice are:

- promoting with the offender a responsibility for his actions;

- making reparation to the victim or wider community; and

- reintegrating the offender into the law-abiding community.

---

79. *Youth Court Bench Book 2001* JSB.
80. This is within the contract agreed by the offender and the youth offender panel and does not form part of the court order. Its inclusion here is for convenience. See the section headed *Contract* below at page XX.

These aims are achieved through a contract entered into between the offender and the panel.

Effect of Referral Order

Successful completion[81] of the contract results in the discharge of the order. As soon as the order is discharged the conviction will be spent for the purposes of the Rehabilitation of Offenders Act 1974.

Rehabilitation of
Offenders Act 1974

The Contract

The contract between the offender and the youth offender panel is the key to the success of the referral order. The contract is a negotiated document focusing on the specific experiences and needs of the child or young person, the victim and the wider community. The contract will be drawn up between the offender and the community members of the youth offender panel with the advice and assistance of the youth offending team.

The contract' terms will depend on the programme of intervention deemed necessary and agreed with the young person to deal with offending behaviour and the risk of re-offending.[82] The terms should not be out of proportion to the seriousness of the offence or to the risk of re-offending. Two main aspects will be included in all contracts:

(1) Reparation to the victim or wider community.

(2) A programme of intervention delivered or organised by the youth offending team addressing factors likely to be associated with re-offending.

Within each contract there will be a series of review and progress meetings. The meetings are held between the offender and the youth offender panel. The purpose of each meeting is to review the offender's progress. A progress meeting may be requested at any time by the offender and such a meeting is able to deal with the following issues:

•   Review the offender's progress;

•   Discuss with the offender any breach of the terms of the contract which it appears to the panel that he has committed;

---

81. Successful completion of the contract is determined at a final meeting between the offender and the panel in accordance with section 27, Powers of Criminal Courts (Sentencing) Act 2000.

82. Section 23(2), Powers of Criminal Court (Sentencing) Act 2000.

- Consider any variation in the terms of the contract sought by the offender or which it appears to the panel to be expedient to make in the light of any such review or discussion;

- Consider whether to accede to any request by the offender that he be referred back to the appropriate court on account of a significant change in his circumstances (such as his being taken to live abroad) making compliance with any contract impractical.[83]

Failure to Agree a Contract

The contract between the child or young person and the youth offender panel is crucial to the order. It sets out the terms of the intervention to be employed in the offender's case. The contract should generally be agreed upon at the first meeting of the panel with the offender. If it is not agreed, the panel may end the meeting and postpone reaching agreement until a further meeting.[84] Once an agreement has been reached, a record of it must be signed by the offender as must any subsequent variation to it.

Breach of a Referral Order

Schedule 1, Part I, Powers of Criminal Courts (Sentencing) Act 2000

Schedule 1, Part 1, Powers of Criminal Courts (Sentencing) Act 2000 deals with the circumstances where the youth offender panel refers the offender back to the appropriate court. The power to do so arises in a number of circumstances including an apparent breach of the terms of the contract.

The circumstances are:

- Failure by the offender to attend panel meeting;

- Where it appears to the panel that there is no prospect of reaching an agreement with the offender within a reasonable period after the making of the referral order;

- Where agreement has been reached between the panel and the offender but he fails unreasonably to sign the record;

- Where the offender has breached the contract;

- Where a variation of the contract has been agreed between the panel and the offender but he fails unreasonably to sign the record;

---

83. Section 26, Powers of Criminal Courts (Sentencing) Act 2000.
84. Section 25(1), Powers of Criminal Courts (Sentencing) Act 2000.

- Where there has been a change in the offender's circumstances and the panel is satisfied that the offender should be referred back to court;

- Where the panel are not satisfied that the offender's compliance with the terms of the contract have been such as to justify its discharge at the final meeting.[85]

The Appropriate Court

In the case of an offender aged under 18 at the time (in pursuance of the referral back) he first appears before the court, the appropriate court is the youth court where he is usually resident; otherwise the appropriate court is an adult magistrates' court.[86]

The Referral Back Procedure

Where one of the circumstances allowing an offender to be referred back to the appropriate court obtains, the panel sends to the court a report explaining why the offender is being returned to court.[87] The court must then issue proceedings to secure the attendance of the offender. This may be by way of summons or, if the report is substantiated on oath, by warrant.[88] Provision is also made for the detention and arrest of an arrested offender where the court has issued a warrant to secure his attendance.[89]

An offender arrested under a warrant issued in these proceedings may be detained for up to 72 hours from the time of his arrest and may be detained in a place of safety as defined in section 107(1) of the Children and Young Persons Act 1933. Within that time the offender shall be brought before a court:

Section 107(1),
Children and Young
Persons Act 1933

- In the case of a person under 18, that court shall be a youth court;

- In the case of a person aged 18 or over, that court shall be an adult court.

The court has power to deal with the offender if it is also the appropriate court. Where it is not the court before which he

---

85. Paragraph 1(1), Part 1, Schedule 1, Powers of Criminal Courts (Sentencing) Act 2002.
86. Paragraph 1(2), Part 1, Schedule 1, Powers of Criminal Courts (Sentencing) Act 2002.
87. Paragraph 2, Part 1, Schedule 1, Powers of Criminal Courts (Sentencing) Act 2002.
88. Paragraph 3(2), Part 1, Schedule 1, Powers of Criminal Courts (Sentencing) Act 2002.
89. Paragraph 4, Part 1, Schedule 1, Powers of Criminal Courts (Sentencing) Act 2002.

appears has power to release him forthwith or to remand him, either in custody, to accommodation provided by the local authority or on bail to appear before the appropriate court.[90]

The power to deal with an offender only arises in the appropriate court.

The Court's Role where an Offender has been Referred Back

The appropriate court does not act on the decision of the panel to refer an offender back to it.

The court's first task is to determine whether it has power to revoke the order. This power arises only where it is proved to the court's satisfaction that:

- So far as the decision relied on any finding of fact by the panel, the panel was entitled to make that finding in the circumstances; and

- So far as the decision involved any exercise of discretion by the panel, the panel reasonably exercised that discretion in the circumstances.[91]

Effectively, the appropriate court has to conduct a limited judicial review of the panel's decision to refer the offender back. The review has two possible outcomes: either the court will be so satisfied or it will not.

Where the Court Upholds the Panel's Decision

Where the court upholds the decision of the panel it may decide to revoke the referral order and deal with the offender in any way in which he could have been dealt with for that offence by the court which made the order.[92] In dealing with him, the court is required to have regard to the circumstances of his

---

90. Paragraph 4, Part 1, Schedule 1, Powers of Criminal Courts (Sentencing) Act 2002.
91. Paragraph 5(1), Part 1, Schedule 1, Powers of Criminal Courts (Sentencing) Act 2002.
92. The making of a referral order is effectively the only disposal available to the court dealing with an offender appearing in court for the first time. However, the sentencing court has the option of either absolutely discharging the offender or, where the offence is so serious that only custody can be justified, imposing a detention and training order. It may be argued with some considerable force that once the sentencing court has rejected the custodial option and proceeded to make a referral order, that it would not be open for the court on a referral back to impose such a sentence. Whether this approach is correct will doubtless be tested in the High Court in due course.

referral back to court and the extent of his compliance with any part of the terms of the contract.[93]

The power to re-sentence is only exercisable in the presence of the offender but can be exercised even where the contract, if ever established has expired either before or after the referral back to court.[94]

There is a right of appeal to the Crown Court against sentence imposed after revocation but there does not appear to be a similar power to appeal against the decision of the appropriate court to uphold the decision of the panel under paragraph 5(1) of Part 1 Schedule 1, Powers of Criminal Courts (Sentencing) Act 2002.

Paragraph 5(1), Part I Schedule I, Powers of Criminal Courts (Sentencing) Act 2002

The court also has power to uphold the panel's decision and to decide (for any reason) not to revoke the order.[95] The consequences of taking this decision are similar to the situation where the court does not uphold the panel's decision.

Where the Court does not Uphold the Panel's Decision

Paragraph 5(1)(a) or (b) Part 1 Schedule 1

Where the appropriate court is not satisfied that the panel's decision is correct having regard to paragraph 5 (1)(a) or (b) of Part 1 Schedule 1, Powers of Criminal Courts (Sentencing) Act 2002, or being so satisfied decides not to revoke the referral order, the offender shall continue to be subject to the referral order as if he had not been referred back to the court.[96]

If the contract had taken effect but expired in such circumstances the court shall discharge the referral order.[97]

Referrals Back under Section 27(4) of the Powers of Criminal Courts (Sentencing) Act 2000

Where an offender has been referred back to the appropriate court on the basis that the panel cannot discharge the order on the grounds that the offender has failed to comply with its terms sufficient to justify discharge, the appropriate court may decide that the offender's compliance has been sufficient.

---

93. Paragraph 5(5), Part 1, Schedule 1, Powers of Criminal Courts (Sentencing) Act 2002.
94. Paragraph 5(6), Part 1, Schedule 1, Powers of Criminal Courts (Sentencing) Act 2002.
95. Paragraph 7(1)(b), Part 1, Schedule 1, Powers of Criminal Courts (Sentencing) Act 2002.
96. Paragraph 7(2), Part 1, Schedule 1, Powers of Criminal Courts (Sentencing) Act 2002.
97. Paragraph 7(3), Part 1, Schedule 1, Powers of Criminal Courts (Sentencing) Act 2002.

Where the court so decides it may make an order discharging the referral order.[98]

The Effect of Further Convictions

The referral order scheme is further complicated by convictions recorded against an offender subject to a referral order after the order has been made. Part II of Schedule 1, Powers of Criminal Courts (Sentencing) Act 2000 provides for the consequences of offending not dealt with by way of the referral order.

Part II of Schedule 1, Powers of Criminal Courts (Sentencing) Act 2000

Offences Committed before Referral

Where an offender commits an offence before the making of the referral order the court which sentences him for it may sentence him by extending the compliance period[99] of the referral order. This power only exists[1] in relation to the offence if the offender's only other occasion on which he has been dealt with for an offence was the occasion when he was made the subject of the referral order.[2]

Offences Committed after Referral

Where an offender commits an offence after the making of the referral order, the court which sentences him for it may extend the period of compliance. This power only exists in relation to the offence if the offender's only other occasion on which he has been dealt with for an offence was the occasion when he was made the subject of the referral order.

Additionally the court must be satisfied, on the basis of a report made to it by the relevant body[3] that there are exceptional circumstances which indicate that, even though the offender has re-offended since being referred to the panel, extending his compliance period is likely to help prevent further re-offending

---

98. Paragraph 8, Part 1, Schedule 1, Powers of Criminal Courts (Sentencing) Act 2002.
99. Compliance period means the period for which any youth offender contract taking effect in his case has (or would have) effect: Paragraph 15(2), Part II, Schedule 1, Powers of Criminal Courts (Sentencing) Act 2000.
1. For these purposes any occasion on which the offender was discharged absolutely in respect of an offence shall be disregarded but any occasion on which he was bound over shall be regarded: Paragraph 13(6) and (7), Part II, Schedule 1, Powers of Criminal Courts (Sentencing) Act 2000.
2. Paragraph 11, Part II, Schedule 1, Powers of Criminal Courts (Sentencing) Act 2002.
3. If a contract has been agreed the relevant body is the panel. If no contract yet exists the relevant body is the youth offending team. Paragraph 12(3), Part II, Schedule 1, Powers of Criminal Courts (Sentencing) Act 2000.

by him. The court is required to state in open court that it is so satisfied and why it is.[4]

Maximum Period of Extension

An order extending the compliance period under these provisions cannot extend the referral order beyond twelve months.[5]

Effect of an Order to Extend

In respect of the new offence the court is not required to extend the referral order and may decide to sentence the offender to any of the other usual sentencing options.

Where the court extends the period of compliance in respect of an offence committed either before or after the referral order was made, the offender may not be otherwise sentenced. Any connected offence must be either dealt with by the order to extend the period of compliance or by way of absolute discharge.[6]

The power to impose a parental bind-over or make a parenting order is also disapplied where the court decides to extend the period of compliance.[7]

Effect of Not Making an Order to Extend

Where the court dealing with an offence committed either before or after the making of a referral order does not decide to either make an order to extend the compliance period, any other sentence or order has the effect of revoking the referral order.[8]

Where any order is revoked by the commission of offences either before or after the making of the order the court may sentence the offender for the offence in respect of which the revoked order had been made where it appears to be in the interests of justice to do so. In determining the appropriate sentence on revocation the court shall have regard to the extent of his compliance with the terms of the contract.[9]

---

4. Paragraph 12(1) and (2), Part II, Schedule 1, Powers of Criminal Courts (Sentencing) Act 2000.
5. Paragraph 13, Part II, Schedule 1, Powers of Criminal Courts (Sentencing) Act 2000.
6. Paragraph 13(4), Part II, Schedule 1, Powers of Criminal Courts (Sentencing) Act 2000.
7. Paragraph 13(5), Part II, Schedule 1, Powers of Criminal Courts (Sentencing) Act 2000.
8. Paragraph 14, Part II, Schedule 1, Powers of Criminal Courts (Sentencing) Act 2000.
9. Paragraph 14(3), Part II, Schedule 1, Powers of Criminal Courts (Sentencing) Act 2000.

Amendment of Referral Orders

Where it appears to the court which made a referral order that, by reason of either a change or prospective change in the offender's place or intended place of residence, the youth offending team named in the order will not have the function of implementing the order, the court may amend the order to specify the youth offending team for the place the offender is now or will reside.[10]

Where the court makes such an amendment – on application by the youth offending team[11] – any contract subsisting with the original youth offender panel is to be treated as if it were a contract between the offender and the panel established by the substituted youth offending team.[12]

Sentencing Options in the Youth Court

In the case of children and young persons appearing before the court for the first time, legislation requires the court on a guilty plea to impose either an absolute discharge, a custodial sentence or a referral order.

In the case of children and young persons found guilty after trial or appearing in circumstances which bring them outside the referral order scheme, the court has a range of other sentences available to deal with the offender.

The majority of sentences are also available in the adult court and many of them share characteristics. However, there are also certain specific sentences only available in the youth court such as reparation orders, action plan orders, supervision orders and detention and training orders.

An adult magistrates' court also has limited powers to sentence a convicted child or young person appearing before it.

Deferment of Sentence

It is possible to defer sentence in respect of a child or young person convicted of any offence.[13] Sentence may be deferred only where the offender consents and the court is satisfied,

---

10. Section 21(5), Powers of Criminal Courts (Sentencing) Act 2000.
11. The legislation appears silent on the actual procedure to be followed. However, similar applications in respect of community orders may be made on notice by application and it would seem appropriate to deal with this type of amendment in the same way.
12. Section 21(6), Powers of Criminal Courts (Sentencing) Act 2000.
13. Section 1, Powers of Criminal Courts (Sentencing) Act 2000.

having regard to the nature of the offence and the character and circumstances of the offender, that it would be in the interests of justice to exercise the power.[14]

Any deferment has to be to a specific date although there is no power to remand the offender to that date and can be for no longer than 6 months after the date on which the deferment is announced.[15]

The deferment of sentence allows the court to set goals for an offender to be completed during the period of the deferment. The court which falls to deal with him at the end of the period may have regard to his conduct after conviction including where appropriate, any reparation he has undertaken and any changes in the offender's circumstances.

At the end of the deferment period the court has power to deal with the offender in any way in which it could have dealt with him if it had not deferred passing sentence.[16] Usually, if the offender has complied with the conditions or terms of the deferment he can expect a lesser sentence than perhaps the seriousness of the offence initially merited.

The powers of the court to deal with additional offending during the period of the deferment in the case of a youth are the same as for dealing with an adult.[17]

Whether it is appropriate to defer sentence in the case of a youth must be doubted given the principles acting in the youth justice system. There is a clear objective to visit the consequences of offending on the child or young person and to deal with him as close to the commission of offence as practical. Although deferment of sentence may be hedged with conditions, the sentence (or rather lack of it) does not fit comfortably with the scheme of intervention and diversion operating in the youth courts. However, in the right case (and usually when other sentencing options appear as poor an option) the court may consider deferment.

Absolute Discharge

A child or young person may be absolutely discharged in respect of any offence of which he has been convicted either after trial or following a guilty plea. An absolute discharge is appropriate where the court is of the opinion, having regard to the circumstances

---

14.   Section 1(2), Powers of Criminal Courts (Sentencing) Act 2000.
15.   Section 1(3), Powers of Criminal Courts (Sentencing) Act 2000.
16.   Section 1(5), Powers of Criminal Courts (Sentencing) Act 2000.
17.   Section 2, Powers of Criminal Courts (Sentencing) Act 2000.

including the nature of the offence and the character of the offender, that it is inexpedient to inflict punishment.[18]

As a general rule an absolute discharge is usually reserved for those occasions where an offender is morally if not legally blameless for the offence.

An absolute discharge may be imposed on a child or young person by the adult magistrates' court.

An absolute discharge does not prevent a court from imposing orders of costs, compensation, disqualification, deprivation or restitution.[19]

The use of an absolute discharge as a sentence is likely to increase as courts begin to use referral orders. There may be a range of offences which do not merit consideration of a custodial sentence where the making of a referral order for the minimum period of three months might be regarded as disproportionate. In such circumstances the court may be more amenable to making orders absolutely discharging the offender.

Conditional Discharge

A conditional discharge is also available as a sentence where the court considers that it is inexpedient to inflict punishment.[20] The discharge is subject to the condition that during the period of the discharge the offender does not commit further offences. If during that period he commits a further offence the court sentencing him for that offence may revoke the conditional discharge and sentence him for the original offence.[21]

Before making a conditional discharge the court is under a duty to explain the terms of the order to the defendant.[22] Consequently, an order of conditional discharge cannot properly be imposed in the absence of the defendant.

The maximum period of a conditional discharge is three years. There is no minimum period.[23]

A conditional discharge does not prevent a court from imposing orders of costs, compensation, disqualification, deprivation or

18.   Section 12(1)(a), Powers of Criminal Courts (Sentencing) Act 2000.
19.   Section 12(7), Powers of Criminal Courts (Sentencing) Act 2000.
20.   Section 12(1)(b), Powers of Criminal Courts (Sentencing) Act 2000.
21.   Section 12(6), Powers of Criminal Courts (Sentencing) Act 2000.
22.   Section 12(4), Powers of Criminal Courts (Sentencing) Act 2000.
23.   Section 12(1)(b), Powers of Criminal Courts (Sentencing) Act 2000.

restitution.[24] The court also has power to allow any person who so consents to give security for the good behaviour of the offender.[25]

Prohibition on the Use of Conditional Discharge

Where, under the statutory diversion from court procedure, a child or young person is convicted by a court of an offence within two years of a warning, the court may not conditionally discharge the offender unless it is of the opinion that there are exceptional circumstances relating to the offence or the offender which justify its doing so. The opinion has to be stated in open court.[26]

Further Offences Committed during the period of Discharge

The key to the conditional discharge is the power of the court to re-sentence the child or young person if further offending takes place during the period of the discharge.

If it appears to the court that an offender subject to a conditional discharge has been convicted of an offence committed during the period of the conditional discharge and has been dealt with for that offence, it may issue a summons or warrant to secure the offender's attendance[27] before the court which made the original order. A warrant may only be issued if information has been laid in writing on oath.[28]

Where an offender was made subject to a conditional discharge by the Crown Court and is convicted by a magistrates' court of an offence during the currency of the discharge, the court has power to commit him either in custody or on bail to appear before the Crown Court.[29] This applies only where the offender was convicted in the Crown Court on indictment. Where the Crown Court imposes a conditional discharge in its appellate capacity in determining appeals against sentence from the magistrates' court, the order is treated as if it were made by the magistrates' court.[30]

---

24. Section 12(7), Powers of Criminal Courts (Sentencing) Act 2000.
25. See Section 12(6), Powers of Criminal Courts (Sentencing) Act 2000 but note the decision of the Court of Human Rights in *Hashman and Harrup* v *UK* [2000] 30 EHRR 241 where it was doubted that the term 'good behaviour' was sufficiently certain to found criminal proceedings under Article 7 of the European Convention of Human Rights.
26. Section 66(4), Crime and Disorder Act 1998.
27. Section 13(1), Powers of Criminal Courts (Sentencing) Act 2000.
28. Section 13(3), Powers of Criminal Courts (Sentencing) Act 2000.
29. Section 13(5), Powers of Criminal Courts (Sentencing) Act 2000.
30. Section 15(3), Powers of Criminal Courts (Sentencing) Act 2000.

Where the court sentencing the offender for an offence committed during the period of conditional discharge is not the court which imposed the conditional discharge, the sentencing court may, with the consent of the original court, deal with the breach.[31]

Section 13(6), Powers of Criminal Courts (Sentencing) Act 2000

The power to deal with the offender is set out in section 13(6), Powers of Criminal Courts (Sentencing) Act 2000 which provides that where it is proved to the satisfaction of the court able to deal with the conditional discharge that the person in whose case the order was made has been convicted of an offence committed during the period of conditional discharge, the court may deal with him, for the offence for which the order was made, in any way in which it could deal with him if he had just been convicted by or before that court of that offence.

Accordingly for the purpose of determining what sentences are available to the sentencing court, the relevant age of the offender is the age at which he appears to be sentenced and not the age at which the original conditional discharge was imposed.

Where an offender was aged under 18 when a conditional discharge was imposed by a magistrates court (including a youth court) in respect of an offence triable only on indictment in the case of an adult and the offender falls to be dealt with by a court having attained 18 years of age, the sentencing court may do either or both of the following:

- Impose a fine not exceeding £5000 for the offence in respect of which the order was made

- Deal with the offender for that offence in any way in which a magistrates' court could deal with him if it had just convicted him of an offence punishable with imprisonment for a term not exceeding 6 months.[32]

The Effect of a Discharge

Section 13(6)

Where a court imposes either an absolute or conditional discharge the conviction shall be deemed not to be a conviction for any purpose other than the purpose of the proceedings in which the order was made.[33] If the offender, however, offends during the period of a conditional discharge and is dealt with under section 13(6), Powers of Criminal Courts Act (Sentencing) 2000 this restriction on the purpose of the conviction ceases to

---

31. Section 13(8), Powers of Criminal Courts (Sentencing) Act 2000.
32. Section 13(9), Powers of Criminal Courts (Sentencing) Act 2000.
33. Section 14(1), Powers of Criminal Courts (Sentencing) Act 2000.

Section 151,
Powers of Criminal
Courts (Sentencing)
Act 2000
Section 14(1)

have effect.[34] In any event, the restriction does not prevent the court from making such other orders as are available upon conviction such as costs and disqualification.[35] By virtue of section 151, Powers of Criminal Courts (Sentencing) Act 2000 orders of absolute discharge or conditional discharge may be taken into account in sentencing as if they were both convictions and sentences notwithstanding section 14(1).

Fines

The adult magistrates' court and youth court may fine a child or young person. Before fixing the amount of any fine a court shall inquire into the financial circumstances of the child or young person[36] and where the order is to be made against the offender's parent or guardian, their financial circumstances.[37] In fixing the amount of any fine, the court shall take into account the circumstances of the case including the financial circumstances of the offender or his parent or guardian so far as they are known, or appear, to the court.[38]

Section 126,
Powers of Criminal
Courts (Sentencing)
Act 2000

In order to ascertain the offender's or his parent or guardian's financial circumstances the court may make a financial circumstances order under section 126, Powers of Criminal Courts (Sentencing) Act 2000.[39] Where a parent or guardian fails to comply with a financial circumstances order or otherwise fails to co-operate with the court's inquiry and the court considers that it has insufficient information to make a proper determination of the parent or guardian's financial circumstances, it may make such determination as it thinks fit.[40]

The amount of any fine shall be such as, in the opinion of the court reflects the seriousness of the offence.[41]

The Amount of Fine

The magistrates' court and the youth court's power to impose fines is limited by statute. The majority of offences are punishable by way of maximum fines set out in terms of levels on a standard scale. In the case of an adult this allows maximum

34.   Section 14(2), Powers of Criminal Courts (Sentencing) Act 2000.
35.   Section 14(3), Powers of Criminal Courts (Sentencing) Act 2000.
36.   Section 128(1), Powers of Criminal Courts (Sentencing) Act 2000.
37.   Section 138(1), Powers of Criminal Courts (Sentencing) Act 2000.
38.   Section 128(3), Powers of Criminal Courts (Sentencing) Act 2000.
39.   Section 136(1), Powers of Criminal Courts (Sentencing) Act 2000.
40.   Section 138(3), Powers of Criminal Courts (Sentencing) Act 2000.
41.   Section 128(2), Powers of Criminal Courts (Sentencing) Act 2000.

fines to be imposed at one of five levels between £200 for a level one offence and £5,000 for a level 5 offence.

The maximum fine which may be imposed on a child or young person depends upon their age.

In the case of a child aged 10 to 13 years the maximum fine is £250. In the case of a young person aged 14 to 17 years the maximum fine is £1,000.[42]

The same maxima apply where the court requires the offender's parent or guardian to pay.

Power to Order Parent or Guardian to Pay

The court has power to order that a parent or guardian pay any order of fine, compensation or costs made on conviction of a child or young person. The power arises in relation to orders made on conviction of any offence[43] or on breach of other community based penalties.[44]

Where the child or young person is under 16 years of age, the power is a duty unless the court is satisfied that the parent or guardian cannot be found or that it would be unreasonable to make an order for payment having regard to the circumstances of the case.[45]

Where the child is aged 16 years or over the duty converts to a power.[46]

No order may be made against a parent or guardian without giving them the opportunity to attend court[47] but where they fail to do so, the court may proceed to deal with the order in their absence.[48]

In the case of an order made by the magistrates' or youth court there is power to appeal to the Crown Court against the order requiring a parent or guardian to pay any fine etc.. In the case of such an order made in the Crown Court on indictment there is power to appeal to the Court of Appeal.[49]

---

42.   Section 135, Powers of Criminal Courts (Sentencing) Act 2000.
43.   Section 137(1), Powers of Criminal Courts (Sentencing) Act 2000.
44.   Section 137(2), Powers of Criminal Courts (Sentencing) Act 2000.
45.   Section 137(1), Powers of Criminal Courts (Sentencing) Act 2000.
46.   Section 137(3), Powers of Criminal Courts (Sentencing) Act 2000.
47.   Section 137(4), Powers of Criminal Courts (Sentencing) Act 2000.
48.   Section 137(5), Powers of Criminal Courts (Sentencing) Act 2000.
49.   Section 137(6) and (7), Powers of Criminal Courts (Sentencing) Act 2000.

Where a child or young person is in the care of a local authority or is provided with accommodation by a local authority in the exercise of statutory functions and that local authority has parental responsibility for the child or young person, references to parent and guardian are to be construed as references to that authority.[50]

Generally, it is an accepted principle that the powers of the local authority to control the conduct of those children and young persons for whom it has parental responsibility are likely to be limited. Where the local authority is found to have done everything it reasonably and properly could do to prevent the offender from offending, it would be unreasonable to impose the burden of payment on the local authority.[51]

Enforcement of Fines etc

In the case of a child or young person responsible to make payments to the court, enforcement takes place in the youth court[52] until he attains the age of 18 years when proceedings are dealt with in the adult court. As far as parents and guardians are concerned, enforcement takes place in the adult court.[53]

As far as enforcement in the youth court is concerned against a child or young person in default the court has powers additional to those available in the case of an adult. These powers are:

• To make an attendance centre order;

• To make an order requiring the defaulter's parent or guardian to enter into a recognizance to ensure that the defaulter pays;

• To make an order directing the parent or guardian to pay the reminder of the sum instead of the defaulter.[54]

Compensation

The adult and youth court have power to make a compensation order against a child or young person on conviction either

---

50.   Section 137(8), Powers of Criminal Courts (Sentencing) Act 2000.
51.   D v DPP [1995] 3 FCR 725.
52.   Where there is no power to impose a term of detention in default of payment. R v Basid [1996] 1 Cr App Rep (S) 421. It may be argued that once enforcement transfers to the adult court, Article 7 of the European Convention of Human Rights – which prohibits exposure to penalties more severe than available at the time of the commission of an offence – might act to prevent the adult court imposing detention in default.
53.   The powers of the court to enforce fines, including the powers of remission are dealt with elsewhere in this text at page XX.
54.   Section 81, Magistrates' Courts Act 1980.

instead of or in addition to any other sentence.[55] Where the court does not make an order for compensation it must give reasons for its failure to do so.

Compensation is available in respect of:

- Personal injury, loss or damage resulting from the offence or any other offence which is taken into consideration by the court in determining sentence; or

- To make payments for funeral expenses or bereavement in respect of a death resulting from any such offence, other than death due to an accident arising out of the presence of a motor vehicle on the road.[56]

The maximum amount of compensation to be paid in respect of any offence of which the court has convicted the offender shall not exceed £5,000.[57]

The total compensation made by a magistrates' court including a youth court in respect of any offence taken into consideration shall not exceed the difference (if any) between the amount or total amount which is the maximum for the offence or offences of which the offender has been convicted and the amount or total amounts which are in fact ordered to be paid in respect of that offence or those offences.[58]

In determining whether to make a compensation order against an offender and in determining the amount to be paid, the court shall have regard to his means so far as they appear or are known to the court.[59]

Where the court considers that it would be appropriate both to impose a fine and to make a compensation order but the offender has insufficient means to pay both, the court shall give preference to compensation (though it may impose a fine as well).[60]

The court has the same powers and duties in respect of making a parent or guardian responsible for paying the compensation as it does in relation to fines.[61]

---

55. Section 130(1), Powers of Criminal Courts (Sentencing) Act 2000.
56. Such loss being dealt with by a state approved scheme with the Motor Insurers Bureau.
57. Section 131(1), Powers of Criminal Courts (Sentencing) Act 2000.
58. Section 131(2), Powers of Criminal Courts (Sentencing) Act 2000.
59. Section 130(11), Powers of Criminal Courts (Sentencing) Act 2000.
60. Section 130(12), Powers of Criminal Courts (Sentencing) Act 2000.
61. See above at page XX.

A local authority with parental responsibility for a child or young person in whose care or accommodation the child or young person was placed at the time of the offence may be ordered to pay any order for compensation.[62] Where a child has been remanded to accommodation provided by the local authority under section 23 of the Children and Young Persons Act 1969 so that the local authority has assumed a responsibility for the child or young person but has not acquired parental responsibility for him, the court may not order that local authority to pay.[63] In such circumstances it may also be unreasonable to make an order against a parent or guardian.[64]

Section 23 Children and Young Persons Act 1969

Procedure for Making the Local Authority Responsible for Compensation

In *Bedfordshire County Council* v *DPP*[65] the following procedure was set down in relation to the exercise of the court's powers to fix the local authority with responsibility for paying compensation ordered against a child or young person for whom it has parental responsibility:

- When considering making a compensation order against a local authority, normally a court should find some causative link between any fault proved and the offences committed;

- The role of the prosecution is strictly neutral, confining itself to:

  - Presenting the facts to the court on the extent of the loss;

  - Presenting evidence to support the value of that loss;

  - Elucidating for the assistance of the court any matters affecting the reasonableness of making a compensation order;

- If the court is considering making an order against the local authority, it must notify the local authority in writing confirming the right of the local authority:

  - To make representations;

  - To produce evidence;

  - To be legally represented;

---

62.   Section 137(8), Powers of Criminal Courts (Sentencing) Act 2000.
63.   *North Yorkshire County Council* v *Selby Youth Court Justices* [1994] 1 All ER 991.
64.   *TA* v *DPP* (1996) 160 JP 736.
65.   (1996) 160 JP 248.

This notice should include a copy of any documents supplied to the court by the prosecution in support of the application for compensation;

- The local authority should notify the court in writing whether there is likely to be a dispute about the amount of the compensation or whether an order should be made;

- If there is a dispute, a hearing must be arranged with reasonable notice to the local authority;

- In advance of the hearing the local authority should supply the court and the prosecution with copies of any documents relied on to support their case;

- The hearing should be kept as simple as possible;

- Where, in exceptional circumstances, the guidelines are not appropriate, the court must act fairly and reasonably.

Enforcement of Compensation

The enforcement of compensation orders including the powers available to the court to re-visit the order in certain circumstances are dealt with elsewhere in this guide.

Costs

Where any person is convicted of an offence before a magistrates' court including a youth court, the court may make such order as to costs[66] to be paid by the accused to the prosecutor, as it considers just and reasonable.[67] The power to award costs arises in respect of any conviction and such an order may be additional to any other sentence. An order for costs cannot, unlike compensation be a penalty in its own right.

The court has power to require payments to be made by a parent or guardian including a local authority with parental responsibility in the same way as it does for other financial penalties.[68]

Where the offender is under the age of 18 years, the amount of costs shall not exceed the amount of any fine imposed on him.[69]

---

66. See also the section on costs elsewhere in this text at page XX.
67. Section 18, Prosecution of Offences Act 1985.
68. Section 137, Powers of Criminal Courts (Sentencing) Act 2000.
69. Section 18(5), Prosecution of Offences Act 1985.

Reparation Orders

A reparation order is a sentence only available in the youth court. In terms of its status a reparation order is equivalent to a fine or discharge in that the court does not have to be satisfied that the offence to which it is to relate is either serious enough for a community penalty or so serious that only a custodial sentence can be justified.

A reparation order may require the offender to make reparation to a person or persons specified in the order and identified by the court as a victim of the offence or a person otherwise affected by it, or to the community at large[70] under the supervision of a responsible officer.[71]

Reparation is a key component of restorative justice and includes making reparation otherwise than by the payment of compensation.[72]

A reparation order may not be combined with custodial sentence or with a community punishment order, a community rehabilitation and punishment order, a supervision order, an action plan order or a referral order.[73]

Before making a reparation order the court must obtain a report[74] in writing from the youth offending team indicating the type of work suitable for the offender and the attitude of the victim to the requirements proposed to be included in the order.[75] If the reparation order is to include direct reparation to the victim of an offence, that person must consent to the order.[76] Victim reparation is considered to be more effective in confronting a child or young person with the consequences of his crime but such interaction between offender and victim requires careful thought.

The court is required to explain the effect of the order in ordinary language to the offender and tell him of the

---

70. Section 73, Powers of Criminal Courts (Sentencing) Act 2000.
71. A probation officer, a social worker or a member of the youth offending team: section 74(5), Powers of Criminal Courts (Sentencing) Act 2000.
72. Section 73(3), Powers of Criminal Courts (Sentencing) Act 2000.
73. Section 73(4), Powers of Criminal Courts (Sentencing) Act 2000.
74. Such a report may be a pre-sentence report compiled to national standards although a Specific Sentence Report would more usually encompass those features which must be included. Completion of such a report on the day may be impractical especially where the court is considering direct reparation.
75. Section 73(5), Powers of Criminal Courts (Sentencing) Act 2000.
76. Section 74(1)(b), Powers of Criminal Courts (Sentencing) Act 2000.

consequences of failing to comply with the order and the power to seek a review of the order.[77]

The court is also required to state its reasons for not making a reparation order where it has power to do so.[78]

A reparation order shall not require the offender to work for more than 24 hours[79] and must be completed within 3 months of the date on which the order was made.[80]

Although the order is available in relation to any offence, the requirements specified in the order shall be such as in the opinion of the court are commensurate with the seriousness of the offence, or the combination of the offence and one or more offences associated with it.[81] Any requirements in the reparation order shall, as far as practicable, be such as to avoid conflict with the offender's religious beliefs or with the requirements of any community order to which he may be subject and any interference with the times at which he normally works or attends school.[82]

Breach, Revocation and Amendment of Reparation Orders

Schedule 8,
Powers of Criminal
Courts (Sentencing)
Act 2000

Schedule 8, Powers of Criminal Courts (Sentencing) Act 2000 deals with the rules relating to the breach, revocation and amendment of reparation orders. This schedule also deals with similar arrangements for action plan orders. For convenience the powers relating to reparation orders are dealt with after the section of action plan orders.

Community Sentences

A community sentence means a sentence which consists of or includes one or more community orders.[83] A community order means one of the following orders:[84]

•   An action plan order

•   A curfew order

•   A rehabilitation order

77.   Section 73(7), Powers of Criminal Courts (Sentencing) Act 2000.
78.   Section 73(8), Powers of Criminal Courts (Sentencing) Act 2000.
79.   Section 74(1)(a), Powers of Criminal Courts (Sentencing) Act 2000.
80.   Section 74(8), Powers of Criminal Courts (Sentencing) Act 2000.
81.   Section 74(2), Powers of Criminal Courts (Sentencing) Act 2000.
82.   Section 74(3), Powers of Criminal Courts (Sentencing) Act 2000.
83.   Section 33(2), Powers of Criminal Courts (Sentencing) Act 2000.
84.   Section 33(1), Powers of Criminal Courts (Sentencing) Act 2000.

- A punishment order

- A rehabilitation and punishment order

- An attendance centre order

- A supervision order

- A drug treatment and testing order

A court shall not pass a community sentence on an offender unless it is of the opinion that the offence, or the combination of the offence and one or more offences associated with it, was serious enough to warrant such a sentence.[85]

Where a court passes a community sentence the particular order or orders comprising or forming part of the sentence shall be such as in the opinion of the court is, or taken together are, the most suitable for the offender and the restrictions on liberty imposed by the order or orders shall be such as in the opinion of the court are commensurate with the seriousness of the offence or the combination of the offence and one or more offences associated with it.[86]

As a rule of thumb the court should obtain a pre-sentence report before forming the opinion as to the suitability of the offender of one or more of the community orders.[87] A report may be furnished in the form of a pre-sentence report or a specific sentence report where the court has indicated the type of community penalty under consideration. Orders involving direct reparation may be difficult to complete no the day as the consent of the victim or person affected by the crime must be obtained before such a requirement can be included. Failure to obtain a report however does not invalidate any community sentence.[88]

In the case of an adult the court may forgo obtaining a pre-sentence report if in the circumstances of the case, the court is of the opinion that it is unnecessary to obtain a pre-sentence report.[89] However, in the case of an offender aged under 18 the court shall not form an opinion as to the suitability of an offender for a community order unless there exists a previous

---

85. Section 35(1), Powers of Criminal Courts (Sentencing) Act 2000.
86. Section 35(3), Powers of Criminal Courts (Sentencing) Act 2000.
87. A rehabilitation order or a supervision order without conditions may be imposed without first obtaining a pre-sentence report as such orders are specifically not mentioned in section 36(3), Powers of Criminal Courts (Sentencing) Act 2000 which otherwise requires the court to obtain reports prior to sentence.
88. Section 36(7), Powers of Criminal Courts (Sentencing) Act 2000.
89. Section 36(5), Powers of Criminal Courts (Sentencing) Act 2000.

pre-sentence report obtained in respect of the offender and the court has had regard to the information contained in that report or, if there is more than one such report, the most recent report.[90]

Where the sentencing court has passed a community sentence without reports, in the course of appeal proceedings against sentence the appeal court is required to obtain a pre-sentence report unless the court is of the opinion that it is unnecessary to do so. Again in the case of a child or young person the appeal court may not form such an opinion unless there exists a recent pre-sentence report to which it has had regard.[91]

Powers of Criminal Courts (Sentencing) Act 2000

Subject to these general statutory provisions regarding community sentences, the Powers of Criminal Courts (Sentencing) Act 2000 provides the consolidated framework for sentencing in the serious enough range.

The range of sentencing options may be further defined by an age restriction on some orders. Where the offender is aged 16 years or over the court may make a series of orders usually regarded as part of the adult sentencing regime. These orders are:

• Rehabilitation orders

• Punishment orders

• Rehabilitation and punishment orders

• Drug treatment and testing orders.

The remaining community orders may be made in respect of a child or young person at any age.

Action Plan Orders

An action plan order may be made by a court[92] in respect of any child or young person provided the offence is serious enough to merit a community sentence[93] and the court is of the opinion that the making of an action plan order is desirable in the interests of securing the rehabilitation of the offender or preventing the commission by him of further offences.[94]

---

90.   Section 36(6), Powers of Criminal Courts (Sentencing) Act 2000.
91.   Section 36(9), Powers of Criminal Courts (Sentencing) Act 2000.
92.   In this context the phrase means either the youth court or the Crown Court on indictment subject to earlier discussed restrictions relating to the sentencing of children and young persons in the Crown Court. The phrase does not include adult magistrates' courts unless the contrary is indicated.
93.   Section 35, Powers of Criminal Courts (Sentencing) Act 2000.
94.   Section 69(3), Powers of Criminal Courts (Sentencing) Act 2000.

An action plan order requires the offender for a period of three months from the date of the order, to comply with an action plan and places the offender under the supervision of a responsible officer usually from the local youth offending team. The action plan order includes a specific programme or series of requirements as to the offender's actions and whereabouts.[95]

An action plan order may not be made if the offender is already subject to such an order or if the court proposes to pass on him a custodial sentence, a rehabilitation order, a punishment order, a rehabilitation and punishment order, an attendance centre order, a supervision order or a referral order.[96]

Before making an action plan order the court shall obtain and consider a written report usually from the youth offending team. The report should indicate:[97]

- The requirements proposed to be included in the order;

- The benefits to the offender that the proposed requirements are designed to achieve;

- The attitude of the offender's parent or guardian to the proposed requirements;

- Where the offender is aged under 16, information about the offender's family circumstances and the likely effect of the order on those circumstances.

The court is also under a duty to explain in ordinary language to the offender the effect of the order, the consequences of breach and the power of the court to review the order at either the offender's or the responsible officer's application.[98]

The action plan order may contain requirements on the offender:[99]

- To participate in activities specified in the requirements or directions at a time or times so specified;

- To present himself to a person or persons specified in the requirements or directions at a place or places and at a time or times so specified;

- To attend at an attendance centre specified in the requirements or directions for a number of hours so specified.

95. Section 69(1), Powers of Criminal Courts (Sentencing) Act 2000.
96. Section 69(5), Powers of Criminal Courts (Sentencing) Act 2000.
97. Section 69(6), Powers of Criminal Courts (Sentencing) Act 2000.
98. Section 69(11), Powers of Criminal Courts (Sentencing) Act 2000.
99. Section 70(1), Powers of Criminal Courts (Sentencing) Act 2000.

(This requirement may only be inserted in to an action plan order if the offence committed by the child or young person is punishable with imprisonment.);[1]

- To stay away from a place or places specified in the requirements or directions;

- To comply with any arrangements for his education specified in the requirements or directions;

- To make reparation specified in the requirements or directions to a person or persons so specified or to the community at large;

- To attend any hearing fixed to review the order by the court.

Where one of the proposed requirements is to make personal reparation, the requirement may only be included in the order if the person to whom reparation is to be made is the victim of the offence or a person otherwise affected by it and that person has consented to direct reparation.[2]

Any requirements in an action plan order shall as far as practicable be such as to avoid any conflict with the offender's religious beliefs or with the requirements of any other community order to which he may be subject and interference with the times at which he normally works or attends school or any other educational establishment.[3]

Review of Action Plan Orders

Immediately after making an action plan order the court may fix a further hearing not more than 21 days after the making of the order for the purposes of a review of the order. The court has discretion whether to fix a review hearing and local practice across the country can vary. The court may also direct the responsible officer to make a report as to the effectiveness of the order and the extent to which it has been implemented.[4]

At the review hearing the court shall consider the report from the responsible officer and may on the application of either that officer or the offender amend the order by cancelling or inserting any provision in to the plan.[5]

---

1. Section 70(2)), Powers of Criminal Courts (Sentencing) Act 2000.
2. Section 70(4), Powers of Criminal Courts (Sentencing) Act 2000.
3. Section 70(5), Powers of Criminal Courts (Sentencing) Act 2000.
4. Section 71(1), Powers of Criminal Courts (Sentencing) Act 2000.
5. Section 71(2), Powers of Criminal Courts (Sentencing) Act 2000.

Breach, Amendment and Revocation of Reparation and Action Plan Orders

Schedule 8, Powers of Criminal Courts (Sentencing) Act 2000

Schedule 8, Powers of Criminal Courts (Sentencing) Act 2000 makes provision for dealing breach, amendment and revocation of both reparation orders and action plan orders.[6]

The power to deal with breach, amendment and revocation arises in the appropriate court. The appropriate court is the youth court acting for the petty sessions area named in the order in question.[7] The youth court retains jurisdiction to deal with breach, amendment and revocation where the offender has attained the age of 18 years.

Breach Proceedings and Powers

The appropriate court may deal with a breach of the order while an action plan order or reparation order is in force.[8] The court's powers depend on a finding that the order, or a requirement of the order has been breached. If it is proved to the satisfaction of the court, on the application of the responsible officer that the offender has failed to comply with any requirements included the order, the court has a number of options,[9] it may:

(1) Whether or not it also makes an order to revoke or amend the order:

   • Order the offender to pay a fine of an amount not exceeding £1,000;[10]

   • May make a curfew order in respect of him;

   • May make an attendance centre order in respect of him; or

(2) If the action plan or reparation order was made by a magistrates' court, may revoke the order and deal with the offender, for the offence in respect of which the order was

---

6.   Section 72, Powers of Criminal Courts (Sentencing) Act 2000.

7.   Paragraph 1, Schedule 8, Powers of Criminal Courts (Sentencing) Act 2000.

8.   The court does not appear to have power to consider whether the order has been breached after the expiry of the relevant order. Arguably, the court must deal with the offender while the order is in force. However, the court would have power to deal with an offender at any time after the order has expired so long as it was proved to the satisfaction of the court that the offender was in breach of the order, while the order was in force. In such circumstances the court would be unable to revoke, amend or continue the order in question because it no longer exists. Nevertheless the court could order the offender to be fined, undertake a curfew order or make an attendance centre order.

9.   Paragraph 2(2), Schedule 8, Powers of Criminal Courts (Sentencing) Act 2000.

10. £250 in the case of a child aged under 14.

made, in any way in which he could have been dealt with for that offence by the court which made the order if the order had not been made; or

(3) If the action plan order or reparation order was made by the Crown Court, may commit him in custody or release him on bail until he can be brought or appear before the Crown Court.

Where the offender is brought or appears before the Crown Court and it is proved to the satisfaction[11] of the court that he has failed to comply with the requirement in question that court may deal with him, for the offence in respect of which the order was made, in any way in which it could have dealt with him for that offence if it had not made that order.[12] Where the Crown Court does so, it shall also revoke the order in question.[13]

In dealing with an offender for breach of the terms of an action plan order or a reparation order, the court shall take into account the extent to which he has complied with the requirements.[14]

Where either order was originally made on appeal against sentence by the Crown Court the orders are to be treated for the purposes of these provisions as if made by the magistrates' court.[15]

Schedule 8, Powers of Criminal Courts (Sentencing) Act 2000

Schedule 8, Powers of Criminal Courts (Sentencing) Act 2000 also provides for certain amendments to the those parts of the same act which deal with curfew orders and attendance centre orders made to punish the breach of an action plan order or reparation order.[16] The amendments are mainly procedural.

---

11. Where the magistrates' court deals with an offender under the provision committing him to the Crown Court a justice of the peace certifies in a certificate the particulars of the offender's failure to comply with the requirement in question and such other particulars of the case as may be desirable. The signed certificate is admissible as evidence of the failure before the Crown Court: Paragraph 2(3), Schedule 8, Powers of Criminal Courts (Sentencing) Act 2000.
12. Paragraph 2(4), Schedule 8, Powers of Criminal Courts (Sentencing) Act 2000.
13. Paragraph 2(5), Schedule 8, Powers of Criminal Courts (Sentencing) Act 2000.
14. Paragraph 2(7), Schedule 8, Powers of Criminal Courts (Sentencing) Act 2000.
15. Paragraph 2(8), Schedule 8, Powers of Criminal Courts (Sentencing) Act 2000.
16. Paragraphs 3 and 4, Schedule 8, Powers of Criminal Courts (Sentencing) Act 2000.

Revocation and Amendment of Action Plan Orders and Reparation Orders

The appropriate court has power to revoke an action plan order or reparation order on the application of either the responsible officer or the offender during the currency of the order.[17] The court may also amend the order by cancelling or inserting any requirement in the order.

Where an application for revocation is dismissed no further application to revoke may be made by any person except with the consent of the appropriate court.[18]

Securing Attendance of the Offender in Breach Proceedings

Paragraphs 4 to 8 of Schedule 8,

Section 55, Magistrates' Courts Act 1980

In order to secure the attendance of the offender before the appropriate court the court may issue a summons or warrant.[19] Paragraphs 4 to 8 of Schedule 8, Powers of Criminal Courts (Sentencing) Act 2000 makes provision for the arrest, detention and remand of an offender arrested under a warrant issued to secure his attendance.[20] Section 55, Magistrates' Courts Act 1980 is appropriately amended to include warrants of this type. Where an offender is arrested under a warrant of this type he may be detained for up to 72 hours in a place of safety and, within that period, appear before a youth court.[21] The youth court, if it is not the appropriate court may either direct his immediate release (and impose bail upon him) or remand him to accommodation provided by the local authority.[22] In the case of an offender so arrested and over the age of 18 the court may remand him to a remand centre or prison.[23]

Section 55(5), Magistrates' Courts Act 1980

If, however the offender is brought before the appropriate court the Schedule does not empower the court to remand the offender. Where proceedings are adjourned however section 55(5), Magistrates' Courts Act 1980 permits the court to remand and further remand the defendant.

---

17. Paragraph 5(1), Schedule 8, Powers of Criminal Courts (Sentencing) Act 2000.
18. Paragraph 5(3), Schedule 8, Powers of Criminal Courts (Sentencing) Act 2000.
19. Paragraph 6(2), Schedule 8, Powers of Criminal Courts (Sentencing) Act 2000.
20. In some areas, youth courts are taking the view that a warrant to secure the attendance of an offender alleged to be in breach of an order may only be issued and remain in force while the order itself is in force unless the offender has, during that period, been found to be in breach of the order. As a result, it would seem at least arguable that the arrest and detention of an offender where the breach has not been proved to the satisfaction of the court, after the order has expired would be unlawful.
21. Paragraph 5(4), Schedule 8, Powers of Criminal Courts (Sentencing) Act 2000.
22. Paragraph 5(5), Schedule 8, Powers of Criminal Courts (Sentencing) Act 2000.
23. Paragraph 5(7), Schedule 8, Powers of Criminal Courts (Sentencing) Act 2000.

The court's powers to make an order on finding that the order has been breached or to revoke or amend an order may only be exercised in the presence of the offender.[24]

The court may however make an order for revocation or amendment in the absence of the offender provided that the effect of the order is confined to:[25]

- Revoking the action plan order or reparation order;

- Cancelling a requirement included in the action plan order or reparation order;

- Altering in the action plan order or reparation order the name of any (petty sessions) area;

- Changing the responsible officer.

An offender may appeal to the Crown Court against any order arising out of breach proceedings or amendment and revocation except where the order made could have been made in his absence. The offender may also appeal to the Crown Court against the dismissal of an application to revoke an action plan order or reparation order made on either his or the responsible officer's application.[26]

Supervision Orders

Where a child or young person is convicted by a court of an offence, the court (either the youth court or the Crown Court after conviction on indictment) may make an order placing him under the supervision of a local authority designated by the order, a probation officer or a member of the youth offending team.[27] This type of sentence is a supervision order and is only available where the court is satisfied that the offending is serious enough to merit a community sentence[28] and that the order is suitable for the offender and commensurate with the seriousness of the offending.[29]

The supervision order shall name the local authority and the petty sessions area in which it appears to the court that the offender resides or will reside and may contain such prescribed

---

24. Paragraph 6(1), Schedule 8, Powers of Criminal Courts (Sentencing) Act 2000.
25. Paragraph 6(9), Schedule 8, Powers of Criminal Courts (Sentencing) Act 2000.
26. Paragraph 7, Schedule 8, Powers of Criminal Courts (Sentencing) Act 2000.
27. Section 63(1), Powers of Criminal Courts (Sentencing) Act 2000.
28. Section 35(1), Powers of Criminal Courts (Sentencing) Act 2000.
29. Section 35(3), Powers of Criminal Courts (Sentencing) Act 2000.

provisions as the court considers appropriate.[30] Specific requirements which may be included in a supervision order are set out in Schedule 6, Powers of Criminal Courts (Sentencing) Act 2000.[31]

Schedule 6, Powers of Criminal Courts (Sentencing) Act 2000

The maximum period of a supervision order is three years or such shorter period as may be specified in the order. The order begins on the day it is made.[32]

Where a supervision order has been made the court is under a duty to send a copy of the order forthwith to the offender and if he is aged under 14 years, to his parent or guardian. The order must also be copied to the supervisor, the relevant local authority, any person in charge of a place where the offender has been directed to reside and where the court making the order is not the court where the offender resides or will reside, to the justices' chief executive for that supervising court.[33]

A supervision order shall not designate a local authority as the supervisor of an order unless the local authority agrees or it appears to the court that the offender resides or will reside in the area of that authority.[34]

Schedule 7

Schedule 7, Powers of Criminal Courts (Sentencing) Act 2000 provides for the court's powers top deal with breach, revocation and amendment of supervision orders.

Requirements of a Supervision Order

It is the duty of the supervisor to advise, assist and befriend the offender and the order may include such provisions[35] as the court considers appropriate for facilitating the performance by the supervisor of his functions including provisions for the offender to receive visits at home from his supervisor.[36]

Schedule 6

Schedule 6, Powers of Criminal Courts (Sentencing) Act 2000 details the requirements which may be included in a supervision order. The insertion of requirements into supervision orders allows the court to tailor make a community sentence suitable to the criminal justice needs of the offender.

---

30. Section 63(6), Powers of Criminal Courts (Sentencing) Act 2000.
31. Section 63(4), Powers of Criminal Courts (Sentencing) Act 2000.
32. Section 63(7), Powers of Criminal Courts (Sentencing) Act 2000.
33. Section 63(8), Powers of Criminal Courts (Sentencing) Act 2000.
34. Section 64, Powers of Criminal Courts (Sentencing) Act 2000.
35. The range of provisions which may be included under this general power are set out in the Magistrates' Courts (Children and Young Persons) Rules 1992.
36. Sections 64(4) and 63(3)(b), Powers of Criminal Courts (Sentencing) Act 2000.

The basic contents of the requirements which may be inserted are described in the Schedule so as to include:

- Requirements to reside with a named individual;

- Requirements to comply with directions of supervisor;

- Requirements as to activities, reparation, night restrictions etc;

- Requirement to live for specified period in local authority accommodation;

- Requirements as to treatment for mental condition;

- Requirements as to education.

Requirements to reside with a named individual

So long as the person with whom it is proposed that the offender is to reside agrees, a requirement may be imposed requiring the offender to reside with a named individual. The requirement is however subject to other requirements which may be imposed under other parts of the schedule.[37]

Requirements to comply with directions of supervisor

Requirements imposed under this part of the schedule are often referred to as intermediate treatment at the direction of the supervisor to distinguish it from the intermediate treatment required specifically by the court. A supervision order may require the offender to comply with any directions given from time to time by the supervisor and requiring him to do all or any of the following things:

- To live at a place or places specified in the directions for a period or periods so specified;

- To present himself to a person or persons specified in the directions at a place or places and on a day or days so specified.

---

37. Paragraph 1, Schedule 6, Powers of Criminal Courts (Sentencing) Act 2000.

Section 66, Powers
of Criminal Courts
(Sentencing)
Act 2000

Such a requirement may only be inserted into a supervision order if there exist appropriate facilities for enabling the directions to be carried out effectively in accordance with section 66, Powers of Criminal Courts (Sentencing) Act 2000.

It is a matter for the supervisor to decide whether and to what extent he exercises the powers to make directions under this part of the Schedule. However the total number of days on which an offender may be required to comply with the directions must be specified in the order and may be for a maximum of 90 days. Days on which the directions do not take place having been planned to take place may be disregarded in calculating the period.

Any requirements shall as far as practicable be such as to avoid any conflict with the offender's religious beliefs or with the requirements of any other community order to which he may be subject and interference with the times at which he normally works or attends school or any other educational establishment.[38]

Requirements as to activities, reparation, night restrictions etc

Requirements under this part of the schedule are usually referred to as intermediate treatment at the direction of the court. The supervisor does not have any general powers to determine what requirements should be undertaken by the offender. The requirements are inserted by the court. Where a supervision order does not contain requirements to comply with the directions of a supervisor, the following requirements may be included to require the offender:

• To live at a place or places specified in the order for a period or periods so specified;

• To present himself to a person or persons specified in the order at a place or places and on a day or days so specified;

• To participate in activities specified in the order on a day or days so specified;

• To make reparation specified in the order to a person or persons so specified or to the community at large;

---

38.   Paragraph 2, Schedule 6, Powers of Criminal Courts (Sentencing) Act 2000.

- To remain for specified periods between 6 p.m. and 6 a.m.:

  - At a place specified in the order; or

  - At one of several places so specified;

- To refrain from participating in activities specified in the order:

  - On a specified day or days during the period for which the supervision is in force; or

  - During the whole of that period or a specified portion of it.

The total number of days in respect of which an offender may be subject to all but the last of such requirements shall not exceed 90 days.

The court may not include requirements of this kind unless:

- it has first consulted the supervisor as to the offender's circumstances and the feasibility of securing compliance with the requirements and is satisfied, having regard to the supervisor's report, that it is feasible to secure compliance with them;

- having regard to the circumstances of the case, it considers the requirements necessary for securing the good conduct of the offender or for preventing a repetition by him of the same offence or the commission of other offences; and

- if the offender is aged under 16, it has obtained and considered information about his family circumstances and the likely effect of the requirements on those circumstances.

Where a requirement involves the co-operation of a third party, the court may only impose the direction if that person has agreed to its inclusion. Any requirement involving direct reparation may only be included if the victim or person affected by the offence has agreed to such reparation. The court may not use its powers under this part of the Schedule to require the offender to reside with a specified individual or to make provision for the treatment of an offender's mental condition.

As with all such requirements and community orders generally, any requirements shall as far as practicable be such as to avoid any conflict with the offender's religious beliefs or with the requirements of any other community order to which he may be subject and interference with the times at which he normally works or attends school or any other educational establishment.

It is not possible to include any requirement that would involve the offender in absence from home for more than two consecutive nights or for more than two consecutive nights in any one week or any requirement where the offender is of compulsory school age, to participate in activities during normal school hours unless the court making the order is satisfied that the facilities for use would accord with those established under section 66, Powers of Criminal Courts (Sentencing) Act 2000. This last restriction does not apply where the proposed activity is made or approved by the local education authority.

Section 66,
Powers of Criminal
Courts (Sentencing)
Act 2000

The requirement to remain in a specified place during a night restriction shall be observed at the place where the offender lives. Where the night restriction relates to a number of different places, on of them must be where the offender lives. The following rules also apply to night restrictions:

- it may not require the offender to remain at a place for longer than ten hours on any one night;

- it shall not be imposed in respect of any day which falls outside the period of three months beginning with the date when the supervision order is made;

- it may not be imposed in respect of more than 30 days;

- a night restriction imposed in respect of a period of time beginning in the evening and ending in the morning shall be treated as imposed only in respect of the day upon which the period begins;

- an offender who is required by a night restriction to remain at a place may leave it if he is accompanied by his parent or guardian, his supervisor or by some other person specified in the supervision order.[39]

---

39.   Paragraphs 3 and 4, Schedule 1, Powers of Criminal Courts (Sentencing) Act 2000.

Requirement to live for specified period in local authority accommodation

Provided that certain criteria are met, the court may impose a requirement in a supervision order requiring the offender to live for a specified period in local authority accommodation.

The criteria are that:

- a supervision order has previously been made in respect of the offender;

- that order imposed a requirement under paragraph 1, 2, 3 or 7 of the schedule;[40] or a local authority residence requirement;

- the offender fails to comply with that requirement, or is convicted of an offence committed while that order was in force; and

- the court is satisfied that:

  - the failure to comply with the requirement, or the behaviour which constituted the offence, was due to a significant extent to the circumstances in which the offender was living; and

  - save that this condition does not apply where the previous supervision order contained a local authority residence requirement, the imposition of a local authority residence requirement will assist in his rehabilitation.

The supervision order must designate the local authority who are to receive the offender but such an order cannot be made without first consulting with the local authority.[41]

The maximum period of local authority residence which may be stipulated is 6 months and no order may be made under this part of the Schedule upon an offender who is not legally represented unless, having been informed of his right to apply, he has failed to apply for representation or has been granted it but it has been withdrawn because of his conduct.

A requirement to reside in local authority accommodation may specify that the offender is not to be placed with a named individual; otherwise the placement is for the local authority to

---

40. That is to say, requirements to reside with a named individual, requirements to comply with directions of supervisor, requirements as to activities, reparation, night restrictions etc, requirements as to education.
41. But there is no requirement that the local authority consent to the placement.

determine according to its resources. Where such an order is made, the court may also attach such requirements as are mentioned ion paragraphs 2, 3, 6 and 7 of the Schedule.[42]

Requirements as to treatment for mental condition

Section 12, Mental Health Act 1983

Where the court is satisfied on the evidence[43] of a registered medical practitioner approved for the purposes of section 12, Mental Health Act 1983 that the mental condition of the offender is such as requires and may be susceptible to treatment but is not such as to warrant the making of a hospital order or guardianship order within the meaning of that Act, the court may insert a requirement as to treatment for that condition into a supervision order.

The court may include a requirement that the offender shall, for a period specified in the order submit to treatment of one of the following descriptions:

Mental Health Act 1983

- treatment as a resident patient in a hospital or mental nursing home within the meaning of the Mental Health Act 1983, but not a hospital at which high security psychiatric services within the meaning of that Act are provided;

- treatment as a non-residential patient at an institution or place specified in the order;

- treatment by or under the direction of a registered medical practitioner specified in the order;

- treatment by or under the direction of a chartered psychologist specified in the order.

Such a requirement may not be included in a supervision order unless the court is satisfied that arrangements have been or can be made for the treatment in question and, in the case of treatment as a resident patient, for the reception of the patient.

Where the offender is aged 14 or over, his consent to such a requirement is required.

The requirement may not continue in force after the offender attains the age of 18 years and is also subject to the length of the supervision order in which the requirements are attached.[44]

---

42. Paragraph 5, Schedule 6, Powers of Criminal Courts (Sentencing) Act 2000.
43. Section 54(2) and (3), Mental Health Act 1983 have effect with respect to proof of an offender's mental condition.
44. Paragraph 6, Schedule 6, Powers of Criminal Courts (Sentencing) Act 2000.

Requirements as to education

The court has power to make a supervision order with requirements as to the provision of education for the offender provided that the order does not contain a requirement requiring the offender to comply with directions of the supervisor under paragraph 2.

A supervision order may require the offender, if he is of compulsory school age, to comply, for as long as he is of that age and the order remains in force, with such arrangements for his education as may from time to time be made by his parent being arrangements for the time being approved by the local education authority.

The court shall not include such a requirement unless it has consulted the local education authority with regard to its proposals to include the requirement and is satisfied that in the view of the local education authority arrangements exist for the offender to receive efficient full-time education suitable to his age, ability and aptitude and to any special educational need he may have.

Additionally, the court may not include such a requirement unless it has first consulted the supervisor as to the offender's circumstances and having regard to the circumstances of the case, it considers the requirement necessary for securing the good conduct of the offender or for preventing a repetition by him of the same offence or the commission of other offences.[45]

Breach, Revocation and Amendment of Supervision Orders

Schedule 7, Powers of Criminal Courts (Sentencing) Act 2000

Schedule 7, Powers of Criminal Courts (Sentencing) Act 2000 provides for the court's powers to deal with breach, amendment and revocation of supervision orders.

The court with power to deal with breach, amendment, or revocation of a supervision order, including the requirements of such an order is termed the relevant court.[46]

The relevant court where the offender is under the age of 18 years is a youth court acting for the petty sessions area for the time being named in the order.

45. Paragraph 7, Schedule 6, Powers of Criminal Courts (Sentencing) Act.
46. Paragraph 1, Schedule 7, Powers of Criminal Courts (Sentencing) Act 2000.

The relevant court where the offender has attained the age of 18 years is a magistrates' court other than a youth court, being a magistrates' court acting for the petty sessions area for the time being so named.

Where the offender attains the age of 18 while the application is pending, the relevant court is the youth court.

Breach Proceedings

Paragraphs 1, 2, 3, 5 or 7 of Schedule 6, Powers of Criminal Courts (Sentencing) Act 2000

The relevant court is empowered to deal with breaches of supervision orders if it is proved to the satisfaction of the court that the offender has failed to comply with any requirement included in the supervision order in pursuance of paragraphs 1, 2, 3, 5 or 7 of Schedule 6, Powers of Criminal Courts (Sentencing) Act 2000 or section 63(6)(b), Powers of Criminal Courts (Sentencing) Act 2000 which provides for meetings and visits between the offender and the supervisor.

The court's powers are as follows:

Paragraph 5(1)

- whether or not it makes an order under paragraph 5(1), Powers of Criminal Courts (Sentencing) 2000 (revocation or amendment):

  - may order the offender to pay a fine of an amount not exceeding £1000 (£250 in the case of a child aged under 14);

  - may make a curfew order in respect of the offender; or

  - may make an attendance centre order in respect of him;

- if the supervision order was made by a magistrates' court, may revoke the supervision order and deal with the offender, for the offence in respect of which the order was made, in any way in which he could have been dealt with for that offence by the court which made the order if the order had not been made;[47] or

- if the supervision order was made by the Crown Court after conviction on indictment,[48] may commit him in custody or release him on bail until he can be brought or appear before the Crown Court.

---

47. Accordingly, an offender who has attained 18 years of age and who appears in the adult court may be sentenced against the youth court regime and is not subject to adult powers of punishment.

48. A supervision order made in the Crown Court on appeal against sentence from a magistrates' court is deemed to be an order of the magistrates' court; Paragraph 2(8), Schedule 7, Powers of Criminal Courts (Sentencing) Act 2000.

The Crown Court has power to deal with the offender for the offence in respect of which the supervision order was made in any way in which it could have dealt with him for that offence if it had not made the order.[49] If the supervision order is in force the Crown Court may revoke it.[50] In any event the Crown Court may only exercise its powers to re-sentence where the failure of the offender to comply with the requirements has been proved to its satisfaction. On committal a certificate signed by a justice of the peace giving particulars of the offender's failure and such other particulars of the case as may be desirable is admissible as evidence of his failure before the Crown Court.[51]

In dealing with an offender a court shall take into account the extent to which he has complied with the requirements of the supervision order.[52]

Where the relevant court makes a curfew order or an attendance centre order, the relevant legislation governing each order is amended to take into account the origins of the orders.[53]

Revocation and Amendment of Supervision Orders

While a supervision order is in force either the supervisor or the offender may apply to the court for revocation or amendment of the order.[54]

On such an application, the court may:

- revoke the supervision order;

- make an order amending it:

  - Schedule 6 or section 63(6)(b), Powers of Criminal Courts (Sentencing) Act 2000

  - by cancelling any requirement included in it by virtue of Schedule 6 or section 63(6)(b), Powers of Criminal Courts (Sentencing) Act 2000;

  - by inserting in it (either in addition to or in substitution for any of its provisions) any provision which could have been included in the order if the court had then had power to make it and were exercising the power.

The power of amendment does not include power to insert in the supervision order a requirement to comply with treatment

---

49. Paragraph 2(4), Schedule 7, Powers of Criminal Courts (Sentencing) Act 2000.
50. Paragraph 2(5), Schedule 7, Powers of Criminal Courts (Sentencing) Act 2000.
51. Paragraph 2(3), Schedule 7, Powers of Criminal Courts (Sentencing) Act 2000.
52. Paragraph 2(7), Schedule 7, Powers of Criminal Courts (Sentencing) Act 2000.
53. Paragraphs 3 and 4, Schedule 7, Powers of Criminal Courts (Sentencing) Act 2000.
54. Paragraph 5, Schedule 7, Powers of Criminal Courts (Sentencing) Act 2000.

for a mental condition after the end of three months beginning with the date when the order was originally made unless it is in substitution for such a requirement already included in the order. The power to amend does not include the power to insert in the supervision order a night restriction in respect of days which fall outside the period of three months beginning with the date on which the order was originally made.[55]

If the court dismisses an application to revoke the supervision order, no further application may be made by any person within three months of the date of dismissal without the consent of the court having jurisdiction to entertain such an application.[56]

A youth court shall not:

• make an order revoking a supervision order, inserting a requirement or varying or cancelling such a requirement except in a case where it is satisfied that the offender either is unlikely to receive the care or control[57] he needs unless the court makes the order or is likely to receive it notwithstanding the order;

• exercise its powers to make an order cancelling or varying a condition of treatment for mental condition except where this caveat applies;

• exercise its powers to make an order inserting a requirement to comply with treatment for a mental condition unless the court is satisfied that the criteria for making such an order originally now exist based on such evidence as is prescribed in paragraph 6 of Schedule 6, Powers of Criminal Courts (Sentencing) Act 2000.

Paragraph 6 of Schedule 6, Powers of Criminal Courts (Sentencing) Act 2000

Where the court is considering exercising its powers to insert a condition requiring the offender to comply with treatment for his mental condition and the offender is aged 14 years or over, the court must first obtain his consent. His consent is also required if the court proposes to alter such a requirement other than by removing it or reducing its duration.[58]

The offender may appeal to the Crown Court against an order made on breach, revocation or amendment (or refusal to do either) or in relation to the amendment of a requirement

---

55. Paragraph 5(3), Schedule 7, Powers of Criminal Courts (Sentencing) Act 2000.
56. Paragraph 5(4), Schedule 7, Powers of Criminal Courts (Sentencing) Act 2000.
57. Care includes protection and guidance and control includes discipline; Paragraph 8(2), Schedule 7, Powers of Criminal Courts (Sentencing) Act 2000.
58. Paragraph 8(9), Schedule 7, Powers of Criminal Courts (Sentencing) Act 2000.

requiring compliance with treatment for mental condition unless the order made was one which could have been made in his absence under paragraph 7(9) of Schedule 7, Powers of Criminal Courts (Sentencing) Act 2000.[59]

Paragraph 7(9) of
Schedule 7

The power to seek revocation or amendment is also exercisable on behalf of the offender by his parent or guardian at the time the order was originally made.[60]

Securing Attendance of the Offender in Breach Proceedings

The provisions relating to securing the attendance of an offender before the court under schedule 7 are similar to the powers available to the court in the case of an action plan order or reparation order. However there are certain differences.

In order to secure the attendance of the offender before the relevant court the court may issue a summons or warrant Paragraph 7 of Schedule 7, Powers of Criminal Courts (Sentencing) Act 2000 makes provision for the arrest, detention and remand of an offender arrested under a warrant issued to secure his attendance. Section 55, Magistrates' Courts Act 1980 is appropriately amended to include warrants of this type. Where an offender is arrested under a warrant of this type he may be detained for up to 72 hours in a place of safety and, within that period, appear before either the relevant court or a justice of the peace.[61] The offender's case may then be adjourned to the relevant court. The justice of the peace may either direct his immediate release (and impose bail upon him) or remand him to accommodation provided by the local authority.[62] In the case of an offender so arrested and over the age of 18 the justice of the peace may remand him to a remand centre or prison.[63]

Paragraph 7 of
Schedule 7

Section 55,
Magistrates'
Courts Act 1980

If, however the offender is brought before the relevant court the Schedule permits the court to remand or further remand the offender to enable information to be obtained which is likely to assist the court in deciding whether and if so, how to exercise its powers on breach.[64]

59. Paragraph 11, Schedule 7, Powers of Criminal Courts (Sentencing) Act 2000.
60. Paragraph 12, Schedule 7, Powers of Criminal Courts (Sentencing) Act 2000.
61. Paragraphs 7(3) and (4), Schedule 7, Powers of Criminal Courts (Sentencing) Act 2000.
62. Paragraph 7(5), Schedule 7, Powers of Criminal Courts (Sentencing) Act 2000.
63. Paragraph 7(7), Schedule 7, Powers of Criminal Courts (Sentencing) Act 2000.
64. Paragraph 7(6)(b), Schedule 7, Powers of Criminal Courts (Sentencing) Act 2000.

The court's powers to make an order on finding that the order has been breached or to revoke or amend an order may only be exercised in the presence of the offender.[65]

The court may however make an order for revocation or amendment in the absence of the offender provided that the effect of the order is confined to:

- Revoking the supervision order;

Schedule 6 or
Section 63(6)(b),
Powers of Criminal
Courts (Sentencing)
Act 2000

- Cancelling a provision included in the supervision order in pursuance of Schedule 6 or section 63(6)(b), Powers of Criminal Courts (Sentencing) Act 2000;

- Reducing the duration of the supervision order or any provisions included in it;

- Altering in the supervision order the name of any area;

- Changing the supervisor.[66]

Curfew Orders

Where a child or young person is convicted by a court of an offence, the court (either the youth court or the Crown Court after conviction on indictment) may make an order requiring him to him to remain for periods specified in the order, at a place also specified in the order. This order is called a curfew order. It is only available where the court is satisfied that the offending is serious enough to merit a community sentence and that the order is suitable for the offender and commensurate with the seriousness of the offending.[67]

A curfew order requires an offender to remain at a specified place for up to 6 months but the order may not require him to remain there for less than 2 hours nor more than 12 hours per day.[68] Effectively this allows a court to impose an order of curfew of up to 2,232 hours.[69]

The order may be made in respect of children and young persons but before making a curfew order in respect of an offender who on conviction is under 16, the court shall obtain and consider information about his family circumstances and the likely effect of such an order on those circumstances.[70]

65. Paragraph 7(1), Schedule 7, Powers of Criminal Courts (Sentencing) Act 2000.
66. Paragraph 7(9), Schedule 7, Powers of Criminal Courts (Sentencing) Act 2000.
67. Section 37, Powers of Criminal Courts (Sentencing) Act 2000.
68. Section 37(3), Powers of Criminal Courts (Sentencing) Act 2000.
69. That is to say, 186 days (6 months) × 12 hours per day.
70. Section 37(9), Powers of Criminal Courts (Sentencing) Act 2000.

Compliance with the order may be secured by monitoring of the curfew period either directly or electronically.[71]

Breach, amendment and revocation

Schedule 3, Powers of Criminal (Sentencing) Act 2000

Schedule 3, Powers of Criminal Courts (Sentencing) Act 2000 makes provision for the powers of the court to deal with breach, amendment and revocation of community punishment orders. The schedule also makes provision for the court's powers to deal with other community sentences. For convenience and to avoid repetition, material relating to breach, amendment and revocation of all community sentences is set out elsewhere in this work at pages XX–XX.

Attendance Centre Orders

Where a child or young person is convicted by a court of an offence, the court (either the youth court or the Crown Court after conviction on indictment) may make an order requiring him to attend an attendance centre for such hours as may be specified in the order.[72] It is only available where the court is satisfied that the offending is serious enough to merit a community sentence and that the order is suitable for the offender and commensurate with the seriousness of the offending.[73]

The order is only available where the offence of which the offender has been convicted is punishable in the case of an adult by imprisonment.[74]

The aggregate number of hours for which an attendance centre order may require a person to attend at an attendance centre shall not be less than 12 except where the offender is aged under 14 and the court is of the opinion that 12 hours would be excessive having regard to his age or any other circumstances.[75]

The aggregate number of hours shall not exceed 12 except where the court is of the opinion, having regard to all the circumstances, that 12 hours would be inadequate and in that case shall not

---

71. Section 40, Powers of Criminal Courts (Sentencing) Act 2000.
72. An attendance centre order is another order available to both the adult and youth courts. In the context of this section, the procedures described apply to children and young persons. They may or may not be the same as for adult offenders and practitioners are warned to examine the procedure in detail before applying principles detailed here for youth offenders in the case of an adult offender.
73. Section 60, Powers of Criminal Courts (Sentencing) Act 2000.
74. Section 60(1)(a), Powers of Criminal Courts (Sentencing) Act 2000.
75. Section 60(3), Powers of Criminal Courts (Sentencing) Act 2000.

exceed 24 hours where the person is aged under 16 and shall not exceed 36 hours where the person is aged 16 or over.[76]

Notwithstanding the restrictions as to hours, a court may make an attendance centre order where the offender is already subject to a current attendance centre order without regard to the number of hours of the existing order or the fact that the order is still in force.[77]

The order may only be made where the court is satisfied that the attendance centre is reasonably accessible to the person concerned having regard to his age, the means of access available to him and any other circumstances.[78] Guidance has been issued by the Home Office translating this provision into practical arrangements. Where the offender is aged below 14 years he may be expected to travel up to 10 miles or for 45 minutes. If he is 14 years or older he may be expected to travel up to 15 miles or for 90 minutes. It is usually thought that the distance and journey times relate to travel to or from the attendance centre and not the combined journey.[79]

The first time the offender attends the attendance centre is specified in the order made by the court.[80] Subsequent requirements to attend may be imposed by the officer in charge of the centre[81] but a person may not be required to attend more than once on any day and not for more than three hours on any occasion.[82]

The times at which a person is required to attend at an attendance centre shall, as far as practicable, be such as to avoid any conflict with his religious beliefs or with the requirements of any other community order to which he is subject and interference with the times at which he normally works or attends school or any other educational establishment.[83]

Whilst subject to an attendance centre order the offender is not only required to attend but he is also given under supervision appropriate occupation or instruction according to the regime of the centre.[84] To this end the Secretary of State has power to regulate the management and regime at attendance centres.[85]

76. Section 60(4), Powers of Criminal Courts (Sentencing) Act 2000.
77. Section 60(5), Powers of Criminal Courts (Sentencing) Act 2000.
78. Section 60(6), Powers of Criminal Courts (Sentencing) Act 2000.
79. Home Office Circulars No 22/1986 and 72/1992.
80. Section 60(8), Powers of Criminal Courts (Sentencing) Act 2000.
81. Section 60(9), Powers of Criminal Courts (Sentencing) Act 2000.
82. Section 60(10), Powers of Criminal Courts (Sentencing) Act 2000.
83. Section 60(7), Powers of Criminal Courts (Sentencing) Act 2000.
84. Section 62(2), Powers of Criminal Courts (Sentencing) Act 2000.
85. Attendance Centre Rules 1995.

Schedule 5, Powers of Criminal Courts (Sentencing) Act 2000

Schedule 5, Powers of Criminal Courts (Sentencing) Act 2000 makes provision for the powers of the court to deal with breach, amendment and revocation of attendance centre orders.

Breach

A summons or a warrant may be issued by a magistrate where it appears on information that an offender has failed to attend in accordance with an attendance centre order or has breached the rules of the centre which cannot be adequately dealt with under the Attendance Centre Rules.[86] Where the information is laid on oath the court may issue a warrant for the arrest of the offender.

The court before which a child or young person is to be brought for breach of an order is the court exercising jurisdiction over the place where the attendance centre is located. In the case of a child or young person, the court would be the youth court so acting but where the offender attains the age of 18 years the appropriate court would be the adult magistrates' court.[87]

If it is proved to the satisfaction of the magistrates' court before which the offender appears that he has failed without reasonable excuse to attend or has committed a breach of the rules the court may deal with him in any one of the following ways:[88]

- It may impose a fine not exceeding £1000. Where the court chooses this as the way of dealing with a breach of the order it shall be without prejudice to the continuation of the order;[89]

- Where the attendance centre order was made by a magistrates' court including a youth court, it may deal with him for the offence in respect of which the order was made, in any way in which he could have been dealt with for that offence by the court which made the order if the order had not been made. Where the court deals with the offender by way of re-sentence it shall revoke the attendance centre order;[90]

- Where the order was made by the Crown Court, it may commit him to custody or release him on bail until he can be brought or appear before the Crown Court.

---

86. Paragraph 1(1), Schedule 5, Powers of Criminal Courts (Sentencing) Act 2000.
87. Paragraph 1(2), Schedule 5, Powers of Criminal Courts (Sentencing) Act 2000.
88. Paragraph 2(1), Schedule 5, Powers of Criminal Courts (Sentencing) Act 2000.
89. Paragraph 2(2), Schedule 5, Powers of Criminal Courts (Sentencing) Act 2000.
90. Paragraph 2(4), Schedule 5, Powers of Criminal Courts (Sentencing) Act 2000.

Where the court decides to deal with the breach by way of re-sentence the court shall take into account the extent to which the offender has complied with the requirements of the order and in the case of an offender who has wilfully and persistently failed to comply with those requirements, may impose a custodial sentence[91] whether or not the offence was so serious that such a sentence could only be justified.[92]

There exists a right of appeal against the decision of the magistrates' court in respect of orders made on proof of breach of an attendance centre order to the Crown Court.[93]

Where the order was made in the Crown Court other than by way of an appeal, the magistrates' court has no power to re-sentence the offender for breaching the order. Instead the offender may be committed to the Crown Court.[94] In such a case the court shall send to the Crown Court a certificate signed by a justice of the peace giving particulars of the offender's failure to attend or as the case may be the breach of the rules which he has committed and such other particulars of the case as may be desirable.[95] The certificate is admissible in evidence of the failure or the breach before the Crown Court.

The Crown Court's powers to deal with breach of an attendance centre order arise where the breach is proved to its satisfaction. Where the breach is denied the court itself is required to determine the issue and the decision is not to be made by verdict of a jury.[96]

The Crown Court may then deal with the offender for the offence in respect of which the order was made in any way in which it could have dealt with him for that offence if it had not made the order.[97] In doing so the Crown Court is required to revoke the order if it is still in force.

Where the Crown Court decides to deal with the breach by way of re-sentence the court shall take into account the extent to which the offender has complied with the requirements of the order and in the case of an offender who has wilfully and

---

91. But note that the power of the youth court to impose a custodial sentence is limited to the making of a Detention and Training Order and this paragraph does not affect the limitation as to the periods of such an order.
92. Paragraph 2(5), Schedule 5, Powers of Criminal Courts (Sentencing) Act 2000.
93. Paragraph 2(6), Schedule 5, Powers of Criminal Courts (Sentencing) Act 2000.
94. Orders made on appeal are treated as orders of the court against whose decision the appeal was brought: Paragraph 6, Powers of Criminal Courts (Sentencing) Act 2000.
95. Paragraph 2(7), Schedule 5, Powers of Criminal Courts (Sentencing) Act 2000.
96. Paragraph 3(4), Schedule 5, Powers of Criminal Courts (Sentencing) Act 2000.
97. Paragraph 3(1), Schedule 5, Powers of Criminal Courts (Sentencing) Act 2000.

persistently failed to comply with those requirements, may impose a custodial sentence[98] whether or not the offence was so serious that such a sentence could only be justified.[99]

Revocation with or without re-sentencing

Where an attendance centre order is in force an appropriate court may, on an application by the offender or by the officer in charge of the relevant attendance centre, revoke the order. The appropriate court means

- The magistrates' court acting for the petty sessions area where the centre is situated; or

- The court which made the order; or

- Where the court which made the order was the Crown Court other than on appeal and there is included in the order a direction that the power to revoke the order is reserved to that court, the Crown Court.[1]

Any power conferred on a court to revoke an attendance centre order includes power to deal with the offender, for the offence in respect of which the order was made, in any way in which he could have been dealt with for that offence by the court which made the order if the order had not been made.[2]

Amendment

Where an attendance centre order is in force an appropriate magistrates' court may, on an application by the offender or by the officer in charge of the relevant centre, by order:

- Vary the day or hour specified in the order for the offender's first attendance at the centre; or

- Substitute for the relevant attendance centre an attendance centre which the court is satisfied is reasonably accessible to the offender having regard to his age, the means of access available to him and any other circumstances.

The appropriate magistrates' court means either the court acting for the petty sessions area in which the centre is located or the

---

98. But note that the power of the Crown Court to impose a custodial sentence is limited to the making of a Detention and Training Order and this paragraph does not affect the limitation as to the periods of such an order.
99. Paragraph 3(3), Schedule 5, Powers of Criminal Courts (Sentencing) Act 2000.
1. Paragraphs 4(1) and (2), Schedule 5, Powers of Criminal Courts (Sentencing) Act 2000.
2. Paragraph 4(3), Schedule 5, Powers of Criminal Courts (Sentencing) Act 2000.

court which made the order. If the order was made in the Crown Court it is the former magistrates' court which has power to deal with amendments.[3]

Offenders Aged 16 or Over

The following community orders may be made by the youth court after conviction in the case of a child or young person aged 16 years or over. These orders move the child or young person towards the adult offender sentencing regime and they may not be appropriate where the child or young person's development or maturity is not commensurate with his age.

Community Punishment Orders

Where a child or young person is convicted by a court of an offence, the court (either the youth court or the Crown Court after conviction on indictment) may make an order requiring him to perform unpaid work in the community. This order was previously referred to a community service order but is presently called a community punishment order. It is only available where the court is satisfied that the offending is serious enough to merit a community sentence and that the order is suitable for the offender and commensurate with the seriousness of the offending.

A community punishment order is only available in respect of an offender aged 16 years or over. Below that age the court may not make such an order.[4]

A community punishment order is only available in respect of an offence which is punishable in the case of an adult by imprisonment.[5]

The number of hours which a person may be required to work under a community punishment order shall be specified in the order and shall be in the aggregate not less than 40 and not more than 240.[6] A community punishment order made in respect of a child or young person is otherwise the same as an order made in respect of an adult.

The following differences exist:[7]

- Before making a community punishment order the court is required to consider an assessment from the appropriate

---

3. Paragraph 5, Schedule 5, Powers of Criminal Courts (Sentencing) Act 2000.
4. Section 46(1), Powers of Criminal Courts (Sentencing) Act 2000.
5. Section 46(1), Powers of Criminal Courts (Sentencing) Act 2000.
6. Section 46(2), Powers of Criminal Courts (Sentencing) Act 2000.
7. Sections 46 and 47, Powers of Criminal Courts (Sentencing) Act 2000.

officer of the offender's suitability for such an order. In the case of an offender aged under 18 the appropriate officer may be either a probation officer, a social worker or a member of the youth offending team;

- A copy of the order must be given by the court to the probation officer or the youth offending team; and

- The responsible officer under whose supervision the order is to be performed will be either a probation officer, a person appointed by the probation committee for the purpose of taking on the role of responsible officer or a member of the youth offending team.

Breach, amendment and revocation

Schedule 3,
Powers of Criminal
Courts (Sentencing)
Act 2000

Schedule 3, Powers of Criminal Courts (Sentencing) Act 2000 makes provision for the powers of the court to deal with breach, amendment and revocation of community punishment orders. The Schedule also makes provision for the court's powers to deal with other community sentences. For convenience and to avoid repetition, material relating to breach, amendment and revocation of all community sentences is set out elsewhere in this work at pages XX–XX.

Rehabilitation Orders

Where a child or young person is convicted by a court of an offence, the court (either the youth court or the Crown Court after conviction on indictment) may make an order placing him under the supervision of a probation officer. This order was previously referred to as a probation order but is presently called a community rehabilitation order. It is only available where the court is satisfied that the offending is serious enough to merit a community sentence and that the order is suitable for the offender and commensurate with the seriousness of the offending.[8]

A rehabilitation order is similar in nature to a supervision order. However, a rehabilitation order may only be imposed where the offender is aged 16 years or over and the court is of the opinion that his supervision is desirable in the interests of securing his rehabilitation or protecting the public from harm from him or preventing the commission by him of further offences.[9]

---

8. Section 41, Powers of Criminal Courts (Sentencing) Act 2000.
9. Section 41(1), Powers of Criminal Courts (Sentencing) Act 2000.

The minimum period of a rehabilitation order is 6 months and the maximum period 3 years.[10]

If the offender is aged under 18 at the time the order is made he shall be required to be under the supervision of a probation officer or a member of the youth offending team. In either case the relevant authority will be the authority exercising its powers over the petty sessions area where the offender resides or will reside.

The court is under a duty to give a copy of the order to the probation officer or member of the youth offending team assigned in the order.

Otherwise a rehabilitation order operates in the case of a young person in the same way as a rehabilitation order made in respect of an adult.

Schedule 2, Powers of Criminal Courts (Sentencing) Act 2000

The court may attach directions or requirements to a rehabilitation order. The additional requirements are set out in Schedule 2, Powers of Criminal Courts (Sentencing) Act 2000 and may be imposed where the court considers it desirable in the interests of securing the rehabilitation of the offender or protecting the public from harm from him or preventing the commission by him of further offences.[11]

Requirements of a Rehabilitation Order

The court may impose a range of requirements into a rehabilitation order. The requirements which may be included in an order made in respect of a child or young person are the same as may be included in the case of an order made in respect of an adult and, where appropriate, subject to the following amendments:

- Requirements as to residence;

- Requirements as to activities;

- Provided that before the court imposes such a requirement it has, in the case of an offender under 18 consulted either a probation officer or a member of the youth offending team.

- Requirements as to attendance at probation centre;

  Provided that before the court imposes such a requirement it has, in the case of an offender under 18 consulted either a probation officer or a member of the youth offending team

10.   Section 41(3), Powers of Criminal Courts (Sentencing) Act 2000.
11.   Section 42(1), Powers of Criminal Courts (Sentencing) Act 2000.

- Requirement as to treatment for mental condition etc.;

- Requirement as to treatment for drug or alcohol dependency.

Breach, amendment and revocation

Schedule 3,
Powers of Criminal
Courts (Sentencing)
Act 2000

Schedule 3, Powers of Criminal Courts (Sentencing) Act 2000 makes provision for the powers of the court to deal with breach, amendment and revocation of community rehabilitation orders. The Schedule also makes provision for the court's powers to deal with other community sentences. For convenience and to avoid repetition, material relating to breach, amendment and revocation of all community sentences is set out elsewhere in this work at pages XX–XX.

Community Rehabilitation and Punishment Orders

Where a child or young person is convicted by a court of an offence, the court (either the youth court or the Crown Court after conviction on indictment) may make an order placing him under the supervision of a probation officer and requiring him to perform unpaid work in the community. This order was previously referred to as a combination order but is presently called a community rehabilitation and punishment order. It is only available where the court is satisfied that the offending is serious enough to merit a community sentence and that the order is suitable for the offender and commensurate with the seriousness of the offending.[12]

Additionally the court must be satisfied that the making of such an order is desirable in the interests of securing the rehabilitation of the offender or protecting the public from harm from him or preventing the commission by him of further offences.[13]

The order is only available in respect of a child or young person aged 16 or over at conviction.[14]

A rehabilitation and punishment order is only available in respect of an offence punishable in the case of an adult by imprisonment.[15]

The supervisory aspect of a community rehabilitation and punishment order may be for a minimum period of 12 months and a maximum period of 3 years. The punishment element is

---

12. Section 51, Powers of Criminal Courts (Sentencing) Act 2000.
13. Section 51(3), Powers of Criminal Courts (Sentencing) Act 2000.
14. Section 51(1), Powers of Criminal Courts (Sentencing) Act 2000.
15. Section 51(1), Powers of Criminal Courts (Sentencing) Act 2000.

less than is available for a simple punishment order, being between 40 and 100 hours.[16]

It is open to the sentencing court to impose such requirements as appear suitable under Schedule 2, Powers of Criminal Courts (Sentencing) Act 2000 and the legislation which affects such requirements applies with equal force to the combined order.[17]

Breach, amendment and revocation

Schedule 3, Powers of Criminal Courts (Sentencing) Act 2000 makes provision for the powers of the court to deal with breach, amendment and revocation of community rehabilitation and punishment orders. The Schedule also makes provision for the court's powers to deal with other community sentences. For convenience and to avoid repetition, material relating to breach, amendment and revocation of all community sentences is set out elsewhere in this work at pages XX–XX.[18]

Drug Treatment and Testing Orders

Where a child or young person is convicted by a court of an offence, the court (either the youth court or the Crown Court after conviction on indictment) may make an order requiring him to submit to treatment by or under the direction of a specified person having the necessary qualifications or experience with a view to the reduction or elimination of the offender's dependency on or propensity to misuse drugs. It is only available where the court is satisfied that the offending is serious enough to merit a community sentence and that the order is suitable for the offender and commensurate with the seriousness of the offending.[19]

Additionally the court shall not make a drug treatment and testing order unless it is satisfied that the offender is dependent on or has a propensity to misuse drugs and that his dependency or propensity is such as requires and may be susceptible to treatment.[20]

The order may be made in respect of children and young persons aged 16 or over at conviction.[21]

---

16.   Section 51(1), Powers of Criminal Courts (Sentencing) Act 2000.
17.   Section 51(4), Powers of Criminal Courts (Sentencing) Act 2000.
18.   Sections 51(5) and (6), Powers of Criminal Courts (Sentencing) Act 2000.
19.   Section 52, Powers of Criminal Courts (Sentencing) Act 2000.
20.   Section 52(3), Powers of Criminal Courts (Sentencing) Act 2000.
21.   Section 52(1), Powers of Criminal Courts (Sentencing) Act 2000.

The powers of the court to make and regulate a drug treatment and testing order are generally the same for a child or young person as they are for an adult.

Where an order has been made by a magistrates' court (adult or youth) against a child or young person in respect of an indictable offence who attains the age of 18 and appears subsequently at a review meeting but fails to express his willingness to comply with the amended requirement as may be proposed by the court, the court may re-sentence him for the original offence by either a fine of up to £5,000 or dealing with him in any way in which the court could deal with him if it had just convicted him of an offence punishable with imprisonment for a term not exceeding six months.[22]

Breach, amendment and revocation

Schedule 3, Powers of Criminal Courts (Sentencing) Act 2000

Schedule 3, Powers of Criminal Courts (Sentencing) Act 2000 makes provision for the powers of the court to deal with breach, amendment and revocation of drug treatment and testing orders. The Schedule also makes provision for the court's powers to deal with other community sentences. For convenience and to avoid repetition, material relating to breach, amendment and revocation of all community sentences is set out elsewhere in this work at pages XX–XX.[23]

Custody

A court may pass a custodial sentence in respect of offences punishable with imprisonment. The youth court and Crown Court have different custodial sentencing options. The Powers of Criminal Courts (Sentencing) Act 2000 imposes certain restrictions on the use of custody. Certain of these restrictions apply in the Crown Court; others only in the youth court.

As far as the youth court is concerned, the only custodial sentence available in respect of children and young persons under 18 is the detention and training order.

---

22. Section 55(5), Powers of Criminal Courts (Sentencing) Act 2000.
23. Section 56, Powers of Criminal Courts (Sentencing) Act 2000.

When Custody may be imposed

Before any court may pass a custodial sentence it must be of the opinion:[24]

- that the offence, or the combination of the offence and one or more offences associated with it, was so serious that only such a sentence can be justified for the offence; or

- where the offence is a violent or sexual offence, that only such a sentence would be adequate to protect the public from serious harm from him.

Nothing in this statement of the custody threshold prevents the court from passing a custodial sentence on the offender if he fails to express his willingness to comply with a requirement which is proposed by the court to be included in a rehabilitation or supervision order and which requires an expression of such willingness or a requirement which is proposed to be included in a drug treatment and testing order or an order to provide samples.[25]

Section 79(2),
Powers of Criminal
Courts (Sentencing)
Act 2000

Where a court passes a custodial sentence, the court must explain to the offender in open court and in ordinary language why it is passing such a sentence and must state in open court why it is of the opinion that only a custodial sentence is appropriate having regard to the tests in section 79(2), Powers of Criminal Courts (Sentencing) Act 2000.[26] In the case of a magistrates' court, including a youth court, such reasons are required to specified in the court register and in the warrant of commitment.[27]

Length of Sentence

A custodial sentence shall be:

- for such term (not exceeding the permitted maximum) as in the opinion of the court is commensurate with the seriousness of the offence, or the combination of the offence and one or more offences associated with it; or

- where the offence is a violent or sexual offence, for such longer term (not exceeding that maximum) as in the opinion of the court is necessary to protect the public from serious harm from the offender.

---

24. Section 79(2), Powers of Criminal Courts (Sentencing) Act 2000.
25. Section 79(3), Powers of Criminal Courts (Sentencing) Act 2000.
26. Section 79(4), Powers of Criminal Courts (Sentencing) Act 2000.
27. Section 79(4), Powers of Criminal Courts (Sentencing) Act 2000.

Where the court passes a sentence for a term longer than is commensurate with the seriousness of the offence the court shall state in open court and explain to the offender in ordinary language why it is of that opinion and why the sentence is for such a term.

Procedural Safeguards

Before passing a custodial sentence a court shall obtain and consider a pre-sentence report[28] unless in the circumstances of the case, the court is of the opinion that it is unnecessary to obtain such a report.[29]

Where the offender is aged under 18 and the offence or any associated offence is not triable only on indictment, the court may not dispense with a pre-sentence report unless:

• there exists a previous pre-sentence report obtained in respect of the offender; and

• the court has had regard to the information contained in that report or, if there is more than one such report, the most recent report.[30]

Failure to obtain and consider a pre-sentence report does not invalidate the custodial sentence[31] but any court on appeal must obtain such a report unless it is of the opinion that the court below was justified in dealing without such a report.[32] In the case of a child or young person the court may only form such an opinion if it has considered the most recent pre-sentence report available in respect of the child or young person.[33]

Generally an offender without legal representation may not be sentenced to custody unless having been granted state funded representation his conduct is such that it has been withdrawn or having been informed of his right to apply for such representation, and having the opportunity to apply for it, the offender refuses or fails to apply.[34]

28.   Section 81(1), Powers of Criminal Courts (Sentencing) Act 2000.
29.   Section 81(2), Powers of Criminal Courts (Sentencing) Act 2000.
30.   Section 81(3), Powers of Criminal Courts (Sentencing) Act 2000.
31.   Section 81(5), Powers of Criminal Courts (Sentencing) Act 2000.
32.   Section 81(6), Powers of Criminal Courts (Sentencing) Act 2000.
33.   Section 81(7), Powers of Criminal Courts (Sentencing) Act 2000.
34.   Section 83, Powers of Criminal Courts (Sentencing) Act 2000.

Detention in the Crown Court

The Crown Court and the youth court have power to order a child or young person to be detained only in the circumstances set out above.

The type of order for detention depends on the manner of conviction.

Where a person convicted of murder appears to the court to have been under 18 at the time of the offence, the court shall sentence him to be detained during Her Majesty's pleasure.[35] This is equivalent to a sentence of imprisonment for life in the case of an adult. This sentence is only available in the Crown Court.

Section 24, Magistrates' Courts Act 1980, Section 91(3), Powers of Criminal Courts (Sentencing) Act 2000

Where a person aged under 18 is convicted of a relevant offence on indictment, the youth court having determined that the offence is a grave crime under section 24, Magistrates' Courts Act 1980, Section 91(3), Powers of Criminal Courts (Sentencing) Act 2000 provides that if the Crown Court is of the opinion that none of the other methods in which the case may legally be dealt with is suitable, the court may sentence the offender to be detained for such period, not exceeding that maximum term of imprisonment with which the offence is punishable in the case of a person aged 21 or over, as may be specified in the sentence.

The relevant offences are:[36]

- An offence punishable in the case of a person aged 21 or over with imprisonment for 14 years or more, not being an offence the sentence for which is fixed by law;

- An offences of indecent assault on a woman;

- An offence of indecent assault on a man;

- Where the person is at least 14 but under 18 an offence of:

    - Causing death by dangerous driving;

    - Causing death by careless driving while under the influence of drink or drugs.

Where an offender aged under 18 years is convicted by the Crown Court of any one of the offences listed above as a grave crime, the court may sentence him to be detained for such period, not exceeding the maximum term of imprisonment available in respect of an adult. This power only arises where the court is of

---

35.   Section 90, Powers of Criminal Courts (Sentencing) Act 2000.
36.   Section 91, Powers of Criminal Courts (Sentencing) Act 2000.

Section 91,
Powers of Criminal
Courts (Sentencing)
Act 2000

the opinion that none of the other methods in which the case may legally be dealt with is suitable.[37] Thus a judge considering his powers under section 91, Powers of Criminal Courts (Sentencing) Act 2000 must consider and reject other methods of sentence including the making of a detention and training order before moving to impose detention under this section.

Section 90 or 91,
Powers of Criminal
Courts (Sentencing)
Act 2000

A person sentenced to be detained under either section 90 or 91, Powers of Criminal Courts (Sentencing) Act 2000 is liable to be detained in such place and under such conditions as the Secretary of State may direct or arrange with any person.[38] Unlike other custodial sentences available in respect of an adult, detention may be served at any secure institution and not necessarily in a young offender institution.[39]

Section 91,
Powers of Criminal
Courts (Sentencing)
Act 2000

Where a child or young person is convicted on an indictment linked to an adult, the Crown Court may impose a custodial sentence but such a sentence would be limited to the making of a detention and training order and the use of detention for grave crimes would not be available unless the joint or linked offence was deserving of punishment under section 91, Powers of Criminal Courts (Sentencing) Act 2000.

Detention and Training Orders

A detention and training order is a custodial sentence available in the Crown Court and the only custodial sentence available in the youth court.[40] The passing of a custodial sentence in the youth court is subject to the restrictions on custodial sentences in general.[41]

Provided that the general restrictions on passing a custodial sentence are met, the court may pass a detention and training order.

The court shall not make a detention and training order:

- In the case of an offender under the age of 15 at the time of the conviction, unless it is of the opinion that he is a persistent offender;

---

37. Section 91(3), Powers of Criminal Courts (Sentencing) Act 2000.
38. Section 92, Powers of Criminal Courts (Sentencing) Act 2000.
39. At the time of writing, offenders aged between 8 and 21 may not be sentenced to imprisonment and are instead liable to serve any period of detention in a young offender's institution whereas offenders aged over 21 serve their detention in prison. Proposals exist to narrow the range of institutional options by replacing young offender institution accommodation with imprisonment.
40. Section 100, Powers of Criminal Courts (Sentencing) Act 2000.
41. See above.

- In the case of an offender under the age of 12 at that time unless it is of the opinion that only a custodial sentence would be adequate to protect the public from further offending by him.

The court is required to state in open court the reasons for passing a detention and training order.

What is a Persistent Offender?

There is no statutory definition of the term persistent offender. The definition of a persistent young offender provided by government for the purposes of the administration of the youth justice system[42] should not be confused with the term persistent offender. In *R v Charlton*[43] the Court of Appeal held that the non-statutory definition in the circular did not apply to help define the term persistent offender for this purpose.[44]

A persistent offender for the purposes of triggering the power of the court to pass a detention and training order on a child or young person under 15 years includes:

- A child who had no previous convictions but who committed a series of robberies over two days;[45]

- A child who has been cautioned by the police but not previously prosecuted;[46]

- A child with no previous warnings or convictions who commits offences after the offence for which the detention and training order is to be imposed;[47]

- A child with previous convictions.[48]

Where a child under the age of 15 years does not fall within the definition of a persistent offender, the court has no power to pass

---

42. See above.
43. [2000] All ER (D) 1254.
44. See below.
45. *R v Smith* (2000) 164 JP 681.
46. *R v D* [2000] Crim LR 867.
47. *R v B* [2001] Crim LR 50.
48. Although where the previous convictions are of a dissimilar nature it may be possible to avoid falling within the definition on the facts of the case: *R v JD* (2000) 165 JP 1.

a custodial sentence. Where the offence is one which can be described as a grave crime, the Crown Court would have available to it the power of passing a sentence of detention under section 91, Powers of Criminal Courts (Sentencing) Act 2000.[49]

Section 91, Powers of Criminal Courts (Sentencing) Act 2000

Length of Detention and Training Orders

The term of a detention and training order may not exceed the maximum term of imprisonment that the Crown Court could, in the case of an offender aged 21, impose for the offence.[50] The term should also be commensurate with the seriousness of the offence or be for a period necessary to protect the public from an offender convicted of a violent or sexual offence.

The term of a detention and training order, whether made by the Crown Court or the youth court shall be one of certain specified periods. The periods are either 4, 6, 8, 10, 12, 18, or 24 months.[51] No other period may be imposed. Half of the sentence is served in a secure institution and half under supervision in the community.[52]

If the offence in respect of which the court is considering the passing of a detention and training order is not sufficiently serious to merit a sentence of 4 months or more, the court has no power to impose a custodial sentence of any kind.

Subject to an overall limit of 24 months, the court may impose consecutive detention and training orders[53] or order that any detention and training order commence on the expiry of the term of any other detention and training order. In passing a sentence combining detention and training orders either concurrently or consecutively, the court must select a period for each separate order from the menu of available terms. However, the court is not limited to imposing a consecutive sentence of a term that will create an aggregate sentence that itself equals one of the permitted totals.[54] Any period which exceeds the 24-month ceiling is treated as remitted.[55] However, a court making a detention and training order shall not order that its term shall commence on the expiry of the term of a detention and training order under which the period of supervision has already begun.[56]

---

49. See above.
50. Section 101(2), Powers of Criminal Courts (Sentencing) Act 2000.
51. Section 101(1), Powers of Criminal Courts (Sentencing) Act 2000.
52. See below.
53. Section 101(3), Powers of Criminal Courts (Sentencing) Act 2000.
54. *R v Norris* (2000) 164 JP 689.
55. Section 101(5), Powers of Criminal Courts (Sentencing) Act 2000.
56. Section 101(6), Powers of Criminal Courts (Sentencing) Act 2000.

Where the new order is made in respect of an offender who is subject to an order under which the supervision part has begun, the old order shall be disregarded in determining whether the effect of the new order would be that the offender would be subject to a term which, overall, exceeds 24 months.[57]

In determining the length of the detention and training order the court shall take account of any period for which the offender has been remanded in custody in connection with the offence or any other offence the charge for which was founded on the same facts or evidence.[58] Where the court proposes to make orders in respect of an offender for two or more offences, the court shall take account of any such periods as they relate to any of those offences. For the purposes of this calculation the court may includes any period when the offender was:

Police and Criminal Evidence Act 1984 Prevention of Terrorism (Temporary Provisions) Act 1989

- Held in police detention, including time so detained under the Police and Criminal Evidence Act 1984 or the Prevention of Terrorism (Temporary Provisions) Act 1989;

- Remanded in or committed to custody by an order of a court;

- Remanded in or committed to accommodation provided by the local authority and placed and kept in secure accommodation; or

Sections 35, 36, 38 or 48, Mental Health Act 1983

- Remanded, admitted or removed to hospital under sections 35, 36, 38 or 48, Mental Health Act 1983.[59]

Once a period of remand has been taken account of, it shall not be subsequently taken account of in relation to such an order made in respect of the offender for any other offence or offences.[60]

The court is not required to precisely reflect mathematically all periods spent on remand in order to take account periods on remand in determining the length of the detention and training order. No rule of general application could be devised to cover the infinitely various situations which might arise. Where the

57.   Section 101(7), Powers of Criminal Courts (Sentencing) Act 2000.
58.   Section 101(8), Powers of Criminal Courts (Sentencing) Act 2000.
59.   Section 101(11), Powers of Criminal Courts (Sentencing) Act 2000.
60.   Section 101(10), Powers of Criminal Courts (Sentencing) Act 2000.

period of remand is approximately equal the difference between two terms for which the order may be made, the court should **Section 101(7),** pass the lesser sentence. Shorter periods of remand may be **Powers of Criminal** effectively ignored in determining the term of the order **Courts (Sentencing)** notwithstanding section 101(7), Powers of Criminal Courts **Act 2000** (Sentencing) Act 2000.[61]

A similar problem arises in relation to the duty of the court **Section 152,** under section 152, Powers of Criminal Courts (Sentencing) Act **Powers of Criminal** 2000 to take into account the timing of a guilty plea. Where a **Courts (Sentencing)** defendant pleads guilty he can expect to receive a discount on **Act 2000** sentence of up to one third. This does not sit comfortably with the quanta of available terms. In *R* v *Kelly*[62] the Court of Appeal found no reason to not allow credit for a guilty plea to reduce a sentence of 24 months to 18 months notwithstanding that the reduction in sentence necessitated by the legislation was disproportionate and unjustified.[63]

If however credit for pleading guilty is to be given, many summary only offences will effectively be removed from the range of offences for which detention is a realistic option.

Sections 102 to For the purposes of any reference in sections 102 to 105, Powers **105, Powers of** of Criminal Courts (Sentencing) Act 2000 to the term of an **Criminal Courts** order, consecutive terms or terms which are wholly or partly **(Sentencing) Act** concurrent shall be treated as a single term if they were made on **2000** the same occasion or where they were made on different occasions the offender has not been released at any time during the period beginning with the first and ending with the last of those occasions.[64]

The Period of Detention and Training

The detention and training order comprises two parts. The first half of the term will be served in such secure accommodation as may be determined by the Secretary of State.[65] Arrangements are usually made on a contingency basis in advance between the youth offending team and the Youth Justice Board centrally. The court has no power to determine the type or location of the secure institution where the offender will serve the detention part of his sentence.

61. *R* v *Inner London Crown Court ex parte N and S* [2000] Crim LR 871 and *R* v *Fieldhouse and Watts* [2000] Crim LR 1020.
62. [2001] Crim LR 583.
63. An alternative approach would be to accord the reduction in sentence similar status to the period spent on remand. The court might properly take account of a guilty plea without giving specific credit for it.
64. Section 101(13), Powers of Criminal Courts (Sentencing) Act 2000.
65. Section 102(2), Powers of Criminal Courts (Sentencing) Act 2000.

The Secretary of State may increase or decrease the custodial part of the term.

- He may at any time release the offender if he is satisfied that exceptional circumstances exists which justify the offender's release on compassionate grounds;[66]

- He may release the offender in the case of an order for a term of 8 months or more but less than 18 months, one month before the half-way point of his term of the order; and

- In the case of an order for a term of 18 months or more, one month or two months before that point;[67]

- He may also apply to the youth court for an order that he shall release the offender:

  - In the case of an order for a term of 8 months or more but less than 18 months, one month after the half-way point of the term of the order; and

  - In the case of an order for a term of 18 months or more, one month or two months after that point.[68]

The Period of Supervision

The second part of a detention and training order is served in the community under supervision. The period of supervision begins with the offender's release and ends when the term of the order ends.[69] The Secretary of State has power to order that the period of supervision comes to an earlier end.[70]

The offender will be supervised by either a probation officer, a social worker or a member of the youth offending team.[71] The Secretary of State determines who will supervise the offender and may add requirements to be complied with during the remaining period of the order's term.[72] This information must be given to the offender in writing prior to his release from the detention part of the term although the supervising officer may be changed from time to time.

---

66. Section 102(3), Powers of Criminal Courts (Sentencing) Act 2000.
67. Section 102(4), Powers of Criminal Courts (Sentencing) Act 2000.
68. Section 102(5), Powers of Criminal Courts (Sentencing) Act 2000.
69. Section 103(1), Powers of Criminal Courts (Sentencing) Act 2000.
70. Section 103(2), Powers of Criminal Courts (Sentencing) Act 2000.
71. Sections 103(3) and (4), Powers of Criminal Courts (Sentencing) Act 2000.
72. Section 103(6), Powers of Criminal Courts (Sentencing) Act 2000.

Breach of Supervision Requirements

Application may be made to a justice of the peace to issue either a summons or where the application is in writing and on oath, warrant to secure the attendance of an offender subject to a detention and training order before the relevant court, where it is alleged that the offender has failed to comply with the terms of his supervision.[73]

The relevant court is the youth court[74] which either made the detention and training order or in whose area the offender resides for the time being.[75]

If it is proved to the satisfaction of the youth court that the child or young person has failed to comply with requirements imposed by the Secretary of State, the court may:

- Order the offender to be detained for such period, not exceeding the shorter of three months or the remainder of the term of the detention and training order, as the court may specify; or

- Impose on the offender a fine not exceeding level 3 on the standard scale.[76]

The child or young person dealt with under these powers has a right of appeal to the Crown Court.[77]

Offences During the Currency of the Order

Section 105, Powers of Criminal Courts (Sentencing) Act 2000

A child or young person who commits offences punishable with imprisonment after his release but before the expiry of the term of the order and who is convicted either before or after the order expires, is at risk of being dealt with by the court under section 105, Powers of Criminal Courts (Sentencing) Act 2000.

Subject to the duty of adult magistrates' courts to remit young offenders to the youth court for sentence, the court by or before which a person is convicted of the new offence may, whether or not it passes any other sentence on him, order him to be

---

73. Section 104(1), Powers of Criminal Courts (Sentencing) Act 2000.
74. Unlike other breach proceedings relating to community orders, section 104, Powers of Criminal Courts (Sentencing) Act 2000 does not contain any provisions governing the power of the relevant authority to detain or produce the offender after arrest under the warrant to court; nor does it provide for the court to remand an offender arrested on warrant to the relevant court if produced before an alternative court.
75. Section 104(2), Powers of Criminal Courts (Sentencing) Act 2000.
76. Section 104(3), Powers of Criminal Courts (Sentencing) Act 2000.
77. Section 104(6), Powers of Criminal Courts (Sentencing) Act 2000.

detained in such secure accommodation as the Secretary of State shall determine for the whole or any part of the period which:

- Begins with the date of the court's order; and

- Is equal in length to the period between the date on which the new offence was committed and the date on which the order expires.[78]

The period for which a person is ordered to be detained in secure accommodation shall, as the court may direct, either be served before and be followed by, or be served concurrently with, any sentence imposed for the new offence and shall be disregarded in determining the appropriate length of that sentence.[79]

For the purposes of calculating the period for which the offender may be ordered to be detained, offences committed over a period of days or between dates are treated as having been committed on the last of those days.[80]

Interaction between Detention and Training Orders and Detention in a Young Offender's Institution

Where a court passes a sentence of detention in a young offender institution[81] in the case of an offender who is subject to a detention and training order, the new sentence takes effect as follows:

- If the offender has been released under supervision, at the beginning of the day on which it is passed;

- If not, or if the court so orders, at the time when the offender would otherwise have been released from the custodial part of the order to begin his supervision.

Where a court makes a detention and training order in the case of an offender who is subject to detention in a young offender institution, the order takes effect as follows:

- If the offender has been released under the early release of prisoner provisions, at the beginning of the day on which it is made;

- If not, or if the court so orders, at the time when the offender would otherwise have been released under the same provisions.

---

78. Section 105(1), Powers of Criminal Courts (Sentencing) Act 2000.
79. Section 105(3), Powers of Criminal Courts (Sentencing) Act 2000.
80. Section 105(4), Powers of Criminal Courts (Sentencing) Act 2000.
81. Section 106(1), Powers of Criminal Courts (Sentencing) Act 2000.

Where at any time an offender is subject concurrently to a detention and training order and detention in a young offender's institution he shall be treated as if he were subject only to the one of them that was imposed on the later occasion.

Where, by virtue of any enactment giving a court power to deal with a person in a way in which a court on a previous occasion could have dealt with him, a detention and training order for any term is made in the case of a person who has attained the age of 18, the person shall be treated as if he had been sentenced to detention in a young offender institution.[82] This provision deals with the situation where an offender is sentenced for breaching a community order. The court has power to re-sentence the offender to any of the orders available at the time when the relevant order was made. In the case of a child or young person the only custodial sentence available is a detention and training order. Where such an order is made, this provision converts the order into an order of detention in a young offender's institution.

Section 29,
Children and
Young Persons
Act 1963

The effect of this provision should not be confused with the situation where a young person attains the age of 18 before trial. Section 29, Children and Young Persons Act 1963 allows the court to deal with him as if he not yet attained that age, and to make orders which are available in respect of offenders of the lower age. Accordingly it is permissible to pass a detention and training order on an offender who has attained 18 in court proceedings so long as he was under that age when the offence was committed and when the court determined mode of trial.[83]

Secure Accommodation

The Secretary of State has power to determine the type and location of accommodation within the secure estate in which a child or young person will serve the custodial element of the detention and training order. Secure accommodation in this context means:

- A secure training centre;

- A young offender institution;

- Accommodation provided by the local authority for the purposes of restricting the liberty of children and young persons;

---

82. Section 106(6), Powers of Criminal Courts (Sentencing) Act 2000.
83. *Aldis v DPP Divisional Court* 2002 February 11.

Section 82,
Children Act 1989

- Accommodation provided for that purpose with financial support by the Secretary of State under section 82, Children Act 1989;

- Such other accommodation provided for the purpose of restricting liberty as the Secretary of State may direct.[84]

Chapter III of
Part V, Powers of
Criminal Courts
(Sentencing)
Act 2000

Chapter III of Part V, Powers of Criminal Courts (Sentencing) Act 2000 provides for minimum sentences to be imposed in respect of certain offences where an offender has previously been convicted of the same or similar serious offences. The provisions do not apply in connection with children or young persons aged under 18.

Orders against Parents

Parents have responsibilities and duties towards their children. The youth justice system acknowledges these duties and fixes legal consequences to their discharge.

A parent may be engaged through the youth justice system in one or more of the following ways:

- By his attendance at court;

- By his involvement in a referral order;

- By the making of a bind over in respect of the future conduct of his child;

- By the making of a parenting order;

Attendance at Court

Where a child or young person is charged with an offence or is for any other reason brought before a court, the court may in any case and shall in the case of a child or a young person who is under the age of 16 years require a parent or guardian to attend court during all the stages of the proceedings.[85] This duty is qualified and parental attendance may be dispensed with to the extent that the court is satisfied that it would be unreasonable to require such attendance, having regard to the circumstances of the case. Where the child is accommodated by a local authority or is in its care and that local authority has parental responsibility for the child or young person references to a parent or guardian are to be construed as a reference to that authority.[86]

---

84. Section 107(1), Powers of Criminal Courts (Sentencing) Act 2000.
85. Section 34A(1), Children and Young Persons Act 1933.
86. Section 34A(2), Children and Young Persons Act 1933.

In order to secure the attendance of a parent or guardian, the court may issue a summons against him. The court has power to issue a warrant for the arrest of a parent or guardian who fails to attend court.[87]

Parents and Referral Orders

A court making a referral order may make an order requiring an appropriate person or persons to attend meetings of the youth offender panel.[88] The power to do so is converted into a duty where the offender is aged under 16 when the court makes the referral order in his case.[89] Usually the appropriate person would be a parent or guardian[90] although the legislation does not limit the category of persons against whom such an order may be made. The court is not required to exercise its power or duty if it is satisfied that it would be unreasonable to do so or to an extent which the court is satisfied would be unreasonable.[91]

The court may make such an order in the absence of a parent or guardian (or other appropriate person) but must send a copy of the order forthwith.[92]

Parental Bind Overs

In certain circumstances the court has either a power or duty to impose upon a parent or guardian a bind over to take proper care of, and to exercise proper control over, an offender.[93] In this context 'care' includes giving the offender protection and guidance and 'control' includes discipline.[94] In addition, if the court also imposes a community penalty it may include in the bind over a duty to ensure that the offender complies with the requirements of that sentence.

The power arises where a child or young person is convicted of an offence and is exercisable by the court which sentences the child or young person.[95] The power may be exercised where the court is satisfied, having regard to the circumstances of the case, that it would be desirable in the interests of preventing the commission of further offences by the offender. In the case of a

---

87. Rule 26, Magistrates' Courts (Children and Young Persons) Rules 1992.
88. Section 20(1), Powers of Criminal Courts (Sentencing) Act 2000.
89. Section 20(2), Powers of Criminal Courts (Sentencing) Act 2000.
90. Section 20(4), Powers of Criminal Courts (Sentencing) Act 2000.
91. Section 20(3), Powers of Criminal Courts (Sentencing) Act 2000.
92. Section 20(7), Powers of Criminal Courts (Sentencing) Act 2000.
93. Section 150(2), Powers of Criminal Courts (Sentencing) Act 2000.
94. Section 150(11), Powers of Criminal Courts (Sentencing) Act 2000.
95. Section 150(1), Powers of Criminal Courts (Sentencing) Act 2000.

child or young person aged under 16 the power is converted into a duty.[96]

As far as the case of an offender aged under 16 is concerned, if the court is not satisfied that it would be desirable to impose a bind over on the offender's parent or guardian it must state in open court why it is not of that opinion. Provided the court reaches such a negative view, a bind over may not be imposed.[97]

An order of this kind may not exceed three years in length.[98] Where the offender will attain 18 years of age in a period shorter than three years, the order may not exceed that shorter period.[99]

The recognisance may not exceed £1,000[1] and an unreasonable refusal to consent to a bind over is punishable by way of a fine not exceeding £1,000.[2] In fixing the amount of the recognisance, the court shall take into account the means of the parent so far as they are known whether this results in increasing or decreasing the amount of the recognisance.[3]

A parent or guardian has a right of appeal to the Crown Court against an order made by the magistrates' (or youth) court and where the order was made by the Crown Court, a right of appeal to the Court of Appeal.[4]

The court has power to vary or revoke the order from time to time on the application of the parent or guardian if it appears to the court, having regard to any change of circumstances, to be in the interests of justice to do so.[5]

Section 120, Magistrates' Courts Act 1980

An order under this section will be breached if the offender is brought before a court and convicted of further offences committed during the currency of the bind over. Section 120, Magistrates' Courts Act 1980 applies in relation to forfeiture proceedings and requires proceedings to be brought by way of complaint.[6] The court does not have power[7] of its own motion

---

96.   Section 150(1), Powers of Criminal Courts (Sentencing) Act 2000.
97.   Section 150(1)(a), Powers of Criminal Courts (Sentencing) Act 2000.
98.   Section 150(4)(a), Powers of Criminal Courts (Sentencing) Act 2000.
99.   Section 150(4)(b), Powers of Criminal Courts (Sentencing) Act 2000.
 1.   Section 150(3), Powers of Criminal Courts (Sentencing) Act 2000.
 2.   Section 150(2)(b), Powers of Criminal Courts (Sentencing) Act 2000.
 3.   Section 150(7), Powers of Criminal Courts (Sentencing) Act 2000.
 4.   Sections 150(8) and (9), Powers of Criminal Courts (Sentencing) Act 2000.
 5.   Section 150(10), Powers of Criminal Courts (Sentencing) Act 2000.
 6.   Section 150(5), Powers of Criminal Courts (Sentencing) Act 2000.
 7.   This is an arguable proposition but it would be inappropriate for the court to be seen to enter into the arena and bring enforcement proceedings itself. A court purporting to do so is likely to lose its cloak of impartiality and may find itself in breach of Article 6 of the European Convention on Human Rights.

to forfeit the recognisance and the legislation is silent as to whose duty it is to bring proceedings to estreat the recognisance. Neither the Crown Prosecution Service nor the police appear to have adopted a consistent approach to this issue with the result that very few (if any) parental bind overs are enforced.

Parenting Orders

In certain circumstances the court has either a power or a duty to make a parenting order[8] against a parent or guardian, or relevant person[9] of a child or young person in relation to whom criminal proceedings have been taken.

The power or duty to make such an order arises where in any court proceedings:[10]

- A child safety order is made in respect of a child;

- An anti-social behaviour order or sex offender order is made in respect of a child or young person;

- A child or young person is convicted of an offence; or

Section 443 or 444   • A person is convicted of an offence under either section 443
Education Act 1996   or 444, Education Act 1996.[11]

A parenting order is an order which requires the parent (or other relevant person) to comply, for a period not exceeding twelve months, with such requirements as are specified in the order and to attend, if the order so specifies,[12] for a concurrent period not exceeding three months and not more than once in any week, such counselling or guidance sessions as may be specified in directions given by the responsible officer.[13]

The requirements that may be specified in the order are those which the court considers desirable in the interests of preventing the repetition of such behaviour as led to the making of one of the trigger orders or, as the case may be, the commission of any further offences by the child or young person (or offences under the Education Act 1996 by the relevant person).[14]

---

8. Section 8(1), Crime and Disorder Act 1998.
9. In this context a person convicted of specified offences under the Education Act 1996.
10. Section 8, Crime and Disorder Act 1998.
11. Respectively, offences of failing to comply with a school attendance order or failing to secure regular attendance at school of a registered pupil.
12. Section 8(5), Crime and Disorder Act 1998.
13. Section 8(4), Crime and Disorder Act 1998.
14. Section 8(7), Crime and Disorder Act 1998.

The responsible officer is a person specified in the order and will be either a probation officer, a local authority social worker or a member of the youth offending team.[15]

A parenting order may only be made if the court is satisfied that the relevant condition is fulfilled. The relevant condition varies depending on the triggers which allow the court to exercise its power (or duty) to make such an order:[16]

- Where the court is empowered to make a parenting order by the making of a child safety order, an anti-social behaviour order or a sex offender order, it may do so only where it would be desirable in the interests of preventing any repetition of the kind of behaviour which led to the relevant order being made.

- Where the court is empowered to make a parenting order on the conviction of a child or young person, it may do so only where it would be desirable in the interests of preventing the commission of further offences by the child or young person.

- Where the court is empowered to make a parenting order on the conviction of a relevant person under the Education Act 1996, it may do so only where it would be desirable in the interests of preventing the commission of any further offences under the relevant sections of the Education Act 1996.

The court has power to make a parenting order where any child or young person is convicted of an offence. The power is converted into a duty where the offender is aged under 16 at the time of conviction. A parenting order must be made if the court is satisfied that the relevant condition is fulfilled and if the court is not so satisfied, it must state in open court its reasons for its opinion.[17] Provided the court explains its negative view a parenting order need not be made.

---

15.   Section 8(8), Crime and Disorder Act 1998.
16.   Section 8(2), Crime and Disorder Act 1998.
17.   Section 9(1), Crime and Disorder Act 1998.

Parental Involvement in Court

Section 47
(Children and Young
Persons) Act 1993
Rule 10(2)(e),
Magistrates' Courts
(Children and Young
Persons) Rules 1992

A parent's presence in the youth court may be secured in the manners described above. The right of a parent to be present arises out of their deemed status as party to the proceedings as appropriate adult. Accordingly the restrictions on persons present in section 47, Children and Young Persons Act 1933 do not apply. However, Rule 10(2)(e), Magistrates' Courts (Children and Young Persons) Rules 1992 provides that a parent or guardian may be excluded after a finding of guilt if it is necessary in the interests of the minor.

Rule 10(1),
Magistrates' Courts
(Children and Young
Persons) Rules 1992

Rule 10(1), Magistrates' Courts (Children and Young Persons) Rules 1992 provides that where a child or young person is found guilty of an offence or appears in court for certain breach proceedings, the relevant minor and his parent or guardian, if present, shall be given the opportunity of making a statement.

A parent or guardian is entitled to receive copies of any written report. Where such a report has not been made available to a parent or guardian and has not been read aloud to the court,[18] the parent or guardian shall be told the substance of any part of such information which the court considers material. If, as a result of hearing those matters which the court considers to be material a parent or guardian wishes to adduce further evidence the court shall adjourn for this purpose if it considers that further evidence would be material. If the child or young person is legally represented this cumbersome procedure need not be followed.[19]

The court has also a duty to explain the manner in which it proposes to deal with a case before it does so.[20] The explanation has to be given to both the child or young person and his parent or guardian. The purpose of this curious provision is to allow further representations to be made before sentence is finalised.[21]

Rule 15

Rule 15, Magistrates' Courts (Children and Young Persons) Rules 1992 provides that without prejudice to any provision of the

---

18. It is highly unlikely that such a report would be read out in court even in the circumstances envisaged by this legislation.
19. Rules 10(3) and (4), Magistrates' Courts (Children and Young Persons) Rules 1992. A similar provision in Rule 21 deals with secure accommodation.
20. Rule 11, Magistrates' Courts (Children and Young Persons) Rules 1992.
21. The duty to provide this information arises whether the child or young person is represented or not. In busy youth courts the provision is honoured more in the breach. It is unlikely that a failure to comply with the rule would render the sentence of the court unlawful. It could however be argued that a court has compromised the right to fair trial by failing to follow this provision where it could be shown that as a result of the failure the child or young person has been prejudiced.

rules a parent or guardian shall be entitled to make representations to the court at any stage after the conclusion of the evidence in the hearing as the court considers appropriate.

Appendix A

Offence Seriousness Indicators for Use in The Youth Court

These guidelines are available for use by the court to obtain a preliminary indication of the level of seriousness of an average offence of the type described. Aggravating and mitigating factors relevant to the offence and the offender may act to increase or decrease this assessment

Offence	Level of seriousness
A	
Abandoning a child under the age of two years	High
Abduction of a female	High
Absconding from bail	Medium
Absconding from lawful custody	High
Abstracting electricity	Low
Administering poison with intent to injure or annoy	High
Affray	Medium
Aggravated burglary of a dwelling	High
Aggravated burglary of non dwelling	High
Aggravated vehicle taking (Driving)	High
Aggravated vehicle taking (Allowing oneself to be carried)	High
Air Weapons offences	Low
Allowing him herself to be carried in stolen vehicle	Medium
Arson endangering life	High
Arson nor endangering life	High
Assault occasioning actual bodily harm	High
Assault occasioning actual bodily harm — racially aggravated	High
Assault on a Police constable	High
Assault with intent to commit rape	High
Assault with intent to resist apprehension or assault on person assisting a constable	High
Assault with intent to rob	High
Attempt murder	High
Attempt rape	High

B

Blackmail	High
Bomb hoax	High
Burglary of a dwelling	High
Burglary of a non dwelling	High

C

Careless driving	Low
Causing death by dangerous driving	High
Causing death by careless driving when under the influence of drink or drugs (aged 14–17)	High
Causing explosion or casting corrosive fluids with intent to do grievous bodily harm	High
Child abduction	High
Common assault	Medium
Common assault — racially aggravated	High
Conspiracy to defraud	High
Conspiring or soliciting to commit murder	High
Counterfeiting	High
Criminal damage	Low
Criminal damage — racially aggravated	High
Criminal damage endangering life	High
Cultivation of cannabis	Medium

D

Demanding money with menaces	High
Driving whilst disqualified	Medium
Drunk and disorderly	Low
Drunkenness	Low

E

Endangering life or causing harm by administering poison	High
Endangering railway passenger by placing anything on rail, taking up rail, changing points or signals	High
Endangering railway passenger by throwing anything at railway carriage	High
Excess alcohol — driving	Medium
Excess alcohol — in charge	Medium

F

False fire alarm	Medium
False imprisonment	High
Forgery	High
Forgery of prescription	Medium

G

Genocide	High
Going equipped to steal	Medium

Grievous bodily harm with intent	High
Gross indecency with children	High

H

Handling stolen goods	High
Harassment	Medium
Harassment racially aggravated	High
Harassment with intent	High
Harassment with intent — racially aggravated	High
Hijacking	High

I

Importation/exportation of controlled drug	High
Incest with female under 13 years	High
Inciting female aged under 16 years to have incestuous sexual intercourse	High
Indecent photographs — making or possession	High
Indecent assault on female aged 16 or over	High
Indecent assault on female under 16	High
Indecent assault on male aged 16 or over	High
Indecent assault on male aged under 16	High
Indecent exposure	Medium
Infanticide	High
Interfering with a motor vehicle	Medium

K

Kidnapping	High

M

Making off without payment	Low
Making written or verbal threats to kill	High
Malicious wounding grievous bodily harm	High
Malicious wounding grievous bodily harm — racially aggravated	High
Manslaughter	High
Murder	High

O

Obstruct Police	Low
Obtaining pecuniary advantage by deception	Medium
Obtaining property by deception	Medium
Offensive weapon	Medium

P

Permitting use of premises for use of class A drug	High
Permitting use of premises for use of class B drug	Low
Perverting the course of justice	High
Possession of an article with a blade or point	Medium
Possession firearm/imitation firearm with intent to commit an indictable offence or resist arrest	High

Possession firearm/imitation firearm with intent to endanger life or injure property	High
Possession firearm imitation with intent to cause violence	High
Possession of class A drug	Medium
Possession of class B drug	Low
Possession of class C drug	Low
Possession of controlled drug with intent to supply it to another	High
Possession of explosive weapon	High
Possession of explosive weapon with intent to endanger life	High
Possession of firearm/imitation firearm at time of committing or being arrested for an offence under schedule I of Firearms Act 1968	High
Production of Class A or B drugs	High
Prostitution	Low

R

Railway frauds	Low
Rape — female	High
Rape — male	High
Riot	High
Robbery	High

S

Section 4 Public Order Act	Medium
Section 4 Public Order Act — racially aggravated	High
Section 4(a) Public Order Act	Low
Section 4(a) Public Order Act — racially aggravated	Medium
Section 5 Public Order Act	Low
Section 5 Public Order Act — Racially Aggravated	Low
Sending articles — offensive/indecent	Medium
Supplying or offering to supply controlled drug or being concerned in the doing of either activity by another	High

T

Telephone calls — making obscene	Low
Theft by an employee	High
Theft	Medium
Theft from the person	High
Theft from a shop	Low
Theft or unauthorized taking of mail	Medium
Threat or conspiracy to murder	High
Threat to commit criminal damage	Low
Trespass on a railway	Low
Taking a vehicle without consent TWOC	Medium

U
Unlawful sexual intercourse with female under 13   High
Using false prescription   Medium

V
Violent Disorder   High

W
Wasting police time   Medium
Witness intimidation   High
Wounding with intent to do grievous bodily harm   High

Youth Court Sentencing Matrix

	Low Risk of Re-offending	Medium Risk of Re-offending	High Risk of Re-offending
Offences of Low Level Seriousness	• Conditional discharge • Fine • Compensation • Reparation Order	• Conditional discharge • Fine • Compensation • Reparation Order	• Fine • Compensation • Reparation Order
Offences of Medium Level Seriousness	• Action Plan Order • Attendance Centre Order • Reparation Order	• Action Plan Order • Attendance Centre Order • Supervision Order • Rehabilitation Order • Community Punishment Order	• Action Plan Order • Drug Treatment and Testing Order • Supervision Order • Rehabilitation Order (with requirements) • Rehabilitation Order • Curfew Order
Offences of High Level Seriousness	• Action Plan Order • Supervision Order • Rehabilitation Order • Community Punishment Order • Community Rehabilitation and Punishment Order • Detention and Training Order	• Action Plan Order (high requirements) • Supervision Order • Rehabilitation Order • Community Punishment Order • Community Rehabilitation and Punishment Order • Detention and Training Order	• Drug Treatment and Testing Order • Supervision Order • Rehabilitation Order (with requirements) • Community Rehabilitation and Punishment Order • Detention and Training Order

The purpose of this table is to guide the court towards an appropriate sentence. The court must exercise judgement in deciding the type and length of sentence. The sentence must be suitable to the needs of the offender. Reparation orders must reflect the needs and wishes of the victim. Requirements in Action Plan Orders and Supervision Orders must address the causes of offending.

Reproduced from the Youth Court Bench Book published by the Judicial Studies Board.

CHAPTER 10
COSTS IN THE
MAGISTRATES' COURT

Introduction

The award of costs is an area of sentencing often overlooked by practitioners. This chapter examines the powers and procedures in the magistrates' court to make orders for costs in favour of the prosecution in addition to reviewing orders for costs which may be made by justices during the course of proceedings.[1] The power to award costs is set in statute and the justices' powers are often similar to the powers available in respect of costs in the Crown Court and the Court of Appeal. Although this book is aimed primarily at practitioners in the magistrates' court, statutory provisions relating to the superior courts have also been included for ease of reference.

Costs in Favour of the Prosecution

A convicted person may be ordered to pay costs towards the prosecution. The power to make such an award arises out of section 18, Prosecution of Offences Act 1985.

Section 18,
Prosecution of
Offences Act 1985   Where:

- any person is convicted of an offence before a magistrates' court;

- the Crown Court dismisses an appeal against such a conviction or against the sentence imposed on that conviction; or

- any person is convicted of an offence before the Crown Court;

---

1.   Part of this chapter has been taken from materials presented by the authors on behalf of Central Law Training and Progressive Legal Training in 2001 and 2002.

the court may make such order as to the costs to be paid by the accused to the prosecutor as it considers just and reasonable.

Where the Court of Appeal dismisses:

- an appeal or application for leave to appeal under Part I of the Criminal Appeal Act 1968; or

- an application by the accused for leave to appeal to the House of Lords under Part II of that Act; or

- an appeal or application for leave to appeal under section 9(11) of the Criminal Justice Act 1987;

it may make such order as to the costs to be paid by the accused, to such person as may be named in the order, as it considers just and reasonable.

The amount to be paid by the accused in pursuance of an order under this section shall be specified in the order.

Where any person is convicted of an offence before a magistrates' court and under the conviction the court orders payment of any sum as a fine, penalty, forfeiture or compensation and the sum so ordered to be paid does not exceed £5, the court shall not order the accused to pay any costs under this section unless in the particular circumstances of the case it considers it right to do so.

Where any person under the age of 18 is convicted of an offence before a magistrates' court, the amount of any costs ordered to be paid by the accused under this section shall not exceed the amount of any fine imposed on him.

Costs ordered to be paid may include the reasonable costs of any transcript of a record of proceeding made in accordance with rules of court.

An award of costs from the defendant to a prosecuting authority may only be made in the circumstances set out in the Act. The precedent for the making of such an order is that the defendant must be convicted in the course of proceedings in respect of which the order is to be made. There is no power for the amount of the order to be taxed and accordingly the amount payable must be stated in the order of the court. The amount ordered must be of a just and reasonable amount. The justices have no power to make an order for costs of their own motion and may not award a sum higher than that which is sought on application by the prosecution.

Where the total financial penalty ordered by the court[2] does not exceed £5 no order for costs can be made. Where a youth offender under 17 years of age is sentenced to a fine, the amount of costs may not exceed the amount of the fine.

Practice varies between the prosecuting agencies. It would seem that the Crown Prosecution Service seek a contribution towards costs rather than a sum reflecting the actual expenses incurred in bringing the case. Other central government agencies either follow the same practice or seek to recover in full the costs of the prosecution. Experience suggests that full orders are often sought on behalf of agencies such as the Environmental Agency, local authorities and the RSPCA.

There is no power to order payment of a prosecutor's costs from central funds where the prosecutor is a public authority. In the limited number of cases in which a private prosecutor is involved (i.e. not a public authority) his costs may be met from central funds. An order should be made save where there is good reason for not doing so where for example proceedings have been instituted or continued without good cause. The power to award a private prosecutor's costs is not therefore dependant on his securing a conviction however, the power to make such an award does not extend to the prosecution costs of summary trial.[3]

The award of costs is often an overlooked feature of the sentencing exercise. There is no power to remit an order for costs subsequently; although many court's adopt the practice where appropriate of seeking a consent from prosecuting authorities so to do. A prosecutor should ensure that he has full details of his claim for costs and the defence should be given an opportunity at the earliest time to consider the claim and be allowed to make representations to the court.[4]

A costs order may be made in respect of the costs incurred by the prosecution in the investigation of a case which results in the commencement of proceedings and a conviction. This principle appears more applicable to those situations where the investigating authority and the prosecuting agency are the same agency; for example the police are responsible for investigating crime and the CPS are responsible for conducting the prosecution. Accordingly, this principle would seem to prohibit an application for costs on conviction which included any

---

2.   Fine, compensation, forfeiture, confiscation of other penalty.
3.   See *Practice Note* [1991] 2 All ER 924.
4.   *R v Coventry Magistrates' Court ex parte DPP* [1990] 154 JP 765.

element relating to the investigation by the police. However, a prosecution by the Department of Trade and Industry is conducted, albeit through an agent, by the same department as is responsible for the investigation and accordingly a costs order in respect of both aspects appears lawful.[5]

Section 12,
Magistrates'
Courts Act 1980

Where a prosecution has been brought utilising the procedure in section 12, Magistrates' Courts Act 1980 the claim for prosecution costs must be notified in writing on the same document as contains the statement of facts. The clerk of the court conducting proceedings is under a duty to bring to the attention of the court such a claim for costs.

The Amount of Costs

Section 18,
Prosecution of
Offences Act 1985

Under section 18, Prosecution of Offences Act 1985 the sum payable to the prosecution on conviction must be limited to such an amount which is just and reasonable. A number of cases heard by the High Court have added further principles and explanations to the statute. Of particular recent importance is the decision in *R v North Allerton Magistrates' Court, ex parte Dove*.[6]

The principles in the *Dove* case together with others are summarised below:

- Costs should be kept in step with the level of the fine; however, where the defendant has the means to pay there is nothing wrong in principle with making an order which is substantially larger than the amount of the fine.

- Any order for costs should be within the means of the offender to pay so that it can be paid off within about 12 months. Recent decisions from the Court of Appeal have suggested that the period can extend to 2 or even 3 years but such an order would be exceptional.

- It is unlawful to make an order in such a sum where the offender has no realistic prospect of paying or in the belief that the sum will be met by a third party.

- Costs should only be ordered after a proper examination of the offender's means and where a custodial sentence is imposed an order should only be made if there are assets out of which the order can be paid.

- An order to pay costs to the prosecutor should never exceed the sum which, having regard to the defendant's means and

---

5.   *R v Associated Octel* [1997] Crim LR 144.
6.   [1999] Crim LR 760.

any other financial order imposed on him, the defendant is able to pay and which is reasonable to order him to pay.

- Such an order should never exceed the sum which the prosecutor has actually and reasonably incurred.

- Where the defendant has, by his conduct, put the prosecutor to avoidable expense, he may, subject to his means, be ordered to pay some or all of that sum to the prosecutor. But he is not to be punished for exercising a constitutional right to defend himself.

- The costs ordered to be paid should not, in the ordinary way, be grossly disproportionate to the fine.

- It is for the defendant facing a financial penalty, by way of a fine or an order for costs, to disclose to the justices such data relevant to his financial position as will enable the justices to assess what he can reasonably afford to pay. In the absence of such disclosure, the justices may draw reasonable inferences as to the defendant's means from evidence they have heard and from all the circumstances of the case.

- It is incumbent on any court, which proposes to make any financial order against a defendant, to give him a fair opportunity to adduce any relevant financial information and make appropriate submissions. If the court has it in mind to make ay unusual or unconventional order potentially adverse to a defendant, it should alert him and his advisers to that possibility.

- Where there are several accused it would be usual to consider what order would be appropriate if each defendant had been tried on their own but this principle could be applied differently where the principal offender was of sufficient means to bear the costs of the prosecution and stood to gain financially from the offences.

Accordingly a court should look at more than merely the claim for costs made by the prosecutor. The sum sought may be just and reasonable in terms of the sums incurred in the conduct of the proceedings but justices are able and required to assess any order by reference to wider issues in the proceedings. It is therefore legitimate to invite the court to take the following factors, amongst other things into account:

- The offender's plea;

- Any earlier tendered plea which was rejected by the Crown at an earlier hearing but which was accepted on the day of trial;

- The substantive sentence imposed;

- The conduct of the defence;

- The conduct of the prosecution; and

- Apportionment between defendants especially where sentencing takes place separately.

There appears to be authority for taking into account the reasonableness of the defence.[7] This may present some risks as a court must recognise and not punish the constitutional right to defend an allegation. Similarly the presumption of innocence recognised by Article 6(2) of the European Convention may impact on a court over-relying on this as a principle to determine costs. Nevertheless there is something apparently reasonable in linking the payment of additional costs in respect of unreasonable defences where such costs are directly incurred to meet such a defence.

Section 108(3)(a), Magistrates' Courts Act 1980

By virtue of section 108(3)(a), Magistrates' Courts Act 1980 there is no right of appeal against an order for costs *simpliciter* although an appeal against conviction or sentence is likely to result in a review of all penalties including costs.[8]

Defence Costs Orders from Central Funds

Section 16, Prosecution of Offences Act 1985

Costs may be ordered from central funds in favour of the defence in accordance with section 16, Prosecution of Offences Act 1985 where:

- any information laid before a justice of the peace for any area, charging any person with an offence, is not proceeded with;

- a magistrates' court inquiring into an indictable offence as examining justices determines not to commit the accused for trial;

---

7.   *R v Mountain* [1978] 68 Cr App Rep 41.
8.   See the section on appeals at page XX–XX above.

- a magistrates' court dealing summarily with an offence dismisses the information;

that court or a magistrates' court for that area, may make an order in favour of the accused for a payment to be made out of central funds in respect of his costs (a 'defendant's costs order').

Where:

- any person is not tried for an offence for which he has been indicted or committed for trial; or

- a notice of transfer is given under a relevant transfer provision but a person in relation to whose case it is given is not tried on a charge to which it relates; or

- any person is tried on indictment and acquitted on any account of the indictment;

the Crown Court may make a defendant's costs order in favour of the accused.

Section 108, Magistrates' Court Act 1980

Where a person convicted of an offence by a magistrates' court appeals to the Crown Court under section 108, Magistrates' Courts Act 1980 and, in consequence of the decision on appeal:

- his conviction is set aside; or

- a less severe punishment is awarded;

the Crown Court may make a defendant's costs order in favour of the accused.

Where the Court of Appeal

Part I, Criminal Appeal Act 1968

- allows an appeal under Part I, Criminal Appeal Act 1968 against

  - conviction;

  - a verdict of not guilty by reason of insanity; or

Section 4, Criminal Procedure (Insanity) Act 1964

- a finding under section 4, Criminal Procedure (Insanity) Act 1964 that the appellant is under disability that he did the act or made the omission charged against him; or

Section 8(1B),
Criminal Appeal
Act 1968
- directs under section 8(1B), Criminal Appeal Act 1968 the entry of a judgment and verdict of acquittal;

- on an appeal under that part against conviction:

  - substitutes a verdict of guilty of another offence;

  - in a case where a special verdict has been found, orders a different conclusion on the effect of that verdict to be recorded; or

Section 6(1)
  - is of the opinion that the case falls within paragraph (a) or (b) of section 6(1) of that Act (cases where the court substitutes a finding of insanity or unfitness to plead); or

Section 11(3)
  - on an appeal under that part against sentence, exercises its powers under section 11(3) of that Act (powers where the court considers that the appellant should be sentenced differently for an offence for which he was dealt with by the court below);

the court may make a defendant's costs order in favour of the accused.

Section 11(4),
Criminal Justice
Act 1987
The court may also make a defendant's costs order in favour of the accused on an appeal under section 11(4), Criminal Justice Act 1987 (appeals against orders or rulings at preparatory hearings) where:

- any proceedings in a criminal cause or matter are determined before a Divisional Court of the Queen's Bench Division;

- the House of Lords determines an appeal, or application for leave to appeal, from such a Divisional Court in a criminal cause or matter;

Part II, Criminal
Appeal Act 1968
- the Court of Appeal determines an application for leave to appeal to the House of Lords under Part II, Criminal Appeal Act 1968; or

- the House of Lords determines an appeal, or application for leave to appeal, under Part II of that Act;

the court may make a defendant's costs order in favour of the accused.

A defendant's costs order shall, subject to the following provisions of this section, be for the amount out of central funds, to the person in whose favour the order is made, of such amount as the court considers reasonably sufficient to compensate him for any expenses properly incurred by him in the proceedings.

Where a court makes a defendant's costs order but is of the opinion that there are circumstances which make it inappropriate that the person in whose favour the order is made should recover the full amount the court shall:

- assess what amount would, in its opinion, be just and reasonable; and

- specify the amount in the order.

The amount to be paid out of central funds in pursuance of a defendant's costs order shall:

- be specified in the order, in any case where the court considers it inappropriate for the amount to be so specified and the person in whose favour the order is made agrees the amount; and

- in any other case, be determined in accordance with regulations made by the Lord Chancellor for the purposes of this section.

Where a person ordered to be retried is acquitted at his retrial, the costs which may be ordered to be paid out of central funds under this section shall include:

- any costs which, at the original trial, could have been ordered to be so paid under this section if he had been acquitted; and

- if no order was made under this section in respect of his expenses on appeal, any sums for the payment of which such an order could have been made.

Part III, Costs in
Criminal Cases
(General)
Regulations 1986

Part III, Costs in Criminal Cases (General) Regulations 1986 apply to the making of costs orders out of central funds. They provide that costs shall be determined by the appropriate authority which shall be

- the registrar of criminal appeals in the case of proceedings in the Court of Appeal;

- the master of the Crown Office in the case of proceedings in a Divisional Court of the Queen's Bench Division;

- an officer appointed by the Lord Chancellor in the case of proceedings in the Crown Court;

- the justices' clerk in the case of proceedings in a magistrates' court.

The appropriate authority may appoint or authorise the appointment of determining officers to act on its behalf under these Regulations in accordance with directions given by it or on its behalf.

Timeliness

Subject to regulation 12, no claim for costs shall be entertained unless it is submitted within three months of the date on which the costs order was made.[9]

A claim for costs shall be submitted to the appropriate authority in such form and manner as it may direct and shall be accompanied by receipts and other evidence of the applicant(s) payment of the costs claimed, and any receipts or other documents In support of any disbursements claimed.

A claim shall:

- summarise the items of work done by a solicitor;

- state, where appropriate, the dates on which items of work were done, the time taken and the sums claimed;

- specify any disbursements claimed, including counsel's fees, the circumstances in which they were incurred and the amounts claimed in respect of them and

---

9.   Regulation 6, Costs in Criminal Cases (General) Regulations 1986.

Regulation 44(7),
Legal Aid in Criminal
and Care Proceedings
(General)
Regulations 1989

- contain either full particulars, including the date and outcome of any claim that Regulation 44(7), Legal Aid in Criminal and Care Proceedings (General) Regulations 1989 should be applied in respect of any work comprised in the claim under the Regulations, or a certificate by the solicitor that he has not made, and will not make, any such claim.

Where there are any special circumstances which should be drawn to the attention of the appropriate authority, the applicant shall specify them.

The applicant shall supply such further particulars, information and documents as the appropriate authority may require.

The amount of costs

The appropriate authority shall consider the claim, any further particulars, information or documents submitted by the applicant and shall allow such costs in respect of:

- such work as appears to have been actually and reasonably done; and

- such disbursements as appear to have been actually and reasonably incurred

as it considers reasonably sufficient to compensate the applicant for any expenses properly incurred by him in the proceedings.[10]

In determining costs the appropriate authority shall take into account all the relevant circumstances of the case including the nature, importance, complexity or difficulty of the work and the time involved.

When determining costs for the purpose of this regulation, there shall be allowed a reasonable amount in respect of all costs reasonably incurred and any doubts which the appropriate authority may have as to whether the costs were reasonably incurred or were reasonable in amount shall be resolved against the applicant.

---

10. Regulation 7, Costs in Criminal Cases (General) Regulations 1986.

Extension of time allowed

The time limit within which there must be made or instituted:

- a claim for costs by an applicant an application for a redetermination or a request for an appropriate authority to give reasons for its decision on a redetermination;

- an appeal to a costs judge or an application for a certificate under regulation 11; or

- an appeal to the High Court under regulation 11;

may, for good reason, be extended by the appropriate authority, the Senior Costs Judge or the High Court as the case may be.[11]

Where an applicant without good reason has failed (or, if an extension were not granted, would fail) to comply with a time limit, the appropriate authority, the Senior Costs Judge or the High Court as the case may be, may, in exceptional circumstances, extend the time limit.

An applicant may appeal to the Senior Costs Judge against a decision made under this regulation by an appropriate authority in respect of proceedings other than proceedings before a magistrates' court and such an appeal shall be instituted within 21 days of the decision being given by giving notice in writing to the Senior Costs Judge specifying the grounds of the appeal.

The powers set out in the Act and subordinate legislation are complemented by the 1991 Practice Note. This Note is not reproduced in these materials and practitioners should therefore familiarise themselves with it rather than relying wholly or in part on the summary provided in this text.

A number of principles have emerged in the application of these powers which are summarised below:

- The sum of costs ordered from central funds may be specified in the defendant's costs order or be postponed pending determination by the justices' clerk or his delegated determining officer.

- Once a costs order has been so determined an aggrieved applicant may seek its re-determination by that officer and/or obtain his reasons for his decision. There does not appear to be an obvious avenue of appeal unless the

---

11.   Regulation 12, Costs in Criminal Cases (General) Regulations 1986.

decision was taken in such a way as to invoke the jurisdiction of the High Court by way of an application for judicial review.

- The amount payable is such a sum as the court considers reasonably sufficient to compensate him for any expenses properly incurred in the proceedings. Accordingly not all expenses incurred by a defendant are necessarily recoverable from central funds. The taxing authority has first to resolve whether work has been actually and reasonably done and then consider what sum is reasonably sufficient to compensate the applicant for the expenses properly incurred.[12]

- The making of an order from central funds is discretionary. There exists no right to such an award. The certainty of this principle may be called into doubt by Article 6 of the European Convention where the failure to make an order may appear to be adverse to the presumption of innocence.[13] However the right is a limited right and the proper question is whether the approach under English law is incompatible with it.

- Generally a costs order from central funds should be made upon acquittal. In this sense acquittal includes the discontinuance, withdrawal, dismissal or staying of a charge or summons against the accused. In the Practice Note 1991 three situations were identified illustratively of circumstances where there may be reason to refuse to make a defendant's costs order. These were:

  (1) Where the defendant's own conduct has brought suspicion on himself and has misled the prosecution into thinking that the case against him is stronger than it is;

  (2) Where there is ample evidence to support a conviction but the defendant is acquitted on a technicality which has no merit;

  (3) Where the defendant is convicted of some charges but acquitted of others, the order may be for only part of the costs incurred where the court thinks it would be inappropriate for the defendant to recover all the costs.

---

12. *R v Leeds Magistrates' Court ex parte Castle* [1991] Crim LR 770.
13. *Sekanina v Austria* (1993) 17 EHRR 221.

- No order may be made in respect of a publically funded defendant. It seems likely that a similar arrangement will be in place to prevent an order being made where representation has been otherwise funded by the state after contracting.

- A claim for pre-representation order costs may be entertained provided that the representative can show that he has not and will not be making a claim to have that part of the costs paid for under retrospective funding arrangements. The position of this proposition was at the time of writing unclear as the Justices Clerks Society had issued guidance to magistrates courts' doubting whether there is power to deal with costs incurred ahead of the grant of a representation order, or in other circumstances where public funds are not available to cover expenses incurred in proceedings.

- Where a defendant is publicly funded there is no power to make an application in respect of costs which are covered by the representation order (this is the case where the fees provided through state funded representation are less than the actual commercial costs of representation. In other words central funds cannot be used to 'top-up' a public fund payment), nor can central funds be used to pay for costs not covered by the representation order, such as counsel not mentioned on the certificate.[14]

- A parent or guardian of a youth may also seek a defence costs order from central funds in the same way as any other applicant. This allows a local authority to make such an application.[15]

- Costs are incurred by a defendant within the meaning of section 16 if he is contractually obliged to pay them. Accordingly the court cannot require evidence to show that a defendant has actually paid his solicitor before making payment from central funds.[16] However, in *R v Miller*[17] the Divisional Court had regard to the Costs in Criminal Cases Act 1973. This legislation provided the scheme for defence costs orders prior to the Prosecution of Offences Act 1985. It was held that costs were incurred by an accused if he, as the client, was responsible or liable to his solicitors for the costs of his defence, even if a third party had in fact undertaken, or was also liable, to pay the costs. It was only

Costs in Criminal
Cases Act 1973
Prosecution of
Offences Act 1985

14. *R v Liverpool Crown Court ex parte the Lord Chancellor* (1993) 158 JP 821.
15. *R v Preston Crown Court ex parte Lancashire County Council* [1998] 3 All ER 765.
16. *R v Clerk to Liverpool Magistrates' Court ex parte Mccormick* (2001) *The Times* 12 January.
17. [1983] 3 All ER 186.

where there was an express or implied agreement which was binding on the accused's solicitors to the effect that in no circumstances would they seek to recover the costs from the accused that the costs ceased to be incurred by him.

- Compensation for a successful defendant's loss of earnings is not recoverable from central funds as it is not a 'cost incurred' in the proceedings. However, his reasonable subsistence and travel costs may be allowed.

- Generally courts will require sight of any correspondence between solicitor and client exhibiting the contract between them. Clearly it would be inappropriate for a court to award costs in excess of any agreed fee or in excess of any agreed hourly rate.

- In principle and practice a costs order from central funds need not be limited to public funds or equivalent rates, however the determining officer will usually apply rates of remuneration employed by the local taxing master as a starting point taking into account the complexity of the work.

- The Royal Courts of Justice have published a guide: *A Guide to the Award of Costs in Criminal Proceedings* (RCJ 1991 HMSO) setting out the statutory provisions and the practice direction together with further explanatory notes.

- The Justices' Clerks' Society has also published a guide to all magistrates' courts; *Taxation of Costs in Magistrates' Courts A Good Practice Guide 2002*. The Guide deals with documentation usually required, the determination stage including fees payable, the standard basis, the hourly rate and the assessment of work done, letters and telephone calls, care and conduct and disbursements. Although the Guide is not binding on magistrates' courts it provides the basis of the procedure usually adopted.

- In addition to the Good Practice Guide, many magistrates' courts have also published details of local arrangements and usually a copy can be obtained from the magistrates' courts office.

- As a general rule the determining officer will tax a bill of costs according to the type of work and the status of the solicitor he believes should have been reasonably able to conduct the case. This is known as the broad average costs basis. For example, a fee earner of partner status or with 10 years experience can expect to be granted a higher hourly rate than an assistant solicitor. However a partner would not necessarily have to be engaged to deal with a straightforward charge of driving without due care and attention. Such a case could be properly conducted by an assistant and accordingly the applicable hourly rate would be for an assistant notwithstanding that a partner in fact conducted the case. Letters and phone calls are generally allowed at a rate of one tenth of the applicable hourly rate. An uplift representing care and conduct is usually allowed on appropriate work excluding travel and waiting. This broad description applies to all claims but details may vary with each determining officer and practitioners would be advised to check local arrangements.

- Where a client and solicitor agree an hourly rate, it is appropriate for the claim for costs to be taxed on the basis of the agreement. The only question for the determining officer is whether it was reasonable for the client to have instructed the advocate in question. If it was, it is not appropriate for the determining officer to conclude that the advocate's hourly rate is unreasonable. Accordingly, costs should be awarded on the basis of the hourly rate. However, no allowance will then be made for care and conduct as may have been allowed on the broad average basis of costs method.

- Where an application for a defence costs order is delayed regulation 12(1) allows the court to extend the period for good reason. This power applies to the making of the initial application for costs and for the submission of the bill after the application has been granted.

- Regulation 12(2) is dealing with cases where there is no good reason for failure to comply with the time limit, in other words procedurally unmeritorious cases. The 'exceptional circumstances' must relate to something other than explanations for failing to submit the application in time.[18]

- Where a court makes an order for costs out of central funds, it must direct that the determining officer disallow any costs where it is plain that those costs were not properly incurred. It may also direct that the determining officer investigate the issue as to whether costs were properly incurred. According to paragraph 5.1 of the 1991 Practice

---

18. *R v Clerk to the North Kent Justices, ex parte McGoldrick* (1995) 160 JP 30.

Direction the determining officer should disclose the findings of his investigation to the party against whom the finding has been made and an opportunity provided to the applicant to make representations in respect of any sum it is proposed to disallow.

Costs Improperly Incurred

Section 19, Prosecution of Offences Act 1985

Section 19, Prosecution of Offences Act 1985 makes provision for orders as to costs in a number of different situations.

The Lord Chancellor may by regulation make provision empowering magistrates' courts, the Crown Court and the Court of Appeal, in any case where the court is satisfied that one party to criminal proceedings has incurred costs as a result of an unnecessary or improper act or omission by, or on behalf of, another party to the proceedings, to make an order as to the payment of those costs.

Regulations may, in particular:

• allow the making of such an order at any time during the proceedings;

• make provision as to the account to be taken, in making such an order, of any other order as to costs which has been made in respect of the proceedings or any grant of representation for the purposes of the proceedings which has been made under the Legal Aid Act 1988;

• make provision as to the account to be taken of any such order in the making of any other order as to costs in respect of the proceedings;

The Lord Chancellor may by regulations make provision for the payment out of central funds, in such circumstances and in relation to such criminal proceedings as may be specified, of such sums as appear to the court to be reasonably necessary:

• to compensate any witness in the proceedings, and any other person who in the opinion of the court necessarily attends for the purpose of proceedings otherwise than to give evidence, for the expense, trouble or loss of time properly incurred in or incidental to his attendance;

- to cover the proper expenses of an interpreter who is required because of the accused's lack of English;

- to compensate a duly qualified medical practitioner who

Section 11, Powers
of Criminal Courts
(Sentencing) Act 2000

- makes a report otherwise than in writing for the purpose of section 11, Powers of Criminal Courts (Sentencing) Act 2000 (remand for medical examination); or

Section 32(2),
Criminal Justice
Act 1967

- makes a written report to a court in pursuance of a request to which section 32(2), Criminal Justice Act 1967 (report by medical practitioner on medical condition of offender) applies;

- for the expenses properly incurred in or incidental to his reporting to the court.

Section 4A,
Criminal Procedure
(Insanity) Act 1964

- to cover the proper fee or costs of a person appointed by the Crown Court under section 4A, Criminal Procedure (Insanity) Act 1964 to put the case for the defence.

The Court of Appeal may order the payment out of central funds of such sums as appear to it to be reasonably sufficient to compensate an appellant who is not in custody and who appears before it on, or in connection with, his appeal under

Part I, Criminal
Appeal Act 1968
Part I, Criminal Appeal Act 1968.

Costs in Criminal
Cases (General)
Regulations 1986
Regulation 3
The Costs in Criminal Cases (General) Regulations 1986 apply.

Regulation 3 that where at any time during criminal proceedings:

- a magistrates' court,

- the Crown Court, or

- the Court of Appeal

is satisfied that costs have been incurred in respect of the proceedings by one of the parties as a result of an unnecessary or improper act or omission by, or on behalf of, another party to the proceedings, the court may, after hearing the parties, order that all or part of the costs so incurred by that party shall be paid to him by the other party.

Before making an order, the court shall take into account any other order as to costs (including any legal aid order) which has been made in respect of the proceedings.

An order shall specify the amount of costs to be paid in pursuance of the order.

Where an order has been made, the court may take that order into account when making any other order as to costs in respect of the proceedings.

No order shall be made by a magistrates' court which requires a person under the age of seventeen who has been convicted of an offence to pay an amount by way of costs which exceeds the amount of any fine imposed on him.

Paragraph 7.5,
1991 Practice Note

Paragraph 7.5, 1991 Practice Note supplements the regulations and provides that such an order is appropriate only where the failure is that of the defendant or of the prosecutor. Where the failure is that of the legal representative powers under section 19A to make a wasted costs order may be exercised.

Section 19A

Section 19

Under section 19 of the Act an order to pay costs thrown away may be made at any time during the proceedings. This allows the court to exercise its jurisdiction even after a notice of discontinuance has been served where the proceedings themselves were adjourned to a subsequent date.[19]

The amount of the costs to be paid must be specified in the order. There is no power to defer the order for taxation by the clerk to the justices or a determining officer. Before specifying the amount of costs the court should ensure that a bill of costs has been drawn up by the party claiming such costs and that the bill has been shown to the defaulting party. The party against whom an order is sought should have the opportunity to make representations on both the appropriateness of the order and on the sum in question.[20]

An order can only be made under this section where the costs in question have been incurred as a result of an unnecessary or improper act or omission. The word 'improper' does not denote some grave impropriety but is intended to cover an act or omission which would not have incurred if the party concerned had conducted his case properly; *DPP* v *Denning* (above). There must be a causal relationship between the unnecessary or

---

19. *DPP* v *Denning* [1991] 2 QB 532.
20. *Hutber* v *Gabriele* (1997) *The Times* 19 August.

improper act and the incurring of the costs to be paid under the order.[21]

It remains in dispute whether an order can be properly made under this section against the Crown Prosecution Service where the fault lies with the police. In some areas it is conceded by CPS that an order can be made in the course of ordinary prosecutions but not where the relationship between the police and CPS is more akin to a private client relationship such as in proceedings for a bind over. The difficulty of course is that if such an order cannot be made against CPS for the default of the police then the court has no power to mark improper acts or omissions as the police are not party to the proceedings. It would seem strange if the court can 'punish' a negligent review of a file by CPS but not the dilatory failure to provide video tapes by the police.[22]

It is also surprising to note how infrequently the magistrates' court resorts to using its powers to make orders as to costs thrown away. An improper act or omission can arise at any stage in the proceedings. If a party as a result incurs costs he would not otherwise have incurred an order should, at the least be considered by the court or sought by the 'innocent' party. The making of an order is not connected with a final determination of guilt or innocence although the court is required to take into account any other order as to costs in the proceedings.

Wasted Costs in Criminal Proceedings

Section 19A, Prosecution of Offences Act 1985

In criminal proceedings there is power to make a wasted costs order against a legal representative under section 19A, Prosecution of Offences Act 1985 which provides as follows. In any criminal proceedings:

- the Court of Appeal;

- the Crown Court; or

- a magistrates' court,

may disallow, or (as the case may be) order the legal or other representative concerned to meet, the whole of any wasted costs or such part of them as may be determined in accordance with regulations.

---

21. *R v Wood Green Crown Court ex parte DPP* [1993] 1 WLR 723.
22. The criminal justice legislation promised in the 2002 Queen's Speech is likely to include a power to make an order in respect of costs thrown away against a third party. If such a provision is enacted, this debate is likely to be consigned to the history books.

In this provision 'legal or other representative', in relation to any proceedings, means a person who is exercising a right of audience, or a right to conduct litigation, on behalf of any party to the proceedings;

The term 'wasted costs' means any costs incurred by a party:

• as a result of any improper, unreasonable or negligent act or omission on the part of any representative or any employee of a representative; or

• which, in the light of any such act or omission occurring after they were incurred, the court considers it is unreasonable to expect that party to pay.

Part IIA, Costs in Criminal Cases (General) Regulations 1986

Part IIA, Costs in Criminal Cases (General) Regulations 1986 deal with the making of wasted costs orders in criminal proceedings. This part of the Regulations applies to actions taken by a court under section 19A of the Act and

• 'wasted costs order' means any action taken by a court under section 19A of the Act; and

• 'interested party' means the party benefiting from the wasted costs order and, where he was legally aided, or an order for the payment of costs out of central funds was made in his favour, shall include the authority responsible for determining costs payable in respect of work done under the legal aid order or out of central funds as the case may be.

A wasted costs order may provide for the whole or any part of the wasted costs to be disallowed or ordered to be paid and the court shall specify the amount of such costs.

Before making a wasted costs order the court shall allow the legal or other representative and any party to the proceedings to make representations.

When making a wasted costs order the court may take into account any other order as to costs in respect of the proceedings and may take the wasted costs into account when making any other such order.

Where a wasted costs order has been made the court shall notify any interested party of the order and the amount disallowed or ordered to be paid.

Appeals

A legal or other representative against whom the wasted costs order is made may appeal:[23]

- in the case of an order made by a magistrates' court, to the Crown Court, and

- in the case of an order made at first instance by the Crown Court, to the Court of Appeal

An appeal shall be instituted within 21 days of the wasted costs order being made by the appellant's giving notice in writing to the court which made the order, stating the grounds of the appeal.

The appellant shall serve a copy of the notice of appeal and grounds, including any application for an extension of time in which to appeal, on any interested party.

The time limit within which an appeal may be instituted may, for good reason, be extended before or after it expires:

- in the case of an appeal to the Crown Court, by a judge of that court;

- in the case of an appeal to the Court of Appeal, a judge of the High Court or Court of Appeal,

and in each case the court to which the appeal is made shall give notice of the extension to the appellant, the court which made the wasted costs order and any interested party.

The court shall give notice of the hearing date to the appellant, the court made the wasted costs order and any interested party and shall allow the interested party to make representations which may be made orally or in writing.

The court may affirm, vary or revoke the order as it thinks fit and shall notify its decision to the appellant, any interested party and the court which made the order.

Recovery of wasted costs

Where the person required to make a payment in respect of sums due under a wasted costs order fails to do so, the payment may be recovered summarily as a sum adjudged to be paid as a civil debt by order of a magistrates' court by the party benefiting from

---

23.   See *Civil Appeals*, Chapter 4E (ed Sir Michael Burton, EMIS, Looseleaf) on Costs for more on such appeals.

the order, save that where he was legally aided or an order for the payment of costs out of central funds was made in his favour, the power to recover shall be exercisable by the Lord Chancellor.

In addition to the power to make a wasted costs order the Crown Court has an inherent jurisdiction to order a solicitor to pay costs thrown away by his or his staff's improper act or omission. No such power exists in the case of a magistrates' court other than the statutory power in section 19A of the Act.

Where a court is minded to consider the making of a wasted costs order it would be usual to hold the hearing in chambers and in the presence of a shorthand writer. In a magistrates' court such a hearing may also be held in camera and the clerk of the court should take at the very least a note of the proceedings. In any event a court making a wasted costs order should give its reasons in public.

The Court of Appeal gave guidance on the procedure under section 19A as also described in the 1991 Practice Note in *Re a Barrister (Wasted Costs Order)(No. 1 of 1991) 1993 QB 293*:

- There was a clear need for any judge or court intending to exercise the wasted costs jurisdiction to formulate carefully and concisely the complaint and grounds upon which such an order might be sought. Those measures were draconian, and, as in contempt proceedings, the grounds had to be clear and particular.

- Where necessary a transcript of the relevant part of the proceedings under discussion should be available. And, in accordance with the rules, a transcript of any wasted costs hearing has to be made.

- A defendant involved in a case where such proceedings were contemplated should be present if, after discussion with counsel, it was thought that his interests might be affected. And he should certainly be present and represented if the matter might affect the course of his trial. Regulation 3B(2) furthermore required that before a wasted costs order was made ' the court shall allow the legal or other representative and any party to the proceedings to make representations'. There might be cases where it might be appropriate for counsel for the Crown to be present.

- A three stage test or approach was recommended when a wasted costs order was contemplated:

  i. Had there been an improper, unreasonable or negligent act or omission?

  ii. As a result, had any costs been incurred by a party?

  iii. If the answers to (i) and (ii) were yes; should the court exercise its discretion to disallow or order the representative to meet the whole or any part of the relevant costs, and if so what specific sum was involved?

- It was inappropriate to propose any deal or settlement, for example that the representative might forgo fees. The judge should formally state his complaint, in chambers, and invite the representative to make his own comments. After any other party had been heard the judge should give his formal ruling. Discursive conversations might be unfair and should certainly not take place.

The Court of Appeal gave further guidance in *Ridehalgh* v *Horsefield 1994 Ch 205*.[24] The case arose in the course of civil proceedings but it was made clear that the principles set out by the then Master of the Rolls were equally applicable to wasted costs orders in the criminal jurisdiction.

1. 'Improper' covered any significant breach of a substantial duty imposed by the relevant code of professional conduct, as well as conduct which would be improper according to the consensus of professional opinion, whether it violated the letter of the professional code or not.

2. 'Unreasonable' described conduct which was vexatious, designed to harass the other side rather than advance the resolution of the case, and it made no difference that the conduct was the product of excessive zeal and not improper motive, since the acid tests was whether the conduct permitted of a reasonable explanation.

3. 'Negligent' was to be understood in an untechnical way to denote failure to act with the competence reasonably expected of ordinary members of the profession.

4. A legal representative was not acting improperly, unreasonably or negligently simply because he acted for a party whose action was bound to fail.

---

24.   Reported in full in *Costs Law Reports* Care Volume, EMIS Professional Publishing.

5. However a representative could not assist in proceedings which amounted to an abuse of process and was not entitled to use litigation in a manner for which it was not intended

6. The court deciding whether to make a wasted costs order should make full allowance for the fact that an advocate in court often had to make decisions quickly and under pressure.

7. The court should also take into account and make full allowance for legal professional privilege which might inhibit the advocate from making full explanation for his conduct. Having made such an allowance in cases of this type the court should make a wasted costs order only where the representative's conduct was plainly unjustifiable.

8. A solicitor seeking counsel's opinion did not abdicate his own professional responsibility. However the more specialist the advice the more reasonable it was for him to accept it.

9. The threat of wasted costs should not be used to intimidate a representative or to seek to exert undue pressure on a party to the proceedings.

10. Generally applications for wasted costs orders should not interrupt the course of a trial and should be dealt with at its conclusion.

11. The representative against whom the making of an order was being considered should be told very clearly what it was he was said to have done wrong. There was no right to disclosure generally and it was not appropriate for the applicant to interrogate the respondent. However he should have the opportunity to show cause why an order should not be made but this did not mean that the burden was on him to exculpate himself.

The Court of Appeal has offered further comments on the use of wasted costs orders and an order may be appropriate even where the representative concerned has no personal responsibility for the improper, unreasonable or negligent act or omission. For example where counsel failed to appear in court as a result of an error by his clerk a wasted costs order was properly made against him.[25] Similarly a sole practitioner could not rely on information given to him by instructing solicitors.[26]

---

25.   *Rodney (Wasted Costs Order)* Unreported December 9 1996.
26.   *Re a Barrister (Wasted Costs Order)(No 4 of 1992)* 1994 *The Times* 15 March.

In *Re a Barrister (Wasted Costs Order No 4 of 1993) 1995 The Times 21 April* the Court of Appeal again emphasised that before making such a Draconian penalty as a wasted costs order the court should fully take into account the daily demands of practice and the difficulties associated with time estimates.

In *Re P (A Barrister) (Wasted Costs Order) 2001 The Times July 31* counsel was acting for the defence in a criminal trial. His final speech to the jury gave the judge cause to abort the trial at a cost of £1,500. Counsel had, unwittingly, put forward his client as being of good character in contra-distinction to the victim. In fact the defendant had previous convictions but they were not before the jury. The judge decided that it was not possible to allow the prosecution to put the defendant's convictions before the jury and that it was improper to allow counsel's address to create the impression with the jury that the defendant was untainted as against the main prosecution witness' character. The judge went on to make a wasted costs order against counsel. On appeal it was argued that the judge should not have made the order because she had effectively made up her mind as to counsel's responsibility. This was dismissed. The trial judge was in the best position to have regard to all the parties conduct. The aim of the order was to compensate a side put to unnecessary expense rather than to punish the culpable and the jurisdiction was to be exercised fairly but summarily.

Although a Chancery case, further light was thrown on the extent of the power to make wasted costs by the decision of the Divisional Court in *Brown v Bennett 2001 The Times November 21.* In this case it was held against a complicated background of fraud and negligence that the court had power to make a wasted costs order against any lawyer in the proceedings and not only against the legal representative of the party making the wasted costs order. The liability of a barrister for a wasted costs order was not limited to his conduct of the proceedings in court but extended to his involvement in acting or advising on the proceedings in any connection, including his involvement in drafting or settling any document in the proceedings. An application for wasted costs was to be determined by reference to the question of whether, but for the conduct complained of, the costs in question would, on the balance of probabilities have been incurred.

Practitioners need to be able to identify when a wasted costs order is appropriate as opposed to an order for costs thrown away. Costs thrown away are ordered where the act or omission is of the party's making and wasted costs where the act or omission is of the representative's making.

Costs Paid by the Court

Section 19, Prosecution of Offences Act 1985

In certain circumstances costs may be recovered from the court in accordance with section 19, Prosecution of Offences Act 1985 and regulations made thereunder. Section 19 is reproduced in full above at page XX.

Part V, Costs in Criminal Cases (General) Regulations 1986

Part V, Costs in Criminal Cases (General) Regulations 1986 empowers the court to make an order for payment out of central funds of

* witness expenses

* the cost of obtaining medical reports, and

* interpreter fees.

Paragraph 4.1, 1991 Practice Note

Regulations 15 to 25 govern the payment of fees and expenses incurred by both professional and lay witnesses. Paragraph 4.1, 1991 Practice Note provides that if, and only if the court directs that such expenses as provided for in the regulations are not to be allowed can the expense of the witness be claimed as a disbursement out of legal aid. A witness includes any person properly attending to give evidence whether or not he gives evidence or is called, but it does not include a character witness unless the court has certified that the interests of justice require his attendance.

The award of expenses under this provision applies regardless of the outcome of the case against the defendant and whether or not the witness is required by either the prosecution or the defence.

A witness attending court to give a character reference is only entitled to receive witness expenses if the court has certified that his attendance was in the interests of justice. It is therefore important to obtain such a certification in the case of character witnesses.

The expenses set out in the order are met from central funds and the court is only able to authorise payment in accordance with the regulations. This may result in the order not meeting the actual expenses incurred and there appears to be no power to make any additional order in respect of the deficit. In the case of medical reports this can cause insurmountable difficulties for the practitioner.

The rates of allowance are set out in further regulations which change from time to time. Practitioners should ensure they are familiar with the financial constraints imposed on the court by the regulations before embarking upon the obtaining of reports or the attendance of witnesses. This may be of even more importance under the contracting system for state funded representation. The regulations in question are the *Costs in Criminal Cases (General) Regulations 1986 – Rates of Allowance.*

Civil Costs and Fees

Section 64,
Magistrates'
Courts Act 1980

Section 64, Magistrates' Courts Act 1980 provides for the power for justices to award costs in civil proceedings. Whilst the civil jurisdiction of magistrates has diminished over recent years the Crime and Disorder Act 1998 has created a number of preventative orders, applications for which are made in civil proceedings often based on criminal facts.[27]

On the hearing of a complaint a magistrates' court shall have power in its discretion to make such order as to costs to be paid either by the complainant to the defendant or by the defendant to the complainant as it thinks just and reasonable.

The amount of the order must be specified in the order[28] and there is no power to order taxation other than in the case of costs ordered by the Licensing Committee where there is power for taxation to be confirmed by the Committee at an adjourned hearing. The sum ordered should not be in excess of the proper costs incurred; not a penalty in the guise of costs.[29]

The amount ordered may include the expenses of the complainant's witnesses as well as the fee for his representative. The overall test is to award such costs as appear just and reasonable.

---

27. For example, anti-social behaviour orders, sex offender orders. For this reason it is not inappropriate to include the powers to make orders for costs in civil proceedings in a book on sentencing practice.
28. *R v Pwllheli Justices ex parte Soane* [1948] 2 All ER 815.
29. *R v Highgate Justices ex parte Petrou* [1954] 1 All ER 406.

Costs ordered in civil proceedings are *inter partes* and any enforcement measure depends on an application to the court under sections 92, 96, Magistrate's Courts Act 1980.

Costs, in civil proceedings generally follow the event and accordingly only the successful party to an action can be awarded costs. This rule does not apply in respect of licensed premises.

In the licensing jurisdiction costs may be awarded by the licensing justices. On any substantive application made to them (that is to say not in respect of matters falling within the competence of justices sitting in petty sessions) the licensing justices may make such order as they think just and reasonable for the payment of costs by the applicant to an objector or by an objector to an applicant: section 193B, Licensing Act 1964.

The application on which any order for costs depends must be in respect of licensed premises and accordingly no order can be made where the premises in question are merely proposed to be licensed. Costs do not follow the event and an unsuccessful objector could recover his costs from the successful applicant. The test to be applied is simply whether an order is just and reasonable. As a general rule the police should not be ordered to pay costs where they have fairly and reasonably objected to an application in line with their duty to prevent abuses of the licensing system.[30]

The amount of any costs to be paid must be specified in the order and there is no power for taxation. However there appears to be nothing wrong in principle with a bill of costs being considered by a determining officer who makes an assessment for comment, representation and affirmation by the licensing justices at a subsequent meeting.

Wasted Costs in Civil Proceedings

A provision similar to section 19A, Prosecution of Offences Act 1985 exists to allow the court to make wasted costs orders against a legal representative in civil proceedings. Section 145A, Magistrates' Courts Act 1980 provides as follows.

In any civil proceedings, a magistrates' court may disallow or (as the case may be) order the legal or other representative concerned to meet the whole of any wasted costs or such part of them as may be determined in accordance with rules.

Sections 92, 96, Magistrate's Courts Act 1980

Section 193B, Licensing Act 1964

Section 19A, Prosecution of Offences Act 1985 Section 145A, Magistrates' Courts Act 1980

---

30. *R v Crown Court at Merthyr Tydfil ex parte Chief Constable of Dyfed Powys Police* (1998) 46 LS Gaz R 35.

The term 'wasted costs' means any costs incurred by a party:

- as a result of any improper, unreasonable or negligent act or omission on the part of any legal or other representative or any employee of such a representative; or

- which, in the light of any such act or omission occurring after they were incurred, the court considers it unreasonable to expect that party to pay.

The term 'legal or other representative', in relation to any proceedings, means any person who is exercising a right of audience, or a right to conduct litigation, on behalf of any party to the proceedings.

Rules made by virtue of this section may, in particular, make provision as to the destination of any payments required to be made under the rules (including provision for the reimbursement of sums paid by the Legal Services Commission).

Rules made by virtue of this section:

- shall require a magistrates' court which proposes to act under the rules against a legal or other representative to allow him a reasonable opportunity to appear before it and show cause why it should not do so;

- shall provide that action may be taken under the rules either on the application of any party to the proceedings or on the motion of the court;

- shall provide that no such action shall be taken after the end of the period of six months beginning with the date on which the proceedings are disposed of by the court; and

- shall provide that a legal or other representative against whom action is taken under the rules may appeal to the Crown Court

The *Magistrates' Courts (Costs Against Legal Representatives in Civil Proceedings) Rules 1991* have been made.

The principles governing the making of wasted costs orders in criminal proceedings apply equally to civil proceedings and the rules have similar effect to Regulations 3A to 3D, Costs in Criminal Cases (General) Regulations 1986. As the majority of applications for wasted costs in the magistrates' court arise in criminal proceedings practitioners are advised to consider those principles.

Regulations 3A to 3D, Costs in Criminal Cases (General) Regulations 1986

The Enforcement of Costs

Where a defendant is ordered to pay the costs of the prosecution under section 17 of the Act or where he is ordered to pay costs thrown away under section 19 of the Act the order for costs shall be treated as if it had been adjudged to be paid on conviction. Accordingly its enforcement is by way of Part III, Magistrates' Courts Act 1980 in the same way as a fine or other financial penalty is enforced. There does not appear to be any power to remit an order for costs although a party may be invited to agree to such an action where enforcement is otherwise impracticable or impossible. Again the propriety of such a procedure may be questionable especially in the case of costs thrown away.

Part III, Magistrates' Courts Act 1980

An order that costs are to be paid by the prosecutor under section 19 for costs thrown away or under section 19A of the Act for wasted costs are enforced as a civil debt. Such orders are *inter partes* and it is unusual for a court to be invited to exercise its powers of enforcement under sections 92, 96, Magistrates' Courts Act 1980.

Sections 92, 96, Magistrates' Courts Act 1980

A Note on State Funded Representation, Article 6 of the European Convention

Article 6(3)(c) of the European Convention on Human Rights provides for the state's obligation to provide state funded legal representation to individuals charged with a criminal offence subject to the interests of justice and their financial means. The importance of legal aid, as it is effectively regarded in the United Kingdom is part of the limited right to a fair trial. In practice this means that not every case requires the state to provide legal representation and that not every case requires the provision of state facilitated legal representation to be free to the accused. Since the Human Rights Act 1998 came into force, the national courts in both Scotland and England and Wales have considered the compatibility of the national legislative system with this aspect of the right to a fair trial.

State funded representation of person's unable to afford their own representation where the interests of justice require it, is a fundamental aspect of the right to a fair trial in Article 6 of the European Convention. It follows that the legal system must have in place a process by which the costs of representation and the employment of resources in that regard are met either from state funds specifically designated for the purpose or from the resources of the agencies responsible for bringing criminal charges. Where an individual is party to civil proceedings there must be a system in place under which proper provision is made for the recovery of certain costs incurred in stating the case for judicial determination.

In *McLean* v *Buchanan 2001 The Times June 4* the Privy Council dealt with a case arising in Scotland. Advocates acting under the equivalent of legal aid found that their costs were likely to exceed the maximum fee payable for the type of offence faced by their client. The advocates continued to work after the maximum fee had been exceeded and claimed that the client's right to a fair trial was compromised by the cap on the maximum fee allowable under the legal aid order. It was conceded that the defendant could not fund the costs of his own representation and that the interests of justice required that he be provided with state funded representation. The Privy Council held that where an accused was entitled to legal aid and the expenditure likely to be incurred in conducting his defence would far exceed the fixed fee payable to his solicitor, it would not be incompatible with the right to a fair trial to continue when he had solicitors who were acting competently and had given no indication that they intended to withdraw. This decision sidesteps the genuine issue. Would there have been a breach if the solicitors had withdrawn and the defendant appeared in person claiming that his right to obtain legal aid had been violated?

In *R* v *Oates 2002 The Times May 20* the Court of Appeal decided there was nothing incompatible with Article 6 of the European Convention to suggest that justice required legal aid to be extended, in the absence of exceptional circumstances, to cover legal representation to present an oral argument to a full Court of Appeal on a renewed application for leave to appeal against conviction.

Costs on Appeal

Broadly speaking costs on appeal to the Crown Court against conviction and sentence follow the same principles described above. An appeal by way of case stated and applications for judicial review are made to the High Court and the principles governing costs are again broadly the same. The 1991 Practice Note provides additional guidance for practitioners. Of interest however may be the position of justices who decide to appear before the High Court in one form or another and their liability for costs.

Liability of Justices for Costs in Judicial Review

In *R v Newcastle-under-Lyme Justices ex parte Massey 1994 158 JP 1037* the Divisional Court decided that the following principles should be applied when determining the liability of justices for costs in judicial review proceedings.

1. the High Court has jurisdiction to award costs against justices in judicial review proceedings and on appeals by way of case stated and the Divisional Court has suggested that there is no reason for applying, at least in civil cases, different principles to each.

2. It is not in every case that a successful litigant can expect to recover his costs against anyone.

3. Justices who merely file affidavits and do not appear before the Court will not, without more, normally be visited with a costs order. This is so despite the fact that in judicial review proceedings justices are served with notice of the proceedings and are therefore party to them within the Supreme Court Act 1981.

4. Justices should not generally appear in the Court unless their *bona fides* are called into question or there are other exceptional circumstances. If they do appear they are unlikely to recover costs if successful, and they will be at risk of costs if they lose.

5. If justices do not appear, an order for costs in relation to the merits of the application or appeal is only likely to be made against them in exceptional circumstances, but justices should first be invited by the Court to appear to explain their apparently unreasonable behaviour.

6. Justices and other tribunals who decline to sign a consent in Crown Office civil proceedings in accordance with Practice Direction (Crown Office List: Consent Orders), so that costs of appearing before the Court are unnecessarily incurred by other parties, may, in an appropriate case, have an order for such costs made against them even if they do not appear.

7. An order for costs should be made where the justices behaved unreasonably in all the circumstances. The quality of the original decision, for example whether it was merely wrong in law or flagrantly perverse, albeit one of the factors for consideration, should not be determinative of the result. It is necessary to look at all the circumstances in which the justices or tribunal were invited to consent; these will include the attitude to the judicial review or appeal proceedings of the prosecution or other body which instituted the original proceedings, the information provided to the justices or tribunal and the time given to them to consider whether to consent, the type of consideration needed and the nature of the flaw in the challenged decision. The more obviously perverse, the more readily should consent be given and, if withheld, the more readily should costs be ordered.

8. No final costs order should be made by the Divisional Court or the High Court against justices without giving them the opportunity to be heard. The preferable route of challenge to such an order is an application to set aside rather than an appeal to the Court of Appeal. The time limit for an application to set aside is usually 7 days but it is appropriate for this to be extended to 21 days where the justices did not appear. The 21 day period runs from the receipt of the transcript by the justices.

Where justices have refused to state a case for the opinion of the High Court on the ground that the application was frivolous and have been informed that a High Court judge has subsequently granted leave to apply for judicial review, the justices must give proper weight to that decision. If they fail to do so and persist in the view that the application to state a case is frivolous, they may be ordered to pay costs of the substantive application for *mandamus*.

CHAPTER 11
ENFORCEMENT OF FINANCIAL PENALTIES

Preliminary issues

Two defendants face an identical offence, and their financial circumstances are the same. One is fined £100 and pays the fine in full, the other is ordered to pay £700, pays £10 and steps are needed to enforce the balance. Which of the fines has been most successful? The point being made is that collection of fines begins with the imposition of the initial figure. It is far more likely that a fine that is realistic will be paid than one that is beyond the means of the offender. It is a valuable point: when fixing a fine, the court is required to inquire into the financial position of the defendant.[1] Whilst the court must have regard to all the circumstances of the case, and the seriousness of the matter before it,[2] fixing an unrealistic fine might be the first factor in the need to issue enforcement proceedings.

However, it would be foolish to suppose that all fines will be paid, no matter how reasonable, and therefore a statutory framework has been created to allow magistrates' courts the means to enforce financial penalties. It should be noted that the magistrates are required to enforce Crown Court fines in addition to those imposed by the magistrates' court itself.[3]

This section does not consider the imposition of fines, which is covered elsewhere in this work, but instead considers the case of the defendant who has defaulted in payment of a financial penalty (including compensation and costs).

---

1. Section 128(1), Powers of Criminal Courts (Sentencing) Act 2000.
2. Sections 128(2) and (3), Powers of Criminal Courts (Sentencing) Act 2000.
3. Section 140(1), Powers of Criminal Courts (Sentencing) Act 2000.

First steps

When a sum to be paid is imposed, both the magistrates' and Crown Court have the power to dispense with immediate payment, and may order the sum be paid by a certain date, or be paid in instalments.[4] The same is true of compensation and costs.[5] This course of action should, however, be avoided if the sum can be satisfied forthwith.

It is possible for imprisonment in lieu of payment of fines to be imposed by a magistrates' court on the occasion of conviction. This may occur in the following circumstances:

(a) In the case of an offence punishable with imprisonment, the defendant appears to have sufficient means to pay the sum forthwith;

(b) It appears to the court to the court that the defendant is unlikely to remain long enough at a place of abode in the United Kingdom to enable payment of the sum to be enforced by other methods; or

(c) On the occasion of conviction the court sentences him to immediate imprisonment, detention in a young offender institution for that or another offence or he is already serving a sentence of custody for life, or a term of imprisonment, detention in a young offender institution, or detention in such an institution for life.[6]

In addition magistrates in lieu of payment of a financial penalty can order detention until 8 o'clock in the evening on the occasion of conviction.[7] They also have the power to issue a warrant of arrest that operates in a similar fashion (although in the case of such a warrant, the period of detention is until 8 o'clock in the morning of the day following arrest or, if the defendant is arrested between midnight and eight o'clock in the morning, until 8 o'clock on the day he was arrested.[8]

Where the Crown Court imposes a financial penalty, and circumstances similar to those matters listed at (a) to (c) above apply, it is required to consider whether a period of

4. In the Magistrates' Court this power is found in section 75(1) and (2), Magistrates' Courts Act 1980. For the Crown Court see section 139(1), Powers of Criminal Courts (Sentencing) Act 2000.
5. For example, see section 141, Powers of Criminal Courts (Sentencing) Act 2000.
6. Section 82(1), Magistrates' Courts Act 1980.
7. Section 135(1), Magistrates' Courts Act 1980.
8. Section 136, Magistrates' Courts Act 1980.

imprisonment should be imposed, suspended until such time that there is any default of any payment terms set.[9]

It is also worth noting another "enforcement" step that can be taken on the occasion of conviction and that is the power of both the Crown and magistrates' courts to order a defendant to be searched and to apply the monies to the sum imposed.[10] In addition, the magistrates are empowered to order such a search at a later hearing where the defendant is said to be in default of payments (a "means inquiry"hearing).[11] In either court, the money may be applied to the sum imposed or outstanding.

Notification of penalties

Where a magistrates' court:

(a) is tasked to collect a financial penalty imposed by a Crown Court, or

(b) has allowed time to pay a sum adjudged to be paid by summary conviction, or

(c) has allowed payments by instalments, or

(d) where a fine has been imposed in the absence of a defendant

that court must serve written notice on the defendant, stating the amount of the sum and, if applicable, the amount of any instalments, and the date on which any payment or instalments are to be paid. Such notice must be served on the defendant last known or usual place of abode, and if this is not done, a distress warrant cannot be issued.[12]

Enforcement powers

It is appropriate at this stage to consider those powers available to the court to enforce sums owed to it. It should be remembered that the chief role of the court in enforcement proceedings is to secure the payment of financial penalties, rather than to punish for non-payment. As a result, the ultimate step that may be taken in respect of outstanding financial orders (that of imprisonment)

---

9. Section 139, Powers of Criminal Courts (Sentencing) Act 2000.
10. Section 80(1), Magistrates' Courts Act 1980 and section 142, Powers of Criminal Courts (Sentencing) Act 2000.
11. Section 80(1), Magistrates' Courts Act 1980.
12. Rules 46(1) and (2), Magistrates' Courts Rules 1981.

should only be utilised where the court has tried, or for good reason ruled out, all other enforcement options.

Allowing further time to pay

The fact that there has been default in payment of a fine does not necessarily mean that the defaulter will go to prison or other drastic step must be taken. There may be a reasonable explanation for the default. In such circumstances, the court is able to simply order that there be further payments without any other sanction.[13] The court could consider setting a date to review whether payments have been made as required, and is empowered to issue a warrant in the event of non-attendance by the defaulter (assuming the sum remains outstanding). There would be no requirement to attend if the sum has been paid in full by the date scheduled for the hearing to take place.[14]

Distress Warrant

A distress warrant is a warrant issued, usually to bailiffs, to seize goods belonging to the defaulter and for these to be sold to satisfy the amount outstanding. Due to the fact that many courts use private firms of bailiffs, who will also seek to recover their costs in executing the warrant, and are entitled to do so, this is likely to be an expensive exercise for any defendant. It should be noted that if any person responsible for the actual execution of a distress warrant wilfully retains from the proceeds of the sale on which distress is levied, or otherwise extracts, any greater costs and charges than those properly payable, or makes any improper charge, he shall be liable on summary conviction to a fine not exceeding £200.[15]

Section 76, Magistrates' Courts Act 1980

The power for magistrates' courts to issue a distress warrant is found in section 76, Magistrates' Courts Act 1980. There is no requirement for the court to conduct a means inquiry before issuing a distress warrant,[16] and many courts consider such a

---

13. Section 75, Magistrates' Courts Act 1980.
14. Section 86, Magistrates' Courts Act 1980.
15. Section 78(5), Magistrates' Courts Act 1980.
16. *R* v *Hereford and Worcester Magistrates' Court, ex parte MacRae* (1998) 163 JP 433. However, where the court is considering the issue of a distress warrant at a means inquiry and the defendant is present, it would be appropriate to notify him of the court's intention to issue a distress warrant and to give him the opportunity of making representations (per *R* v *Guildford Justices, ex parte Rich* [1997] 1 Cr App R (S) 49). In *R* v *Hereford and Worcester, ex parte MacRae* (above) there was clear notification in the paperwork sent out by the court to defaulters that a distress warrant would be issued in the event of a default in payments, thus making the issue of the warrants without any hearing an open process.

warrant to be the first stage in the enforcement process.[17] That being said, it is still permissible to issue a distress warrant at a means inquiry, and the execution of the warrant can be suspended upon payment terms.[18] This can be particularly effective where the defaulter is ordered to make periodical payments whilst having sufficient goods to levy to satisfy the sum outstanding.

The issue of a distress warrant allows the person executing it to enter premises (and will not be deemed to be a trespasser in these circumstances even if there is a defect in the warrant).[19] The warrant:

(a) shall name or otherwise describe the person against whom the distress is to be levied; and

(b) shall be directed to constables or (more usually) civilian enforcement officers or private bailiffs named in the warrant and shall require them to levy the sum adjudged to be paid by conviction.[20]

Any goods seized must be sold by public auction or in such other manner as the defaulter, in writing, permits.[21] This auction will take place not earlier than the sixth day after the execution of the warrant as may be specified in the warrant, or in any other case, within a period beginning on the sixth day and ending on the fourteenth day after execution.[22] If the distress warrant is executed, but the sum to which the warrant was issued (and any charges in taking or keeping the goods) are paid before the auction or sale, the goods shall not be sold.[23]

In any event, a distress warrant does not authorise the person or persons executing it to seize the clothing or bedding of a defaulter or his family, nor any tools, books, vehicles or other equipment which he personally needs to use in his employment, business or vocation (unless the defaulter is a corporation).[24]

Once a distress warrant has been issued, part payment may be made to the person holding the warrant.[25]

---

17. See, for example, *R* v *Hereford and Worcester Magistrates' Court, ex parte MacRae* (above).
18. Section 77, Magistrates' Courts Act 1980.
19. Section 78(2), Magistrates' Courts Act 1980.
20. Rule 54(1), Magistrates' Courts Rules 1981.
21. Rule 54(6), Magistrates' Courts Rules 1981.
22. Rule 54(5), Magistrates' Courts Rules 1981.
23. Rule 54(7), Magistrates' Courts Rules 1981.
24. Rule 54(4), Magistrates' Courts Rules 1981.
25. Rule 55(1)(c), Magistrates' Courts Rules 1981.

Attachment of earnings orders

A magistrates' court may make an attachment of earnings order (AEO) in respect of any sum adjudged to be paid on conviction or treated as adjudged to be so paid.[26] Such an order is a direction to a defendant's employer to deduct a sum from the earnings of the defaulter to satisfy the outstanding sum.[27] An order cannot be made in respect of a person who is self-employed. This order does not require that there has to have been any default in payment, and the defendant can consent to the making of such an order.[28] However, if the court is intending to make an AEO of its own motion (rather than upon the application of, or with the consent of, the debtor) it must appear to the court that the defendant has failed to make one or more payments required by the court.[29]

When making an AEO, the court must fix a "normal deduction rate" and "protected earnings rate".

A normal deduction rate is the rate (expressed as a sum of money per week, month or other period) at which the court thinks it reasonable for the debtor's earnings to be applied to meeting his liability.[30] The protected earnings rate is the rate below which, having regard to the debtor's resources and needs, the court thinks it reasonable that the earnings actually paid to him should not be reduced (i.e. to protect the defendants take home pay, after the AEO has operated, from falling below the amount he requires to feed and clothe himself, etc.).[31]

An attachment of earnings order must contain sufficient information to enable an employer to identify the debtor.[32] Accordingly, the court may require the debtor to sign a statement detailing:[33]

a)   the name and address of any person by whom earnings are paid to him; and

b)   specified particulars for the purpose of enabling identification by the employer.

The court may also require this statement to provide specified particulars as to the defendant's earnings and anticipated

---

26.   Section 1(3)(b), Attachment of Earnings Act 1971.
27.   Section 6(1), Attachment of Earnings Act 1971.
28.   Sections 3(3B) and (3C), Attachment of Earnings Act 1971.
29.   Section 3(3), Attachment of Earnings Act 1971.
30.   Section 6(5)(a), Attachment of Earnings Act 1971.
31.   Section 6(5)(b), Attachment of Earnings Act 1971.
32.   Section 6(3), Attachment of Earnings Act 1971.
33.   Section 14(1), Attachment of Earnings Act 1971.

earnings, and his resources and needs.[34] In addition, the court may require any person appearing to be the debtor's employer to give to the court, within a specified period, a signed statement of specified particulars of the defendant's earnings and anticipated earnings.[35]

Deductions from benefits order

Where a defaulter is on income support or a jobseeker's allowance, a court may apply to the secretary of state, asking him to deduct sums from any amounts payable to the offender by way of those benefits.[36] The amount that will be deducted will be a fixed figure and this sum is altered periodically. It should be noted that the court may only *apply* to the Secretary of State for such deductions to be made – it cannot order that the deductions should occur. In addition, the court must enquire into the defendant's means before making such an application.[37]

Deductions from benefits may be applied for in respect of fines (including Crown Court fines), compensation, costs, and vehicle excise back duty and additional excise duties.[38]

Where an application is made for such an order, the court shall send a form to the Secretary of State detailing the following matters:

a) the name and address of the offender, and, if known, his date of birth;

b) the date when the fine was imposed of the compensation order made;

c) the name and address of the court imposing the fine or making the compensation order;

d) the amount of the fine or the amount payable by the compensation order as the case may be;

e) the date on which the application is made;

f) the date on which the court enquired into the defendant's means;

---

34. Section 14(1)(a)(ii), Attachment of Earnings Act 1971.
35. Section 14(1)(b), Attachment of Earnings Act 1971.
36. Section 24(1), Criminal Justice Act 1991.
37. Regulation 2(2), Fines (Deductions from Income Support) Regulations 1992.
38. Sections 24(3) and (4), Criminal Justice Act 1991.

g)   whether the defendant has defaulted in paying the fine, compensation order or any instalment of either;[39]

If the Secretary of State feels that insufficient information has been provided, he may request the court to provide further details.[40] It should be noted that there is no power for the Secretary of State to deduct from benefits unless the offender has defaulted in payments in respect of the fine, etc and he is aged at least eighteen years.[41]

Once an adequate application is received, it is forwarded to an adjudication officer who will in turn determine whether there is sufficient entitlement to income support or income-based jobseeker's allowance to enable deductions to be made.[42] The decision will then be notified to the court within 14 days of the Secretary of State receiving notification from the adjudication officer.[43] If other deductions are being made from the benefit, deductions in respect of fines may not be allowed.[44]

Where deductions are being made in respect of a financial order, those deductions will cease if:

a)   there is no longer sufficient entitlement to income support to enable deductions to be made;

b)   entitlement to income support ceases;

c)   a court withdraws it application for deductions to be made;

d)   the liability to make payment of the fine or under the compensation order has ceased.[45] The court should, so far as practicable, give the Secretary of State 21 day's notice of the whole of any sum having been paid.[46]

Payments of sums deducted from the relevant benefits shall be made to the court at intervals of 13 weeks.[47]

The fact that the court cannot control the amount of the deductions from benefits is not an attractive one to many magistrates. In addition, the court may find that some offenders, whilst receiving benefits, are able to pay more than

39.   Regulation 3(1), Fines (Deductions from Income Support) Regulations 1992.
40.   Regulation 3(3), Fines (Deductions from Income Support) Regulations 1992.
41.   Regulation 7(2), Fines (Deductions from Income Support) Regulations 1992.
42.   Regulation 4(1), Fines (Deductions from Income Support) Regulations 1992.
43.   Regulation 5, Fines (Deductions from Income Support) Regulations 1992.
44.   Regulation 7(1)(b), Fines (Deductions from Income Support) Regulations 1992.
45.   Regulation 7(4), Fines (Deductions from Income Support) Regulations 1992.
46.   Regulation 7(7), Fines (Deductions from Income Support) Regulations 1992.
47.   Regulation 7(6), Fines (Deductions from Income Support) Regulations 1992.

the statutory amount fixed by the legislation in any event, meaning it is more likely that "unsecured" higher payments are ordered by the court. However, given that magistrates are increasingly being told to ensure that all enforcement options are considered before imprisonment for default is imposed, a previous argument for not applying for deductions from benefits (being that the sum to be paid was too large and would therefore take a significant period of time to collect) has had significant doubt cast upon it. The option preferred by the appeal courts, where the sum is outstanding is large but where deductions from benefits have not been attempted, is to remit such of the outstanding sum as it is possible to do to leave a reasonable figure for payment.

Money payment supervision order

Magistrates may make a money payment supervision order (MPSO) on the occasion of conviction or on a subsequent occasion (so long as a period of imprisonment for non-payment is not being imposed).[48] A MPSO will place the defendant under the supervision of a person that the court will appoint (often a probation officer, although there is nothing in the legislation to require this). Where a defaulter is under the age of twenty-one, the court is prohibited from imposing imprisonment in default of payment unless it has first made a MPSO, unless a MPSO has previously been attempted, or where the court feels it is impracticable or undesirable to do so.[49] Where the court detains a young person without having made a MPSO, the reasons must be stated.[50] However, where the court wishes to utilise sections 135 or 136, Magistrates Courts Act 1980 (short periods of detention in court or police cells) it does not have to make a MPSO before doing so.[51]

Sections 135 or 136, Magistrates Courts Act 1980

Whilst a MPSO is in force, the offender cannot be committed to prison in respect of the outstanding sum unless the court has first taken reasonable steps to obtain an oral or written report from the person responsible for supervision.[52] This report should address the offender's means and conduct.

Whilst a MPSO is in force, it shall be the duty of the person with responsibility for supervision to advise and befriend the offender with a view to inducing him to pay the sum adjudged to be paid and thereby avoid committal to custody. That supervisor is also

48.   Section 88(1), Magistrates' Courts Act 1980.
49.   Section 88(4), Magistrates' Courts Act 1980.
50.   Section 88(5), Magistrates' Courts Act 1980.
51.   Sections 135(1) and 136(1), Magistrates' Courts Act 1980.
52.   Section 88(6), Magistrates' Courts Act 1980.

under a duty to give any information required by a magistrates' court about the offenders conduct and means.[53]

Attendance Centre Order

The court is able to make an attendance centre order in respect of an offender who is below twenty-five years of age and who has defaulted in payments. The court must first be satisfied that imprisonment for default is appropriate.

Enforcement in the High and County Court

It is possible for enforcement to be effected in the High and County Court, although given the complexity, time and expense, this type of enforcement would normally be considered where there is a substantial sum to be collected. Such proceedings take the form of an application by the Justices' Chief Executive of the Magistrates' Courts Committee for a judgment order. Such proceedings can only be taken where an inquiry into the defendant's means has taken place in accordance with section 82, Magistrates' Courts Act 1980 and it appears to the court that the defendant has sufficient means to pay the sum outstanding forthwith (i.e. that he has defaulted with no good reason).

Section 82, Magistrates' Courts Act 1980

The types of order that may be applied for under these provisions are:

a)   a garnishee order (allowing the debtor's bank and/or building society accounts to be frozen, and the funds from such accounts to be paid to the court in satisfaction of the amount payable);

b)   placing a charge on land or interest;

c)   the appointment of a receiver for land or rents and profits.

The power to remit

Whilst the power to order the remission of any fine would not appear to be on the face of it an enforcement power, it has a role to play when considering means inquiries. Reference has been made to the use of the power in conjunction with applications for deductions from benefits (see above).

---

53.   Rule 56, Magistrates' Courts Rules 1981.

Section 85, Magistrates' Courts Act 1980

The power of remission under section 85, Magistrates' Courts Act 1980 does not apply to orders for costs, nor vehicle excise back duty or confiscation orders, but only to fines.[54] There is a separate power to review compensation orders under section 133, Powers of Criminal Courts (Sentencing) Act 2000, although this is available where civil proceedings reveal the extent of a loss to be less than awarded by way of compensation; that the property in respect of which compensation was ordered has been recovered; where the means of the person ordered to pay compensation are not sufficient to meet both that order and any confiscation order made in the same proceedings; or where the offender has suffered a substantial reduction in his means (that was unexpected when the compensation was imposed and is unlikely to improve for a considerable period) (per section 133(3)(a)–(d), Powers of Criminal Courts (Sentencing) Act 2000).

Section 133, Powers of Criminal Courts (Sentencing) Act 2000

Section 133(3) (a)–(d), Powers of Criminal Courts (Sentencing) Act 2000)

The power to remit in relation to fines may be exercised at any time if the court thinks it just to do so having regard to a change of circumstances which has occurred since the date of conviction, or since a suspended period of imprisonment has been imposed.[55] An order to remit fines may be an order to remit the whole or any part of the sum outstanding. If a magistrates' court is considering the remission of a fine imposed by the Crown Court, it must first obtain the consent of that other court.[56]

In addition to the power to remit a fine due to a change in circumstances, the amount of any fine imposed can also be adjusted by remission where more information as to an offender's financial circumstances have come to light.[57] This power is may be exercised if, having imposed a fine, the court subsequently inquires into the defendant's financial circumstances, it is satisfied that it would have fixed a smaller sum or not imposed a fine, the court may remit the whole or any part of the amount outstanding.

In the case of any decision to remit an outstanding sum, if the court has previously fixed a period of committal in respect of non-payment, the balance to be served under the order for committal shall be reduced to take into account the adjustment.

---

54. Whilst the definition of "fine" found in section 150(1), Magistrates' Court Act 1980 includes any pecuniary penalty or pecuniary forfeiture or pecuniary compensation payable under a conviction this wider definition is disapplied for the purposes of the power to remit a fine by virtue os section 85(4), Magistrates' Courts Act 1980.
55. Section 85(1), Magistrates' Courts Act 1980.
56. Section 140(5), Powers of Criminal Courts (Sentencing) Act 2000.
57. Section 129, Powers of Criminal Courts (Sentencing) Act 2000.

Imprisonment

As mentioned above, this is the ultimate sanction so far as enforcement of financial penalties is concerned.

In this part, the term imprisonment and committal may be used for ease of reference to describe a custodial disposal in respect of non-payment of financial orders. However, the term "imprisonment" would apply where the offender is aged twenty-one years or older. Where committal takes place in respect of an offender aged twenty years or younger, the term "detention" would apply. It is important to note that there is no power to order the committal of an offender aged 17 years or less.

Assuming that the court did not utilise its limited powers to order committal on the occasion of the defendant's conviction (see above), the court must have held an inquiry into the defendant's financial circumstances, in his presence, on at least one occasion before any committal can be ordered (unless the offender is a serving prisoner).[58] At this means inquiry, or on a later occasion, the court must not issue a warrant committing the defendant to custody unless:

a) where the offence is punishable with imprisonment, the offender appears to have sufficient means to pay the sum forthwith; or

b) the court –

  i.   is satisfied that the default is due to the offender's wilful refusal or culpable neglect; and

  ii.   has considered or tried all other methods of enforcing payment of the sum and it appears to the court that they are inappropriate or unsuccessful.[59]

When considering the question of culpable neglect and wilful refusal, the court must be satisfied that there is some causative link between the neglect or refusal, and the failure to make payment.[60]

The other methods of enforcement that must be expressly considered by the court before imposing any committal are a distress warrant, application for enforcement to the High Court or County Court, attachment of earnings order and, if the offender is below twenty-five years of age, an attendance centre order.[61] It will be noted from this list that not all other

---

58. Section 82(3), Magistrates' Courts Act 1980.
59. Section 82(4), Magistrates' Courts Act 1980.
60. *R v Manchester City Magistrates' Court, ex parte Davies* [1989] 1 All ER 90.
61. Section 82(4A), Magistrates' Courts Act 1980.

enforcement measures need to be considered. However, as a matter of good practice we are of the opinion that the court should, for example, explain why deductions from benefit should not be applied for and, even in the case of an adult offender, why a MPSO is not appropriate. The reasons for not utilising these other enforcement methods, or the failure of these measures, should be recorded and be marked on the face of any committal warrant.[62] When considering the enforcement options, we would also suggest that the court make reference to the power to remit, and explain why this power has not been used.

Where the court determines that a period of imprisonment should be imposed, but suspends the operation of this committal upon payments or such other terms as it thinks fit,[63] and there is further default, the court can then issue a warrant of commitment. However, the court must not issue such a warrant unless the defendant has been served with written notice of the date and time and place when this warrant will be considered.[64] The defendant is entitled to attend the hearing, or make representations in writing, if he contends that there are grounds why the warrant should not be issued.[65] However, where a defaulter does not attend, not having made written representations, the court should consider issuing a warrant[66] to secure his attendance at a means inquiry hearing before moving on to actually issue the committal warrant.

At any hearing where committal is being considered, the court[67] may order the offender to furnish it with a statement of means.[68] A failure to comply with such an order is an offence, punishable with a fine of up to £1000.[69] Further, if false information is knowingly or recklessly provided, or an attempt is made to conceal a material particular an offence punishable with 4 months imprisonment and/or a fine of up to £1000 is committed.[70]

Where committal takes place, the sums in respect of that committal are wiped out. This also applies where the committal is

62. In re *Cawley and others* (1995) 28 November.
63. In accordance with section 77(2), Magistrates' Courts Act 1980.
64. Section 82(5A) and (5C)(a), Magistrates' Courts Act 1980.
65. Section 82(5C)(b).
66. A power conferred on the court by virtue of section 83, Magistrates' Courts Act 1980.
67. This power is also exercisable by a single justice by virtue of section 84(1), Magistrates' Courts Act 1980, and also a Justices Clerk or Justices' Clerk's assistant so delegated (Justices Clerks Rules 1999).
68. Section 84(1), Magistrates' Courts Act 1980.
69. Section 84(2), Magistrates' Courts Act 1980.
70. section 84(3), Magistrates' Courts Act 1980.

in respect of costs and compensation. In the event that a defendant is committed in respect of compensation, the compensatee would have to recover his losses through the civil courts.

Schedule 4,
Magistrates'
Courts Act 1980

Schedule 4, Magistrates' Courts Act 1980 and section 319, Powers of Criminal Courts Sentencing Act 2000 provide the relevant maximum periods of committal that may be imposed in respect of a sum of money. These are:

Magistrates' Courts:	
An amount not exceeding £200	7 days
An amount exceeding £200 but not exceeding £500	14 days
An amount exceeding £500 but not exceeding £1,000	28 days
An amount exceeding £1,000 but not exceeding £2,500	45 days
An amount exceeding £2,500 but not exceeding £5,000	3 months
An amount exceeding £5,000 but not exceeding £10,000	6 months
An amount exceeding £10,000	12 months
Crown Court	
An amount not exceeding £200	7 days
An amount exceeding £200 but not exceeding £500	14 days
An amount exceeding £500 but not exceeding £1,000	28 days
An amount exceeding £1,000 but not exceeding £2,500	45 days
An amount exceeding £2,500 but not exceeding £5,000	3 months
An amount exceeding £5,000 but not exceeding £10,000	6 months
An amount exceeding £10,000 but not exceeding £20,000	12 months
An amount exceeding £20,000 but not exceeding £50,000	18 months
An amount exceeding £50,000 but not exceeding £100,000	2 years
An amount exceeding £100,000 but not exceeding £250,000	3 years
An amount exceeding £250,000 but not exceeding £1 million	5 years
An amount exceeding £1 million	10 years

Section 140,
Powers of Criminal
Courts (Sentencing)
Act 2000

Where magistrates are required to enforce a sum imposed by the Crown Court in accordance with section 140, Powers of Criminal Courts (Sentencing) Act 2000 they may use the Crown Court period described above where the figure is sufficiently large to require this. It should be noted, however that the periods are the *maximum* period, rather than the period that automatically applies. The court must still apply its mind judicially to the length of any period of committal. The only caveat to this is that 7 days is the *minimum* period that can be imposed in respect of non-payment of financial penalties.[71]

As mentioned elsewhere in this part, the key aim of enforcement is to secure payment. In such circumstances, and differentiating the position of the offender who is already serving a custodial sentence, there is strong argument for suggesting that in the first instance committal should be suspended to give the defaulter an opportunity to make payments. In any event, given that there is a problem with prison overcrowding, the appeal courts are likely to find fault with an order for committal unless the processes leading up to that decision have been rigorous. Fault could lie in something apparently as simple as not having warned the offender of the sanctions available to the court and enquiring whether he wishes to be represented by a solicitor in those circumstances.

---

71.   Paragraph 2(2), Schedule 4, Magistrates' Courts Act 1980.

CHAPTER 12
ROAD TRAFFIC

Introduction

The majority of offences under the road traffic legislation are punishable by fine only. Certain offences, however, are punishable with imprisonment and therefore all penalties in the community punishment range of orders are potentially available to the sentencing court. The punishment of road traffic offences falls within the usual approach to sentencing and accordingly, sentencers will have regard to the seriousness of the offence and aggravating and mitigating factors associated with it.

The most important feature of road traffic offences is that many offences carry obligatory endorsement and discretionary disqualification from driving. Certain offences carry mandatory disqualification. In either case, the offender's past record, as it relates to road traffic offences is of significance in the sentencing process. The sentencing regime is set out in the Road Traffic Offenders Act 1988.

Road Traffic
Offenders Act 1988

The following text sets out the sentencing regime for road traffic offences.

Endorsement of licences

Where a person is convicted of an offence involving obligatory endorsement, the court must order there to be endorsed on any licence held by him particulars of the conviction[1] and also:

- if the court orders him to be disqualified, particulars of the disqualification; or

---

1. Section 44, Road Traffic Offenders Act 1988.

- if the court does not order him to be disqualified:

  - particulars of the offence, including the date when it was committed; and

  - the penalty points to be attributed to the offence.

Where the court does not order the person convicted to be disqualified, it need not make an order for endorsement if for special reasons it thinks fit not to do so.

Effect of endorsement

An order that any particulars or penalty points are to be endorsed on any licence held by the person convicted shall, whether he is at the time the holder of a licence or not, operate as an order that any licence he may then hold or may subsequently obtain is to be so endorsed until he becomes entitled to have a licence issued to him free from the particulars or penalty points.

On the issue of a new licence to a person, any particulars or penalty points ordered to be endorsed on any licence held by him shall be entered on the licence unless he has become entitled to have a licence issued to him free from those particulars or penalty points.

If a person whose licence has been ordered to be endorsed with any particulars or penalty points applies for or obtains a licence without giving particulars of the order when he has not previously become entitled to have a licence issued to him free from those particulars or penalty points, he is guilty of an offence and any licence so obtained shall be of no effect.

A person whose licence has been ordered to be endorsed is entitled to have a new licence issued to him free from the endorsement if, after the end of the period for which the endorsement remains effective, he applies for a new licence, surrenders any subsisting licence, pays the fee prescribed by regulations and satisfies the other general requirements for the grant of a licence.

An endorsement ordered on a person's conviction of an offence remains effective until:

- if an order is made for the disqualification of the offender, four years have elapsed since the conviction; and

- if no such order is made, either:

  - until four years have elapsed since the commission of the offence; or

  - such an order is made.

Where the offence was one of causing death by dangerous driving or dangerous driving, the endorsement remains in any case effective until four years have elapsed since the conviction.

Where the offence was one of driving when under influence of drink or drugs or driving with alcohol concentration above prescribed limit or failing to provide specimen involving obligatory disqualification, the endorsement remains effective until eleven years have elapsed since the conviction.[2]

Production of licence

Section 44

Where a person who is the holder of a licence is convicted of an offence involving obligatory endorsement, the court must, before making any order under section 44 of the Act, require the licence to be produced to it.[3]

If the holder of the licence has not caused it to be delivered, or posted it, and does not produce it as required then, unless he satisfies the court that he has applied for a new licence and has not received it:

- he is guilty of an offence; and

- the licence shall be suspended from the time when its production was required until it is produced to the court and shall, while suspended, be of no effect.

The suspension of the offender's driving licence is automatic and does not require the court to make an order. Upon suspension, an offender's insurance to drive is likely to be ineffective, as the majority of policies require the driver to hold a valid licence. An offender who drives whilst his licence is suspended is driving otherwise in accordance with a driving licence and is not driving whilst disqualified. The suspension appears to lapse as soon as the licence is produced to the court

---

2. Section 45, Road Traffic Offenders Act 1988.
3. Section 27, Road Traffic Offenders Act 1988.

Section 56, Road
Traffic Offenders
Act 1988

The suspension does not apply where the holder of the licence has caused a current receipt for the licence issued under section 56, Road Traffic Offenders Act 1988 to be delivered to the clerk of the court not later than the day before the date appointed for the hearing, or has posted such a receipt, at such time that in the ordinary course of post it would be delivered not later than that day, in a letter duly addressed to the clerk and either registered or sent by the recorded delivery service, or surrenders such a receipt to the court at the hearing, and produces the licence to the court immediately on its return.

Penalty points to be attributed to an offence

Where a person is convicted of an offence involving obligatory or discretionary disqualification, the number of penalty points to be attributed to the offence, is:

Schedule 2, Road
Traffic Offenders
Act 1988

- the number shown against the provision or offence in the last column of Schedule 2, Road Traffic Offenders Act 1988,[4] where a range of numbers is so shown, a number falling within the range; and

- in the case of an offence committed by aiding, abetting, counselling or procuring, or inciting to the commission of, an offence involving obligatory disqualification, ten penalty points.

For example, an offender convicted of speeding may be fined and his licence endorsed with between 3 and 6 penalty points.

Where a person is convicted (whether on the same occasion or not) of two or more offences committed on the same occasion, and involving obligatory endorsement, the total number of penalty points to be attributed to them is the number or highest number that would be attributed on a conviction of one of them (so that if the convictions are on different occasions the number of penalty points to be attributed to the offences on the later occasion or occasions shall be restricted accordingly).

For example, an offender convicted of speeding and driving with a defective tyre on the same occasion may be fined and his licence endorsed with a maximum between 3 and 6 penalty points. In order to exceed 3 penalty points the points would have to be attributed to the speeding offence. The driving licence is also endorsed with the offence to which penalty

---

4. In addition to specifying the penalty points attributable to offences, the Schedule describes the maximum penalties for each offence under the road traffic legislation.

points are not attributed, in this example the defective tyre, but no penalty points are shown against the endorsement.

However, section 28(5), Road Traffic Offenders Act 1988 allows the court, if it thinks fit, to disapply this protection. If an offender is convicted of two or more endorseable offences committed on the same occasion, the court may order penalty points to be attributed to both (or as many offences as there might be).

For example, in the previous example, the court could order that penalty points be attributed to both offences. If this was the order of the court, the offender's driving licence would be endorsed with both offences and penalty points in the range of 3 to 6 for the speeding offence plus 3 penalty points for the defective tyre, giving a total of 9 penalty points to be taken into account on subsequent conviction in respect of these offences.

Where a court uses these additional powers, it must state in open court its reasons for doing so and must record the reasons in the register.

The term 'same occasion' is not defined but it has been persuasively suggested[5] that there must be a physical nexus between offences in order that they be properly considered to be committed on the same occasion. For the practitioner, one of the issues to be considered here is whether offences detected by way of unmanned camera can be considered to have been committed on the same occasion where they are committed in the course of a single journey but separated by several miles.

Penalty points to be taken into account on conviction

Where a person is convicted of an offence involving obligatory or discretionary disqualification, the penalty points to be taken into account on that occasion[6] are:

- any that are to be attributed to the offence or offences of which he is convicted; and

---

5.   *Johnson* v *Over* (1984) 149 JP 286.
6.   Section 29, Road Traffic Offences Act 1988.

- any that were on a previous occasion ordered to be endorsed on any licence held by him, unless the offender has since that occasion and before the conviction been disqualified under section 34 or 35, Road Traffic Offenders Act 1988.

Section 34 or 35,
Road Traffic
Offenders Act 1988

If any of the offences was committed more than three years before another, the penalty points in respect of that offence shall not be added to those in respect of the other.

For example, an offender is convicted of two offences of speeding committed on different occasions. The penalty points to be taken into account on conviction will be those attributed to each offence, namely between 6 and 12 penalty points (3 to 6 on each offence totalled together).

For example, an offender is convicted of driving with a defective tyre. The offence was committed on 1 February 2003. He was convicted on 1 March 2003. His driving licence shows that he has previously committed the like offence on two occasions in the past. The first endorsement shows an offence on 31 January 2000 and the second on 12 March 2000. On each occasion the court imposed 3 penalty points.

For the purpose of taking into account penalty points on conviction the court must add those imposed for an offence within 3 years of the commission of the offence for which the offender is to be sentenced. This can be expressed as date of offence to date of offences within three years. In the example, there would be 6 penalty points to be taken into account (3 for the new offence and 3 in respect of the offence 12 March 2000).

Penalty points: modification where fixed penalty also in question

Where:

- a person is convicted of an offence involving obligatory or discretionary disqualification; and

Section 57 or 77,
Road Traffic
Offenders Act 1988

- the court is satisfied that his licence has been or is liable to be endorsed under section 57 or 77, Road Traffic Offenders Act 1988 (penalty points imposed on the acceptance of a fixed penalty) in respect of an offence (the "connected offence") committed on the same occasion as the offence of which he is convicted;

- the number of penalty points to be attributed to the offence of which he is convicted is;

Section 28(1)
- the number of penalty points to be attributed to that offence under section 28(1) of the Act apart from this section; less

the number of penalty points required to be endorsed on his licence in respect of the connected offence.

For example, an offender is stopped by the police for speeding. He is offered and accepts a fixed penalty carrying 3 penalty points but is also reported for driving the vehicle without insurance. On conviction for no insurance he is liable to between 6 and 8 penalty points. The court is required to determine the number of points to be attributed to the offence and then to deduct the points attributed by virtue of the fixed penalty. Thus, where the court decides to impose 6 penalty points for no insurance, it will order the licence to be endorsed with only 3 to reflect the fact that a fixed penalty was imposed at the same time, leaving the licence endorsed with the correct number of penalty points required by section 28 of the Act (6 − 3 (+3 fixed penalty) = 6).

Court may take particulars endorsed on licence into consideration

Where a person is convicted of an offence involving obligatory endorsement and his licence is produced to the court:

- any existing endorsement on his licence is *prima facie* evidence of the matters endorsed; and

- the court may, in determining what order to make in pursuance of the conviction, take those matters into consideration.

Disqualification

The court may disqualify an offender from driving in respect of any endorseable offence. The court may also disqualify an offender in respect of certain offences which do not carry endorsement such as taking a vehicle without the consent of the owner under section 12, Theft Act 1968. The court also has power to disqualify without endorsement in respect of certain offences in the course of which the offender used a motor vehicle.[7]

Section 12,
Theft Act 1968

---

7.   See the section of ancillary orders above at page XX.

The court is also required to disqualify an offender from driving in respect of certain offences unless there exist special reasons to avoid disqualification.

Disqualification for certain offences

Compulsory disqualification

Where a person is convicted of an offence involving obligatory disqualification, the court must order him to be disqualified for such period not less than twelve months as the court thinks fit unless the court for special reasons thinks fit to order him to be disqualified for a shorter period or not to order him to be disqualified.[8]

Schedule 2 to the Act sets out those offences to which this provision applies.

Discretionary disqualification

Where a person is convicted of an offence involving discretionary disqualification, and either:

• the penalty points to be taken into account on that occasion number fewer than twelve; or

• the offence is not one involving obligatory endorsement,[9]

the court may order him to be disqualified for such period as the court thinks fit.[10]

Schedule 2 to the Act sets out those offences to which this provision applies.

Increase in minimum period of mandatory disqualification

Road Traffic Act 1988

Where a person convicted of an offence under any of the following provisions of the Road Traffic Act 1988:

Section 4(1)

• section 4(1) (driving or attempting to drive while unfit);

Section 3A

• section 3A (causing death by careless driving when under the influence of drink or drugs);

Section 5(1)(a)

• section 5(1)(a) (driving or attempting to drive with excess alcohol); and

---

8. Section 34(1), Road Traffic Offenders Act 1988.
9. Such as an offence allowing the court to impose a period of disqualification but which does not carry an endorsement.
10. Section 34(2), Road Traffic Offenders Act 1988.

Section 7(6)

- section 7(6) (failing to provide a specimen) where that is an offence involving obligatory disqualification,

has within the ten years immediately preceding the commission of the offence been convicted[11] of any such offence, the minimum period of disqualification is increased from twelve months to three years.

In relation to a person convicted of

- manslaughter, or in Scotland culpable homicide, or

Section 1, Road
Traffic Act 1988

- an offence under section 1, Road Traffic Act 1988 (causing death by dangerous driving), or

- an offence under section 3A of that Act (causing death by careless driving while under the influence of drink or drugs); and

in relation to a person on whom more than one disqualification for a fixed period of 56 days or more has been imposed within the three years immediately preceding the commission of the offence, the minimum period of twelve months is increased to two years.

Section 26
Section 147
Section 223A or
436A,

Section 12 or 25
Section 178

For these purposes there shall be disregarded any disqualification imposed under section 26, Road Traffic Offences Act 1988 or section 147, Powers of Criminal Courts (Sentencing) Act 2000 or section 223A or 436A, Criminal Procedure (Scotland) Act 1975 (offences committed by using vehicles) and any disqualification imposed in respect of an offence of stealing a motor vehicle, an offence under section 12 or 25, Theft Act 1968, an offence under section 178, Road Traffic Act 1988, or an attempt to commit such an offence.

Section 35, Road
Traffic Offenders
Act 1988
Section 34(2),
Road Traffic
Offenders Act 1988

Subject to the increase in minimum periods of disqualification under section 35, Road Traffic Offenders Act 1988, there are no specific consequences for repeated offences giving rise to discretionary disqualification under section 34(2), Road Traffic Offenders Act 1988.

---

11. Note that it is the fact of conviction and not disqualification that triggers the increased period of disqualification. Thus an offender may be liable to the increased period of disqualification for a subsequent offence even where there were found to be special reasons to avoid disqualification for the first offence: *Bolliston* v *Gibbons* (1985) RTR 176.

Reduced period of disqualification for attendance on prescribed courses

Following a successful 6 year pilot, all courts in the the United Kingdom have power to reduce the compulsory period of disqualification in respect of certain offences.[12]

Courses for drink-drive offenders

Courses can be used where a person is convicted of an offence under section 3A (causing death by careless driving when under influence of drink or drugs), 4 (driving or being in charge when under influence of drink or drugs), 5 (driving or being in charge with excess alcohol) or 7 (failing to provide a specimen) of the Road Traffic Act 1988, and the court makes an order under section 34(1) of the Road Traffic Offenders Act 1988 disqualifying him for a period of not less than twelve months.

The court may make an order that the period of disqualification shall be reduced if, by a date specified in the order under this section, the offender satisfactorily completes a course approved by the Secretary of State for the purposes of this section and specified in the order.

The reduction made by an order under this section in a period of disqualification shall be a period specified in the order of not less than three months and not more than one quarter of the unreduced period (and accordingly where the period imposed is twelve months, the reduced period shall be nine months).

The court shall not make an order under this section unless:

- it is satisfied that a place on the course specified in the order will be available for the offender;[13]

- the offender appears to the court to be of or over the age of 17;

- the court has explained the effect of the order to the offender in ordinary language, and has informed him of the amount of the fees for the course and of the requirement that he must pay them before beginning the course; and

- the offender has agreed that the order should be made.

The date specified in an order under this section as the latest date for completion of a course must be at least two months

---

12. Section 34A, Road Traffic Offenders Act 1988.
13. At the time of writing the Secretary of State had not made an order activating the order in respect of drugs.

before the last day of the period of disqualification as reduced by the order.

For example, an offender disqualified on 1 September 2003 for twelve months will be banned until 31 August 2004. If an order is made in his case, he will be eligible for a 3 month reduction so long as he completes the drink drive rehabilitation course by 31 March 2004 (3 months + 2 months).

Section 26(2), Road Traffic Offenders Act 1988

If, in the same example, the offender had pleaded guilty at an earlier hearing on 1 August 2003 and been made the subject of an interim order for disqualification under section 26(2), Road Traffic Offenders Act 1988, the period of disqualification would commence from the date of the interim disqualification. Accordingly the offender would be disqualified until 31 July 2004 and would be eligible for a 3 month reduction provided the relevant course was complete by 28 February 2004.

Once an offender has completed the drink drive rehabilitation course, the organisers provide to him and the court which made the order, a certificate of completion. The certificate is brought to the notice of the Secretary of State and the offender may then apply for his driving licence subject to any additional requirements to which he may be subject.

If the organisers do not issue a certificate of completion, the offender may appeal to the magistrates' court in whose area the offender resides (and will have taken the course) against the refusal to issue a certificate of completion. The purpose of the two-month period in section 34A of the Road Traffic Act 1998 is to allow such an appeal to be determined. If the offender is successful in his appeal, the court's decision to allow the appeal acts as a certificate of completion allowing the offender to reapply for his driving licence.[14]

Disqualification for repeated offences

Where:

- a person is convicted of an offence involving obligatory or discretionary disqualification; and

- the penalty points to be taken into account on that occasion number twelve or more;

---

14.   Sections 34A, B and C, Road Traffic Offenders Act 1988.

the court must order him to be disqualified for not less than the minimum period unless the court is satisfied, having regard to all the circumstances, that there are grounds for mitigating the normal consequences of the conviction and thinks fit to order him to be disqualified for a shorter period or not to order him to be disqualified.[15]

The minimum period is:

- six months if no previous disqualification imposed on the offender is to be taken into account; and

- one year if one, and two years if more than one such disqualification is to be taken into account;

and a previous disqualification imposed on an offender is to be taken into account if it was imposed within the three years immediately preceding the commission of the latest offence in respect of which penalty points are taken into account under section 29, Road Traffic Offenders Act 1988.

Section 29, Road Traffic Offenders Act 1988

Where an offender is convicted on the same occasion of more than one offence involving obligatory or discretionary disqualification:

- not more than one disqualification shall be imposed on him;

- in determining the period of the disqualification the court must take into account all the offences; and

- for the purposes of any appeal any disqualification imposed shall be treated as an order made on the conviction of each of the offences.

Discretionary disqualification and disqualification for repeat offenders

Where an offender has, for example, 9 relevant penalty points and is convicted of another endorseable offence, for example speeding, the court may be faced with a dilemma. The court has power to impose a period of disqualification for the new offence in which case the usual number of penalty points attributable to the offence (3 to 6) would not be taken into account in deciding whether the offender has accumulated 12 or more penalty points and is therefore liable for disqualification under section 35, Road Traffic Offenders Act 1988.

Section 35, Road Traffic Offenders Act 1988

---

15.   Section 35, Road Traffic Offenders Act 1988.

If the court decides to impose a short period of disqualification, the offender apparently 'escapes' the penalty Parliament has prescribed for multiple offending within a certain period. Does the court have power to decide between a short period of disqualification and the imposition of penalty points leading to the longer mandatory period?[16]

The answer to this dilemma is provided in the case of *Jones* v *DPP (2000) The Times 20 October*. The court should look at the whole record and decide whether to impose a discretionary disqualification for the current offence before considering in the light of the whole record whether to go on to consider a disqualification as a repeat offender.[17]

The hardship exception

No account is to be taken of any of the following circumstances:

• any circumstances that are alleged to make the offence or any of the offences not a serious one;

• hardship, other than exceptional hardship; or

• any circumstances which, within the three years immediately preceding the conviction, have been taken into account in ordering the offender to be disqualified for a shorter period or not ordering him to be disqualified.

Disqualification until test is passed

Where a person is convicted of an offence involving obligatory or discretionary disqualification, the court may order him to be disqualified until he passes the appropriate test of competence to drive.

This power is exercisable by the court whether or not the person convicted has previously passed that test and whether or not the court makes an order for disqualification under section 34 or 35 of the Act.[18]

---

16. This is of particular difficulty where the offender has driven in excess of 100 mph. Usually the court would impose a period of disqualification. If, however the offender would otherwise be liable for a disqualification as a totter (i.e. he has accumulated 12 or more penalty points) the court's decision to impose the shorter period is an incentive to drive faster!

17. Although apparently favourable to the risks described in the preceding footnote, practitioners should note that if the court imposes a discretionary period of disqualification for more than 56 days there may be consequences for subsequent minimum periods of disqualification as a repeat offender.

18. Section 36, Road Traffic Offenders Act 1988.

An order to take a driving test applies in respect of the following circumstances.

Compulsory retest

The court must order an offender to be disqualified until he passes the appropriate driving test where:

- a person who is disqualified under section 34 of this Act on conviction of manslaughter, or in Scotland culpable homicide, by the driver of a motor vehicle; or

- an offence under section 1 (causing death by dangerous driving) or section 2 (dangerous driving) of the Road Traffic Act 1988;

- to a person who is disqualified under section 34 or 35 of this Act in such circumstances or for such period as the Secretary of State may by order prescribe; or

- to such other persons convicted of such offences involving obligatory endorsement as may be so prescribed.

Where a person is convicted of an offence to which the preceding provisions do not apply, involving obligatory endorsement, the court may order him to be disqualified until he passes the appropriate driving test (whether or not he has previously passed any test).

The term "appropriate driving test" means:

- an extended driving test, where a person is convicted of an offence involving obligatory disqualification or is disqualified under section 35 of the Act;

- a test of competence to drive, other than an extended driving test, in any other case.

In determining whether to make an order for an offender to take a test of competence to drive the court shall have regard to the safety of road users.

Where a person is disqualified until he passes the extended driving test any earlier order under this section shall cease to have effect and a court shall not make a further order under this section while he is so disqualified.

Effect of order of disqualification

Where the holder of a licence is disqualified by an order of a court, the licence shall be treated as being revoked with effect from the beginning of the period of disqualification.

Where the holder of the licence appeals against the order and the disqualification is suspended under section 39 of the Act, the period of disqualification shall be treated as beginning on the day on which the disqualification ceases to be suspended.

Appeal against disqualification

A person disqualified by an order of a magistrates' court under section 34 or 35 of the Act may appeal against the order in the same manner as against a conviction.[19]

Suspension of disqualification pending appeal

Any court in England and Wales (whether a magistrates' court or another) which makes an order disqualifying a person may, if it thinks fit, suspend the disqualification pending an appeal against the order.

Power of appellate courts in England and Wales to suspend disqualification

Where a person has been convicted by or before a court in England and Wales of an offence involving obligatory or discretionary disqualification and has been ordered to be disqualified and appeals to the Crown Court, or appeals or applies for leave to appeal to the Court of Appeal, against his conviction or his sentence, the Crown Court or, as the case may require, the Court of Appeal may, if it thinks fit, suspend the disqualification.

Section 11, Magistrates' Courts Act 1980 Section 28, Supreme Court Act 1981

Where a person ordered to be disqualified makes an application in respect of the decision of the court in question under section 11, Magistrates' Courts Act 1980 (statement of case by magistrates' court) or section 28, Supreme Court Act 1981 (statement of case by Crown Court) the High Court may, if it thinks fit, suspend the disqualification.

---

19. Section 38, Road Traffic Offenders Act 1988.

Where a person ordered to be disqualified:

- applies to the High Court for an order of *certiorari* to remove into the High Court any proceedings of a magistrates' court or of the Crown Court, being proceedings in or in consequence of which he was convicted or his sentence was passed; or

- applies to the High Court for leave to make such an application;

the High Court may, if it thinks fit, suspend the disqualification.

Any power of a court under the preceding provisions of this provision to suspend the disqualification of any person is a power to do so on such terms as the court thinks fit.

Removal of disqualification

A person who by an order of a court is disqualified may apply to the court by which the order was made to remove the disqualification.

On any such application the court may, as it thinks proper having regard to:

- the character of the person disqualified and his conduct subsequent to the order;

- the nature of the offence; and

- any other circumstances of the case;

either by order remove the disqualification as from such date as may be specified in the order or refuse the application.

No application shall be made for the removal of a disqualification before the expiration of whichever is relevant of the following periods from the date of the order by which the disqualification was imposed, that is:

- two years, if the disqualification is for less than four years;

- one half of the period of disqualification, if it is for less than ten years but not less than four years;

- five years in any other case;

and in determining the expiration of the period after which under this subsection a person may apply for the removal of a disqualification, any time after the conviction during which the disqualification was suspended or he was not disqualified shall be disregarded.

Where an application is refused, a further application shall not be entertained if made within three months after the date of the refusal.

Sentences and disqualification

Combination of disqualification and endorsement with probation orders and orders for discharge

A court in England and Wales which on convicting a person of an offence involving obligatory or discretionary disqualification makes

* a probation order; or

* an order discharging him absolutely or conditionally;

may on that occasion also exercise any power conferred, and must also discharge any duty imposed, on the court by sections 34, 35, 36 or 44 of this Act.

A conviction in respect of which a court in England and Wales has ordered a person to be disqualified or of which particulars have been endorsed on any licence held by him, is to be taken Section 13(1), into account, notwithstanding anything in section 13(1), Powers of Criminal Powers of Criminal Courts Act 1973 (conviction of offender Courts Act 1973 placed on probation or discharged to be disregarded for the purpose of subsequent proceedings), in determining his liability to punishment or disqualification for any offence involving obligatory or discretionary disqualification committed subsequently.[20]

Exemption from disqualification and endorsement for certain offences against construction and use regulations

Section 40A or Where a person is convicted of an offence under section 40A or section 41A, Road section 41A, Road Traffic Act 1988 the court must not: Traffic Act 1988

* order him to be disqualified; or

---

20. Section 46, Road Traffic Offenders Act 1988.

- order any particulars or penalty points to be endorsed on any licence held by him;

if he proves that he did not know, and had no reasonable cause to suspect, that the facts of the case were such that the offence would be committed.[21]

Offender escaping consequences of endorseable offence by deception

This provision applies where in dealing with a person convicted of an offence involving obligatory endorsement a court was deceived regarding any circumstances that were or might have been taken into account in deciding whether or for how long to disqualify him.

If:

- the deception constituted or was due to an offence committed by that person; and

- he is convicted of that offence;

the court by or before which he is convicted shall have the same powers and duties regarding an order for disqualification as had the court which dealt with him for the offence involving obligatory endorsement but must, in dealing with him, take into account any order made on his conviction of the offence involving obligatory endorsement.

Notification of disability

Section 22, Road Traffic Offenders Act 1988
Section 92, Road Traffic Act 1988

Section 22, Road Traffic Offenders Act 1988 provides that the court must advise the Secretary of State if it appears that a person accused of an offence in respect of a motor vehicle is suffering from a disability. Disability is defined in section 92, Road Traffic Act 1988 to include disease and the persistent misuse of drugs or alcohol, whether or not such a misuse amounts to dependency. The term relevant disability means any prescribed disability and any other disability likely to cause the driving of a vehicle by him in pursuance of a licence to be a source of danger to the public.

Once the Secretary of State has been notified by the court he will make enquiries with the person to see if action needs to be taken

---

21.   Section 48, Road Traffic Offenders Act 1988.

to revoke the driving licence or substitute an existing driving licence for one with conditions.

This court power applies whether or not the accused person is convicted of any offence.

Probationary drivers

Newly qualified drivers are subject to a period of probation. The probationary period is the period of two years beginning with the day on which he becomes a qualified driver.

A person becomes a qualified driver on the first occasion on which he passes any test of competence to drive mentioned in the Road Traffic Act 1988 or any test of competence to drive conducted under the law of another EEA State or Gibraltar.

Revocation of licences and re-testing

- Where a person is the holder of a licence, he is convicted of an offence involving obligatory endorsement and the penalty points to be taken into account on that occasion number six or more;

Section 44(1)(b),
Road Traffic
Offenders Act 1988

- the court makes an order falling within section 44(1)(b), Road Traffic Offenders Act 1988 in respect of the offence;

- the person's licence shows the date on which he became a qualified driver, or that date has been shown by other evidence in the proceedings; and

- it appears to the court, in the light of the order and the date so shown, that the offence was committed during the person's probationary period.

the Secretary of State must by notice served on that person revoke the licence.[22]

The Secretary of State may not grant a person whose licence has been revoked a full licence to drive any class of vehicles in relation to which the revoked licence was issued as a full licence unless he satisfies the Secretary of State that within the relevant period he has passed a relevant driving test.

---

22. The decision to revoke is administrative and does not involve judicial discretion. It may therefore sometimes be better to invite the court to impose a short period of disqualification rather than penalty points to avoid the revocation of a new driver's licence. However, courts will be aware that the legislation was enacted to protect road safety and may not be persuaded to get round the safety features of requiring a new driver to have his competence to drive tested again.

Exceptional Hardship: In Practice

The sentencing court has discretion to disqualify an offender from holding or obtaining a driving licence in addition to any other sentence made in respect of any endorseable offence of which he has been convicted. The decision to disqualify will be informed by the presence of aggravating or mitigating factors relating to the offence and possibly to the offender. The exercise of this discretion to disqualify is unfettered.

Section 35, Road
Traffic Offenders
Act 1988

Where, however, the penalty points to be taken into account amount to 12 or more, there is a statutory presumption that the court will impose a period of disqualification according to section 35, Road Traffic Offenders Act 1988. The presumption may only be displaced if the offender can show that he will suffer exceptional hardship if he were to be so disqualified.

Where the court finds exceptional hardship, it may decide not to disqualify the offender or it may decide to reduce the minimum period of diqualification it would otherwise have to impose.

If an offender is successful in putting forward an argument based on exceptional hardship, the court is under a duty to note the grounds on the offender's licence. An offender is precluded from using the same grounds to establish exceptional hardship if the grounds have been taken into account by a court considering disqualification under section 35 of the Road Traffic Offenders Act 1988 within the three years immediately preceding the conviction which gives rise to the new consideration of disqualification. It is for the offender to show that the reasons put forward on such a second occasion are different from those originally relied upon.[23]

The court is not required to hear evidence[24] from an offender before it finds exceptional hardship although it would be imprudent to dismiss exceptional hardship without allowing an offender to present evidence and make representations on the point.

Establishing exceptional hardship is effectively a special form of plea in mitigation. Accordingly there do not appear to be any restrictions on the facts on which such a plea can be based. It may include the effect of disqualification on the offender or on others who rely on his ability to drive.

23.   *R v Sandbach Justices, ex parte Pescaud* [1983] 5 Cr App Rep (S) 177.
24.   *Owen v Jones* [1988] RTR 102.

Practitioners need to be able to present an effective plea which shows that the offender (or another) will suffer more than mere hardship. The legislation requires the court to have regard only to exceptional hardship. There is good argument to ask how the hardship caused by an inability to drive to an individual who relies on his ability to drive can be described as exceptional. Practitioners need therefore to be actively seeking information which will establish that the offender (or another) will suffer hardship plus. For example, a professional driver may suffer hardship if he is disqualified. Losing his job as a driver may be hard but may not be sufficient to demonstrate exceptional hardship. If, however, evidence were to be given that as a result he will be unable to meet his mortgage, this may be the kind of hardship which can be properly described as exceptional.

Practitioners, however, should also be aware of the risk in putting forward grounds establishing exceptional hardship. If one ground will suffice to establish exceptional hardship, it would be unfortunate if the court were to listen to other equally valid arguments and base its decision on all the grounds put forward. The court would then be obliged to record all the grounds in open court, on the register and driving licence and the offender would be unable to rely on these grounds again for a period of three years, if he was unfortunate enough to appear in court again. The practitioner has difficult advice to give as the grounds he intends to rely upon may not, of course amount to exceptional hardship in the eyes of the court and by the time that is clear, it may be too late to put forward further reasons.

Special Reasons in Practice

An offender may seek to establish special reasons for not endorsing his driving licence with penalty points or to establish special reasons for not disqualifying him from driving where the court is otherwise under a mandatory duty to disqualify him.

Section 40A and 41A, Road Traffic Act 1988 Section 48, Road Traffic Act 1988 — Practitioners should ensure they have considered whether any special reasons exist in the circumstances of all endorseable offences. Where the offences arise under section 40A and 41A, Road Traffic Act 1988, practitioner's attention is drawn to section 48, Road Traffic Act 1988 as an alternative procedure to avoid endorsement.[25]

---

25.   See above.

Special reasons may only be established by evidence.[26] The burden of proof lies on the offender and he must show that the relevant conditions exist on a balance of probabilities.[27] The successful establishment of special reasons does not require the court to not impose penalty points, endorse or disqualify; it merely opens the gate to the court exercising its discretion. In other words, there is a two-stage process.[28] Firstly, the court must decide on evidence whether there exist in fact, special reasons. If the offender fails to prove on a balance of probabilities what he has to prove, the court must proceed to endorse and/or disqualify. If the offender establishes that special reasons exist as a matter of fact, the court has then to decide whether this is the type of case where it should exercise its discretion in favour of the offender.[29] This is the second stage of the procedure. The discretion should only be exercised in clear and compelling cases.[30]

Sentencers have been reminded by the High Court on a number of occasions that Parliament wishes offenders who commit certain serious offences to be disqualified from driving and have provided a very limited opportunity to avoid such a consequence after conviction. Sentencers have been regularly reminded of their duty to give effect to Parliament's intention and generally the court will anxiously scrutinise any grounds put forward to establish special reasons. The High Court will not generally interfere with findings made by sentencers so long as they can show they have properly and judicially directed their mind to the right considerations even if the High Court itself would have reached a different conclusion.

A special reason must fulfil four general criteria.[31] These are:

(1) It must be a mitigating or extenuating circumstance.

(2) It must not amount in law to a defence to the allegation.

(3) It must be directly connected with the commission of the offence.

---

26. *Jones* v *English* [1951] 2 All ER 853.
27. *Pugsley* v *Hunter* [1973] 1 WLR 578.
28. *DPP* v *O Connor* [1992] RTR 66.
29. For example, an offender may be able to establish that his drinks were spiked and that he did not know at the time he drove that he was drink driving. This would be capable of amounting to a special reason but it would be open to the court to decide that the offender should still be disqualified if the offender was aware that something was not right but went onto take the risk nonetheless.
30. *Vaughan* v *Dunn* [1984] RTR 376.
31. *R* v *Wickins* [1958] 42 Cr App Rep 236.

(4) It must be a matter which the court ought properly to take into consideration when sentencing the offender.

Where a court has previously found special reasons, and an offender is convicted of a second relevant offence so that the minimum period of disqualification increases to 3 years under

Section 34(3), section 34(3), Road Traffic Offenders Act 1998, the court is
Road Traffic required to impose the longer period (unless it finds special
Offenders Act 1998 reasons relating to the new offence). A finding of special reasons for one offence does not excuse the offender of the consequences of a second conviction.[32]

Circumstances where special reasons may exist

It is impossible to exhaustively list all the circumstances which may or may not amount to special reasons. However, the majority of decisions concerning special reasons fall into the following range of categories:

- A police driver undertaking realistic driver training is not able to establish a special reason for avoiding endorsement as the safety of other road users is more important.[33]

- A doctor is not able to establish as a special reason that there is a shortage of doctors in the area and therefore his disqualification may place patients at risk.[34]

- An unexpected episode of hypoglycaemia in a diabetic controlled by insulin is not capable of amounting to a special reason.[35]

- A disabled driver is not able to put forward the severity of a period of disqualification as a special reason to avoid it.[36]

In each of these examples, the grounds of the special reasons were based on the personal characteristics of the offender. Generally, such personal characteristics are not capable of amounting to special reasons.

---

32. *Bolliston v Gibbons* [1985] RTR 176.
33. *Agnew v DPP* (1990) 155 JP 927.
34. *Holroyd v Berry* [1973] Crim LR 118.
35. *Jarvis v DPP* (2000) 165 JP 15.
36. *Williamson v Wilson* [1947] 1 All ER 306.

However, ignorance may be relevant:

- An offender who relied on a third party on whom it was reasonable to rely may successfully establish special reasons where he was ignorant of the true position.[37]

- A driver who did not know that a system of street lights imposed a certain speed limit was not successful in establishing special reasons.[38]

- An offender who drove the morning after consuming alcohol and did not believe he was over the limit has no special reason.[39]

- An offender who relies on an earlier negative breath specimen does not have a special reason.[40]

- The fact that the offence is trivial (just over the speed limit, just over the drink drive limit) is not capable of providing a special reason.[41]

- An offender who can show that his drinks were spiked may have a special reason but he must show that he was unaware of the third party's intervention. An offender drinking alcohol which is spiked is under a heavy responsibility. If he is drinking non-alcoholic drinks which are spiked, the question has to be asked whether he would not have become aware of the influence of alcohol. It is not enough for him to do nothing. The offender has the burden to show that the additional alcohol which he did not know about was responsible for the excess alcohol in his system.[42] As previously suggested, even if an offender is able to establish that his drinks were spiked and he did not know, the court may decide that this is not the type of case in which it should exercise its discretion. The court is entitled to take into account whether the offender should have known that he was not fit to drive.

37.   For example, an offender who arranges insurance cover over the telephone with a broker who assures his that he is insured to drive a vehicle may be able to put forward special reasons if it subsequently transpires that the broker was wrong in his assertion and the offender reasonably relied on what he had been told and had no other way of checking the facts he was given.
38.   *Walker v Rawlinson* [1957] Crim LR 523.
39.   *DPP v O Meara* [1989] RTR 24.
40.   *DPP v White* [1988] RTR 267.
41.   *Marks v West Midlands Police* [1981] RTR 471.
42.   *R v Newton* [1974] RTR 451; *Weatherson v Cannop* [1975] Crim LR 239.

- An offender may be able to establish that he drove because of an emergency. This is an extremely difficult ground to prove even on the lower standard. The offender must show that:

    - he had no intention to drive the vehicle after he had been drinking;

    - that the situation created an urgent and compelling need to drive;

    - that the situation was not foreseeable and continued to subsist throughout the period of driving;

    - that there was no alternative means of dealing with the emergency;

    - that there were no other traffic offences committed.[43]

    A useful test to employ in deciding whether there exists a true emergency is to ask whether the reasonable, responsible and sober passenger in the vehicle would have advised the offender to drive or not to drive?[44]

- Shortness of distance driven may amount to a special reason. The factors to be taken into account are as follows:[45]

    - how far the vehicle was actually driven;

    - the manner in which the vehicle was driven

    - the state of the vehicle

    - whether the offender intended to drive any further before he was apprehended;

    - the road and traffic conditions;

    - the reason for driving; and

    - whether there was any risk of danger to other road users arising out of the presence of the vehicle.

---

43.   *Taylor v Rajan* [1974] QB 424.
44.   Needless to say, such a passenger does not actually have to be present. He is simply visiting from the Clapham Omnibus (and doubtless wishing he had remained aboard the bus rather that travelling in a car with a drunk driver during an emergency!) *DPP v Bristow* (1996) 161 JP 35.
45.   *Chatters v Burke* [1986] 3 All ER 168.

CHAPTER 13
SENTENCING MENTALLY DISORDERED OFFENDER

Introduction

Mental Health
Act 1983

This section deals with orders which may be made in prescribed circumstances under the Mental Health Act 1983.[1] Practitioners should also have regard to treatment conditions for mental disorder which may be added to community rehabilitation orders.[2]

Remand to hospital for report on accused's mental condition

The Crown Court or a magistrates' court may remand an accused person to a hospital specified by the court for a report on his mental condition.[3]

The power may be exercised at different stages of proceedings depending on the court making the remand:[4]

- In the Crown Court, a remand may be made in respect of any person who is awaiting trial before the court for an offence punishable with imprisonment or who has been arraigned before the court for such an offence and has not yet been sentenced or otherwise dealt with for the offence on which he has been arraigned;

- In the magistrates' court a remand may only be made in respect of any person who has been convicted by the court of an offence punishable on summary conviction with imprisonment and in respect of any person charged with

---

1. This part does not deal with findings of insanity or diminished responsibility.
2. See above at page XX.
3. The accused is entitled to commission an independent report of his own at his own expense: section 35(8), Mental Health Act 1983, and may apply to the court to terminate his remand to hospital accordingly.
4. Section 35, Mental Health Act 1983.

such an offence if the court is satisfied that he did the act or made the omission charged or he has consented to the exercise by the court of these powers.

The power to remand may be exercised if the court is satisfied, on the written or oral evidence of a registered medical practitioner that there is reason to suspect that the accused person is suffering from mental illness, psychopathic disorder, severe mental impairment or mental impairment and the court is of the opinion that it would be impracticable for a report to be made if he were remanded on bail.[5]

The court may not make such an order unless satisfied, on the written or oral evidence of the registered medical practitioner responsible for the report, that arrangements have been made for the admission of the offender within 7 days of the date of remand. The court may also give directions that the accused be conveyed to, and detained in, a place of safety pending his admission within this period.

The accused may be remanded for a maximum of 28 days at a time but his further remand need not take place in his presence. However, a remand under section 35, Mental Health Act 1983 may not exceed 12 weeks overall.[6]

Section 35, Mental Health Act 1983

Remand of accused to hospital for treatment

This power is only available in the Crown Court which may, instead of remanding the accused in custody, remand him to hospital for treatment. Such a remand may only be made if the court is satisfied on the written or oral evidence of two registered practitioners that the accused is suffering from mental illness or severe mental impairment of a nature or degree which makes it appropriate for him to be detained in a hospital for medical treatment.[7]

Again the court must be satisfied that suitable admission arrangements have been made within 7 days of the date of remand and may give directions as to the conveyance to, and detention in, a place of safety pending his admission. The court is also able to further remand the accused if it appears to be warranted on the evidence of the responsible medical officer. The power is subject to the overall remand period of 12 weeks and the accused may only be remanded for a maximum period

5.   The Crown Court may not remand to hospital a person convicted of an offence if the sentence is fixed by law.
6.   Section 35(7), Mental Health Act 1983.
7.   Section 36, Mental Health Act 1983.

of 28 days at any one time although subsequent remands may take place in his absence.

The power may be exercised in respect of any accused person in custody awaiting either trial or sentence for an offence punishable with imprisonment which sentence is not fixed by law.

Interim Hospital Orders

The Crown Court and the magistrates' court may make an interim hospital order[8] in respect of any person convicted of an offence punishable with imprisonment (unless the sentence is fixed by law) provided it is satisfied, on the written or oral evidence of two registered medical practitioners:

• that the offender is suffering from mental illness, psychopathic disorder, severe mental impairment or mental impairment; and

• that there is reason to suppose that the mental disorder from which the offender is suffering is such that it may be appropriate for a hospital order to be made in his case.

An interim hospital order may not be made unless the court is satisfied, on appropriate evidence, that arrangements have been made for the offender's admission to the hospital within 28 days and may give directions for his conveyance to, and detention in, a place of safety pending admission.

An interim hospital order may not be made for longer than 12 weeks but may then be renewed for 28 days at a time in the absence of the offender, provided the court is satisfied, on appropriate evidence from a medical practitioner, that the continuation of the order is warranted. The interim hospital order may not remain in force for more than 12 months and may be brought to an end at any time by the court if the court decides to deal with the offender in some other way.

Before the court can renew an interim hospital order in the absence of the offender, he must be legally represented and the court must provide an opportunity for the representative to make representations on his behalf. In such circumstances, the court is also empowered to make a full hospital order without having the offender brought to court.[9]

---

8. Section 38, Mental Health Act 1983.
9. Section 38(2), Mental Health Act 1983.

Powers of courts to order hospital admission or guardianship

Where a person is convicted before the Crown Court of an offence punishable with imprisonment other than an offence the sentence for which is fixed by law [or falls to be imposed under section 109, Powers of Criminal Courts (Sentencing) Act 2000, or is convicted by a magistrates' court of an offence punishable on summary conviction with imprisonment, and the conditions mentioned in below are satisfied, the court may by order authorise his admission to and detention in such hospital as may be specified in the order or, as the case may be, place him under the guardianship of a local social services authority or of such other person approved by a local social services authority as may be so specified.[10]

Section 109,
Powers of Criminal
Courts (Sentencing)
Act 2000

The conditions referred to above are that:

- the court is satisfied, on the written or oral evidence of two registered medical practitioners, that the offender is suffering from mental illness, psychopathic disorder, severe mental impairment or mental impairment and that either:

  (i) the mental disorder from which the offender is suffering is of a nature or degree which makes it appropriate for him to be detained in a hospital for medical treatment and, in the case of psychopathic disorder or mental impairment, that such treatment is likely to alleviate or prevent a deterioration of his condition; or

  (ii) in the case of an offender who has attained the age of 16 years, the mental disorder is of a nature or degree which warrants his reception into guardianship under the Mental Health Act 1983; and

Mental Health
Act 1983

- the court is of the opinion, having regard to all the circumstances including the nature of the offence and the character and antecedents of the offender, and to the other available methods of dealing with him, that the most suitable method of disposing of the case is by means of an order under this section.[11]

Where a person is charged before a magistrates' court with any act or omission as an offence and the court would have power,

---

10. In the case of an offence the sentence for which would otherwise fall to be imposed under subsection (2) of section 110 or 111, Powers of Criminal Courts (Sentencing) Act 2000, nothing in that subsection shall prevent a court from making an order for the admission of the offender to a hospital.
11. Section 37, Mental Health Act 1983.

on convicting him of that offence, to make an order in his case as being a person suffering from mental illness or severe mental impairment, then, if the court is satisfied that the accused did the act or made the omission charged, the court may, if it thinks fit, make such an order without convicting him.[12]

An order for the admission of an offender to a hospital ("a hospital order") shall not be made under unless the court is satisfied on the written or oral evidence of the registered medical practitioner who would be in charge of his treatment or of some other person representing the managers of the hospital that arrangements have been made for his admission to that hospital within the period of 28 days beginning with the date of the making of such an order. The court may, pending his admission within that period, give such directions as it thinks fit for his conveyance to and detention in a place of safety.

An order placing an offender under the guardianship of a local social services authority or of any other person ("a guardianship order") shall not be made unless the court is satisfied that that authority or person is willing to receive the offender into guardianship.

A hospital order or guardianship order shall specify the form or forms of mental disorder from which, upon the evidence taken into account, the offender is found by the court to be suffering; and no such order shall be made unless the offender is described by each of the practitioners whose evidence is taken into account as suffering from the same one of those forms of mental disorder, whether or not he is also described by either of them as suffering from another of them.

Where an order is made under this section, the court shall not:

- pass sentence of imprisonment or impose a fine or make a probation order in respect of the offence;

- if the order under this section is a hospital order, make a referral order in respect of the offence; or

- make in respect of the offender a supervision order or an order binding over of parent or guardian,

but the court may make any other order which it has power to make apart from this section;[13] and for the purposes of this

---

12. The mode of trial and plea before venue procedure does not apply in such circumstances and the court may proceed to summary trial as if the offender had consented to it. *R v Lincoln Justices ex parte O Connor* (1983) 147 JP 97.
13. Section 37(8), Mental Health Act 1983.

subsection "sentence of imprisonment" includes any sentence or order for detention.

Restriction orders

Power of higher courts to restrict discharge from hospital

Where a hospital order is made in respect of an offender by the Crown Court, and it appears to the court, having regard to the nature of the offence, the antecedents of the offender and the risk of his committing further offences if set at large, that it is necessary for the protection of the public from serious harm so to do,[14] the court may further order that the offender shall be subject to the special restrictions set out in this section, either without limit of time or during such period as may be specified in the order;[15] and an order of this kind shall be known as "a restriction order".[16]

A restriction order shall not be made in the case of any person unless at least one of the registered medical practitioners whose evidence is taken into account by the court for the purpose of making a hospital order has given evidence orally before the court.

The special restrictions applicable to a patient in respect of whom a restriction order is in force are as follows:

Part II, Mental Health Act 1983

- none of the provisions of Part II, Mental Health Act 1983 relating to the duration, renewal and expiration of authority for the detention of patients shall apply, and the patient shall continue to be liable to be detained by virtue of the relevant hospital order until he is duly discharged under Part II or absolutely discharged under sections 42, 73, 74 or 75, Mental Health Act 1983;[17]

Section 42, 73, 74 or 75 Mental Health Act 1983

- none of the provisions of Part II of the Act relating to after-care under supervision shall apply;

Section 66 or 69(1), Mental Health Act 1983

- no application shall be made to a Mental Health Review Tribunal in respect of a patient under section 66 or 69(1), Mental Health Act 1983;

---

14. It is for the court to make an assessment of risk and should not rely on medical opinion as to risk. *R v Birch* [1990] Cr App R 78.

15. The safer course is to make an order of unlimited duration unless medical evidence unequivocally suggests that treatment will be successful within a specified period. *R v Nwohia* [1996] 1 Cr App Rep (S) 170.

16. Section 41, Mental Health Act 1983.

17. These provisions are not considered in this text.

the following powers shall be exercisable only with the consent of the Secretary of State, namely:

- power to grant leave of absence to the patient;

- power to transfer the patient in pursuance of regulations

Section 23

- power to order the discharge of the patient under section 23 above;

and if leave of absence is granted power to recall the patient under that section shall vest in the Secretary of State as well as the responsible medical officer and the power of the Secretary of State to recall the patient and power to take the patient into custody and return him may be exercised at any time.

A hospital order shall not cease to have effect if a restriction order in respect of the patient is in force at the material time. Where a restriction order in respect of a patient ceases to have effect while the relevant hospital order continues in force, the provisions of section 40, Mental Health Act 1983 and Part I, Schedule 1 to the same act shall apply to the patient as if he had been admitted to the hospital in pursuance of a hospital order (without a restriction order) made on the date on which the restriction order ceased to have effect.

Section 40, Mental Health Act 1983 Part I, Schedule 1

While a person is subject to a restriction order the responsible medical officer shall at such intervals (not exceeding one year) as the Secretary of State may direct examine and report to the Secretary of State on that person and every report shall contain such particulars as the Secretary of State may require.

Powers of Secretary of State in respect of patients subject to restriction orders

If the Secretary of State is satisfied that in the case of any patient a restriction order is no longer required for the protection of the public from serious harm, he may direct that the patient cease to be subject to the special restrictions. Where the Secretary of State so directs, the restriction order shall cease to have effect.[18]

At any time while a restriction order is in force in respect of a patient, the Secretary of State may, if he thinks fit, by warrant discharge the patient from hospital, either absolutely or subject to conditions. Where a person is absolutely discharged under this power, he shall thereupon cease to be liable to be detained

---

18.   Section 42, Mental Health Act 1983.

by virtue of the relevant hospital order, and the restriction order shall cease to have effect accordingly.

The Secretary of State may at any time during the continuance in force of a restriction order in respect of a patient who has been conditionally discharged by warrant recall the patient to such hospital as may be specified in the warrant.

If a restriction order in respect of a patient ceases to have effect after the patient has been conditionally discharged under this part of the Mental Health Act 1983, the patient shall, unless previously recalled be deemed to be absolutely discharged on the date when the order ceases to have effect, and shall cease to be liable to be detained by virtue of the relevant hospital order accordingly.

The Secretary of State may, if satisfied that the attendance at any place in Great Britain of a patient who is subject to a restriction order is desirable in the interests of justice or for the purposes of any public inquiry, direct him to be taken to that place; and where a patient is directed under this power to be taken to any place he shall, unless the Secretary of State otherwise directs, be kept in custody while being so taken, while at that place and while being taken back to the hospital in which he is liable to be detained.

Power of magistrates' courts to commit for restriction order

If[19] in the case of a person of or over the age of 14 years[20] who is convicted by a magistrates' court of an offence punishable on summary conviction with imprisonment:

Section 37(1), Mental Health Act 1983

- the conditions which under section 37(1), Mental Health Act 1983 are required to be satisfied for the making of a hospital order are satisfied in respect of the offender; but

- it appears to the court, having regard to the nature of the offence, the antecedents of the offender and the risk of his committing further offences if set at large, that if a hospital order is made a restriction order should also be made,

the court may, instead of making a hospital order or dealing with him in any other manner, commit him in custody to the Crown Court to be dealt with in respect of the offence.

In *R* v *Gardner*[21] the Court of Appeal gave guidance to magistrates on the different effects of a hospital order, which

---

19.   Section 43, Mental Health Act 1983.
20.   Below this age, the court is limited to a hospital or guardianship order.
21.   [1967] 1 All ER 895.

may be made by a magistrates' court, and a restriction order, which may only be made after committal in the Crown Court. In summary the Court of Appeal said that magistrates should bear in mind that a hospital order is of limited duration, usually six months unless requiring further medical treatment in the view of the relevant medical authorities, and may be discharged at any time. A patient discharged under a hospital order is not liable for recall and may cease to be detainable if he leaves the hospital for certain periods. A restriction order, on the other hand, provides for an order of specific duration which can only be discharged by the Secretary of State. A patient who is discharged is liable to be recalled and may be taken into custody at any time if he is absent without leave.

Where an offender is committed to the Crown Court under this section, the Crown Court shall inquire into the circumstances of the case and may:

Section 37(1), Mental Health Act 1983

- if that court would have power so to do under the foregoing provisions of this Part of this Act upon the conviction of the offender before that court of such an offence as is described in section 37(1), Mental Health Act 1983, make a hospital order in his case, with or without a restriction order;

- if the court does not make such an order, deal with the offender in any other manner in which the magistrates' court might have dealt with him.

Sections 35, 36 and 38, Mental Health Act 1983

The Crown Court shall have the same power to make orders under sections 35, 36 and 38, Mental Health Act 1983 in the case of a person committed to the court under this section as the Crown Court has under those sections in the case of an accused person within the meaning of section 35 or 36 or of a person convicted before that court.

Section 3, Powers of Criminal Courts (Sentencing) Act 2000

The power of a magistrates' court under section 3, Powers of Criminal Courts (Sentencing) Act 2000 (which enables such a court to commit an offender to the Crown Court where the court is of the opinion that greater punishment should be inflicted for the offence than the court has power to inflict) shall also be exercisable by a magistrates' court where it is of the opinion that greater punishment should be inflicted as aforesaid on the offender unless a hospital order is made in his case with a restriction order.

The power of the Crown Court to make a hospital order, with or without a restriction order, in the case of a person convicted before that court of an offence may, in the same circumstances and subject to the same conditions, be exercised by such a court in the case of a person committed to the court under section 5, Vagrancy Act 1824 (which provides for the committal to the Crown Court of persons who are incorrigible rogues within the meaning of that section).

Section 5, Vagrancy Act 1824

Committal to hospital under section 43 of the Mental Health Act 1983

Section 43(1), Mental Health Act 1983

Where an offender is committed under section 43(1), Mental Health Act 1983 to the Crown Court and the magistrates' court by which he is committed is satisfied on written or oral evidence that arrangements have been made for the admission of the offender to a hospital in the event of an order being made under this section, the court may, instead of committing him in custody, by order direct him to be admitted to that hospital,[22] specifying it, and to be detained there until the case is disposed of by the Crown Court, and may give such directions as it thinks fit for his production from the hospital to attend the Crown Court by which his case is to be dealt with.

The evidence required shall be given by the registered medical practitioner who would be in charge of the offender's treatment or by some other person representing the managers of the hospital in question.

Appeals from magistrates' courts

Where on the trial of an information charging a person with an offence a magistrates' court makes a hospital order or guardianship order in respect of him without convicting him, he shall have the same right of appeal against the order as if it had been made on his conviction; and on any such appeal the Crown Court shall have the same powers as if the appeal had been against both conviction and sentence.[23]

---

22. The power to give directions under sections 37(4), 37(5) and 40(1), Mental Health Act 1983 shall apply in relation to the order as they apply in relation to a hospital order, but as if references to the period of 28 days were omitted; and subject as aforesaid an order under this section shall, until the offender's case is disposed of by the Crown Court, have the same effect as a hospital order together with a restriction order, made without limitation of time.

23. Section 45, Mental Health Act 1983.

Hospital and limitation directions

Power of higher courts to direct hospital admission

Section 45A,
Mental Health
Act 1983

Section 2,
Crime (Sentences)
Act 1997

Section 45A, Mental Health Act 1983 applies where, in the case of a person convicted before the Crown Court of an offence the sentence for which is not fixed by law the following conditions are fulfilled and except where the offence is one the sentence for which falls to be imposed under section 2, Crime (Sentences) Act 1997, the court considers making a hospital order in respect of him before deciding to impose a sentence of imprisonment ("the relevant sentence") in respect of the offence.

The conditions referred to above are that the court is satisfied, on the written or oral evidence of two registered medical practitioners:

- that the offender is suffering from psychopathic disorder;

- that the mental disorder from which the offender is suffering is of a nature or degree which makes it appropriate for him to be detained in a hospital for medical treatment; and

- that such treatment is likely to alleviate or prevent a deterioration of his condition.

The court may give both of the following directions:

- a direction that, instead of being removed to and detained in a prison, the offender be removed to and detained in such hospital as may be specified in the direction (a "hospital direction"); and

Section 41, Mental
Health act 1983

- a direction that the offender be subject to the special restrictions set out in section 41, Mental Health Act 1983 (a "limitation direction").

A hospital direction and a limitation direction shall not be given in relation to an offender unless at least one of the medical practitioners whose evidence is taken into account by the court has given evidence orally before the court.

A hospital direction and a limitation direction shall not be given in relation to an offender unless the court is satisfied on the written or oral evidence of the registered medical practitioner who would be in charge of his treatment, or of some other person representing the managers of the hospital that arrangements have been made for his admission to that hospital within the period of 28 days beginning with the day of the giving of such directions. The court may, pending his admission within that period, give such directions as it thinks fit for his conveyance to and detention in a place of safety.

If within the period of 28 days it appears to the Secretary of State that by reason of an emergency or other special circumstances it is not practicable for the patient to be received into the hospital specified in the hospital direction, he may give instructions for the admission of the patient to such other hospital as appears to be appropriate instead of the hospital so specified.

Effect of hospital and limitation directions

A hospital direction and a limitation direction[24] shall be sufficient authority

- for a constable or any other person directed to do so by the court to convey the patient to the hospital specified in the hospital direction within a period of 28 days; and

- for the managers of the hospital to admit him at any time within that period and thereafter detain him in accordance with the provisions of this Act.

While a person is subject to a hospital direction and a limitation direction the responsible medical officer shall at such intervals (not exceeding one year) as the Secretary of State may direct examine and report to the Secretary of State on that person; and every report shall contain such particulars as the Secretary of State may require.

Relevant conditions

There is no power to instigate measures under the Mental Health Act 1983 unless the offender is suffering from a recognisable and prescribed condition. The conditions are defined in the Mental Health Act 1983 as follows.[25]

Mental disorder means mental illness, arrested or incomplete development of mind, psychopathic disorder and any other disorder or disability of mind.

Severe mental impairment means a state of arrested or incomplete development of mind which includes severe impairment of

---

24.   Section 45B, Mental Health Act 1983.
25.   Section 1, Mental Health Act 1983.

intelligence and social functioning and is associated with abnormally aggressive or seriously irresponsible conduct on the part of the person concerned.

Mental impairment means a state of arrested or incomplete development of mind (not amounting to severe mental impairment) which includes significant impairment of intelligence and social functioning and is associated with abnormally aggressive or seriously irresponsible conduct on the part of the person concerned.

Psychopathic disorder means a persistent disorder or disability of mind (whether or not including significant impairment of intelligence) which results in abnormally aggressive or seriously irresponsible conduct on the part of the person concerned.

Mental Health
Act 1983

Nothing in these definitions is to be construed as implying that a person may be dealt with under the Mental Health Act 1983 as suffering from mental disorder or from any form of mental disorder by reason only of promiscuity or other immoral conduct, sexual deviancy or dependence on alcohol or drugs.

CHAPTER 14
APPEALS FROM THE
MAGISTRATES' COURT

Introduction

The sentencing process is susceptible to appeals either on fact or on law. The following chapter outlines the appeal process in more detail from the magistrates' court.[1] Practitioners need to be aware of the range of potential appeals both to and from the magistrates' court and for the sake of completeness the following text includes an analysis of the appeals process in so far as it relates to the determination of bail.

The Appellate System in General

Broadly speaking there are three avenues of appeal against decisions made by the magistrates' court. Appeals on the basis of facts,[2] such as appeals against sentence or conviction are made to the Crown Court and usually take the form of a re-hearing of the case and do not involve an assessment of whether the decision at first instance was right or not. Appeals based on a mis-direction as to law or in excess of jurisdiction lie to the High Court either the Queen's Bench Division or the more recently named Administrative Court. The third avenue of reviewing decisions relies on the statutory power of justices themselves to put right errors and to otherwise act in the interests of justice.

This broad description of avenues of appeal does not take into account other powers, such as the obtaining of prerogative orders, statutory declarations and the power to alter sentences during their currency. Practitioners should try to maintain an up to date knowledge of these lesser quasi-appeals procedures as they

---

1. These materials have previously been presented in training courses by Richard Powell and Chris Bazell on behalf of Progressive Legal Training.
2. Appeals on the facts in family proceedings lie to the Family Division of the High Court.

are often more effective, quicker and cheaper to take advantage of rather than pursuing a costly appeal on a point of law.

Other than applications for the prerogative order of mercy the appeals process from the magistrates' court is entirely statutory based. The coming into force of the Human Rights Act 1998 has led some commentators to suggest that the range of remedies available on appeal may not cover all and sundry circumstances and that in order to give effect to Article 6 of the European Convention the courts may need to develop additional remedies for aggrieved persons seeking redress.

Human Rights Act 1998

Appeals in the Criminal Process

Appeals against the Refusal of Bail

Section 81, Supreme Court Act 1981

The Crown Court has jurisdiction to grant bail in the circumstances set out in section 81, Supreme Court Act 1981. The most common exercise of this jurisdiction arises out of the decision to refuse bail by justices when adjourning criminal proceedings.

Section 81(1)(g)

Section 81(1)(g) provides that the Crown Court may grant bail to a person who has been remanded in custody by a magistrates' court on adjourning a case under:

Section 5

- section 5 (adjournment of inquiry into offence);

Section 10

- section 10 (adjournment of trial);

Section 18

- section 18 (initial procedure on information against adult for offence triable either-way); or

Section 30, Magistrates' Courts Act 1980

- section 30 (remand for medical examination), of the Magistrates' Courts Act 1980.

Section 81(1J)

This section is qualified by section 81(1J) which provides that the court can only grant bail if the magistrates' court which remanded him in custody has certified under section 5(6A) of the Bail Act 1976 that it heard full argument on bail.

Section 5(6A), Bail Act 1976

The key characteristic of the decision making by the Crown Court under this part of the Supreme Court Act 1981 is that it takes effect in the course of proceedings which are not yet completed in the magistrates' court. The power of the Crown Court to grant bail under this section arises in relation to proceedings which are otherwise completed in the magistrates' court.

Rules 19 and 20, Crown Court Rules 1982 govern the procedure for seeking bail from the Crown Court. This is supplemented by Practice Direction 1983 2 All ER 261.

This rule applies where an application to the Crown Court relating to bail is made otherwise than during the hearing of proceedings in the Crown Court.

Notice in writing of intention to make such an application to the Crown Court shall, at lease 24 hours before it is made be given to the prosecutor and, if the prosecution is being carried on by the Crown Prosecution Service, to the appropriate Crown prosecutor or, if the application is to be made by the prosecutor or a constable under section 3(8), Bail Act 1976, to the person to whom bail was granted.

On receiving notice, the prosecutor or appropriate Crown Prosecutor or, as the case may be, the person to whom bail was granted shall:

- notify the appropriate officer of the Crown Court and the applicant that he wishes to be represented at the hearing of the application; or

- notify the appropriate officer and the applicant that he does not oppose the application; or

- give to the appropriate officer, for the consideration of the Crown Court, a written statement of his reasons for opposing the application, at the same time sending a copy of the statement to the applicant.

Except in the case of an application made by the prosecutor or a constable under section 3(8), Bail Act 1976, the applicant shall not be entitled to be present on the hearing of his application unless the Crown Court gives him leave to be present.

Where a person is in custody or has been released on bail desires to make an application relating to bail and has not been able to instruct a solicitor to apply on his behalf under the preceding paragraphs of this rule, he may give notice in writing to the Crown Court of his desire to make an application relating to bail, requesting that the Official Solicitor shall act for him in the

Margin notes:

Rules 19 and 20, Crown Court Rules 1982 Practice Direction 1983

Section 3(8), Bail Act 1976

Section 3(8), Bail Act 1976

application and the court may, if it thinks fit, assign the Official Solicitor to act for the applicant accordingly.

Where the Official Solicitor has been assigned the Crown Court may, if it thinks fit, dispense with the requirements to notify the prosecutor or the offender of the hearing and deal with the application in a summary manner.

Article 6, European Convention

The right of the applicant to be present during a bail application made on his behalf was one of the issues thought to be affected by Article 6, European Convention. The Court of Human Rights has long recognised a right of access to court and a right to effectively participate in proceedings as forming part of the right to a fair trial. A number of Crown Courts amended their practice after 2 October 2000 when the Human Rights Act 1998 so as to give effect to these rights. However in recent months the Crown Court appears to have resumed its traditional approach to the attendance of applicants for bail and reverted to the practice of dealing with them in the applicant's presence. The justification for this appears to be based on the premise that Article 6 requires either the presence of the applicant or that he be represented in the proceedings. As by far the majority of applicants are legally represented in bail applications before the Crown Court such a practice does not seem to offend the right to a fair trial.

Another related issue arose under the right to a fair and public hearing under Article 6 and whether the hearing of bail applications in chambers was compatible with the Convention. At present there has been little case law on the subject however practice seems to vary across the country with some Crown Court centres following traditional procedure and others dealing with applications in open court but allowing representatives to appear as if they were in chambers.

Section 3(8), Bail Act 1976

Rule 19 applies also to applications under section 3(8), Bail Act 1976. This section allows the applicant, the prosecutor or a constable to apply to the Crown Court to vary or impose conditions on bail where the court has granted bail after committal for sentence or trial.

Rule 20 provides

Every person who makes an application to the Crown Court relating to bail shall inform the court of any earlier application to the High Court or the Crown Court relating to bail in the course of the same proceedings.

Where the Crown Court grants bail in criminal proceedings, the recognisance of any surety required as a condition of bail may be entered into before an officer of the Crown Court or, where the person granted bail is in a prison or other place of detention, before the governor or keeper of the prison or place as well as before the persons specified in section 8(4), Bail Act 1976.

Section 8(4), Bail Act 1976

Where the Crown Court imposes a requirement to be complied with before a person's release on bail, the court may give directions as to the manner in which and the person or persons before whom the requirement may be complied with.

The remaining parts of Rule 20 deal with the issue of recognisance and fall outside the scope of this book.

An application for bail to the Crown Court is accordingly dependent on two main limbs. Firstly, that an argued application for bail has been heard and refused by the magistrates' court and secondly, that the magistrates have certified this and issued a full argument certificate which should accompany the application for bail. In addition or as an alternative to applying to the Crown Court an application may be made to a High Court judge by virtue of section 22, Criminal Justice Act 1967.

Section 22, Criminal Justice Act 1967

This provision provides that where a magistrates' court withholds bail in criminal proceedings or imposes conditions in granting bail in criminal proceedings the High Court may, subject to section 25, Criminal Justice and Public Order Act 1994 grant bail or vary the conditions.

Section 25, Criminal Justice and Public Order Act 1994

The procedure under this provision however is less effective to the making of an application to the Crown Court under section 81(1)(g), Supreme Court Act 1981. Where justices have imposed conditions on bail upon adjourning a case otherwise on committal to the Crown Court for sentence or trial the High Court may be only court with jurisdiction to hear an appeal against those conditions.

Section 81(1)(g), Supreme Court Act 1981

Appeals against the Imposition of Bail Conditions by the Magistrates' Court

Section 3(8),
Bail Act 1976

Where the magistrates' court grants bail subject to conditions the venue of any appeal depends on the circumstances in which they were imposed. Section 3(8), Bail Act 1976 provides that where a court has granted bail in criminal proceedings that court or, where that court has committed a person on bail to the Crown Court for trial or to be sentenced or otherwise dealt with, that court or the Crown Court may on application:

- by or on behalf of the person to whom bail was granted; or

- by the prosecutor or a constable;

vary the conditions of bail or impose conditions in respect of bail which has been granted unconditionally.

Section 22,
Criminal Justice
Act 1967
Order 79, Rule 9
of the Rules of the
Rules of the
Supreme Court 1965

If the justices decline to vary their own conditions of bail or if they were imposed other than on the committal for trial or sentence to the Crown Court, the High Court alone has jurisdiction to deal with appeals against such conditions by virtue of section 22, Criminal Justice Act 1967. The procedure for making such an application is set out in Order 79, Rule 9 of the Rules of the Supreme Court 1965.

The relevant procedural parts of Order 79 Rule 9 are as follows:

Subject to the provisions of this rule, every application to the High Court in respect of bail in any criminal proceedings:

- where the defendant is in custody, must be made by summons before a judge in chambers to show cause why the defendant should not be granted bail;

- where the defendant has been granted bail, must be made by summons before a judge in chambers to show cause why the variation in the arrangements for bail proposed by the applicant should not be made.

The summons must, at least 24 hours before the day named therein for the hearing, be served:

- where the application was made by the defendant, on the prosecutor and on the Director of Public Prosecutions, if the prosecution is being carried on by him;

- where the application was made by prosecutor or a constable under section 3(8) of the Bail Act 1976, on the defendant.

Every application must be supported by affidavit

Where a defendant is in custody who desires to apply for bail is unable through lack of means to instruct a solicitor, he may give notice in writing to the judge in chambers stating his desire to apply for bail and requesting that the Official Solicitor shall act for him in the application, and the judge may, if he thinks fit, assign the Official Solicitor to act for the applicant accordingly.

The remainder of the rule deals with amendments to the procedure where the Official Solicitor is assigned and with recognisance and arrangements for compliance with pre-release conditions of bail.

The affidavit required under this rule may be sworn by anyone with knowledge of the case. Where the defendant is represented it may be convenient for his solicitor to swear the affidavit in his own name. It should include:

- Present and anticipated charges;

- Likely plea and any mitigation;

- Defendant's personal circumstances and antecedents including previous convictions;

- Complete history of the proceedings including dates so far;

- Statement of prosecutions objections to bail and the defendant's answers; and

- Defendant's proposals if released on bail including names and addresses of proposed sureties.

The affidavit will need to be amended as appropriate to take into account applications to vary conditions of bail or where the application is made by the prosecutor or a constable under section 3(8), Bail Act 1976.

Section 3(8),
Bail Act 1976

Appeal to the Magistrates' Court Against Bail Granted by the Police or Bail Conditions Imposed on Release from the Police Station

Criminal Justice and Public Order Act 1994

Prior to the Criminal Justice and Public Order Act 1994 the custody officer's decision-making over the grant of bail on charge was relatively straightforward. The accused could either be released on unconditional bail or detained pending appearance before the justices at the next available court.

Bail Act 1976

The Bail Act 1976 was amended by the 1994 Act to allow the custody officer to grant bail with conditions. As this process took place often without any input from the prosecution and without a judicial determination a series of safeguards was created to protect the rights of both the defendant and the community at large.

A defendant refused bail is processed in the traditional manner and appears before justices in order that the legality of his detention is scrutinised under the Bail Act 1976. A defendant granted bail with conditions may apply to the magistrates' to review those conditions and similarly the prosecutor may apply to the magistrates' for bail to be withdrawn.

Applications in Respect of Bail Conditions

Section 3A(4), Bail Act 1976

Section 3A(4), Bail Act 1976 provides that where a custody officer has granted bail in criminal proceedings he or another custody officer serving at the same police station may, at the request of the person to whom it was granted vary the conditions of bail; and in doing so he may impose conditions or more onerous conditions.

There exists a similar power to apply to the magistrates' court prior to the first appearance on the charge to vary conditions of bail imposed by the custody officer.

Section 43B, Magistrates' Courts Act 1980
Part IV, Police and Criminal Evidence Act 1984

Section 43B, Magistrates' Courts Act 1980 provides that where a custody officer:

• grants bail to any person under Part IV, Police and Criminal Evidence Act 1984 in criminal proceedings and imposes conditions, or

Section 3(8),
Bail Act 1976

- varies, in relation to any person, conditions of bail in criminal proceedings under section 3(8), Bail Act 1976:

a magistrates' court may, on application by or on behalf of that person, grant bail or vary the conditions.

On an application the court, if it grants bail and imposes conditions or if it varies the conditions, may impose more onerous conditions.

On determining the application the court shall remand the applicant, in custody or on bail in accordance with the determination and, where the court withholds bail or grants bail, the grant of bail made by the custody officer shall lapse.

Rule 84A,
Magistrates'
Courts Rules 1981

Rule 84A, Magistrates' Courts Rules 1981 prescribes the following procedure. An application under shall:

- be made in writing;

- contain a statement of the grounds upon which it is made;

- specify the offence with which the applicant was charged before his release on bail;

- specify, or be accompanied by a copy of the note of, the reasons given by the custody officer for imposing or varying the conditions of bail; and

- specify the name and address of any surety provided by the applicant before his release on bail to secure his surrender to custody.

Any such application shall be sent to the clerk of the magistrates' court (if any) at the court before which the applicant has a duty to appear or if no such court has been appointed, a magistrates' court acting for the petty sessions area in which the police station at which the applicant was granted bail or at which the conditions of bail were varied, as the case may be, is situated and in either case, a copy shall be sent to a custody officer appointed for that police station.

The clerk to whom an application is sent shall send a notice in writing of the date, time and place fixed for the hearing of the application to the applicant, the prosecutor and any surety in connection with bail in criminal proceedings granted to, or the conditions of which were varied by a custody officer in relation to, the applicant.

The time fixed for the hearing shall be not later than 72 hours after receipt of the application. In fixing the hearing no account shall be taken of Saturday, Sunday or any bank holiday.

Any notice required by this rule to be sent to any person shall either be delivered to him or be sent by post in a letter and, if sent by post to the applicant or a surety of his, shall be addressed to him at his last known or usual place of abode.

If the magistrates' court hearing an application under section 43B(1) of the Act of 1980 discharges or enlarges any recognisance entered into by any surety or reduces the amount in which that person is bound, the clerk of the court shall forthwith give notice thereof to the applicant and any such surety.

Reconsideration of Bail

Section 5B,
Bail Act 1976

Section 5B, Bail Act 1976 provides that where a magistrates' court has granted bail in criminal proceedings in connection with an offence, or proceedings for an offence, to which this section applies, or a constable has granted bail in criminal proceedings in connection with proceedings for such an offence, that court or the appropriate court in relation to the constable may, on application by the prosecutor for the decision to be reconsidered:

- vary the conditions of bail;

- impose conditions in respect of bail which has been granted unconditionally; or

- withhold bail.

The offences to which this section applies are offences triable on indictment and offences triable either-way.

No application for the reconsideration of a decision under this section shall be made unless it is based on information which was not available to the court or constable when the decision was taken.

Section 4(1),
Schedule 1,
Bail Act 1976

Whether or not the person to whom the application relates appears before it, the magistrates' court shall take the decision in accordance with section 4(1) (and Schedule 1), Bail Act 1976.

Where the decision of the court on a reconsideration under this section is to withhold bail from the person to whom it was originally granted the court shall:

- if that person is before the court, remand him in custody; and

- if that person is not before the court, order him to surrender himself forthwith into the custody of the court.

Where a person surrenders himself into the custody of the court in compliance with such an order, the court shall remand him in custody.[3]

Rule 93B,
Magistrates'
Courts Rules 1981

The remaining parts of the section deal with the issue of a warrant for such a person's arrest and the obligation of the court to remand in custody on his appearance under that warrant. Rule 93B, Magistrates' Courts Rules 1981 provide for the procedure to be followed in reconsidering bail under this section.

Bail (Amendment)
Act 1993

The reconsideration of the decision to grant bail under section 5B of the Bail Act arises only in respect of indictable and either-way offences and may only be exercised where fresh information has come to light since the decision to grant bail was taken. It seems to be implicit in this concept of fresh information that the information is directly relevant to the issue of bail and is adverse to the accused. The procedure here is not to be confused with the power of the prosecutor to appeal against the grant of bail *per se* under the Bail (Amendment) Act 1993, dealt with below.

Rule 93B,
Magistrates'
Courts Rules 1981
Section 5B,
Bail Act 1976

Rule 93B, Magistrates' Courts Rules 1981 provides that the appropriate court for the purposes of section 5B, Bail Act 1976 in relation to the decision of a constable to grant bail shall be the magistrates' court (if any) appointed by the custody officer as the court before which the person to whom bail was granted has a duty to appear or if no such court has been appointed, a magistrates' court acting for the petty sessions area in which the police station at which bail was granted is situated.

---

3. The section appears too preclude the court from considering bail. It is questionable whether the legislation can displace the right to bail or the right to a review of bail, both of which are protected by Article 5 of the Human Rights Convention.

An application of this kind shall:

- be made in writing;

- contain a statement of the grounds on which it is made;

- specify the offence which the proceedings in which bail was granted were connected with, or for;

- specify the decision to be reconsidered (including any conditions of bail which have been imposed and why they have been imposed); and

- specify the name and address of any surety provided by the person to whom the application relates to secure his surrender to custody.

The clerk of a magistrates' court to which an application has been made under section 5B shall fix a date, time and place for the hearing of the application and shall give notice of the application and of the date, time and place so fixed in the prescribed form[4] to the person affected and send a copy of the notice to the prosecutor who made the application and to any surety specified in the application.

The time fixed for the hearing shall be not later than 72 hours after receipt of the application.

Service of a notice to be given under paragraph (3) to the person affected may be effected by delivering it to him.

At the hearing of an application under section 5B the court shall consider any representations made by the person affected (whether in writing or orally) before taking any decision under that section in respect to him; and, where the person affected does not appear before the court, the court shall not take such a decision unless it is proved to the satisfaction of the court, on oath or in the manner prescribed by paragraph (1) of rule 67,[5] that the notice required to be given was served on him before the hearing.

Where the court proceeds in the absence of the person affected:

- if the decision of the court is to vary the conditions of bail or impose conditions in respect of bail which has been granted unconditionally, the clerk of the court shall notify the person affected in the prescribed form;

---

4.   Magistrates' Courts (Forms) Rules 1981, Form 153A, B, C.
5.   Which provides for proof of service and certification of service.

- if the decision of the court is to withhold bail, the order of the court shall be signed by the justice issuing it or state his name and be authenticated by the signature of the clerk of the court and shall be in the prescribed form;

- Service of any of the documents may be effected by delivering it to the person to whom it is directed or by leaving it for him with some person at his last known or usual place of abode.

Appeals Against the Grant of Bail

Bail (Amendment) Act 1993

The Bail (Amendment) Act 1993 confers upon the prosecution the right to appeal to the Crown Court against a decision by magistrates' to grant bail.

Where a magistrates' court grants bail to a person who is charged with or convicted of:

- an offence punishable by a term of imprisonment of 5 years or more; or

Section 12 or 12A, Theft Act 1968

- an offence under section 12 or 12A, Theft Act 1968,

the prosecution may appeal to a judge of the Crown Court against the granting of bail.

The power applies only where the prosecution is conducted:

- by or on behalf of the Director of Public Prosecutions; or

- by a person who falls within such class or description of person as may be prescribed for the purposes of this section by order made by the Secretary of State.

Such an appeal may be made only if:

- the prosecution made representations that bail should not be granted; and

- the representations were made before it was granted.

In the event of the prosecution wishing to exercise the right of appeal, oral notice shall be given to the magistrates' court at the conclusion of the proceedings in which such bail has been granted and before the release from custody of the person concerned.

Written notice of appeal shall thereafter be served on the magistrates' court and the person concerned within two hours of the conclusion of such proceedings. Upon receipt from the prosecution of oral notice of appeal from its decision to grant bail the magistrates' court shall remand in custody the person concerned, until the appeal is determined or otherwise disposed of.

The hearing of an appeal against a decision of the magistrates' court to grant bail shall be commenced within 48 hours, excluding weekends and any public holidays, from the date on which oral notice of appeal is given.[6] At the hearing of any appeal by the prosecution under this section, such appeal shall be by way of re-hearing, and the judge hearing such an appeal may remand the person concerned in custody or may grant him bail subject to such conditions (if any) as he thinks fit.

Bail (Amendment) Act 1993 The Bail (Amendment) Act 1993 procedure applies equally to youths as if the reference to a remand in custody included a remand to accommodation provided by a local authority. The procedure does not however appear to apply where the justices have refused bail and remanded a youth to local authority accommodation but have declined to impose a security requirement or a direction as to the keeping of the defendant in secure accommodation.

The following prosecuting authorities have been prescribed by the Secretary of State:

- the Director of the Serious Fraud Office;

Section 1(7), Criminal Justice Act 1987

- any person designated under section 1(7), Criminal Justice Act 1987;

- the Secretary of State for Trade and Industry;

- the Commissioners of Customs and Excise;

- the Secretary of State for Social Security;

- the Post Office; and

- the Commissioners of the Inland Revenue.

Magistrates' Courts (Bail)(Amendment) Rules 1994, Rule 93A The Magistrates' Courts (Bail) (Amendment) Rules 1994 made a number of amendments to the Magistrates' Courts Rules 1981. Rule 93A provides as follows.

---

6.   The 48 hour period indicates that the appeal must be heard within two days and not strictly within 48 hours exactly.

Where the prosecution wishes to exercise the right of appeal under section 1 of the Bail (Amendment) Act to a judge of the Crown Court against a decision to grant bail, the oral notice of appeal must be given to the clerk of the magistrates' court and to the person concerned at the conclusion of the proceedings in which such bail was granted and before the release of the person concerned.

When oral notice of appeal is given, the clerk of the magistrates' court shall announce in open court the time at which such notice was given.

A record of the prosecution's decision and the time the oral notice of appeal was given shall be made in the register and shall contain the particulars set out in the appropriate form prescribed for the purpose.

Where an oral notice of appeal has been given the court shall remand the person concerned in custody by way of a warrant of commitment in the appropriate form prescribed for the purpose.

On receipt of the written notice of appeal, the court shall remand the person concerned in custody by a warrant of commitment in the appropriate form prescribed for the purpose, until the appeal is determined or otherwise disposed of.

A record of the receipt of the written notice of appeal shall be made in the same manner as that of the oral notice of appeal.

If, having given oral notice of appeal, the prosecution fails to serve a written notice of appeal within the two hour period, the clerk of the magistrates' court shall, as soon as practicable, by way of written notice to the persons in whose custody the person concerned is, direct the release of the person concerned on bail as granted by the magistrates' court and subject to any conditions which it imposed.

If the prosecution serves notice of abandonment of appeal on the clerk to the magistrates' court, the clerk shall, forthwith, by way of written notice to the Governor of the prison where the person concerned is being held, or the person responsible for any other establishment where such a person is being held, direct his release on bail as granted by the magistrates' court and subject to any conditions which it imposed.

The clerk to the magistrates' court shall record the prosecution's failure to serve a written notice of appeal, or its service of a notice of abandonment, in the appropriate form prescribed for the purpose.

Where a written notice of appeal has been served on the clerk to the magistrates' court, he shall provide as soon as practicable to the appropriate officer of the Crown Court a copy of that written notice and:

• the notes of argument made by the clerk of the court; and

• a note of the date, or dates when the person concerned is next due to appear in the magistrates' court, whether he is released on bail or remanded in custody by the Crown Court.

Rule 11A, Crown Court Rules Bail (Amendment) Act 1993

Rule 11A, Crown Court Rules makes provision for appeals under the Bail (Amendment) Act 1993 as follows:

The written notice of appeal shall be in the prescribed form or a form to the like effect and shall be served on:

• the clerk of the magistrates' court;

• the person concerned.

The appropriate officer of the Crown Court shall enter the appeal and give notice of the time and place of the hearing to:

• the prosecution;

• the person concerned or his legal representative;

• the clerk of the magistrates' court.

The person concerned shall not be entitled to be present at the hearing of the appeal unless he is acting in person or, in any other case of an exceptional nature, a judge of the Crown Court is of the opinion that the interests of justice require him to be present and gives him leave to be so.

Where a person concerned has not been able to instruct a solicitor to represent him at the appeal, he may give notice to the Crown Court requesting that the Official Solicitor shall represent him at the appeal, and the court may, if it thinks fit, assign the Official Solicitor to act for the person concerned accordingly.

At any time after the service of written notice of appeal, the prosecution may abandon the appeal by giving notice in writing in the prescribed form or a form to the like effect. The notice of abandonment shall be served on:

- the person concerned or his legal representative;

- the clerk of the magistrates' court;

- the appropriate officer of the Crown Court.

The appropriate officer of the Crown Court shall, as soon as practicable after the hearing of the appeal, give notice[7] of the decision to:

- the person concerned or his legal representative;

- the prosecution;

- the police;

- the clerk to the magistrates' court;

- the governor of the prison or person responsible for the establishment where the person concerned is being held.

Guidance issued by the CPS states that "the power of appeal against a grant of bail must be used judiciously and responsibly, and the CPS expects the number of appeals to be small. It is not to be used merely because the Crown Prosecutor disagrees with the decision of the magistrates. It should only be used in cases of grave concern." As a general rule approval for the use of this power to appeal can expect to have been given by an experienced Crown Prosecutor of at least four years' standing.

The oral notice of appeal must be given at the conclusion of proceedings and before the person concerned is released on bail. In *R v Isleworth Crown Court ex parte Clarke*[8] notice was served 5 minutes after the bench rose and moments before the person concerned was to be released. On appeal the Divisional Court held that the statutory criteria had been met.

---

7. In addition to the methods of service permitted by rule 28, the notices required by paragraphs (3), (5), (7) and (9) may be sent by way of a facsimile transmission and the notice required by paragraph (3) may be given by telephone.
8. [1998] 1 Cr App R 257.

Where the judge decides to withhold bail the person concerned must be remanded to the next hearing before the magistrates' court. The prosecution should advise the judge to stipulate a date which falls within the time limits set by sections 128 and 129, Magistrates Courts Act 1980.[9]

Sections 128 and 129, Magistrates Courts Act 1980

In *R* v *Middlesex Guildhall Crown Court ex parte Okoli*[10] the Queen's Bench Division held that where an oral notice of appeal against a decision to grant bail had been given, the appeal hearing was to commence within 48 hours of the date and not the time from which notice of appeal was given.

The Right of Appeal to the Crown Court

Section 108, Magistrates' Courts Act 1980

The right to appeal against conviction and/or sentence to the Crown Court is a familiar jurisdiction.[11] Section 108, Magistrates' Courts Act 1980 provides that a person convicted by a magistrates' court may appeal to the Crown Court if he pleaded guilty, against his sentence and if he did not, against the conviction or sentence.

Statutory provisions under which a conviction of an offence for which an order for conditional or absolute discharge is made is deemed not to be a conviction (except for certain purposes) shall not prevent an appeal under this section, whether against conviction or otherwise.

A person sentenced by a magistrates' court for an offence in respect of which an order for conditional discharge has been previously made may appeal to the Crown Court against the sentence.

The term "sentence' includes any order made on conviction by a magistrates' court, not being:

• an order for the payment of costs;

Section 2, Protection of Animals Act 1911

• an order under section 2, Protection of Animals Act 1911 (which enables a court to order the destruction of an animal); or

---

9. *Governor of Pentonville Prison ex parte Bone* (1994) *The Times* 15 November.
10. (2002) *The Times* 2 August.
11. But one which can catch out the unwary. Contrary to popular belief in at least one Crown Prosecution area there is a right of appeal against both conviction and sentence for contempt of court. Similarly there is a right of appeal upon re-sentencing for breach of a community penalty. A Youth Court is a special kind of magistrates' court and as such the appeal provisions apply equally to decisions of the youth court save that any appeal will be before a judge and justices drawn from the Youth Court Panel.

- an order made in pursuance of any enactment under which the court has no discretion as to the making of the order or its terms,

Section 31, Public Order Act 1986 Football Spectators Act 1989

and also includes a declaration of relevance[12] under section 31, Public Order Act 1986 or under the Football Spectators Act 1989.

Whilst there is no right to appeal against an order for costs, the destruction of an animal under the Protection of Animals Act or against a mandatory order made on conviction there is a right to appeal against conviction, subject to the usual bar relating to guilty pleas, which gave rise to the unappealable order.

Guilty Pleas Bar the Right to Appeal Against Conviction

As a general rule a defendant may not appeal against his conviction having entered a lawful guilty plea to the charge. There are three exceptions to this rule although they are not true exceptions as they arise out of a challenge to the legality of the defendant's plea. In each of these situations the Crown Court has power to remit the matter back to the magistrates' court on a not guilty basis and for a trial to take place, or for the case to be otherwise disposed of.

The three situations are:

(1) where the defendant enters an equivocal plea. It would be unusual for the justices to accept an equivocal plea but where they do, and act upon it the Crown Court will remit back to the justices on appeal;

(2) A plea which is unequivocally one of guilty when made may be rendered equivocal by information given to the magistrates before they pass sentence. This information may come from the prosecution or the defence but regard should also be had of any investigations carried out in the preparation of pre-sentence reports. In such situations on appeal the Crown Court should remit the cases back to the magistrates for trial. (E.g. R v Blandford Justices, ex parte G;[13]

(3) Even if a plea of guilty was unequivocal when made and not put in doubt by any developments prior to the passing of sentence, the accused is not debarred from appealing his conviction to the Crown Court if the plea was entered

---

12. See the section on ancillary order at page XX above.
13. [1967] 1 QB 82.

under duress *R* v *Huntingdon Crown Court, ex parte Jordan*.[14] In such circumstances the Crown Court has power to remit the matter for trial back to the justices.

Where a defendant has been committed for sentence the Crown Court retains a general discretion to remit back to the magistrates where the conviction is in doubt as a result of the accused's guilty plea. (*R* v *Inner London Crown Court ex parte Sloper*.[15] This situation seems more likely to arise now that justices are required to take a plea in all either-way offences even those which are certain to be committed for sentence. Strictly this procedure falls outside the scope of this course on appeals but it is an important issue for practitioners to consider.

Human Rights Act 1998

The Human Rights Act 1998 has also potentially affected the issue of whether a defendant should be barred from appealing against conviction after entering a guilty plea. If a guilty plea has been tendered in circumstances where it is not equivocal or made under duress but in the course of a trial procedure which lacks the necessary safeguards to amount to a fair trial for the purposes of Article 6 of the European Convention there may now be grounds to allow an appeal notwithstanding the general bar. In *R* v *Togher and Others*[16] the Court of Appeal recognised this principle in the case of convictions on indictment and it would seem that the same is likely to hold true in the case of appeals from magistrates' courts.

Crown Court directions that magistrates rehear a case on a not guilty basis can lead to certain difficulties if the justices do not accept that the Crown Court's assessment is correct. In *R* v *Plymouth Justices ex parte Hart*[17] the Divisional Court held that provided the Crown Court had made a proper inquiry into whether the accused's plea was equivocal and had sufficient evidence to reach that conclusion, then the order to remit and try the cause had to be obeyed by the magistrates. The magistrates were also held to be under a duty to assist the Crown Court in its investigation of the summary process by supplying relevant affidavits. If the justices in receipt of an order to try the matter refuse to do so an application for judicial review lies to the Administrative Court to either quash the crown court's order or to compel the magistrates to comply with it.

14. [1981] QB 857.
15. [1978] 69 Cr App R 1.
16. (2000) *The Times* 9 November.
17. [1986] QB 950.

The Crown Court Rules and Magistrates' Courts Rules more fully describe the procedure for an appeal to the Crown Court. Rule 74, Magistrates' Courts Rules 1981 provides that a clerk of a magistrates' court shall as soon as practicable[18] send to the appropriate officer of the Crown Court any notice of appeal to the Crown Court given to the clerk of the court.

Rule 74, Magistrates' Courts Rules 1981

The clerk of the magistrates' court shall send to the appropriate officer of the Crown Court, with the notice of appeal, a copy of the extract of the magistrates' courts register relating to that decision and of the last known or usual place of abode of the parties to the appeal.

Where any person, having given notice of appeal to the Crown Court, has been granted bail for the purposes of the appeal the clerk of the court from whose decision the appeal is brought shall before the day fixed for the hearing of the appeal sent to the appropriate officer of the Crown Court

Section 5, Bail Act 1976

- in the case of bail in criminal proceedings, a copy of the record made in pursuance of section 5, Bail Act 1976 relating to such bail;

- in the case of bail otherwise than in criminal proceedings, the recognisance entered into by the appellant relating to such bail.

Where a notice of appeal is given in respect of a hospital order or guardianship order, the clerk of the magistrates' court from which the appeal is brought, shall send with the notice to the appropriate officer of the Crown Court any written evidence considered by the court.

Section 10, Criminal Justice Act 1967

Where a notice of appeal is given in respect of an appeal against conviction by a magistrates' court the clerk of the court shall send with the notice to the appropriate officer of the Crown Court any admission of facts made for the purposes of the summary trial under section 10, Criminal Justice Act 1967.

Where a notice of appeal is given in respect of an appeal against sentence by a magistrates' court, and where that sentence was a custodial sentence, the clerk of the court shall send with the notice to the appropriate officer of the Crown Court, a statement of whether the magistrates' court obtained and considered a pre-sentence report before passing such sentence.

---

18. Emerging national guidelines suggest that all appeals (and committals) to the Crown Court should be processed administratively within 4 working days. This is not a statutory time limit.

The requirements of this rule have to be complied with even where the notice of appeal is given after the 21 days allowed for an appeal to the Crown Court has expired. It will be for the Crown Court to deal with the issue of whether to grant leave to appeal out of time. There is no right to an oral hearing in an application for leave to appeal out of time and, until the incorporation of Article 6 of the European Convention there was no general duty on the Crown Court to give reasons for refusing such an application; R v *Croydon Crown Court ex parte Smith.*[19]

Rule 7, Crown Court Rules 1982

Rule 7, Crown Court Rules 1982 provides that an appeal shall be commenced by the appellant's giving notice of appeal in accordance with the following provisions of this rule.

The notice required by the preceding paragraph shall be in writing and shall be given:

- in a case where the appeal is against a decision of the magistrates' court, to the clerk of the magistrates' court;

- in any other case, to the appropriate officer of the Crown Court;

- in any case, to any other party to the appeal.

Notice of appeal shall be given not later than 21 days after the day on which the decision appealed against is given and, for this purpose, where the court has adjourned the trial of an information after conviction, that day shall be the day on which the court sentences or otherwise deals with the offender. Provided that, where a court exercises its power to defer sentence that day shall, for the purposes of an appeal against conviction, be the day on which the court exercises that power.

A notice of appeal shall state in the case of an appeal arising out of a conviction by a magistrates' court, whether the appeal is against conviction or sentence or both. The time for giving notice of appeal may be extended, either before or after it expires, by the Crown Court, on application. An application for an extension of time shall be made in writing, specifying the grounds of the application and sent to the appropriate officer of the Crown Court.

Where the Crown Court extends the time for giving notice of appeal, the appropriate officer of the Crown Court shall give notice of the extension to

- the appellant;

---

19.   [1983] 77 Cr App R 277.

- in the case of an appeal from a decision of the magistrates' court, to the clerk of the magistrates' court;

and the appellant shall give notice of the extension to any other party to the appeal.

Rule 8

Rule 8 provides that on receiving notice of appeal, the appropriate officer of the Crown Court shall enter the appeal and give notice of the time and place of the hearing to:

- the appellant;

- any other party to the appeal;

- in the case of an appeal from a decision of the magistrates' court, to the clerk of the magistrates' court.

Section 74, Supreme Court Act 1981 Practice Direction (Crown Court: Allocation of Business)

In accordance with section 74, Supreme Court Act 1981 and Practice Direction (Crown Court: Allocation of Business)[20] an appeal is listed before a circuit judge or recorder who normally sits with two lay justices. The magistrates must, of course, not have been concerned with the original case. The justices are expected to take part in the decision making and a majority decision, even if it excludes the professional judge prevails except that in matters of law the justices must defer to the views of the presiding judge; *R* v *Orpin*.[21] Occasions where such a majority view has prevailed are usually obvious to the practitioner!

If the appellant is legally aided he can require the clerk of the relevant magistrates' court to provide him with a note of the evidence at first instance. This right does not extend to a non-legally aided appellant but any such request should be "viewed with sympathy"; *R* v *Highbury Corner Justices ex parte Hussein*.[22]

The appeal against conviction takes the form of a rehearing and the usual rules relating to trial and mitigation apply.[23] Because the appeal is a re-hearing the parties are not limited to the evidence given before the justices and the judge is free to deal with procedural and substantive issue as he sees fit in accordance with usual practice. However, this power is restricted and the judge does not have power to amend the information in respect of which the defendant was convicted in the first place; *R* v *Norwich Crown Court ex parte Russell*[24] and he cannot

---

20.   [1995] 1 WLR 1083.
21.   [1975] QB 283.
22.   [1986] 1 WLR 1266.
23.   Section 79(3), Supreme Court Act 1981.
24.   [1993] Crim LR 518.

strike out amendments made by the justices at the original trial; *Fairgrieve v Newman*.[25]

At an appeal against sentence the prosecution simply outline the facts of the case, the court considers any pre-sentence reports and defence mitigation. The task of the court is to decide whether what it thinks is the appropriate sentence differs significantly from the sentence imposed. Only where it does, should the court allow the appeal and substitute its own sentence. Over the years there has been a marked increase in judicial "tinkering' that is to say alterations to sentences which are not significantly inappropriate.

The justices from whose decision the appeal is being brought, have a right to appear and to call evidence in support of their decision, but in doing so the justices do not make themselves a party to the appeal and, therefore, do not incur a liability in costs. The person who initiated the proceedings is the proper respondent and normally the only respondent to the appeal. Justices generally will not wish to be represented on the hearing of the appeal where the prosecutor is going to be present. However where the justices know that the prosecutor will not appear they have a duty to appear to call evidence to support their original conclusion. If no-one appears to do so the Crown Court will normally allow the appeal. *R v Harrow Crown Court ex parte Dave*.[26]

Section 48, Supreme Court Act 1981

The Crown Court's powers on appeal are set out in section 48, Supreme Court Act 1981, which, in part provides that the Crown Court may, in the course of hearing any appeal, correct any error or mistake in the order or judgment incorporating the decision which is the subject of the appeal.

On the termination of the hearing of an appeal the Crown Court:

- may confirm, reverse or vary any part of the decision appealed against, including a determination not to impose a separate penalty in respect of an offence; or

- may remit the matter with its opinion thereon to the authority whose decision is appealed against; or

- may make such other order in the matter as the court thinks just, and by such order exercise any power which the said authority might have exercised.

25.   [1985] 82 Cr App R 60
26.   [1994] 1 All ER 315.

Section 11(6),
Criminal Appeal
Act 1995

Subject to section 11(6), Criminal Appeal Act 1995, if the appeal is against a conviction or a sentence, the preceding provisions of this section shall be construed as including power to award any punishment, whether more or less severe than that awarded by the magistrates' court whose decision is appealed against, if that is a punishment which that magistrates' court might have awarded.

Effectively an appeal against a decision of the magistrates' court is an appeal against the whole decision made at the relevant hearing. This would permit the Crown Court to allow an appeal against conviction for offence A but to substitute a finding of guilt in respect of offence B which the magistrates had acquitted. More usually the Crown Court exercises its powers under this section to vary or confirm the original decision. Where an appellant successfully appeals against his conviction for an endorseable motoring offence the Crown Court is able to re-sentence in respect of other endorseable offences convicted on the same occasion but where penalty points/disqualification were not imposed as they attached to the offence now successfully appealed against.

Where an appellant fails to appear to prosecute his appeal the Crown Court has power to dismiss the appeal and in so doing may, in appropriate cases increase the sentence; R v *Guildford Crown Court ex parte Brewer*.[27] In this case the prosecutor was present at the appeal and the court was not able to treat the non-appearance of the appellant as an application for leave to abandon the appeal. Where neither the appellant nor the prosecutor appear the proper course is to dismiss the appeal; R v *Croydon Crown Court ex parte Clair*.[28]

When dismissing an appeal against conviction (and probably now when confirming or varying sentence) the Crown Court must give sufficient reasons which do not need to be elaborate, to show that it has identified the main issues in the case and how it has dealt with them.

---

27.   [1987] Cr App R 265.
28.   [1986] 1 WLR 746.

Section 109, Magistrates' Courts Act 1980, Rule 11, Crown Court Rules and Rule 75, Magistrates' Courts Rules make provision for the abandonment of the appeal which may either be effected by obtaining the leave of the Crown Court or by service of a written notice of abandonment.

Section 109, Magistrates' Courts Act 1980, Rule 11, Crown Court Rules and Rule 75, Magistrates' Courts Rules

Appeals Against Binding Over Orders

Section 1(1), Magistrates' (Appeals from Binding Over Orders) Act 1956 provides a separate right of appeal to the Crown Court against an order to be bound over to keep the peace. The appeal is by way of a re-hearing and sufficient evidence to justify the order must be presented unless the appellant admits his behaviour.

Section 1(1), Magistrates' (Appeals from Binding Over Orders) Act 1956

Bail Pending Appeal

Section 113, Magistrates' Court Act 1980 provides that where a person has given notice of appeal to the Crown Court against the decision of a magistrates' court or has applied to a magistrates' court to state a case for the opinion of the High Court, then, if he is in custody, the magistrates' court may grant him bail.[29]

Section 113, Magistrates' Court Act 1980

The magistrates have discretion whether to grant bail pending appeal. The scheme for bail under the Bail Act 1976 as informed by Article 5 of the European Convention applies to the exercise of this discretion except that the right to bail is lost. If bail is withheld on an appeal to the Crown Court the appellant has a right to apply for bail from the Crown Court under section 81, Supreme Court Act 1981 or to the High Court under section 22, Criminal Justice Act 1967. As a general proposition case law tends to favour the justices' refusal of bail pending appeal to the Crown Court: *R v Watton*.[30]

Section 81, Supreme Court Act 1981 Section 22, Criminal Justice Act 1967

Whilst the granting of bail pending appeal inevitably suspends the order of a custodial sentence the lodging of notice of appeal does not suspend any other order of the court. There is specific power to suspend the operation of a disqualification from driving pending appeal but there is non power to suspend the effect of a community penalty and the general principle that a sentence is in force when it is made applies; *Greater Manchester Probation Committee v Best*.[31]

---

29. See above at page XX.
30. [1979] Crim LR 246.
31. (1996) 160 JP 297.

The Enforcement of Orders Made on Appeal

Section 110,
Magistrates'
Courts Act 1980

Section 110, Magistrates' Courts Act 1980 provides that in effect any order made by the Crown Court on appeal is to be treated as if it were made by the magistrates. This prohibits the justices from committing an offender in breach of a community order on appeal to be dealt with at the Crown Court and similarly restricts the power of the judge to reserve re-sentencing to himself under the Crime and Disorder Act 1998.

Crime and
Disorder Act 1998

Criminal Appeal
Act 1968
Section 28,
Supreme Court
Act 1981

Further appeal may lie against the decision of the Crown Court to the Court of Appeal under the Criminal Appeal Act 1968 or to the High Court by way of case stated under section 28, Supreme Court Act 1981.

References from the Criminal Cases Review Commission

The Criminal Cases Review Commission

The Commission has power to refer convictions or sentences in the magistrates' court to the Crown Court. Before it can do so the following conditions must apply:

• there must be a real possibility that the conviction, verdict or sentence would not be upheld;

• conviction cases: there must be evidence or an argument on a point not previously raised, unless there are exceptional circumstances;

• sentence case: there must be information or an argument on a point of law not previously raised;

• there must have been a determined appeal or a refusal of leave to appeal, unless there are exceptional circumstances.

The Commission has wide powers and duties to investigate what can misleadingly be described as "miscarriages of justice'.

The Commission has published an information pack which includes an application form to set in train the Commission's powers. It is available from the Commission at

Alpha Tower,
Suffolk Street,
Queensway,
Birmingham B1 1TT or
DX 715466 Birmingham 41.

Section 11,
Criminal Appeal
Act 1995

Section 108(1),
Magistrates'
Courts Act 1980

If the Commission makes use of its powers under section 11, Criminal Appeal Act 1995 to refer a conviction in the magistrates' court to the Crown Court, then such a reference shall be treated for all purposes as an appeal under section 108(1), Magistrates' Courts Act 1980 against conviction whether he pleaded guilty or not. In such a deemed appeal the Crown Court is not empowered to increase the sentence imposed on the applicant if his referral is unsuccessful.

Appeals by Way of Case Stated

An appeal by way of case stated is an appeal on a point of law. The appeal is to the High Court where a Divisional Court of the Queen's Bench exercises jurisdiction. Provisions of the Magistrates' Courts Act and Rules and the Rules of the Supreme Court govern the procedure.

Section 111,
Magistrates'
Courts Act 1980

Section 111, Magistrates' Courts Act 1980 provides that any person who was a party to any proceeding before a magistrates' court or is aggrieved by the conviction order, determination or other proceeding of the court may question the proceeding on the ground that it is wrong in law or is in excess of jurisdiction by applying to the justices composing the court to state a case for the opinion of the High Court on the question of law or jurisdiction involved; but a person shall not make an application under this section in respect of a decision against which he has a right of appeal to the High Court or which by virtue of any enactment passed after 31 December 1879 is final.

An application to state a case shall be made within 21 days after the day on which the decision of the magistrates' court was given.

For this purpose the day on which the decision of the magistrates' court is given shall, where the court has adjourned the trial of an information after conviction, be the day on which the court sentences or otherwise deals with the offender.

On the making of an application under this section in respect of a decision any right of the applicant to appeal against the decision to the Crown Court shall cease.

If the justices are of the opinion that an application is frivolous, they may refuse to state a case, and, if the applicant so requires, shall give him a certificate stating that the application has been refused; but the justices shall not refuse to state a case if the application is made by or on behalf of the Attorney-General.

Where justices refuse to state a case, the High Court may, on the application of the person who applied for the case to be stated, make an order of *mandamus* requiring the justices to state a case.

Section 113,
Magistrates'
Courts Act 1980

Section 113, Magistrates' Courts Act 1980 allows the justices to grant bail pending an appeal by way of case stated. However the recent decision in *Allen* v *West Yorkshire Probation Service*[32] should be considered in respect of appeals against sentence. The Queen's Bench Division held that appeals by case stated or judicial review were not usually appropriate procedures for appeals against sentence.[33] If a sentence imposed by a magistrates' court was wrong, the defendant should appeal to the Crown Court.

Section 114,
Magistrates'
Courts Act 1980

Section 114, Magistrates' Courts Act 1980 provides as follows. Justices to whom application has been made to state a case for the opinion of the High Court on any proceeding of a magistrates' court shall not be required to state a case until the applicant has entered into a recognisance with or without sureties, before the magistrates' court, conditioned to prosecute the appeal without delay and to submit to the judgment of the High Court and pay such costs as that Court may award; and (except in criminal matters) the clerk of the magistrates' court shall not be required to deliver the case to the applicant until the applicant has paid the fees payable for the case and for the recognisances to the justices' chief executive for the court.

The imposition of sureties to state a case must be carefully handled by the clerk of the magistrates' court. The surety should be sufficiently meaningful to guarantee the swift prosecution of the case but not so heavy so as to amount to an effective bar on the case proceedings. Such a bar could amount to a restriction on the right of access to court protected under Article 6 of the European Convention.

---

32. (2001) *The Times* 20 February.
33. The Lord Chief Justice said that he hoped that a loud and clear signal would be sent to those who had to advise defendants where they contended that something had gone wrong in the sentencing process of a lower court.

The procedure to state a case for the opinion of the High Court is complicated and involves the review of a number of different statutory sources. The following is a guide to the procedure.

Except where there is a right of appeal to the High Court, or where some enactment makes the magistrates' decision final, any person who was a party to any proceeding before a magistrates' court, or is aggrieved by the conviction, order, determination or other proceeding of the court, may question the proceeding on the ground that it is wrong in law or in excess of jurisdiction, by applying to the justices composing the court to state a case for the opinion of the High Court. However, if the defendant is aggrieved by a decision of justices on matters of fact, the proper remedy is by appeal to the Crown Court. Any challenge made to a sentence imposed by justices should be by way of appeal to the Crown Court, rather than by way of case stated to the Divisional Court, in all but the most exceptional case.

An application to state a case must be made within 21 days after the date on which the decision of the magistrates' court was given. The court may refuse to state a case if of the opinion that the application is frivolous, the applicant may then apply for an order of *mandamus* requiring the justices to state a case. An appellant in an appeal by way of case stated is entitled to withdraw his appeal and the leave of the High Court is not required.

As to when a case stated is appropriate, practitioners should understand that it may be applied for only where it is submitted that an order or procedure is wrong in law or in excess of jurisdiction. Justices have no jurisdiction to state a case in criminal proceedings unless and until they have reached a final determination in the case. There is no jurisdiction to state an "interlocutory' case during the hearing. A stated case may be sought by any party or person aggrieved by the decision of the court including the a prosecutor. Questions over the court's jurisdiction cannot be stated unless there has been a hearing in the magistrates' court. It is unlikely that a case may be stated on the basis of the way in which the magistrates' court has exercised its discretion unless the exercise of discretion is so unreasonable that no proper tribunal could have reached that decision.

Section 142,
Magistrates'
Courts Act 1980

A case may be stated even where the court has alternative methods of resolving the error for example by use of its powers under section 142, Magistrates' Courts Act 1980. However, refusal to accept an alternative and more economic way of dispute resolution may be a factor taken into account in determining costs.

It is possible to state a case on the basis that the sentence imposed by the justices on the defendant was harsh and oppressive, or so far outside the normal discretionary limits as to entitle the Divisional Court to say that the decision must involve an error of law. However the general rule has been recently reinforced that where something has gone wrong in the sentence of a defendant by a lower court the usual route of appeal lies to the Crown Court and not by way of case stated or judicial review.

Appeal from the Divisional Court in a criminal matter lies to the House of Lords. The Divisional Court must first certify that a point of law of general public importance is involved in the decision. Leave must then be given to appeal by either the Divisional Court or the House of Lords.

Application to State a Case

The application to state a case must be in writing and signed by or on behalf of the applicant. It has to identify the question of law or jurisdiction on which the opinion of the High Court is sought. The application should be sent to the clerk to the magistrates' court whose decision is questioned. The requirement to identify the question or questions of law or jurisdiction is directory. If no such question is identified the magistrates may decline to state the case. In such circumstances an applicant will need either to redraft his case or seek further order from the High Court. In such an application the High Court will need to decide whether there has been a substantial compliance with the rule. In any event, any failure to comply with the Rules indicating the form of the application, can be corrected at any time before the case comes before the High Court. Indeed it is usual for the questions to be redrafted a number of times by agreement between the parties.

The 21 day limit

The 21 day time limit for applications to state a case is strictly observed. Where an application is sent by post, the application is made when it is posted, provided that in the ordinary course of post it would be received within the 21 day period prescribed, even though, in fact, it is received outside that period.

The High Court has no power to extend the period of 21 days within which the application must be made. For the purposes of the time limit both Christmas Day and Good Friday are counted. The time runs after the day on which the court sentences or otherwise deals with the offender, when the decision was made.

Justices may refuse to state a case where they are of the opinion that the application is frivolous, unless the application is made by or on behalf of the Attorney-General. The word "frivolous' in means that the justices consider the application to be futile, misconceived, hopeless or academic. Justices forming this opinion must indicate their reasons and issue a certificate of refusal. Such a decision is open to appeal by way of judicial review for an order requiring the court to state the case. Where leave is granted for such a judicial review to begin, it would be usual for the justices to act on the grant of leave and state the case.

On the making of an application to state a case, the applicant loses any right of appeal to the Crown Court.

The justices are not required to state the case until the applicant has entered into a recognisance to prosecute the appeal without delay, submit to judgment, and to pay any costs ordered by the High Court. It does not appear to be mandatory for the justices to require a recognisance. In deciding whether to require a recognisance, and if so, in fixing the amount of the recognisance, the justices shall take the applicant's means into account. The fact that the applicant is a man of straw does not mean that the justices cannot impose a requirement that the applicant enter into a recognisance with a surety to prosecute the appeal. The recognisance may be entered into at any time before the case is stated and delivered.

Procedure for Stating a Case

Rules 76 to 81, Magistrates' Courts Rules 1981

The procedure for stating a case is set out in rules 76 to 81, Magistrates' Courts Rules 1981. The following procedure has been judicially approved:

1. On receipt of a proper application, the justices' clerk should prepare a draft case immediately, unless the justices are likely to refuse to state a case.

2. For the purposes of preparing the first draft, the justices' clerk should, if necessary, consult the justices, and may informally discuss the application with either or both parties.

3. The first draft should be sent to the justices and to the parties within 21 days of the application being received.

4. When the draft is sent to the parties they should be specifically reminded that they must make representation within 21 days of receiving the draft case.

5. The justices' clerk may informally discuss the draft case with the parties prior to their making representations.

6. Immediately after the expiry of the date by which representations should be made by the parties, the justices' clerk should notify the justices of any representations, or provide a revised draft of the case, and agree the final form of the case with them.

7. The final form of the draft will be signed by any two of the justices or by the justices' clerk, and sent to the applicant or his solicitor within 21 days of the last day for making representations.

If there has been any delay in complying with the 21 day limits or an extension of time has been agreed, the justices' clerk must attach to the case a statement of the delay and the cause of the delay. Generally, the justices' clerk should prepare the first draft of the case. Although the stated case is that of the justices, it would be highly unusual for lay magistrates to be able to provide a compliant stated case for the opinion of the High Court. Usually a district judge will prepare his own stated case. In the rare circumstances where the justices prepare their own case, their justices' clerk remains under a duty to comply with time limits. It is not relevant that the original decision was by reached by a majority.

The Content of the Case

The content of the case includes the facts found by the court, and the question or questions of law or jurisdiction on which the opinion of the High Court is sought. It should also state the submissions of the parties, and the opinion or decision of the justices. The question stated should reflect the findings of fact. It should also provide an answer to the point at issue, for example whether the conviction is correct in law. There is nothing improper about the justices altering or amending the question so long as the parties, in particular the party seeking the opinion of the High Court have had an opportunity to comment upon it.

Where a document forms a material part of the case stated, the original document or a photocopy of the whole of the document should be appended to the case. The stated case should clearly set out the facts of the case found by the justices and not the evidence upon which their finding is based. The only exception to this is where the whole point of the question is whether there was sufficient evidence on which the justices could come to their decision.

The High Court will not preclude arguments being raised in the stated case which were not raised before the justices originally. However, the High Court will not permit further evidence to be called or allow arguments to be advanced which require further findings of fact. The High Court is a tribunal of law and not fact.

Since the Human Rights Act 1998 came into force it has become common practice for justices to give reasons for convictions and sentence. At the end of a trial good practice has developed whereby the justices' decision includes a summary of the facts as found and how evidence was dealt with. There is nothing in statute requiring justices' reasons to be in any particular form or detail and accordingly there appears to be nothing wrong in principle for those brief reasons to be expanded upon in a case stated. However the findings and reasons set out in a stated case must be consistent with the gist of the decision given at first instance.

Generally, the High Court will not disturb the exercise of judicial discretion or interfere with inferences properly drawn. For example the High Court should not interfere with the justices' decision to exclude or admit evidence under the Police and Criminal Evidence Act 1984 provided the justices have applied the right tests.

The impact of Article 6 of the European Convention on this issue remains to be seen. It would appear likely that if the Divisional Court is of the opinion that the trial was unfair it is under a duty to intervene. The fairness of the trial may well involve the exercise of discretion to exclude/admit evidence and the correctness of the justices' decision in this area may become a province of the Divisional Court especially in the light of the suggested approach of the Court of Appeal to the question of whether a conviction in the Crown Court is unsafe.

The Hearing in the High Court

The hearing of the case stated then takes place in the High Court according to rules and procedures familiar in that jurisdiction and falling outside the scope of this work. It would be unusual for the justices to appear unless their *bona fides* is in question. There is power to join the Secretary of State in proceedings for a declaration of incompatibility under the Human Rights Act 1998.

Having heard and determined the question or questions of law, the court may reverse, affirm or amend the determination in respect of which the case has been stated, or remit the matter to the justices or justices with the opinion of the court thereon, or make such other order in relation to the matter as to the court may seem fit. This does not include a power to order a retrial or to impose a lesser penalty on the appellant. Where the court overturns the decision of the justices to dismiss an allegation, the High Court has power to impose a sentence if it is satisfied that only one sentence was open to the justices had they acted "correctly' in the first place

Section 112,
Magistrates'
Courts Act 1980

Section 112, Magistrates' Courts Act 1980 provides that any conviction, order, determination or other proceeding of a magistrates' court varied by the High Court on an appeal by case stated, and any judgment or order of the High Court on such an appeal may be enforced as if it were a decision of the magistrates' court from which the appeal was brought.

Appeals by Way of Judicial Review

Appeals by way of judicial review engage the inherent jurisdiction of the High Court exercised through the Administrative Court. The procedure is set out in a number of rules under the Rules of the Supreme Court. The following is a guide to the procedure.[34]

RSC Order 53
Practice Note
(Crown Office List:
Preparation for
Hearings)

The High Court has jurisdiction to make orders of *certiorari*, *mandamus* and prohibition, the application for which shall be made in accordance with RSC Order 53, by a procedure known as an application for judicial review. Practice Note (Crown Office List: Preparation for Hearings)[35] sets out the practical arrangements for such an application. Judicial review is limited to considering whether the magistrates' court has failed to exercise its jurisdiction properly or whether it has come to some error of laws which appears on the face of the record. Judicial review is concerned, not with the decision but with the decision-making process; it is the legality of the process which is under review, not whether it is right or wrong. An application for judicial review may be made whether or not other avenues of appeal have been exhausted, although in the case of sentence such applications are generally inappropriate. The most appropriate way of challenging the decisions of magistrates on a point of law is by way of case stated and not by judicial review as the power to review a decision or decision making process is usually an appeal of last resort. Judicial review may not be appropriate in all interlocutory matters in the summary trial of proceedings. Where for example a defendant sought review of the justice's decision to refuse to stay summary proceedings where the Crown had declined to provide advance disclosure and an issue under Article 6 of the Convention arose, the High Court decided that the application was premature and should await the final outcome of the trial in order to ascertain whether the proceedings were fair or otherwise; *R v Stratford Justices ex parte Imbert* (1999).

Leave of the High Court must first be obtained before an application for judicial review may be commenced. The application must be made without delay and normally within three months from the date when grounds for the application first arose. In appropriate circumstances the High Court may direct a stay in the magistrates' court proceedings when it grants leave to bring judicial review proceedings.

---

34.   See, generally, *Civil Appeals*, EMIS Professional Publishing.
35.   [1994] 4 All ER 671.

Judicial review is a discretionary remedy and the principles on which the Divisional Court will exercise that discretion were considered in *R* v *Peterborough Justices ex parte Dowler*[36] and *R* v *Hereford Magistrates' Court ex parte Rowlands*.[37] The availability of other methods of obtaining redress, such as an appeal to the Crown Court may be taken into account in deciding whether to grant leave to bring judicial review proceedings. However, if the applicant can show that there is an arguable case that the decision is untenable, it is likely that judicial review may be commenced notwithstanding those other methods of obtaining relief.

The High Court may, in judicial review proceedings, grant a range of reliefs. These include *Certiorari*, *Mandamus* and *Prohibition*. The nature and availability of such orders fall outside this work and practitioners are advised to seek specialist procedural advice in advance of seeking judicial review

Appearance by Justices

Generally justices will not appear or be represented in the High Court in judicial review proceedings unless their *bona fides* is in question or the Administrative Court wishes them to be present. The justices' clerk is responsible for ensuring that the justices submit affidavits as appropriate

Liability of Justices for Costs in Judicial Review

In *R* v *Newcastle-under-Lyme Justices ex parte Massey*[38] the Divisional Court decided that the following principles should be applied when determining the liability of justices for costs in judicial review proceedings:

- The High Court has jurisdiction to award costs against justices in judicial review proceedings and on appeals by way of case stated and the Divisional Court has suggested that there is no reason for applying, at least in civil cases, different principles to each.

- It is not in every case that a successful litigant can expect to recover his costs against anyone.

- Justices who merely file affidavits and do not appear before the Court will not, without more, normally be visited with a

---

36. [1996] 2 Cr App Rep 561.
37. (1997) 161 JP 258.
38. (1994) 158 JP 1037.

Supreme Court Act 1981

costs order. This is so despite the fact that in judicial review proceedings justices are served with notice of the proceedings and are therefore party to them within the Supreme Court Act 1981.

- Justices should not generally appear in the Court unless their *bona fides* are called into question or there are other exceptional circumstances. If they do appear they are unlikely to recover costs if successful, and they will be at risk of costs if they lose.

- If justices do not appear, an order for costs in relation to the merits of the application or appeal is only likely to be made against them in exceptional circumstances, but justices should first be invited by the Court to appear to explain their apparently unreasonable behaviour.

Practice Direction (Crown Office List: Consent Orders)

- Justices and other tribunals who decline to sign a consent in Crown Office civil proceedings in accordance with Practice Direction (Crown Office List: Consent Orders), so that costs of appearing before the Court are unnecessarily incurred by other parties, may, in an appropriate case, have an order for such costs made against them even if they do not appear.

- An order for costs should be made where the justices behaved unreasonably in all the circumstances. The quality of the original decision, for example whether it was merely wrong in law or flagrantly perverse, albeit one of the factors for consideration, should not be determinative of the result. It is necessary to look at all the circumstances in which the justices or tribunal were invited to consent; these will include the attitude to the judicial review or appeal proceedings of the prosecution or other body which instituted the original proceedings, the information provided to the justices or tribunal and the time given to them to consider whether to consent, the type of consideration needed and the nature of the flaw in the challenged decision. The more obviously perverse, the more readily should consent be given and, if withheld, the more readily should costs be ordered.

- No final costs order should be made by the Divisional Court or the High Court against justices without giving them the opportunity to be heard. The preferable route of challenge to such an order is an application to set aside rather than an appeal to the Court of Appeal. The time limit for an application to set aside is usually 7 days but it is appropriate for this to be extended to 21 days where the justices did not appear. The 21 day period runs from the receipt of the transcript by the justices.

Where justices have refused to state a case for the opinion of the High Court on the ground that the application was frivolous and have been informed that a High Court judge has subsequently granted leave to apply for judicial review, the justices must give proper weight to that decision. If they fail to do so and persist in the view that the application to state a case is frivolous, they may be ordered to pay costs of the substantive application for *mandamus*.

Alternatives to Appeals in the Criminal Jurisdiction of the Magistrates' Court

Not all defects in decisions taken in or by a magistrates' court require the assistance of the appellate courts to resolve. There are a number of procedures within the magistrates' court which can be employed to put right something which has gone wrong.

Power to Correct Mistakes

Section 142, Magistrates' Courts Act 1980

Section 142, Magistrates' Courts Act 1980 provides that a magistrates' court may vary or rescind a sentence or other order imposed or made by it when dealing with an offender if it appears to the court to be in the interests of justice to do so; and it is hereby declared that this power extends to replacing a sentence or order which for any reason appears to be invalid by another which the court has power to impose or make.

The power conferred on a magistrates' court shall not be exercisable in relation to any sentence or order imposed or made by it when dealing with an offender if:

- the Crown Court has determined an appeal against:

  - the sentence or order;

  - the conviction in respect of which that sentence or order was imposed or made; or

  - any other sentence or order imposed or made by the magistrates' court when dealing with the offender in respect of that conviction (including a sentence or order replaced by that sentence or order); or

- the High Court has determined a case stated for the opinion of that court on any question arising in any proceeding leading to or resulting from the imposition or making of the sentence or order.

Where a person is convicted by a magistrates' court and it subsequently appears to the court that it would be in the interests of justice that the case should be heard again by different justices, the court may so direct.

The power conferred on a magistrates' court to reopen a case shall not be exercisable in relation to a conviction if:

- the Crown Court has determined an appeal against any sentence or order imposed or made by the magistrates' court when dealing with the offender in respect of that conviction; or

- the High Court has determined a case stated for the opinion of that court on any question arising in any proceeding leading to or resulting from the imposition or making of the sentence or order.

Where a sentence or order is varied, the sentence or other order as so varied shall take effect from the beginning of the day on which it was originally imposed or made unless the court otherwise directs.

Section 142, Magistrates' Courts Act 1980

The power under section 142, Magistrates' Courts Act 1980 is effectively a slip rule and the justices have a wide discretion over the employment of the section's powers. The provision cannot be used to reinstate a case after acquittal as it applies only in relation to orders on conviction. However the section can be used to rectify mistakes made during the interlocutory stages of summary proceedings. The section acts without prejudice to the various common law powers of the court to put right matters arising out of proceedings which are a nullity.

When exercising its discretion as to whether the interests of justice require a re-hearing the court must act on proper judicial grounds. The section should not be used as a device to get around restrictions imposed on the appeal's process; for example to allow a defendant a rehearing where he is prevented from appealing to the Crown Court on account of an unequivocal guilty plea. Where there is a complaint against the course or outcome of proceedings it can sometimes be difficult to know what is a proper matter for reconsideration under section 142 and what is a proper matter for appeal to the Crown or High Court. However the exercise of the justice' broad discretion must be informed as much by the consequences for the prosecution as the defence.

Altering Crown Court sentences

Section 142, Magistrates' Courts Act 1980

The power to alter sentences available to magistrates' courts under section 142, Magistrates' Courts Act 1980 is a useful device to avoid costly appeals. A similar power exists in relation to sentences imposed by the Crown Court. The power is described here because occasionally orders made in the Crown Court may not be as accurate as they could be, particularly for example orders made involving endorsement and disqualification.

A sentence imposed, or other order made, by the Crown Court when dealing with an offender may be varied or rescinded by the Crown Court within the period of 28 days beginning with the day on which the sentence or other order was imposed or made or, where two or more persons are jointly tried on an indictment, then, subject to the following provisions of this section, a sentence imposed, or other order made, by the Crown Court on conviction of any of those persons on the indictment may be varied or rescinded by the Crown Court not later than the expiry of whichever is the shorter of the following periods, that is:

- the period of 28 days beginning with the date of conclusion of the joint trial;

- the period of 56 days beginning with the day on which the sentence or other order was imposed or made.

For these purposes, the joint trial is concluded on the latest of the following dates, that is any date on which any of the persons jointly tried is sentenced or is acquitted or on which a special verdict is brought in.

A sentence or other order shall not be varied or rescinded under this section except by the court constituted as it was when the sentence or other order was imposed or made, or, where that court comprised one or more justices of the peace, a court so constituted except for the omission of any one or more of those justices.

Where a sentence or other order is varied under this section the sentence or other order, as so varied, shall take effect from the beginning of the day on which it was originally imposed or made, unless the court otherwise directs.

Statutory Declarations

The magistrates' court may also permit a defendant to make a statutory declaration in relation either to his conviction or in relation to the registration of certain financial penalties against him.

Section 14,
Magistrates'
Courts Act 1980
Section 1,
Magistrates'
Courts Act 1980

A statutory declaration may be made where the defendant was not aware of proceedings under section 14, Magistrates' Courts Act 1980 which provides, so far as it is relevant that where a summons has been issued under section 1, Magistrates' Courts Act 1980 and a magistrates' court has begun to try the information to which the summons relates, then, if the accused, at any time during or after the trial, makes a statutory declaration that he did not know of the summons or the proceedings until a date specified in the declaration, being a date after the court has begun to try the information and within 21 days of that date the declaration is served on the justices' chief executive for the court without prejudice to the validity of the information, the summons and all subsequent proceedings shall be void.

The declaration must be served within 21 days of the date specified in the declaration as the date on which he came to know of the summons or the proceeding concerned. A justice may extend this period on application if it was not reasonable to expect the accused to serve the declarations as required.

The making of a declaration renders void the consequences of the trial from the date the declaration is served. However the consequences, including disqualification from driving is not void *ab initio*; *Singh* v *DPP*.[39]

The declaration does not affect the validity of the information and accordingly a further summons can be issued against the accused but justices who adjudicated on the void proceedings may not try the issue again.

---

39.   [1999] Crim LR 914.

Statutory Declarations under the Road Traffic Offenders Act 1988

Sections 72 and 73, Road Traffic Offenders Act 1988

Sections 72 and 73, Road Traffic Offenders Act 1988 allow the making of a statutory declaration to a justice of the peace in relation to fixed penalties which, having been unpaid have been registered as a fine in the magistrates' court for enforcement against the relevant person. Section 72 provides for a person against whom such a fine has been registered to make a declaration that he was not the person to whom the notice was given or that he had requested but not been granted a hearing on the matter. The declaration must be made and served on the proper officer of the court enforcing the fixed penalty within 21 days of the person making it receiving notice of the registration.

Section 73 makes similar provision for those cases where the original notice was affixed to a vehicle in the absence of any person. A declaration may be made subject to the same procedural requirements asserting that the person making the declaration did not know of the fixed penalty until he received notice of the registration, that he was not the owner of the vehicle at the time and has reasonable excuse for failing to comply with the notice or that he requested but was not granted a hearing on the matter.

In either case the period of notice may be extended on application by a justice of the peace. The declaration renders the proceedings void and effectively cancels the consequences flowing from registration.

The grounds for making a statutory declaration under this legislation are strict and the procedure cannot be used to avoid the registration of an unpaid fixed penalty otherwise than in the circumstances prescribed by the legislation.

Statutory Declarations Act 1835

Declarations made under these sections are made by virtue of the Statutory Declarations Act 1835 and a false declaration is punishable of conviction on indictment by imprisonment of up to 2 years and summarily by 6 months imprisonment, a fine or both.

Applications to Alter Sentences

There are several provisions enabling applications to be made to modify sentences. These include:

Remission of
Penalties Act 1859

- the remission of penalties in criminal and quasi-criminal proceedings under the Remission of Penalties Act 1859. The procedure for which is explained in *Todd* v *Robinson*;[40]

Section 85,
Magistrates'
Courts Act 1980

- the remission of a fine in default of payment on inquiry into a defaulter's means under section 85, Magistrates' Courts Act 1980;

- the variation of a fine where the justices were unaware of the defendant's means;

- the discharge or variation of a compensation order on the grounds of a subsequent change in financial circumstances;

- the substitution of a conditional discharge for a probation order;

Section 42,
Road Traffic
Offenders Act 1988

- the removal of any order of disqualification after the passage of certain time periods including driving disqualification under section 42, Road Traffic Offenders Act 1988; and

- the common law power to reject a "guilty' plea and direct a "not guilty' plea at any time up to sentence.

Application for a Pardon

Power exists in the royal prerogative of mercy for a pardon to be given under the sign manual. This course may be used where all proper form was followed in achieving the conviction and no recourse to appeal or review exists, but where it is abundantly clear that the conviction was wrong, for example from unimpeachable evidence which emerges later. The effect of the pardon is to remove from the subject of the pardon " all pains penalties and punishments whatsoever that from the said conviction may

Section 9, Criminal
Justice Act 1967

ensue' but not to eliminate the conviction. Section 9, Criminal Justice Act 1967 pertains to this unusual procedure.

Application for Habeas Corpus

This is an easy and quick mode of challenging the legality of a person's detention. It is not an appropriate means of appealing

---

40.   (1884) 48 JP 692.

Order 54, Rules
of the Supreme
Court 1965

from a sentence of imprisonment nor for securing the release of a person detained for non-payment of fines where the warrant is defective. Order 54, Rules of the Supreme Court 1965 provides for the procedure to be followed in such an application.

International Process

No direct appeal lies against a decision of a magistrates' court to any international judicial forum. However a practitioner should always consider the international angle of any possible appeal. Of particular importance are the roles of the Court of Human Rights and the Court of Justice.

Human Rights Act 1998

Human Rights
Act 1998

Under the Human Rights Act 1998 a magistrates' court is a public authority with a duty to act compatibly with the rights and freedoms set out in the European Convention. Where a public authority does not act compatibly with such rights and freedoms it may be acting unlawfully and can be litigated against. The Act does not provide any remedies additional to those already available in the High Court and accordingly a violation of Convention rights by a public authority may be pursued through, most usually judicial review where the act

Section 6

complained of is under section 6 of the Act.

In this early stage of the Acts currency it is difficult to assess the likelihood of successes against the court as a public authority. Judicial acts are in any event exempted from litigation based on this provision.

The magistrates' court is unable to make a declaration of incompatibility in respect of primary legislation which is not compatible with the European Convention. Accordingly whilst the duty of the court is to strive to find a compatible interpretation of national legislation with Convention rights, where it cannot do so the justices must apply the law as it is.

The decision of the magistrates' court in such circumstances may then be appealed on a point of law either by way of a stated case or by judicial review. The High Court may be able then to find a compatible interpretation of the relevant law but in the rare cases where it is unable to do so the High Court has power to make a declaration of incompatibility which triggers the fast track towards legislative change. However, little immediate comfort is available for the successful appellant under the scheme of the Human Rights Act as the making of a declaration of incompatibility does not affect the enforcement or validity of the proceedings in which it is made and the High Court would be bound to follow the natural meaning of the relevant statute notwithstanding its conclusion that the legislation is incompatible with Convention rights.

In an unreported case – *Craig T and Others* (1999) – the Court of Criminal Appeal declined to take into account apparent violations of Convention rights when considering the seriousness of an offence of gross indecency between a number of men.

Appeals under the Human Rights Act 1998

Sections 7 and 8, Human Rights Act 1988

Sections 7 and 8, Human Rights Act 1998 provide for actions to be brought against a public authority which acts otherwise in accordance with a right protected under the European Convention. Proceedings are commenced under existing heads or causes of action and in many cases the appropriate method of bringing such proceedings will be by way of judicial review. Such an application must be brought within twelve months of the act complained of unless the Court grants an extension.

This process is not an appeal in the strictest sense although decisions of the magistrates' court as a public authority may be properly challenged in this way.

Section 9, Section 7

Section 9 of the Act provides that proceedings under section 7 against a judicial act may only be brought by way of appeal, application for judicial review or by such other form as may be prescribed. The attack envisaged by this provision is on the compatibility of the judicial act with the Convention rights *vis-à-vis* the judicial officer's role as a public authority.

An aggrieved party to a decision of the court in the course of proceedings is more likely to arise out of the court's interpretation or application of law. The magistrates' court has no power to make a declaration of incompatibility and must, in default of finding a compatible interpretation of statutes, apply the law as it is written. As a matter of course such a determination is unlikely to be concerned with the facts of the case such that an appeal to the Crown Court will be appropriate. The determination is more likely to trespass into the domain of the High Court by either judicial review or stated case; however, practitioners should consider whether an appeal to the Crown Court may resolve the complaint without troubling the higher courts and where such an appeal would provide an adequate remedy it is perhaps to be preferred.

On appeal to the High Court there is power for a declaration of incompatibility to be made. The Criminal Appeals (Amendment) Rules 2000 make provision for notice to be given to the Crown and for the joinder of the relevant Secretary of State to such proceedings. Where a declaration of incompatibility is made by the senior appellate court in criminal proceedings the Crown is entitled with leave to appeal against the order directly to the House of Lords. The making of a declaration does not however affect the validity or enforcement of the legislation in the proceedings and does not set a precedent for future cases while the "offending' legislation remains in force. Accordingly an appellant in proceedings where a declaration is made remains subject to the full force of the legislation whether it is subsequently amended or not. At present this issue seems unlikely to be accepted as mitigation by a criminal court after the case of *Craig T and Others* (2000), where defendants convicted of certain sexual offences were unsuccessful in persuading the Court of Appeal that the accepted incompatibility between the Sexual Offences Act 1956 and Article 8 of the Convention was relevant to the sentence. Instead the Court of Appeal held that the sentencing court was right to sentence for the seriousness of the offence and should not undermine the statute unless and until Parliament changed the law to bring it in line with Convention rights.

Criminal Appeals (Amendment) Rules 2000

Sexual Offences Act 1956 Article 8

The Court of Human Rights

The scheme for the protection of rights and freedoms under the European Convention operates outside the overall legal system in the United Kingdom. Save to the extent that it is provided by the Human Rights Act 1998 the Court of Human Rights cannot be regarded as an appeal court from decisions in the United Kingdom.

Human Rights Act 1998

However the Court of Human Rights exists to provide at least a possible but partial remedy to violations of fundamental rights within the criminal process. A practitioner should consider the jurisdiction of the Court of Human Rights once all domestic remedies open are exhausted by way of appeal and where the circumstances of the case disclose a *prima facie* breach of the

Convention. The process should not be lightly embarked upon as it is complex, costly, lengthy and may produce little in terms of tangible redress for the client. However, a finding of the Court of Human Rights that a client's rights or freedoms have been violated may be a useful tool to persuade either the Court of Appeal or the Criminal Cases Review Commission that the decision of the magistrates' court should be reviewed.

In *Rowe, Davis and Johnson* v *UK* (2000) the applicant's before the Court of Human Rights were successful in showing that their trial had been unfair and in violation of Article 6 of the Convention. In this case their earlier appeal had been rejected by the Court of Appeal. Armed with their finding from the Court of Human Rights the three were subsequently successful before a further hearing of the Court of Appeal.

The procedure for taking a case to the Court of Human Rights is complex and falls outside this course. Practitioners considering such a course would be advised to seek assistance from those with familiarity with the procedures and, at the very least, to consult a specialist text on the subject.

The Court of Justice

The Court of Justice is the judicial forum for the European Union. The Court has jurisdiction to give a preliminary ruling on the interpretation of Union treaties, acts of the institutions and the interpretation of Union legislation. National courts are required to separate that which is of purely domestic law from that which falls within the jurisdiction of the Court of Justice. It is not for the national authorities to interpret union legislation. The purpose behind this is to ensure consistent application of Union regulations throughout the Union.

A magistrates' court has power to make a reference to the Court of Justice for a preliminary ruling on the interpretation of union and Union-related law at any stage of proceedings and a case in which such a reference is made may be adjourned to await the outcome of the Court of Justice's deliberations.

Although this procedure cannot be regarded as an appeals process in the strictest sense the process allows a practitioner to vastly expand upon the judicial environment. Again extensive case-law exists on the propriety of seeking a preliminary ruling from the Court of Justice and it would not be unfair to say that the practice is hardly encouraged by the higher courts.

Practitioners should however make themselves aware of the process and should not shrink from urging the procedure upon the magistrates' court in the right cases.

CHAPTER 15
THE MAGISTRATES' COURTS' SENTENCING GUIDELINES

**Issued October 2003 for Implementation date:
1 January 2004**

Public Order Act 1986 s.3 Triable either way – see Mode of Trial Guidelines Penalty: Level 5 and/or 6 months	**Affray**

CONSIDER THE SERIOUSNESS OF THE OFFENCE
(INCLUDING THE IMPACT ON THE VICTIM)

IS DISCHARGE OR FINE APPROPRIATE?
IS IT SERIOUS ENOUGH FOR A COMMUNITY PENALTY?
GUIDELINE: → IS IT SO SERIOUS THAT ONLY CUSTODY IS APPROPRIATE?
ARE YOUR SENTENCING POWERS SUFFICIENT?

THIS IS A GUIDELINE FOR A FIRST-TIME OFFENDER PLEADING NOT GUILTY

✚   CONSIDER AGGRAVATING AND MITIGATING FACTORS   ➖
AND THE WEIGHT TO ATTACH TO EACH

for example	for example
Busy public place	Provocation
Football related	Did not start the trouble
Group action	Stopped as soon as the police arrived
Injuries caused	*This list is not exhaustive*
People actually put in fear	
Vulnerable victim(s)	
This list is not exhaustive	

If racially or religiously aggravated, or offender is on bail, this offence is more serious
If offender has previous convictions, their relevance and any failure to respond to previous
sentences should be considered – they may increase the seriousness. The court should make
it clear, when passing sentence, that this was the approach adopted.

TAKE A PRELIMINARY VIEW OF SERIOUSNESS,
THEN CONSIDER OFFENDER MITIGATION

for example
  Age, health (physical or mental)
  Co-operation with police
  Evidence of genuine remorse
  Voluntary compensation

CONSIDER YOUR SENTENCE

Compare it with the suggested guideline level of sentence and reconsider
your reasons carefully if you have chosen a sentence at a different level.
Consider a reduction for a timely guilty plea.

DECIDE YOUR SENTENCE
NB. COMPENSATION – Give reasons if not awarding compensation

Aggravated vehicle-taking	Theft Act 1968 s.12A as inserted by Aggravated Vehicle-Taking Act 1992 Triable either way – but in certain cases summarily only – consult legal adviser. Penalty: Level 5 and/or 6 months Must endorse and disqualify at least 12 months

CONSIDER THE SERIOUSNESS OF THE OFFENCE
(INCLUDING THE IMPACT ON THE VICTIM)

IS DISCHARGE OR FINE APPROPRIATE?
IS IT SERIOUS ENOUGH FOR A COMMUNITY PENALTY?
GUIDELINE: → IS IT SO SERIOUS THAT ONLY CUSTODY IS APPROPRIATE?
ARE YOUR SENTENCING POWERS SUFFICIENT?

THIS IS A GUIDELINE FOR A FIRST-TIME OFFENDER PLEADING NOT GUILTY

➕ CONSIDER AGGRAVATING AND MITIGATING FACTORS AND THE WEIGHT TO ATTACH TO EACH ➖

for example	for example
Competitive driving: racing, showing off	Passenger only
Disregard of warnings, eg from passengers or others in vicinity	Single incident of bad driving
Group action	Speed not excessive
Police pursuit	Very minor injury/damage
Pre-meditated	*This list is not exhaustive*
Serious injury/damage	
Serious risk	
Trying to avoid detection or arrest	
Vehicle destroyed	
This list is not exhaustive	

If racially or religiously aggravated, or offender is on bail, this offence is more serious
If offender has previous convictions, their relevance and any failure to respond to previous sentences should be considered – they may increase the seriousness. The court should make it clear, when passing sentence, that this was the approach adopted.

TAKE A PRELIMINARY VIEW OF SERIOUSNESS, THEN CONSIDER OFFENDER MITIGATION

for example
    Health (physical or mental)
    Co-operation with police
    Evidence of genuine remorse
    Voluntary compensation

CONSIDER YOUR SENTENCE

Compare it with the suggested guideline level of sentence and reconsider your reasons carefully if you have chosen a sentence at a different level. Consider a reduction for a timely guilty plea. Order a re-test unless good reason not to.

DECIDE YOUR SENTENCE
NB. COMPENSATION – Give reasons if not awarding compensation. In certain cases this offence is summary only – consult legal adviser.

Protection of Animals Act 1911 s.1 Triable only summarily Penalty: Level 5 and/or 6 months with powers to deprive ownership of the relevant animal and disqualify from keeping all or any animals	**Animal cruelty**

CONSIDER THE SERIOUSNESS OF THE OFFENCE

IS DISCHARGE OR FINE APPROPRIATE?
GUIDELINE: → IS IT SERIOUS ENOUGH FOR A COMMUNITY PENALTY?
IS IT SO SERIOUS THAT ONLY CUSTODY IS APPROPRIATE?

THIS IS A GUIDELINE FOR A FIRST-TIME OFFENDER PLEADING NOT GUILTY

➕ CONSIDER AGGRAVATING AND MITIGATING FACTORS AND THE WEIGHT TO ATTACH TO EACH ➖

for example	for example
Adult involving children Animal(s) kept for livelihood Committed over a period or involving several animals Deriving pleasure from torturing or frightening Disregarded warnings of others Group action Offender in position of special responsibility towards the animal Premeditated/deliberate Prolonged neglect Serious injury or death Use of Weapon *This list is not exhaustive*	Ignorance of appropriate care Impulsive Minor injury Offender induced by others Single incident *This list is not exhaustive*

If offender is on bail, this offence is more serious
If offender has previous convictions, their relevance and any failure to respond to previous sentences should be considered – they may increase the seriousness. The court should make it clear, when passing sentence, that this was the approach adopted.

TAKE A PRELIMINARY VIEW OF SERIOUSNESS, THEN CONSIDER OFFENDER MITIGATION

for example
    Age, health (physical or mental)
    Co-operation with police
    Evidence of genuine remorse

CONSIDER YOUR SENTENCE

Compare it with the suggested guideline level of sentence and reconsider your reasons carefully if you have chosen a sentence at a different level.
Consider a reduction for a timely guilty plea.
Always consider disqualifying the offender from having custody of animals, or depriving him or her of owning the animal concerned.

DECIDE YOUR SENTENCE

Assault – actual bodily harm	Offences Against the Person Act 1861 s.47 Triable either way – see Mode of Trial Guidelines Penalty: Level 5 and/or 6 months

CONSIDER THE SERIOUSNESS OF THE OFFENCE
(INCLUDING THE IMPACT ON THE VICTIM)

IS DISCHARGE OR FINE APPROPRIATE?
IS IT SERIOUS ENOUGH FOR A COMMUNITY PENALTY?
GUIDELINE: → IS IT SO SERIOUS THAT ONLY CUSTODY IS APPROPRIATE?
ARE YOUR SENTENCING POWERS SUFFICIENT?

THIS IS A GUIDELINE FOR A FIRST-TIME OFFENDER PLEADING NOT GUILTY

➕ CONSIDER AGGRAVATING AND MITIGATING FACTORS AND THE WEIGHT TO ATTACH TO EACH ➖

for example	for example
Abuse of trust (domestic setting)	Minor injury
Deliberate kicking or biting	Provocation
Extensive injuries (may be psychological)	Single blow
Headbutting	*This list is not exhaustive*
Group action	
Offender in position of authority	
On hospital/medical or school premises	
Premeditated	
Victim particularly vulnerable	
Victim serving the public	
Weapon	
This list is not exhaustive	

If offender is on bail, this offence is more serious
If offender has previous convictions, their relevance and any failure to respond to previous sentences should be considered – they may increase the seriousness. The court should make it clear, when passing sentence, that this was the approach adopted.

TAKE A PRELIMINARY VIEW OF SERIOUSNESS, THEN CONSIDER OFFENDER MITIGATION

for example
Age, health (physical or mental)
Co-operation with police
Evidence of genuine remorse
Voluntary compensation

CONSIDER YOUR SENTENCE

Compare it with the suggested guideline level of sentence and reconsider your reasons carefully if you have chosen a sentence at a different level. Consider a reduction for a timely guilty plea.

DECIDE YOUR SENTENCE
NB. COMPENSATION – Give reasons if not awarding compensation

| Police Act 1996 s.89
Triable only summarily
Penalty: Level 5 and/or 6 months | **Assault on a
police officer** |

CONSIDER THE SERIOUSNESS OF THE OFFENCE
(INCLUDING THE IMPACT ON THE VICTIM)

IS DISCHARGE OR FINE APPROPRIATE?
IS IT SERIOUS ENOUGH FOR A COMMUNITY PENALTY?
GUIDELINE: → IS IT SO SERIOUS THAT ONLY CUSTODY IS APPROPRIATE?

THIS IS A GUIDELINE FOR A FIRST-TIME OFFENDER PLEADING NOT GUILTY

➕   **CONSIDER AGGRAVATING AND MITIGATING FACTORS**   **➖**
AND THE WEIGHT TO ATTACH TO EACH

for example
    Any injuries caused
    Gross disregard for police authority
    Group action
    Premeditated
    Spitting
    This list is not exhaustive

for example
    Impulsive action
    Unaware that person was a police officer
    This list is not exhaustive

If racially or religiously aggravated, or offender is on bail, this offence is more serious
If offender has previous convictions, their relevance and any failure to respond to previous
sentences should be considered – they may increase the seriousness. The court should make
it clear, when passing sentence, that this was the approach adopted.

TAKE A PRELIMINARY VIEW OF SERIOUSNESS, THEN
CONSIDER OFFENDER MITIGATION

for example
    Age, health (physical or mental)
    Co-operation with police
    Evidence of genuine remorse
    Voluntary compensation

CONSIDER YOUR SENTENCE

Compare it with the suggested guideline level of sentence and reconsider
your reasons carefully if you have chosen a sentence at a different level.
Consider a reduction for a timely guilty plea.

DECIDE YOUR SENTENCE
NB. COMPENSATION – Give reasons if not awarding compensation

Breach of a community order	Criminal Justice Act 1991 sch. 2 A fine – maximum £1,000 A Community Punishment Order (up to 60 hours) In certain circumstances, an Attendance Centre Order Revocation of Order and re-sentence for original offence Commit a Crown Court Order to be dealt with at Crown Court

CONSIDER THE EXTENT OF THE BREACH

➕ CONSIDER AGGRAVATING AND MITIGATING FACTORS AND THE WEIGHT TO ATTACH TO EACH ➖

for example	for example
No attempt to start the sentence Unco-operative *This list is not exhaustive*	Completed a significant part of the order *This list is not exhaustive*

CONSIDER OFFENDER MITIGATION
(including timely admission)

DECIDE IF THE ORDER SHOULD CONTINUE

IF THE ORDER SHOULD CONTINUE

   Is a fine appropriate? (Starting Point B)

   Is a community punishment order appropriate?

   Where the order is a community rehabilitation order, is an attendance centre order appropriate?

   Is a curfew order appropriate?

IF THE ORDER SHOULD NOT CONTINUE AND IT IS A MAGISTRATES' COURT ORDER:

   Revoke and re-sentence for original offence (see relevant guideline)

NB. IF THE ORDER WAS MADE BY THE CROWN COURT, MAY FINE AND ALLOW ORDER TO CONTINUE, OR COMMIT TO CROWN COURT TO BE DEALT WITH (CONSULT LEGAL ADVISER)

Crime and Disorder Act 1998 s.1 Triable either way – see Mode of Trial Guidelines Penalty: Level 5 and/or 6 months	**Breach of anti-social behaviour order**

CONSIDER THE SERIOUSNESS OF THE OFFENCE
(INCLUDING THE IMPACT ON THE VICTIM)

IS FINE APPROPRIATE? (NB. A DISCHARGE IS NOT AVAILABLE FOR THIS OFFENCE)
IS IT SERIOUS ENOUGH FOR A COMMUNITY PENALTY?
GUIDELINE: → IS IT SO SERIOUS THAT ONLY CUSTODY IS APPROPRIATE?
ARE YOUR SENTENCING POWERS SUFFICIENT?

THIS IS A GUIDELINE FOR A FIRST-TIME OFFENDER PLEADING NOT GUILTY

➕ CONSIDER AGGRAVATING AND MITIGATING FACTORS ➖
AND THE WEIGHT TO ATTACH TO EACH

for example
    Breach of recently imposed order
    Breach amounted to commission of an
       offence
    Continues the pattern of behaviour the order
       sought to prohibit
    Group action
    Use of violence, threats, intimidation
    This list is not exhaustive

If racially or religiously aggravated, or offender is on bail, this offence is more serious
If offender has previous convictions, their relevance and any failure to respond to previous
sentences should be considered – they may increase the seriousness. The court should make
it clear, when passing sentence, that this was the approach adopted.

TAKE A PRELIMINARY VIEW OF SERIOUSNESS, THEN
CONSIDER OFFENDER MITIGATION

for example
    Age, health (physical or mental)
    Co-operation with police
    Evidence of genuine remorse
    Voluntary compensation

CONSIDER YOUR SENTENCE

Compare it with the suggested guideline level of sentence and reconsider
your reasons carefully if you have chosen a sentence at a different level.
Consider a reduction for a timely guilty plea.

DECIDE YOUR SENTENCE
NB. COMPENSATION – Give reasons if not awarding compensation

Burglary (dwelling)	Theft Act 1968 s.9 Triable either way – see Mode of Trial Guidelines Penalty: Level 5 and/or 6 months

CONSIDER THE SERIOUSNESS OF THE OFFENCE
(INCLUDING THE IMPACT ON THE VICTIM)

IS DISCHARGE OR FINE APPROPRIATE?
IS IT SERIOUS ENOUGH FOR A COMMUNITY PENALTY?
IS IT SO SERIOUS THAT ONLY CUSTODY IS APPROPRIATE?
GUIDELINE: → ARE YOUR SENTENCING POWERS SUFFICIENT?

THIS IS A GUIDELINE FOR A FIRST-TIME OFFENDER PLEADING NOT GUILTY

➕ CONSIDER AGGRAVATING AND MITIGATING FACTORS ➖
AND THE WEIGHT TO ATTACH TO EACH

for example	for example
Force used or threatened Group enterprise High value (in economic or sentimental terms) property stolen More than minor trauma caused Professional planning/organisation/ execution Significant damage or vandalism Victim injured Victim present at the time Vulnerable victim *If ANY of the above factors are present you should commit for sentence.*	First offence of its type AND low value property stolen AND no significant damage or disturbance AND no injury or violence Minor part played Theft from attached garage Vacant property *ONLY if one or more of the above factors are present AND none of the aggravating factors listed are present should you consider NOT committing for sentence.*

If racially or religiously aggravated, or offender is on bail, this offence is more serious
If offender has previous convictions, their relevance and any failure to respond to previous sentences should be considered – they may increase the seriousness. The court should make it clear, when passing sentence, that this was the approach adopted.

TAKE A PRELIMINARY VIEW OF SERIOUSNESS, THEN CONSIDER
WHETHER THE CASE SHOULD BE COMMITTED FOR SENTENCE,
THEN CONSIDER OFFENDER MITIGATION

for example
    Age, health (physical or mental)
    Co-operation with police
    Evidence of genuine remorse
    Voluntary compensation

CONSIDER COMMITTAL OR YOUR SENTENCE

Compare it with the suggested guideline level of sentence and reconsider your reasons carefully if you have chosen a sentence at a different level. Consider a reduction for a timely guilty plea.

DECIDE YOUR SENTENCE
NB. COMPENSATION – Give reasons if not awarding compensation

| Theft Act 1968 S.9
Triable either way – see Mode of Trial Guidelines
Penalty: Level 5 and/or 6 months | **Burglary
(non-dwelling)** |

CONSIDER THE SERIOUSNESS OF THE OFFENCE
(INCLUDING THE IMPACT ON THE VICTIM)

IS DISCHARGE OR FINE APPROPRIATE?
GUIDELINE: → IS IT SERIOUS ENOUGH FOR A COMMUNITY PENALTY?
IS IT SO SERIOUS THAT ONLY CUSTODY IS APPROPRIATE?
ARE YOUR SENTENCING POWERS SUFFICIENT?

THIS IS A GUIDELINE FOR A FIRST-TIME OFFENDER PLEADING NOT GUILTY

➕ CONSIDER AGGRAVATING AND MITIGATING FACTORS ➖
AND THE WEIGHT TO ATTACH TO EACH

for example	for example
Forcible entry	Low value
Group offence	Nobody frightened
Harm to business	No damage or disturbance
Occupants frightened	*This list is not exhaustive*
Professional operation	
Repeat victimisation	
School or medical premises	
Soiling, ransacking, damage	
This list is not exhaustive	

If racially or religiously aggravated, or offender is on bail, this offence is more serious
If offender has previous convictions, their relevance and any failure to respond to previous
sentences should be considered – they may increase the seriousness. The court should make
it clear, when passing sentence, that this was the approach adopted.

TAKE A PRELIMINARY VIEW OF SERIOUSNESS, THEN
CONSIDER OFFENDER MITIGATION

for example
    Age, health (physical or mental)
    Co-operation with police
    Evidence of genuine remorse
    Voluntary compensation

CONSIDER YOUR SENTENCE

Compare it with the suggested guideline level of sentence and reconsider
your reasons carefully if you have chosen a sentence at a different level.
Consider a reduction for a timely guilty plea.

DECIDE YOUR SENTENCE
NB. COMPENSATION – Give reasons if not awarding compensation

Common assault	Criminal Justice Act 1988 s.39 Triable only summarily Penalty: Level 5 and/or 6 months

CONSIDER THE SERIOUSNESS OF THE OFFENCE
(INCLUDING THE IMPACT ON THE VICTIM)

IS DISCHARGE OR FINE APPROPRIATE?
GUIDELINE: → IS IT SERIOUS ENOUGH FOR A COMMUNITY PENALTY?
IS IT SO SERIOUS THAT ONLY CUSTODY IS APPROPRIATE?

THIS IS A GUIDELINE FOR A FIRST-TIME OFFENDER PLEADING NOT GUILTY

**➕   CONSIDER AGGRAVATING AND MITIGATING FACTORS
AND THE WEIGHT TO ATTACH TO EACH   ➖**

for example	for example
Abuse of trust (domestic setting)	Impulsive
Group action	Minor injury
Injury	Provocation
Offender in position of authority	Single blow
On hospital/medical or school premises	*This list is not exhaustive*
Premeditated	
Spitting	
Victim particularly vulnerable	
Victim serving the public	
Weapon	
This list is not exhaustive	

If offender is on bail, this offence is more serious
If offender has previous convictions, their relevance and any failure to respond to previous sentences should be considered – they may increase the seriousness. The court should make it clear, when passing sentence, that this was the approach adopted.

TAKE A PRELIMINARY VIEW OF SERIOUSNESS, THEN
CONSIDER OFFENDER MITIGATION

for example
    Age, health (physical or mental)
    Co-operation with police
    Evidence of genuine remorse
    Voluntary compensation

CONSIDER YOUR SENTENCE

*Compare it with the suggested guideline level of sentence and reconsider
your reasons carefully if you have chosen a sentence at a different level.
Consider a reduction for a timely guilty plea.*

DECIDE YOUR SENTENCE
NB. COMPENSATION – Give reasons if not awarding compensation

Criminal Damage Act 1971 s.1
Triable either way or summarily only. Consult legal adviser
Penalty: Either way – Level 5 and/or 6 months
Summarily – Level 4 and/or 3 months

Criminal damage

CONSIDER THE SERIOUSNESS OF THE OFFENCE
(INCLUDING THE IMPACT ON THE VICTIM)

GUIDELINE: → IS DISCHARGE OR FINE APPROPRIATE?
IS IT SERIOUS ENOUGH FOR A COMMUNITY PENALTY?
IS IT SO SERIOUS THAT ONLY CUSTODY IS APPROPRIATE?
ARE YOUR SENTENCING POWERS SUFFICIENT?

THIS IS A GUIDELINE FOR A FIRST-TIME OFFENDER PLEADING NOT GUILTY

GUIDELINE FINE – STARTING POINT C

⊕ CONSIDER AGGRAVATING AND MITIGATING FACTORS
AND THE WEIGHT TO ATTACH TO EACH ⊖

for example	for example
Deliberate	Impulsive action
Group offence	Minor damage
Serious damage	Provocation
Targeting	*This list is not exhaustive*
Vulnerable victim	
This list is not exhaustive	

If offender is on bail, this offence is more serious
If offender has previous convictions, their relevance and any failure to respond to previous sentences should be considered – they may increase the seriousness. The court should make it clear, when passing sentence, that this was the approach adopted.

TAKE A PRELIMINARY VIEW OF SERIOUSNESS, THEN
CONSIDER OFFENDER MITIGATION

for example
   Age, health (physical or mental)
   Co-operation with police
   Evidence of genuine remorse
   Voluntary compensation

CONSIDER YOUR SENTENCE

Compare it with the suggested guideline level of sentence and reconsider your reasons carefully if you have chosen a sentence at a different level.
Consider a reduction for a timely guilty plea.

DECIDE YOUR SENTENCE
NB. COMPENSATION – Give reasons if not awarding compensation

Disorderly behaviour	Public Order Act 1986 s.5 Triable only summarily Penalty: Level 3

CONSIDER THE SERIOUSNESS OF THE OFFENCE
(INCLUDING THE IMPACT ON THE VICTIM)

GUIDELINE: → IS DISCHARGE OR FINE APPROPRIATE?
IS IT SERIOUS ENOUGH FOR A COMMUNITY PENALTY?
(COMMUNITY REHABILITATION AND CURFEW ORDERS ARE THE ONLY
AVAILABLE COMMUNITY PENALTIES FOR THIS OFFENCE)

THIS IS A GUIDELINE FOR A FIRST-TIME OFFENDER PLEADING NOT GUILTY

GUIDELINE FINE – STARTING POINT B

➕ ## CONSIDER AGGRAVATING AND MITIGATING FACTORS ➖
AND THE WEIGHT TO ATTACH TO EACH

for example	for example
Football related	Stopped as soon as police arrived
Group action	Trivial incident
Vulnerable victim	*This list is not exhaustive*
This list is not exhaustive	

If offender is on bail, this offence is more serious
If offender has previous convictions, their relevance and any failure to respond to previous
sentences should be considered – they may increase the seriousness. The court should make
it clear, when passing sentence, that this was the approach adopted.

TAKE A PRELIMINARY VIEW OF SERIOUSNESS, THEN
CONSIDER OFFENDER MITIGATION

for example
   Age, health (physical or mental)
   Co-operation with police
   Evidence of genuine remorse
   Voluntary compensation

CONSIDER YOUR SENTENCE

Compare it with the suggested guideline level of sentence and reconsider
your reasons carefully if you have chosen a sentence at a different level.
Consider a reduction for a timely guilty plea.

DECIDE YOUR SENTENCE
NB. COMPENSATION – Give reasons if not awarding compensation

Public Order Act 1986 s.4A Triable only summarily Penalty: Level 5 and/or 6 months	**Disorderly behaviour with intent to cause harassment, alarm or distress**

CONSIDER THE SERIOUSNESS OF THE OFFENCE
(INCLUDING THE IMPACT ON THE VICTIM)

IS DISCHARGE OR FINE APPROPRIATE?
GUIDELINE: → IS IT SERIOUS ENOUGH FOR A COMMUNITY PENALTY?
IS IT SO SERIOUS THAT ONLY CUSTODY IS APPROPRIATE?

THIS IS A GUIDELINE FOR A FIRST-TIME OFFENDER PLEADING NOT GUILTY

➕ CONSIDER AGGRAVATING AND MITIGATING FACTORS AND THE WEIGHT TO ATTACH TO EACH ➖

for example
- Football related
- Group action
- High degree of planning
- Night time offence
- Victims specifically targeted
- Weapon
- *This list is not exhaustive*

for example
- Short duration
- *This list is not exhaustive*

If offender is on bail, this offence is more serious
If offender has previous convictions, their relevance and any failure to respond to previous sentences should be considered – they may increase the seriousness. The court should make it clear, when passing sentence, that this was the approach adopted.

TAKE A PRELIMINARY VIEW OF SERIOUSNESS, THEN CONSIDER OFFENDER MITIGATION

for example
- Age, health (physical or mental)
- Co-operation with police
- Evidence of genuine remorse
- Voluntary compensation

CONSIDER YOUR SENTENCE

Compare it with the suggested guideline level of sentence and reconsider your reasons carefully if you have chosen a sentence at a different level. Consider a reduction for a timely guilty plea.

DECIDE YOUR SENTENCE
NB. COMPENSATION – Give reasons if not awarding compensation

Drugs: Class A – possession

Misuse of Drugs Act 1971 s.5
Triable either way – see Mode of Trial Guidelines
Penalty: Level 5 and/or 6 months

CONSIDER THE SERIOUSNESS OF THE OFFENCE

IS DISCHARGE OR FINE APPROPRIATE?
GUIDELINE: → IS IT SERIOUS ENOUGH FOR A COMMUNITY PENALTY?
IS IT SO SERIOUS THAT ONLY CUSTODY IS APPROPRIATE?
ARE YOUR SENTENCING POWERS SUFFICIENT?

THIS IS A GUIDELINE FOR A FIRST-TIME OFFENDER PLEADING NOT GUILTY

➕ CONSIDER AGGRAVATING AND MITIGATING FACTORS AND THE WEIGHT TO ATTACH TO EACH ➖

for example	for example
An amount other than a very small quantity	Very small quantity
This list is not exhaustive	*This list is not exhaustive*

If offender is on bail, this offence is more serious
If offender has previous convictions, their relevance and any failure to respond to previous sentences should be considered – they may increase the seriousness. The court should make it clear, when passing sentence, that this was the approach adopted.

TAKE A PRELIMINARY VIEW OF SERIOUSNESS, THEN CONSIDER OFFENDER MITIGATION

for example
Age, health (physical or mental)
Co-operation with police
Evidence of genuine remorse

CONSIDER YOUR SENTENCE

Compare it with the suggested guideline level of sentence and reconsider your reasons carefully if you have chosen a sentence at a different level. Consider a reduction for a timely guilty plea. Consider forfeiture and destruction.

DECIDE YOUR SENTENCE

Misuse of Drugs Act 1971 s.4 Triable either way – see Mode of Trial Guidelines Penalty: Level 5 and/or 6 months	**Drugs: Class A – production, supply**

CONSIDER THE SERIOUSNESS OF THE OFFENCE
(INCLUDING THE IMPACT ON THE VICTIM)

IS DISCHARGE OR FINE APPROPRIATE?
IS IT SERIOUS ENOUGH FOR A COMMUNITY PENALTY?
IS IT SO SERIOUS THAT ONLY CUSTODY IS APPROPRIATE?
GUIDELINE: → ARE YOUR SENTENCING POWERS SUFFICIENT?

THIS IS A GUIDELINE FOR A FIRST-TIME OFFENDER PLEADING NOT GUILTY

➕ CONSIDER AGGRAVATING AND MITIGATING FACTORS ➖
AND THE WEIGHT TO ATTACH TO EACH

for example	for example
Commercial production	Small amount
Deliberate adulteration	*This list is not exhaustive*
Quantity	
Sophisticated operation	
Supply to children	
Venue, eg prisons, educational	
establishments	
This list is not exhaustive	

If offender is on bail, this offence is more serious
If offender has previous convictions, their relevance and any failure to respond to previous sentences should be considered – they may increase the seriousness. The court should make it clear, when passing sentence, that this was the approach adopted.

TAKE A PRELIMINARY VIEW OF SERIOUSNESS, THEN CONSIDER
WHETHER THE CASE SHOULD BE COMMITTED FOR SENTENCE,
THEN CONSIDER OFFENDER MITIGATION

for example
    Age, health (physical or mental)
    Co-operation with police
    Evidence of genuine remorse

CONSIDER COMMITTAL OR YOUR SENTENCE

*Compare it with the suggested guideline level of sentence and reconsider
your reasons carefully if you have chosen a sentence at a different level.
Consider a reduction for a timely guilty plea. Consider forfeiture and destruction.*

DECIDE YOUR SENTENCE

Drugs: Class B and C – possession	Misuse of Drugs Acts 1971 s.5 Triable either way – see Mode of Trial Guidelines Penalty: Level 4 and/or 3 months

CONSIDER THE SERIOUSNESS OF THE OFFENCE

GUIDELINE: → IS DISCHARGE OR FINE APPROPRIATE?
IS IT SERIOUS ENOUGH FOR A COMMUNITY PENALTY?
IS IT SO SERIOUS THAT ONLY CUSTODY IS APPROPRIATE?
ARE YOUR SENTENCING POWERS SUFFICIENT?

THIS IS A GUIDELINE FOR A FIRST-TIME OFFENDER PLEADING NOT GUILTY

GUIDELINE FINE – STARTING POINT B

➕ CONSIDER AGGRAVATING AND MITIGATING FACTORS ➖
AND THE WEIGHT TO ATTACH TO EACH

for example	for example
Large amount	Small amount
This list is not exhaustive	*This list is not exhaustive*

If offender is on bail, this offence is more serious
If offender has previous convictions, their relevance and any failure to respond to previous sentences should be considered – they may increase the seriousness. The court should make it clear, when passing sentence, that this was the approach adopted.

TAKE A PRELIMINARY VIEW OF SERIOUSNESS, THEN
CONSIDER OFFENDER MITIGATION

for example
  Age, health (physical or mental)
  Co-operation with police
  Evidence of genuine remorse

CONSIDER YOUR SENTENCE

Compare it with the suggested guideline level of sentence and reconsider
your reasons carefully if you have chosen a sentence at a different level.
Consider a reduction for a timely guilty plea. Consider forfeiture and destruction.

DECIDE YOUR SENTENCE

Misuse of Drugs Act 1971 s.4 Triable either way – see Mode of Trial Guidelines Penalty: Level 5 and/or 6 months	**Drugs: Class B and C – supply, possession with intent to supply**

CONSIDER THE SERIOUSNESS OF THE OFFENCE
(INCLUDING THE IMPACT ON THE VICTIM)

IS DISCHARGE OR FINE APPROPRIATE?
IS IT SERIOUS ENOUGH FOR A COMMUNITY PENALTY?
IS IT SO SERIOUS THAT ONLY CUSTODY IS APPROPRIATE?
GUIDELINE: → ARE YOUR SENTENCING POWERS SUFFICIENT?

THIS IS A GUIDELINE FOR A FIRST-TIME OFFENDER PLEADING NOT GUILTY

➕ CONSIDER AGGRAVATING AND MITIGATING FACTORS ➖
AND THE WEIGHT TO ATTACH TO EACH

for example	for example
Commercial supply	No commercial motive
Deliberate adulteration	Small amount
Large amount	*This list is not exhaustive*
Sophisticated operation	
Supply to children	
Venue, eg prisons, educational establishments	
This list is not exhaustive	

If offender is on bail, this offence is more serious
If offender has previous convictions, their relevance and any failure to respond to previous sentences should be considered – they may increase the seriousness. The court should make it clear, when passing sentence, that this was the approach adopted.

TAKE A PRELIMINARY VIEW OF SERIOUSNESS, THEN CONSIDER
WHETHER THE CASE SHOULD BE COMMITTED FOR SENTENCE,
THEN CONSIDER OFFENDER MITIGATION

for example
    Age, health (physical or mental)
    Co-operation with police
    Evidence of genuine remorse

CONSIDER COMMITTAL OR YOUR SENTENCE

Compare it with the suggested guideline level of sentence and reconsider your reasons carefully if you have chosen a sentence at a different level. Consider a reduction for a timely guilty plea. Consider forfeiture and destruction.

DECIDE YOUR SENTENCE

Drugs: Cultivation of cannabis	Misuse of Drugs Act 1971 s.6 Triable either way – see Mode of Trial Guidelines Penalty: Level 5 and/or 6 months

CONSIDER THE SERIOUSNESS OF THE OFFENCE
(INCLUDING THE IMPACT ON THE VICTIM)

IS DISCHARGE OR FINE APPROPRIATE?
GUIDELINE: → IS IT SERIOUS ENOUGH FOR A COMMUNITY PENALTY?
IS IT SO SERIOUS THAT ONLY CUSTODY IS APPROPRIATE?
ARE YOUR SENTENCING POWERS SUFFICIENT?

THIS IS A GUIDELINE FOR A FIRST-TIME OFFENDER PLEADING NOT GUILTY

➕ CONSIDER AGGRAVATING AND MITIGATING FACTORS AND THE WEIGHT TO ATTACH TO EACH ➖

for example	for example
Commercial cultivation	For personal use
Large quantity	Not responsible for planting
Use of sophisticated system	Small scale cultivation
This list is not exhaustive	*This list is not exhaustive*

If offender is on bail, this offence is more serious
If offender has previous convictions, their relevance and any failure to respond to previous sentences should be considered – they may increase the seriousness. The court should make it clear, when passing sentence, that this was the approach adopted.

TAKE A PRELIMINARY VIEW OF SERIOUSNESS, THEN CONSIDER OFFENDER MITIGATION

for example
  Age, health (physical or mental)
  Co-operation with police
  Evidence of genuine remorse

CONSIDER YOUR SENTENCE

Compare it with the suggested guideline level of sentence and reconsider your reasons carefully if you have chosen a sentence at a different level. Consider a reduction for a timely guilty plea. Consider forfeiture and destruction.

DECIDE YOUR SENTENCE

| Criminal Justice Act 1967 s.91
Triable only summarily
Penalty: Level 3 | **Drunk and disorderly** |

CONSIDER THE SERIOUSNESS OF THE OFFENCE

GUIDELINE: → IS DISCHARGE OR FINE APPROPRIATE?
IS IT SERIOUS ENOUGH FOR A COMMUNITY PENALTY?
(COMMUNITY REHABILITATION AND CURFEW ORDERS ARE THE ONLY
AVAILABLE COMMUNITY PENALTIES FOR THIS OFFENCE)

THIS IS A GUIDELINE FOR A FIRST-TIME OFFENDER PLEADING NOT GUILTY

GUIDELINE FINE – STARTING POINT A

CONSIDER AGGRAVATING AND MITIGATING FACTORS AND THE WEIGHT TO ATTACH TO EACH

for example	for example
Offensive language or behaviour	Induced by others
On hospital/medical or school premises	No significant disturbance
On public transport	Not threatening
With group	*This list is not exhaustive*
This list is not exhaustive	

If racially or religiously aggravated, or offender is on bail, this offence is more serious
If offender has previous convictions, their relevance and any failure to respond to previous
sentences should be considered – they may increase the seriousness. The court should make
it clear, when passing sentence, that this was the approach adopted.

TAKE A PRELIMINARY VIEW OF SERIOUSNESS, THEN CONSIDER OFFENDER MITIGATION

for example
    Health (physical or mental)
    Co-operation with police
    Evidence of genuine remorse

CONSIDER YOUR SENTENCE

Compare it with the suggested guideline level of sentence and reconsider
your reasons carefully if you have chosen a sentence at a different level.
Consider a reduction for a timely guilty plea.

DECIDE YOUR SENTENCE

Evasion of duty	Customs and Excise Management Act 1979 s.170 Triable either way – see Mode of Trial Guidelines Penalty: 6 months and/or £5000/or 3 times the value of the goods (whichever is the greater)

CONSIDER THE SERIOUSNESS OF THE OFFENCE

IS DISCHARGE OR FINE APPROPRIATE?
GUIDELINE: → IS IT SERIOUS ENOUGH FOR A COMMUNITY PENALTY?
IS IT SO SERIOUS THAT ONLY CUSTODY IS APPROPRIATE?
ARE YOUR SENTENCING POWERS SUFFICIENT?

THIS IS A GUIDELINE FOR A FIRST-TIME OFFENDER PLEADING NOT GUILTY

➕ CONSIDER AGGRAVATING AND MITIGATING FACTORS ➖
AND THE WEIGHT TO ATTACH TO EACH

for example	for example
Abuse of power (eg use of children/ vulnerable adults) Offender is Customs/Police Officer Playing an organisational role Professional operation Repeated imports over a period of time Substantial amount of duty evaded Threats of violence Two or more types of goods Warning previously given *This list is not exhaustive*	Co-operation with authorities No evidence of pre-planning Small amounts of duty evaded Under pressure from others to commit offence *This list is not exhaustive*

If offender is on bail, this offence is more serious
If offender has previous convictions, their relevance and any failure to respond to previous sentences should be considered – they may increase the seriousness. The court should make it clear, when passing sentence, that this was the approach adopted.

TAKE A PRELIMINARY VIEW OF SERIOUSNESS, THEN
CONSIDER OFFENDER MITIGATION

for example
   Age, health (physical or mental)
   Co-operation with authorities
   Evidence of genuine remorse
   Voluntary restitution

CONSIDER YOUR SENTENCE

Compare it with the suggested guideline level of sentence and reconsider
your reasons carefully if you have chosen a sentence at a different level.
Consider a reduction for a timely guilty plea. Consider forfeiture.

DECIDE YOUR SENTENCE
NB. The guideline above approximates to a low level offender with duty
evaded in the region of £1000 to £10000. Restitution should be made.
For offences above this level seek advice from legal adviser.

Bail Act 1976 s.6 Triable only summarily Penalty: Level 5 and/or 3 months	**Failure to surrender to bail**

CONSIDER THE SERIOUSNESS OF THE OFFENCE

IS DISCHARGE OR FINE APPROPRIATE?
GUIDELINE: → IS IT SERIOUS ENOUGH FOR A COMMUNITY PENALTY?
IS IT SO SERIOUS THAT ONLY CUSTODY IS APPROPRIATE?

THIS IS A GUIDELINE FOR A FIRST-TIME OFFENDER PLEADING NOT GUILTY

➕ CONSIDER AGGRAVATING AND MITIGATING FACTORS ➖
AND THE WEIGHT TO ATTACH TO EACH

for example	for example
Leaves jurisdiction Long term evasion Results in ineffective trial date Wilful evasion *This list is not exhaustive*	Appears late on day of hearing Genuine misunderstanding Voluntary surrender *This list is not exhaustive*

A curfew order may be particularly suitable

Previous convictions for this offence increase the seriousness – consider custody

TAKE A PRELIMINARY VIEW OF SERIOUSNESS, THEN
CONSIDER OFFENDER MITIGATION

for example
    Age, health (physical or mental)
    Co-operation with police
    Evidence of genuine remorse

CONSIDER YOUR SENTENCE

Compare it with the suggested guideline level of sentence and reconsider
your reasons carefully if you have chosen a sentence at a different level.
Consider a reduction for a timely guilty plea.

DECIDE YOUR SENTENCE

Football-related offences: being drunk in, or whilst trying to enter ground	Sporting Events (Control of Alcohol etc) Act 1985 s.2(2) Triable only summarily Penalty: Level 2

CONSIDER THE SERIOUSNESS OF THE OFFENCE

GUIDELINE: → *IS DISCHARGE OR FINE APPROPRIATE?*
IS IT SERIOUS ENOUGH FOR A COMMUNITY PENALTY?
(NB. COMMUNITY REHABILITATION AND CURFEW ORDERS ARE THE ONLY
AVAILABLE COMMUNITY PENALTIES FOR THIS OFFENCE)

THIS IS A GUIDELINE FOR A FIRST-TIME OFFENDER PLEADING NOT GUILTY

GUIDELINE FINE – STARTING POINT A

✚ CONSIDER AGGRAVATING AND MITIGATING FACTORS ✖ AND THE WEIGHT TO ATTACH TO EACH

for example	for example
Group action	No significant disturbance
Offensive language/behaviour used	Not threatening
This list is not exhaustive	*This list is not exhaustive*

If offender is on bail, this offence is more serious
If offender has previous convictions, their relevance and any failure to respond to previous
sentences should be considered – they may increase the seriousness. The court should make
it clear, when passing sentence, that this was the approach adopted.

TAKE A PRELIMINARY VIEW OF SERIOUSNESS, THEN CONSIDER OFFENDER MITIGATION

for example
Age, health (physical or mental)
Co-operation with police
Evidence of genuine remorse

CONSIDER YOUR SENTENCE

Compare it with the suggested guideline level of sentence and reconsider
your reasons carefully if you have chosen a sentence at a different level.
Consider a reduction for a timely guilty plea.

DECIDE YOUR SENTENCE
MUST CONSIDER IMPOSING A BANNING ORDER
IF NO BANNING ORDER IS MADE, COURT MUST GIVE REASONS
Seek advice from the legal adviser

Football (Offences) Act 1991 s.4 Triable only summarily Penalty: Level 3	**Football-related offences: going onto playing area or adjacent area to which spectators are not admitted**

CONSIDER THE SERIOUSNESS OF THE OFFENCE

GUIDELINE: → IS DISCHARGE OR FINE APPROPRIATE?
IS IT SERIOUS ENOUGH FOR A COMMUNITY PENALTY?
(NB. COMMUNITY REHABILITATION AND CURFEW ORDERS ARE THE ONLY
AVAILABLE COMMUNITY PENALTIES FOR THIS OFFENCE)

THIS IS A GUIDELINE FOR A FIRST-TIME OFFENDER PLEADING NOT GUILTY

GUIDELINE FINE – STARTING POINT A

**➕   CONSIDER AGGRAVATING AND MITIGATING FACTORS   ➖
AND THE WEIGHT TO ATTACH TO EACH**

for example	
Being drunk Deliberate provocative act Inciting others *This list is not exhaustive*	

If offender is on bail, this offence is more serious
If offender has previous convictions, their relevance and any failure to respond to previous
sentences should be considered – they may increase the seriousness. The court should make
it clear, when passing sentence, that this was the approach adopted.

TAKE A PRELIMINARY VIEW OF SERIOUSNESS, THEN
CONSIDER OFFENDER MITIGATION

for example
   Age, health (physical or mental)
   Co-operation with police
   Evidence of genuine remorse

CONSIDER YOUR SENTENCE

Compare it with the suggested guideline level of sentence and reconsider
your reasons carefully if you have chosen a sentence at a different level.
Consider a reduction for a timely guilty plea.

DECIDE YOUR SENTENCE
MUST CONSIDER IMPOSING A BANNING ORDER
IF NO BANNING ORDER IS MADE, COURT MUST GIVE REASONS
Seek advice from the legal adviser

Football-related offences: possession of liquor whilst entering or trying to enter the ground	Sporting Events (Control of Alcohol etc) Act 1985 s.2(1) Triable only summarily Penalty: Level 3 and/or 3 months

CONSIDER THE SERIOUSNESS OF THE OFFENCE

GUIDELINE: → IS DISCHARGE OR FINE APPROPRIATE?
IS IT SERIOUS ENOUGH FOR A COMMUNITY PENALTY?
IS IT SO SERIOUS THAT ONLY CUSTODY IS APPROPRIATE?

THIS IS A GUIDELINE FOR A FIRST-TIME OFFENDER PLEADING NOT GUILTY

GUIDELINE FINE – STARTING POINT B

➕ CONSIDER AGGRAVATING AND MITIGATING FACTORS AND THE WEIGHT TO ATTACH TO EACH ➖

for example	for example
Concealed	Low alcoholic-content liquor
Group action	Small amount of alcohol
High alcoholic-content liquor	*This list is not exhaustive*
Large amount of alcohol	
Offensive language/behaviour used	
This list is not exhaustive	

If offender is on bail, this offence is more serious
If offender has previous convictions, their relevance and any failure to respond to previous sentences should be considered – they may increase the seriousness. The court should make it clear, when passing sentence, that this was the approach adopted.

TAKE A PRELIMINARY VIEW OF SERIOUSNESS, THEN CONSIDER OFFENDER MITIGATION

for example
Age, health (physical or mental)
Co-operation with police
Evidence of genuine remorse

CONSIDER YOUR SENTENCE

Compare it with the suggested guideline level of sentence and reconsider your reasons carefully if you have chosen a sentence at a different level.
Consider a reduction for a timely guilty plea.

DECIDE YOUR SENTENCE
MUST CONSIDER IMPOSING A BANNING ORDER
IF NO BANNING ORDER IS MADE, COURT MUST GIVE REASONS
Seek advice from the legal adviser

| Football (Offences) Act 1991 s.2
Triable only summarily
Penalty: Level 3 | **Football-related offences:
throwing missiles** |

CONSIDER THE SERIOUSNESS OF THE OFFENCE

GUIDELINE: → IS DISCHARGE OR FINE APPROPRIATE?
IS IT SERIOUS ENOUGH FOR A COMMUNITY PENALTY?
(NB. COMMUNITY REHABILITATION AND CURFEW ORDERS ARE THE ONLY
AVAILABLE COMMUNITY PENALTIES FOR THIS OFFENCE)

THIS IS A GUIDELINE FOR A FIRST-TIME OFFENDER PLEADING NOT GUILTY

GUIDELINE FINE – STARTING POINT B

⊕   CONSIDER AGGRAVATING AND MITIGATING FACTORS   ⊖
AND THE WEIGHT TO ATTACH TO EACH

| for example | |
| Object likely to cause injury (eg coin,
glass bottle, stone)
This list is not exhaustive | |

If racially or religiously aggravated, or offender is on bail, this offence is more serious
If offender has previous convictions, their relevance and any failure to respond to previous
sentences should be considered – they may increase the seriousness. The court should make
it clear, when passing sentence, that this was the approach adopted.

TAKE A PRELIMINARY VIEW OF SERIOUSNESS, THEN
CONSIDER OFFENDER MITIGATION

for example
  Age, health (physical or mental)
  Co-operation with police
  Evidence of genuine remorse
  Voluntary compensation

CONSIDER YOUR SENTENCE

Compare it with the suggested guideline level of sentence and reconsider
your reasons carefully if you have chosen a sentence at a different level.
Consider a reduction for a timely guilty plea.

DECIDE YOUR SENTENCE
MUST CONSIDER IMPOSING A BANNING ORDER
IF NO BANNING ORDER IS MADE, COURT MUST GIVE REASONS
Seek advice from the legal adviser

Football-related offences: unauthorised sale or attempted sale of ticket

Criminal Justice and Public Order Act 1994 s.166
Triable only summarily
Penalty: Level 5

CONSIDER THE SERIOUSNESS OF THE OFFENCE

GUIDELINE: → IS DISCHARGE OR FINE APPROPRIATE?
IS IT SERIOUS ENOUGH FOR A COMMUNITY PENALTY?
(NB. COMMUNITY REHABILITATION AND CURFEW ORDERS ARE THE ONLY
AVAILABLE COMMUNITY PENALTIES FOR THIS OFFENCE)

THIS IS A GUIDELINE FOR A FIRST-TIME OFFENDER PLEADING NOT GUILTY

GUIDELINE FINE – STARTING POINT B

➕ CONSIDER AGGRAVATING AND MITIGATING FACTORS AND THE WEIGHT TO ATTACH TO EACH ➖

for example	for example
Commercial operation	Single ticket
Counterfeit tickets	*This list is not exhaustive*
In possession of a large number of tickets/ potential high value	
Sophisticated operation	
This list is not exhaustive	

If offender is on bail, this offence is more serious
If offender has previous convictions, their relevance and any failure to respond to previous sentences should be considered – they may increase the seriousness. The court should make it clear, when passing sentence, that this was the approach adopted.

TAKE A PRELIMINARY VIEW OF SERIOUSNESS, THEN CONSIDER OFFENDER MITIGATION

for example
Age, health (physical or mental)
Co-operation with police
Evidence of genuine remorse
Voluntary compensation

CONSIDER YOUR SENTENCE

Compare it with the suggested guideline level of sentence and reconsider your reasons carefully if you have chosen a sentence at a different level.
Consider a reduction for a timely guilty plea.

DECIDE YOUR SENTENCE
MUST CONSIDER IMPOSING A BANNING ORDER
IF NO BANNING ORDER IS MADE, COURT MUST GIVE REASONS
Seek advice from the legal adviser

Theft Act 1968 s.25 Triable either way – see Mode of Trial Guidelines Penalty: Level 5 and/or 6 months May disqualify where committed with reference to the theft or taking of a vehicle	**Going equipped for theft etc.**

CONSIDER THE SERIOUSNESS OF THE OFFENCE

IS DISCHARGE OR FINE APPROPRIATE?
GUIDELINE: → IS IT SERIOUS ENOUGH FOR A COMMUNITY PENALTY?
IS IT SO SERIOUS THAT ONLY CUSTODY IS APPROPRIATE?
ARE YOUR SENTENCING POWERS SUFFICIENT?

THIS IS A GUIDELINE FOR A FIRST-TIME OFFENDER PLEADING NOT GUILTY

➕ CONSIDER AGGRAVATING AND MITIGATING FACTORS ➖
AND THE WEIGHT TO ATTACH TO EACH

for example Group action Number of items People put in fear Sophisticated Specialised equipment *This list is not exhaustive*	

If offender is on bail, this offence is more serious
If offender has previous convictions, their relevance and any failure to respond to previous sentences should be considered – they may increase the seriousness. The court should make it clear, when passing sentence, that this was the approach adopted.

TAKE A PRELIMINARY VIEW OF SERIOUSNESS, THEN
CONSIDER OFFENDER MITIGATION

for example
Age, health (physical or mental)
Co-operation with police
Evidence of genuine remorse

CONSIDER YOUR SENTENCE

Compare it with the suggested guideline level of sentence and reconsider
your reasons carefully if you have chosen a sentence at a different level.
Consider a reduction for a timely guilty plea. Consider forfeiture and destruction.

DECIDE YOUR SENTENCE

Handling stolen goods	**Theft Act 1968 s.22** **Triable either way – see Mode of Trial Guidelines** **Penalty: Level 5 and/or 6 months**

CONSIDER THE SERIOUSNESS OF THE OFFENCE
(INCLUDING THE IMPACT ON THE VICTIM)

IS DISCHARGE OR FINE APPROPRIATE?
GUIDELINE: → *IS IT SERIOUS ENOUGH FOR A COMMUNITY PENALTY?*
IS IT SO SERIOUS THAT ONLY CUSTODY IS APPROPRIATE?
ARE YOUR SENTENCING POWERS SUFFICIENT

THIS IS A GUIDELINE FOR A FIRST-TIME OFFENDER PLEADING NOT GUILTY

⊕ CONSIDER AGGRAVATING AND MITIGATING FACTORS ⊖
AND THE WEIGHT TO ATTACH TO EACH

for example	for example
High level of profit accruing to handler	Isolated offence
High value (including sentimental) of goods	Little or no benefit accruing to handler
Provision by handler of regular outlet for stolen goods	Low monetary value of goods
Proximity of the handler to the primary offence	*This list is not exhaustive*
Seriousness of the primary offence	
Sophistication	
The particular facts, eg the goods handled were the proceeds of a domestic burglary	
Threats of violence or abuse of power by handler in order to obtain goods	
This list is not exhaustive	

If offender is on bail, this offence is more serious
If offender has previous convictions, their relevance and any failure to respond to previous sentences should be considered – they may increase the seriousness. The court should make it clear, when passing sentence, that this was the approach adopted.

TAKE A PRELIMINARY VIEW OF SERIOUSNESS, THEN
CONSIDER OFFENDER MITIGATION

for example
Age, health (physical or mental)
Co-operation with police
Evidence of genuine remorse
Voluntary compensation

CONSIDER YOUR SENTENCE

Compare it with the suggested guideline level of sentence and reconsider your reasons carefully if you have chosen a sentence at a different level. Consider a reduction for a timely guilty plea.

DECIDE YOUR SENTENCE
NB. COMPENSATION – Give reasons if not awarding compensation

Protection from Harrassment Act 1997 s.4 Triable either way Penalty: Level 5 and/or 6 months Consider making a restraining order	**Harassment** Conduct causing fear of violence

CONSIDER THE SERIOUSNESS OF THE OFFENCE
(INCLUDING THE IMPACT ON THE VICTIM)

IS DISCHARGE OR FINE APPROPRIATE?
IS IT SERIOUS ENOUGH FOR A COMMUNITY PENALTY?
GUIDELINE: → IS IT SO SERIOUS THAT ONLY CUSTODY IS APPROPRIATE?
ARE YOUR SENTENCING POWERS SUFFICIENT?

THIS IS A GUIDELINE FOR A FIRST-TIME OFFENDER PLEADING NOT GUILTY

✚ CONSIDER AGGRAVATING AND MITIGATING FACTORS AND THE WEIGHT TO ATTACH TO EACH ⊖

for example	for example

Disregard of warning
Excessive persistence
Interference with employment/business
Invasion of victim's home
Involvement of others
Threat to use weapon or substance
    (including realistic imitations)
Use of violence or grossly offensive material
Where photographs or images of a personal
    nature are involved
This list is not exhaustive
	Initial provocation
	Short duration
	This list is not exhaustive

If offender is on bail, this offence is more serious
If offender has previous convictions, their relevance and any failure to respond to previous sentences should be considered – they may increase the seriousness. The court should make it clear, when passing sentence, that this was the approach adopted.

TAKE A PRELIMINARY VIEW OF SERIOUSNESS, THEN CONSIDER OFFENDER MITIGATION

for example
    Age, health (physical or mental)
    Co-operation with police
    Evidence of genuine remorse
    Voluntary compensation

CONSIDER YOUR SENTENCE

Compare it with the suggested guideline level of sentence and reconsider
your reasons carefully if you have chosen a sentence at a different level.
Consider a reduction for a timely guilty plea.
Restraining order – consider making an order in addition to the sentence to protect
the victim or any named person from further conduct which would amount to harassment,
or which would cause the fear of violence.

DECIDE YOUR SENTENCE
NB. COMPENSATION – Give reasons if not awarding compensation

Harassment Conduct causing harassment	Protection from Harassment Act 1997 s.2 Triable only summarily Penalty: Level 5 and/or 6 months Consider making a restraining order

CONSIDER THE SERIOUSNESS OF THE OFFENCE
(INCLUDING THE IMPACT ON THE VICTIM)

IS DISCHARGE OR FINE APPROPRIATE?
GUIDELINE: → IS IT SERIOUS ENOUGH FOR A COMMUNITY PENALTY?
IS IT SO SERIOUS THAT ONLY CUSTODY IS APPROPRIATE?

THIS IS A GUIDELINE FOR A FIRST-TIME OFFENDER PLEADING NOT GUILTY

➕ CONSIDER AGGRAVATING AND MITIGATING FACTORS ➖
AND THE WEIGHT TO ATTACH TO EACH

for example	for example
Disregard of warning Excessive persistence Interference with employment/business Invasion of victim's home Involvement of others Use of violence or grossly offensive material Where photographs or images of a personal nature are involved *This list is not exhaustive*	Initial provocation Short duration *This list is not exhaustive*

If offender is on bail, this offence is more serious
If offender has previous convictions, their relevance and any failure to respond to previous
sentences should be considered – they may increase the seriousness. The court should make
it clear, when passing sentence, that this was the approach adopted.

TAKE A PRELIMINARY VIEW OF SERIOUSNESS, THEN
CONSIDER OFFENDER MITIGATION

for example
Age, health (physical or mental)
Co-operation with police
Evidence of genuine remorse
Voluntary compensation

CONSIDER YOUR SENTENCE

Compare it with the suggested guideline level of sentence and reconsider
your reasons carefully if you have chosen a sentence at a different level.
Consider a reduction for a timely guilty plea.
Restraining order – consider making an order in addition to the sentence to protect
the victim or any named person from further conduct which would amount to harassment.

DECIDE YOUR SENTENCE
NB. COMPENSATION – Give reasons if not awarding compensation

Sexual Offences Act 1956 ss.14&15 Triable either way – see Mode of Trial Guidelines Penalty: Level 5 and/or 6 months Entry in Sex Offender's Register (consult legal adviser)	**Indecent assault**

CONSIDER THE SERIOUSNESS OF THE OFFENCE
(INCLUDING THE IMPACT ON THE VICTIM)

IS DISCHARGE OR FINE APPROPRIATE?
IS IT SERIOUS ENOUGH FOR A COMMUNITY PENALTY?
GUIDELINE: → IS IT SO SERIOUS THAT ONLY CUSTODY IS APPROPRIATE?
ARE YOUR SENTENCING POWERS SUFFICIENT?

THIS IS A GUIDELINE FOR A FIRST-TIME OFFENDER PLEADING NOT GUILTY

➕ CONSIDER AGGRAVATING AND MITIGATING FACTORS AND THE WEIGHT TO ATTACH TO EACH ➖

for example Age differential Breach of trust Injury (may be psychological) Prolonged assault Very young victim Victim deliberately targeted Victim serving the public Vulnerable victim *This list is not exhaustive*	for example Slight contact *This list is not exhaustive*

If racially or religiously aggravated, or offender is on bail, this offence is more serious
If offender has previous convictions, their relevance and any failure to respond to previous sentences should be considered – they may increase the seriousness. The court should make it clear, when passing sentence, that this was the approach adopted.

TAKE A PRELIMINARY VIEW OF SERIOUSNESS, THEN CONSIDER OFFENDER MITIGATION

for example
Age, health (physical or mental)
Co-operation with police
Evidence of genuine remorse
Voluntary compensation

CONSIDER YOUR SENTENCE

Compare it with the suggested guideline level of sentence and reconsider your reasons carefully if you have chosen a sentence at a different level. Consider a reduction for a timely guilty plea. Entry in Sex Offender's Register (consult legal adviser).

DECIDE YOUR SENTENCE
NB. COMPENSATION – Give reasons if not awarding compensation

Indecent photographs etc.	Protection of Children Act 1978 s.1(1) Criminal Justice Act 1988 s.160(1) Triable either way – see Mode of Trial Guidelines Penalty: Level 5 and/or 6 months Entry in Sex Offender's Register (consult legal adviser)

CONSIDER THE SERIOUSNESS OF THE OFFENCE
(INCLUDING THE IMPACT ON THE VICTIM)

IS DISCHARGE OR FINE APPROPRIATE?
IS IT SERIOUS ENOUGH FOR A COMMUNITY PENALTY?
IS IT SO SERIOUS THAT ONLY CUSTODY IS APPROPRIATE?
GUIDELINE: → ARE YOUR SENTENCING POWERS SUFFICIENT?

THIS IS A GUIDELINE FOR A FIRST-TIME OFFENDER PLEADING NOT GUILTY

➕ CONSIDER AGGRAVATING AND MITIGATING FACTORS ➖
AND THE WEIGHT TO ATTACH TO EACH

for example Abuse of trust Commercial gain Involvement in production Large number of images Particularly young or vulnerable children *This list is not exhaustive*	for example Images at the lowest categories of COPINE* (seek advice from the legal adviser) One photograph only Possession for own use Pseudo images *This list is not exhaustive* **The COPINE (Combating Paedophile Information* *Networks in Europe) Project was founded in 1997,* *and is based in the Department of Applied* *Psychology, University College Cork, Ireland*

If racially or religiously aggravated, or offender is on bail, this offence is more serious
If offender has previous convictions, their relevance and any failure to respond to previous
sentences should be considered – they may increase the seriousness. The court should make
it clear, when passing sentence, that this was the approach adopted.

TAKE A PRELIMINARY VIEW OF SERIOUSNESS, THEN CONSIDER
WHETHER THE CASE SHOULD BE COMMITTED FOR SENTENCE,
THEN CONSIDER OFFENDER MITIGATION

for example
Age, health (physical or mental)
Co-operation with police
Evidence of genuine remorse
Voluntary compensation

CONSIDER COMMITTAL OR YOUR SENTENCE

Compare it with the suggested guideline level of sentence and reconsider
your reasons carefully if you have chosen a sentence at a different level.
Consider a reduction for a timely guilty plea. Consider forfeiture and destruction.
Entry in Sex Offender's Register (consult legal adviser).

DECIDE YOUR SENTENCE

| Theft Act 1978 s.3
Triable either way – see Mode of Trial Guidelines
Penalty: Level 5 and/or 6 months | **Making off without payment** |

CONSIDER THE SERIOUSNESS OF THE OFFENCE
(INCLUDING THE IMPACT ON THE VICTIM)

GUIDELINE: → IS DISCHARGE OR FINE APPROPRIATE?
IS IT SERIOUS ENOUGH FOR A COMMUNITY PENALTY?
IS IT SO SERIOUS THAT ONLY CUSTODY IS APPROPRIATE?
ARE YOUR SENTENCING POWERS SUFFICIENT?

THIS IS A GUIDELINE FOR A FIRST-TIME OFFENDER PLEADING NOT GUILTY

GUIDELINE FINE – STARTING POINT B

➕ **CONSIDER AGGRAVATING AND MITIGATING FACTORS AND THE WEIGHT TO ATTACH TO EACH** **➖**

for example	for example
Deliberate plan	Impulsive action
High value	Low value
Two or more involved	*This list is not exhaustive*
Victim particularly vulnerable	
This list is not exhaustive	

If racially or religiously aggravated, or offender is on bail, this offence is more serious
If offender has previous convictions, their relevance and any failure to respond to previous sentences should be considered – they may increase the seriousness. The court should make it clear, when passing sentence, that this was the approach adopted.

TAKE A PRELIMINARY VIEW OF SERIOUSNESS, THEN CONSIDER OFFENDER MITIGATION

for example
Age, health (physical or mental)
Co-operation with police
Evidence of genuine remorse
Voluntary compensation

CONSIDER YOUR SENTENCE

Compare it with the suggested guideline level of sentence and reconsider your reasons carefully if you have chosen a sentence at a different level. Consider a reduction for a timely guilty plea.

DECIDE YOUR SENTENCE
NB. COMPENSATION – Give reasons if not awarding compensation

Obstructing a police officer	Police Act 1996 s.89(2) Triable only summarily Penalty: Level 3 and/or 1 month

CONSIDER THE SERIOUSNESS OF THE OFFENCE
(INCLUDING THE IMPACT ON THE VICTIM)

GUIDELINE: → IS DISCHARGE OR FINE APPROPRIATE?
IS IT SERIOUS ENOUGH FOR A COMMUNITY PENALTY?
IS IT SO SERIOUS THAT ONLY CUSTODY IS APPROPRIATE?

THIS IS A GUIDELINE FOR A FIRST-TIME OFFENDER PLEADING NOT GUILTY

GUIDELINE FINE – STARTING POINT B

➕ CONSIDER AGGRAVATING AND MITIGATING FACTORS AND THE WEIGHT TO ATTACH TO EACH ➖

for example	for example
Attempt to impede arrest	Genuine misjudgement
Group action	Impulsive action
Premeditated	Minor obstruction
This list is not exhaustive	This list is not exhaustive

If racially or religiously aggravated, or offender is on bail, this offence is more serious
If offender has previous convictions, their relevance and any failure to respond to previous
sentences should be considered – they may increase the seriousness. The court should make
it clear, when passing sentence, that this was the approach adopted.

TAKE A PRELIMINARY VIEW OF SERIOUSNESS, THEN
CONSIDER OFFENDER MITIGATION

for example
Age, health (physical or mental)
Subsequent co-operation with police
Evidence of genuine remorse

CONSIDER YOUR SENTENCE

Compare it with the suggested guideline level of sentence and reconsider
your reasons carefully if you have chosen a sentence at a different level.
Consider a reduction for a timely guilty plea.

DECIDE YOUR SENTENCE

| Theft Act 1968 s.15 Triable either way – see Mode of Trial Guidelines Penalty: Level 5 and/or 6 months | **Obtaining by deception** |

CONSIDER THE SERIOUSNESS OF THE OFFENCE
(INCLUDING THE IMPACT ON THE VICTIM)

IS DISCHARGE OR FINE APPROPRIATE?
GUIDELINE: → IS IT SERIOUS ENOUGH FOR A COMMUNITY PENALTY?
IS IT SO SERIOUS THAT ONLY CUSTODY IS APPROPRIATE?
ARE YOUR SENTENCING POWERS SUFFICIENT?

THIS IS A GUIDELINE FOR A FIRST-TIME OFFENDER PLEADING NOT GUILTY

➕ CONSIDER AGGRAVATING AND MITIGATING FACTORS AND THE WEIGHT TO ATTACH TO EACH ➖

for example	for example
Committed over lengthy period	Impulsive action
Large sums or valuable goods	Short period
Two or more involved	Small sum
Use of stolen credit/debit card, cheque books, or giros	*This list is not exhaustive*
Victim particularly vulnerable	
This list is not exhaustive	

If offender is on bail, this offence is more serious
If offender has previous convictions, their relevance and any failure to respond to previous sentences should be considered – they may increase the seriousness. The court should make it clear, when passing sentence, that this was the approach adopted.

TAKE A PRELIMINARY VIEW OF SERIOUSNESS, THEN CONSIDER OFFENDER MITIGATION

for example
Age, health (physical or mental)
Co-operation with police
Evidence of genuine remorse
Voluntary compensation

CONSIDER YOUR SENTENCE

Compare it with the suggested guideline level of sentence and reconsider your reasons carefully if you have chosen a sentence at a different level. Consider a reduction for a timely guilty plea.

DECIDE YOUR SENTENCE
NB. COMPENSATION – Give reasons if not awarding compensation

Possession of a bladed instrument	Criminal Justice Act 1988 s.139 Triable either way – see Mode of Trial Guidelines Penalty: Level 5 and/or 6 months

CONSIDER THE SERIOUSNESS OF THE OFFENCE
(INCLUDING THE IMPACT ON THE VICTIM)

IS DISCHARGE OR FINE APPROPRIATE?
IS IT SERIOUS ENOUGH FOR A COMMUNITY PENALTY?
GUIDELINE: → IS IT SO SERIOUS THAT ONLY CUSTODY IS APPROPRIATE?
ARE YOUR SENTENCING POWERS SUFFICIENT?

THIS IS A GUIDELINE FOR A FIRST-TIME OFFENDER PLEADING NOT GUILTY

➕ CONSIDER AGGRAVATING AND MITIGATING FACTORS ➖
AND THE WEIGHT TO ATTACH TO EACH

for example	for example
Group action or joint possession	Acting out of genuine fear
Location of offence	Carried only on a temporary basis
Offender under influence of drink or drugs	No attempt to use
People put in fear/weapon brandished	Not premeditated
Planned use	*This list is not exhaustive*
Very dangerous weapon	
This list is not exhaustive	

If racially or religiously aggravated, or offender is on bail, this offence is more serious
If offender has previous convictions, their relevance and any failure to respond to previous sentences should be considered – they may increase the seriousness. The court should make it clear, when passing sentence, that this was the approach adopted.

TAKE A PRELIMINARY VIEW OF SERIOUSNESS, THEN
CONSIDER OFFENDER MITIGATION

for example
Age, health (physical or mental)
Co-operation with police
Evidence of genuine remorse

CONSIDER YOUR SENTENCE

Compare it with the suggested guideline level of sentence and reconsider
your reasons carefully if you have chosen a sentence at a different level.
Consider a reduction for a timely guilty plea. Consider forfeiture and destruction.

DECIDE YOUR SENTENCE

Prevention of Crime Act 1953 s.1 Triable either way – see Mode of Trial Guidelines Penalty: Level 5 and/or 6 months	**Possession of an offensive weapon**

CONSIDER THE SERIOUSNESS OF THE OFFENCE
(INCLUDING THE IMPACT ON THE VICTIM)

IS DISCHARGE OR FINE APPROPRIATE?
IS IT SERIOUS ENOUGH FOR A COMMUNITY PENALTY?
GUIDELINE: → IS IT SO SERIOUS THAT ONLY CUSTODY IS APPROPRIATE?
ARE YOUR SENTENCING POWERS SUFFICIENT?

THIS IS A GUIDELINE FOR A FIRST-TIME OFFENDER PLEADING NOT GUILTY

➕ CONSIDER AGGRAVATING AND MITIGATING FACTORS AND THE WEIGHT TO ATTACH TO EACH ➖

for example	for example
Group action or joint possession Location of offence Offender under influence of drink or drugs People put in fear/weapon brandished Planned use Very dangerous weapon *This list is not exhaustive*	Acting out of genuine fear Carried only on a temporary basis No attempt to use Not premeditated *This list is not exhaustive*

If racially or religiously aggravated, or offender is on bail, this offence is more serious
If offender has previous convictions, their relevance and any failure to respond to previous sentences should be considered – they may increase the seriousness. The court should make it clear, when passing sentence, that this was the approach adopted.

TAKE A PRELIMINARY VIEW OF SERIOUSNESS, THEN CONSIDER OFFENDER MITIGATION

for example
   Age, health (physical or mental)
   Co-operation with police
   Evidence of genuine remorse
   Voluntary compensation

CONSIDER YOUR SENTENCE

Compare it with the suggested guideline level of sentence and reconsider your reasons carefully if you have chosen a sentence at a different level. Consider a reduction for a timely guilty plea. Consider forfeiture and destruction.

DECIDE YOUR SENTENCE

Racially or religiously aggravated assault – actual bodily harm	Offences Against the Person Act 1861 s.47 Crime and Disorder Act 1998 s.29 Anti-Terrorism, Crime and Security Act 2001 Triable either way – see Mode of Trial Guidelines Penalty: Level 5 and/or 6 months

CONSIDER THE SERIOUSNESS OF THE OFFENCE
(INCLUDING THE IMPACT ON THE VICTIM)

IS DISCHARGE OR FINE APPROPRIATE?
IS IT SERIOUS ENOUGH FOR A COMMUNITY PENALTY?
IS IT SO SERIOUS THAT ONLY CUSTODY IS APPROPRIATE?
GUIDELINE: → ARE YOUR SENTENCING POWERS SUFFICIENT?

THIS IS A GUIDELINE FOR A FIRST-TIME OFFENDER PLEADING NOT GUILTY

➕ CONSIDER AGGRAVATING AND MITIGATING FACTORS AND THE WEIGHT TO ATTACH TO EACH ➖

for example	for example
Deliberate kicking or biting Extensive injuries (may be psychological) Group action Headbutting **Motivation** for the offence was racial or religious Offender in position of authority On hospital/medical or school premises Premeditated Setting out to humiliate the victim Victim particularly vulnerable Victim serving the public Weapon *This list is not exhaustive*	Minor injury Provocation Single blow *This list is not exhaustive*

If offender is on bail, this offence is more serious
If offender has previous convictions, their relevance and any failure to respond to previous sentences should be considered – they may increase the seriousness. The court should make it clear, when passing sentence, that this was the approach adopted.

TAKE A PRELIMINARY VIEW OF SERIOUSNESS, THEN CONSIDER WHETHER THE CASE SHOULD BE COMMITTED FOR SENTENCE, THEN CONSIDER OFFENDER MITIGATION

for example	
Age, health (physical or mental) Co-operation with police	Evidence of genuine remorse Voluntary compensation

CONSIDER COMMITTAL OR YOUR SENTENCE

Compare it with the suggested guideline level of sentence and reconsider your reasons carefully if you have chosen a sentence at a different level. Consider a reduction for a timely guilty plea.

DECIDE YOUR SENTENCE
NB. COMPENSATION – Give reasons if not awarding compensation

Criminal Justice Act 1988 s.39 Crime and Disorder Act 1998 s.29 Anti-Terrorism, Crime and Security Act 2001 Triable either way – see Mode of Trial Guidelines Penalty: Level 5 and/or 6 months	**Racially or religiously aggravated common assault**

CONSIDER THE SERIOUSNESS OF THE OFFENCE
(INCLUDING THE IMPACT ON THE VICTIM)

IS DISCHARGE OR FINE APPROPRIATE?
IS IT SERIOUS ENOUGH FOR A COMMUNITY PENALTY?
GUIDELINE: → IS IT SO SERIOUS THAT ONLY CUSTODY IS APPROPRIATE?
ARE YOUR SENTENCING POWERS SUFFICIENT?

THIS IS A GUIDELINE FOR A FIRST-TIME OFFENDER PLEADING NOT GUILTY

➕ CONSIDER AGGRAVATING AND MITIGATING FACTORS ➖
AND THE WEIGHT TO ATTACH TO EACH

for example	for example
Group action	Impulsive
Injury	Minor injury
Motivation for the offence was racial or religious	Provocation
Motivation for the offence was racial or religious	Single blow
Offender in position of authority	*This list is not exhaustive*
On hospital/medical or school premises	
Premeditated	
Setting out to humiliate the victim	
Victim particularly vulnerable	
Victim serving the public	
Weapon	
This list is not exhaustive	

If offender is on bail, this offence is more serious
If offender has previous convictions, their relevance and any failure to respond to previous sentences should be considered – they may increase the seriousness. The court should make it clear, when passing sentence, that this was the approach adopted.

TAKE A PRELIMINARY VIEW OF SERIOUSNESS, THEN
CONSIDER OFFENDER MITIGATION

for example
Age, health (physical or mental)
Co-operation with police
Evidence of genuine remorse
Voluntary compensation

CONSIDER YOUR SENTENCE

Compare it with the suggested guideline level of sentence and reconsider your reasons carefully if you have chosen a sentence at a different level. Consider a reduction for a timely guilty plea.

DECIDE YOUR SENTENCE
NB. COMPENSATION – Give reasons if not awarding compensation

Racially or religiously aggravated criminal damage	Criminal Damage Act 1971 s.1 Crime and Disorder Act 1998 s.30 Anti-Terrorism, Crime and Security Act 2001 Triable either way – see Mode of Trial Guidelines Penalty: Level 5 and/or 6 months

CONSIDER THE SERIOUSNESS OF THE OFFENCE
(INCLUDING THE IMPACT ON THE VICTIM)

IS DISCHARGE OR FINE APPROPRIATE?
GUIDELINE: → IS IT SERIOUS ENOUGH FOR A COMMUNITY PENALTY?
IS IT SO SERIOUS THAT ONLY CUSTODY IS APPROPRIATE?
ARE YOUR SENTENCING POWERS SUFFICIENT?

THIS IS A GUIDELINE FOR A FIRST-TIME OFFENDER PLEADING NOT GUILTY

➕ CONSIDER AGGRAVATING AND MITIGATING FACTORS AND THE WEIGHT TO ATTACH TO EACH ➖

for example	for example
Deliberate	Impulsive action
Group offence	Minor damage
Motivation for the offence was racial or religious	Provocation
Serious damage	*This list is not exhaustive*
Setting out to humiliate the victim	
Vulnerable victim	
This list is not exhaustive	

If offender is on bail, this offence is more serious
If offender has previous convictions, their relevance and any failure to respond to previous sentences should be considered – they may increase the seriousness. The court should make it clear, when passing sentence, that this was the approach adopted.

TAKE A PRELIMINARY VIEW OF SERIOUSNESS, THEN CONSIDER OFFENDER MITIGATION

for example
    Age, health (physical or mental)
    Co-operation with police
    Evidence of genuine remorse
    Voluntary compensation

CONSIDER YOUR SENTENCE

Compare it with the suggested guideline level of sentence and reconsider your reasons carefully if you have chosen a sentence at a different level.
Consider a reduction for a timely guilty plea.

DECIDE YOUR SENTENCE
NB. COMPENSATION – Give reasons if not awarding compensation

Public Order Act 1986 s.5 Crime and Disorder Act 1998 s.31 Anti-Terrorism, Crime and Security Act 2001 Triable only summarily Penalty: Level 4	**Racially or religiously aggravated disorderly behaviour**

CONSIDER THE SERIOUSNESS OF THE OFFENCE
(INCLUDING THE IMPACT ON THE VICTIM)

IS DISCHARGE OR FINE APPROPRIATE?
GUIDELINE: → IS IT SERIOUS ENOUGH FOR A COMMUNITY PENALTY?
(COMMUNITY REHABILITATION AND CURFEW ORDERS ARE THE ONLY
AVAILABLE COMMUNITY PENALTIES FOR THIS OFFENCE)

THIS IS A GUIDELINE FOR A FIRST-TIME OFFENDER PLEADING NOT GUILTY

➕ CONSIDER AGGRAVATING AND MITIGATING FACTORS AND THE WEIGHT TO ATTACH TO EACH ➖

for example	for example
Group action **Motivation** for the offence was racial or religious Setting out to humiliate the victim Vulnerable victim *This list is not exhaustive*	Stopped as soon as police arrived Trivial incident *This list is not exhaustive*

If offender is on bail, this offence is more serious
If offender has previous convictions, their relevance and any failure to respond to previous sentences should be considered – they may increase the seriousness. The court should make it clear, when passing sentence, that this was the approach adopted.

TAKE A PRELIMINARY VIEW OF SERIOUSNESS, THEN CONSIDER OFFENDER MITIGATION

for example
Age, health (physical or mental)
Co-operation with police
Evidence of genuine remorse
Voluntary compensation

CONSIDER YOUR SENTENCE

Compare it with the suggested guideline level of sentence and reconsider your reasons carefully if you have chosen a sentence at a different level. Consider a reduction for a timely guilty plea.

DECIDE YOUR SENTENCE
NB. COMPENSATION – Give reasons if not awarding compensation

Racially or religiously aggravated disorderly behaviour with intent to cause harassment, alarm or distress	Public Order Act 1986 s.4A Crime and Disorder Act 1998 s.31 Anti-Terrorism, Crime and Security Act 2001 Triable either way – see Mode of Trial Guidelines Penalty: Level 5 and/or 6 months

CONSIDER THE SERIOUSNESS OF THE OFFENCE
(INCLUDING THE IMPACT ON THE VICTIM)

IS DISCHARGE OR FINE APPROPRIATE?
IS IT SERIOUS ENOUGH FOR A COMMUNITY PENALTY?
GUIDELINE: → *IS IT SO SERIOUS THAT ONLY CUSTODY IS APPROPRIATE?*
ARE YOUR SENTENCING POWERS SUFFICIENT?

THIS IS A GUIDELINE FOR A FIRST-TIME OFFENDER PLEADING NOT GUILTY

➕ CONSIDER AGGRAVATING AND MITIGATING FACTORS AND THE WEIGHT TO ATTACH TO EACH ➖

for example	for example
Football related	Single incident
Group action	*This list is not exhaustive*
High degree of planning	
Motivation for the offence was racial or religious	
Night time offence	
Setting out to humiliate the victim	
Victims specifically targeted	
Weapon	
This list is not exhaustive	

If offender is on bail, this offence is more serious
If offender has previous convictions, their relevance and any failure to respond to previous sentences should be considered – they may increase the seriousness. The court should make it clear, when passing sentence, that this was the approach adopted.

TAKE A PRELIMINARY VIEW OF SERIOUSNESS, THEN CONSIDER OFFENDER MITIGATION

for example
    Age, health (physical or mental)
    Co-operation with police
    Evidence of genuine remorse
    Voluntary compensation

CONSIDER YOUR SENTENCE

Compare it with the suggested guideline level of sentence and reconsider your reasons carefully if you have chosen a sentence at a different level.
Consider a reduction for a timely guilty plea.

DECIDE YOUR SENTENCE
NB. COMPENSATION – Give reasons if not awarding compensation

Protection from Harassment Act 1997 s.4 Crime and Disorder Act 1998 s.32 Anti-Terrorism, Crime and Security Act 2001 Triable either way – see Mode of Trial Guidelines Penalty: Level 5 and/or 6 months Consider making a restraining order	**Racially or religiously aggravated harassment** Conduct causing fear of violence

CONSIDER THE SERIOUSNESS OF THE OFFENCE
(INCLUDING THE IMPACT ON THE VICTIM)

IS DISCHARGE OR FINE APPROPRIATE?
IS IT SERIOUS ENOUGH FOR A COMMUNITY PENALTY?
IS IT SO SERIOUS THAT ONLY CUSTODY IS APPROPRIATE?
GUIDELINE: → ARE YOUR SENTENCING POWERS SUFFICIENT?

THIS IS A GUIDELINE FOR A FIRST-TIME OFFENDER PLEADING NOT GUILTY

➕ CONSIDER AGGRAVATING AND MITIGATING FACTORS ➖
AND THE WEIGHT TO ATTACH TO EACH

for example	for example
Disregard of warning	Initial provocation
Excessive persistence	Short duration
Interference with employment/business	*This list is not exhaustive*
Invasion of victim's home	
Involvement of others	
Motivation for the offence was racial or religious	
Setting out to humiliate the victim	
Threat to use weapon or substance (including realistic imitations)	
Use of violence or grossly offensive material	
Where photographs or images of a personal nature are involved	
This list is not exhaustive	

If offender is on bail, this offence is more serious
If offender has previous convictions, their relevance and any failure to respond to previous sentences should be considered – they may increase the seriousness. The court should make it clear, when passing sentence, that this was the approach adopted.

TAKE A PRELIMINARY VIEW OF SERIOUSNESS, THEN CONSIDER
WHETHER THE CASE SHOULD BE COMMITTED FOR SENTENCE,
THEN CONSIDER OFFENDER MITIGATION

for example
Age, health (physical or mental)
Co-operation with police
Evidence of genuine remorse
Voluntary compensation

continued on page 505

continued from page 504

CONSIDER COMMITTAL OR YOUR SENTENCE

Compare it with the suggested guideline level of sentence and reconsider your reasons carefully if you have chosen a sentence at a different level.
Consider a reduction for a timely guilty plea.
Restraining order – consider making an order in addition to the sentence to protect the victim or any named person from further conduct which would amount to harassment, or which would cause the fear of violence.

DECIDE YOUR SENTENCE
NB. COMPENSATION – Give reasons if not awarding compensation

Racially or religiously aggravated harassment **Conduct causing harassment**	Protection from Harassment Act 1997 s.2 Crime and Disorder Act 1998 s.32 Anti-Terrorism, Crime and Security Act 2001 Triable either way – see Mode of Trial Guidelines Penalty: Level 5 and/or 6 months Consider making a restraining order

CONSIDER THE SERIOUSNESS OF THE OFFENCE
(INCLUDING THE IMPACT ON THE VICTIM)

IS DISCHARGE OR FINE APPROPRIATE?
IS IT SERIOUS ENOUGH FOR A COMMUNITY PENALTY?
GUIDELINE: → IS IT SO SERIOUS THAT ONLY CUSTODY IS APPROPRIATE?
ARE YOUR SENTENCING POWERS SUFFICIENT?

THIS IS A GUIDELINE FOR A FIRST-TIME OFFENDER PLEADING NOT GUILTY

➕ CONSIDER AGGRAVATING AND MITIGATING FACTORS AND THE WEIGHT TO ATTACH TO EACH ➖

for example	for example
Disregard of warning Excessive persistence Interference with employment/business Invasion of victim's home Involvement of others **Motivation** for the offence was racial or religious Setting out to humiliate the victim Use of violence or grossly offensive material Where photographs or images of a personal nature are involved *This list is not exhaustive*	Initial provocation Short duration *This list is not exhaustive*

If offender is on bail, this offence is more serious
If offender has previous convictions, their relevance and any failure to respond to previous sentences should be considered – they may increase the seriousness. The court should make it clear, when passing sentence, that this was the approach adopted.

TAKE A PRELIMINARY VIEW OF SERIOUSNESS, THEN CONSIDER OFFENDER MITIGATION

for example Age, health (physical or mental) Co-operation with police	Evidence of genuine remorse Voluntary compensation

CONSIDER YOUR SENTENCE

Compare it with the suggested guideline level of sentence and reconsider your reasons carefully if you have chosen a sentence at a different level.
Consider a reduction for a timely guilty plea.
Restraining order – consider making an order in addition to the sentence to protect the victim or any named person from further conduct which would amount to harassment.

DECIDE YOUR SENTENCE
NB. COMPENSATION – Give reasons if not awarding compensation

Public Order Act 1986 s.4 Crime and Disorder Act 1998 s.32 Anti-Terrorism, Crime and Security Act 2001 Triable either way – see Mode of Trial Guidelines Penalty: Level 5 and/or 6 months	**Racially or religiously aggravated threatening behaviour**

CONSIDER THE SERIOUSNESS OF THE OFFENCE
(INCLUDING THE IMPACT ON THE VICTIM)

IS DISCHARGE OR FINE APPROPRIATE?
IS IT SERIOUS ENOUGH FOR A COMMUNITY PENALTY?
GUIDELINE: → IS IT SO SERIOUS THAT ONLY CUSTODY IS APPROPRIATE?
ARE YOUR SENTENCING POWERS SUFFICIENT?

THIS IS A GUIDELINE FOR A FIRST-TIME OFFENDER PLEADING NOT GUILTY

✚ CONSIDER AGGRAVATING AND MITIGATING FACTORS AND THE WEIGHT TO ATTACH TO EACH ➖

for example	for example
Group action	Minor matter
Motivation for the offence was racial or religious	Short duration
On hospital/medical or school premises	*This list is not exhaustive*
People put in fear	
Setting out to humiliate the victim	
Victim serving the public	
Vulnerable victim	
This list is not exhaustive	

If offender is on bail, this offence is more serious
If offender has previous convictions, their relevance and any failure to respond to previous sentences should be considered – they may increase the seriousness. The court should make it clear, when passing sentence, that this was the approach adopted.

TAKE A PRELIMINARY VIEW OF SERIOUSNESS, THEN CONSIDER OFFENDER MITIGATION

for example
Age, health (physical or mental)
Co-operation with police
Evidence of genuine remorse
Voluntary compensation

CONSIDER YOUR SENTENCE

Compare it with the suggested guideline level of sentence and reconsider your reasons carefully if you have chosen a sentence at a different level. Consider a reduction for a timely guilty plea.

DECIDE YOUR SENTENCE
NB. COMPENSATION – Give reasons if not awarding compensation

Racially or religiously aggravated wounding – grievous bodily harm	Offences Against the Person act 1861 s.20 Crime and Disorder Act 1998 s.29 Anti-Terrorism, Crime and Security Act 2001 Triable either way – see Mode of Trial Guidelines Penalty: Level 5 and/or 6 months

CONSIDER THE SERIOUSNESS OF THE OFFENCE
(INCLUDING THE IMPACT ON THE VICTIM)

IS DISCHARGE OR FINE APPROPRIATE?
IS IT SERIOUS ENOUGH FOR A COMMUNITY PENALTY?
IS IT SO SERIOUS THAT ONLY CUSTODY IS APPROPRIATE?
GUIDELINE: → ARE YOUR SENTENCING POWERS SUFFICIENT?

THIS IS A GUIDELINE FOR A FIRST-TIME OFFENDER PLEADING NOT GUILTY

✚　　CONSIDER AGGRAVATING AND MITIGATING FACTORS AND THE WEIGHT TO ATTACH TO EACH　　➖

for example	for example
Deliberate kicking/biting Extensive injuries Group action **Motivation** for the offence was racial or religious Offender in position of authority On hospital/medical or school premises Premeditated Setting out to humiliate the victim Victim particularly vulnerable Victim serving the public Weapon *This list is not exhaustive*	Minor wound Provocation *This list is not exhaustive*

If offender is on bail, this offence is more serious
If offender has previous convictions, their relevance and any failure to respond to previous sentences should be considered – they may increase the seriousness. The court should make it clear, when passing sentence, that this was the approach adopted.

TAKE A PRELIMINARY VIEW OF SERIOUSNESS, THEN CONSIDER WHETHER THE CASE SHOULD BE COMMITTED FOR SENTENCE, THEN CONSIDER OFFENDER MITIGATION

for example
　　Age, health (physical or mental)
　　Co-operation with police
　　Evidence of genuine remorse
　　Voluntary compensation

CONSIDER COMMITTAL OR YOUR SENTENCE

Compare it with the suggested guideline level of sentence and reconsider your reasons carefully if you have chosen a sentence at a different level. Consider a reduction for a timely guilty plea.

DECIDE YOUR SENTENCE
NB. COMPENSATION – Give reasons if not awarding compensation

Education Act 1996 s.444A Penalty: Level 4 and/or 3 months Triable only summarily	School non-attendance

CONSIDER THE SERIOUSNESS OF THE OFFENCE

IS DISCHARGE OR FINE APPROPRIATE?
GUIDELINE: → IS IT SERIOUS ENOUGH FOR A COMMUNITY PENALTY?
IS IT SO SERIOUS THAT ONLY CUSTODY IS APPROPRIATE?

THIS IS A GUIDELINE FOR A FIRST-TIME OFFENDER PLEADING NOT GUILTY

✚ CONSIDER AGGRAVATING AND MITIGATING FACTORS AND THE WEIGHT TO ATTACH TO EACH ➖

for example	for example
Harmful effect on other children in the family Lack of parental effort to ensure attendance Parental collusion Threats to teachers, pupils and/or officials *This list is not exhaustive*	Physical or mental health of child Substantiated history of bullying, drugs etc. *This list is not exhaustive*

If offender is on bail, this offence is more serious
If offender has previous convictions, their relevance and any failure to respond to previous sentences should be considered – they may increase the seriousness. The court should make it clear, when passing sentence, that this was the approach adopted.

TAKE A PRELIMINARY VIEW OF SERIOUSNESS, THEN CONSIDER OFFENDER MITIGATION

for example
    Age, health (physical or mental)
    Co-operation with the Education Authority
    Evidence of genuine remorse

CONSIDER YOUR SENTENCE

Compare it with the suggested guideline level of sentence and reconsider your reasons carefully if you have chosen a sentence at a different level.
Consider a reduction for a timely guilty plea.
Consider a parenting order where appropriate.

DECIDE YOUR SENTENCE
Prosecutions under s.444 are penalty level 3 only – consult legal adviser.

Social Security – false representation to obtain benefit

Social Security Act 1992 s.112
Triable only summarily
Penalty: Level 5 and/or 3 months

CONSIDER THE SERIOUSNESS OF THE OFFENCE

IS DISCHARGE OR FINE APPROPRIATE?
GUIDELINE: → IS IT SERIOUS ENOUGH FOR A COMMUNITY PENALTY?
IS IT SO SERIOUS THAT ONLY CUSTODY IS APPROPRIATE?

THIS IS A GUIDELINE FOR A FIRST-TIME OFFENDER PLEADING NOT GUILTY

➕ CONSIDER AGGRAVATING AND MITIGATING FACTORS AND THE WEIGHT TO ATTACH TO EACH ➖

for example
  Claim fraudulent from the start
  Fraudulent claims over a long period
  Large amount
  Organised group offence
  Planned deception
  This list is not exhaustive

for example
  Misunderstanding of regulations
  Pressurised by others
  Small amount
  This list is not exhaustive

If offender is on bail, this offence is more serious
If offender has previous convictions, their relevance and any failure to respond to previous sentences should be considered – they may increase the seriousness. The court should make it clear, when passing sentence, that this was the approach adopted.

TAKE A PRELIMINARY VIEW OF SERIOUSNESS, THEN CONSIDER OFFENDER MITIGATION

for example
  Age, health (physical or mental)
  Co-operation with police
  Evidence of genuine remorse
  Voluntary compensation

CONSIDER YOUR SENTENCE

Compare it with the suggested guideline level of sentence and reconsider your reasons carefully if you have chosen a sentence at a different level. Consider a reduction for a timely guilty plea.

DECIDE YOUR SENTENCE
NB. COMPENSATION – Give reasons if not awarding compensation

Theft Act 1968 s.12 Triable only summarily Penalty: Level 5 and/or 6 months May disqualify	**Taking vehicle without consent**

CONSIDER THE SERIOUSNESS OF THE OFFENCE
(INCLUDING THE IMPACT ON THE VICTIM)

IS DISCHARGE OR FINE APPROPRIATE?
GUIDELINE: → IS IT SERIOUS ENOUGH FOR A COMMUNITY PENALTY?
IS IT SO SERIOUS THAT ONLY CUSTODY IS APPROPRIATE?

THIS IS A GUIDELINE FOR A FIRST-TIME OFFENDER PLEADING NOT GUILTY

➕ CONSIDER AGGRAVATING AND MITIGATING FACTORS ➖
AND THE WEIGHT TO ATTACH TO EACH

for example	for example
Group action	Misunderstanding with owner
Premeditated	Soon returned
Related damage	Vehicle belonged to family or friend
Professional hallmarks	*This list is not exhaustive*
Vulnerable victim	
This list is not exhaustive	

If offender is on bail, this offence is more serious
If offender has previous convictions, their relevance and any failure to respond to previous sentences should be considered – they may increase the seriousness. The court should make it clear, when passing sentence, that this was the approach adopted.

TAKE A PRELIMINARY VIEW OF SERIOUSNESS, THEN
CONSIDER OFFENDER MITIGATION

for example
    Health (physical or mental)
    Co-operation with police
    Evidence of genuine remorse
    Voluntary compensation

CONSIDER YOUR SENTENCE

*Compare it with the suggested guideline level of sentence and reconsider
your reasons carefully if you have chosen a sentence at a different level.
Consider a reduction for a timely guilty plea.*

DECIDE YOUR SENTENCE
NB. COMPENSATION – Give reasons if not awarding compensation

Theft	**Theft Act 1968 s.1** Triable either way – see Mode of Trial Guidelines Penalty: Level 5 and/or 6 months May disqualify where committed with reference to the theft or taking of a vehicle

CONSIDER THE SERIOUSNESS OF THE OFFENCE
(INCLUDING THE IMPACT ON THE VICTIM)

IS DISCHARGE OR FINE APPROPRIATE?
GUIDELINE: → IS IT SERIOUS ENOUGH FOR A COMMUNITY PENALTY?
IS IT SO SERIOUS THAT ONLY CUSTODY IS APPROPRIATE?
ARE YOUR SENTENCING POWERS SUFFICIENT?

THIS IS A GUIDELINE FOR A FIRST-TIME OFFENDER PLEADING NOT GUILTY

➕ CONSIDER AGGRAVATING AND MITIGATING FACTORS ➖
AND THE WEIGHT TO ATTACH TO EACH

for example	for example
High value	Impulsive action
Planned	Low value
Sophisticated	*This list is not exhaustive*
Adult involving children	
Organised team	
Related damage	
Vulnerable victim	
This list is not exhaustive	

If racially or religiously aggravated, or offender is on bail, this offence is more serious
If offender has previous convictions, their relevance and any failure to respond to previous
sentences should be considered – they may increase the seriousness. The court should make
it clear, when passing sentence, that this was the approach adopted.

TAKE A PRELIMINARY VIEW OF SERIOUSNESS, THEN
CONSIDER OFFENDER MITIGATION

for example
Age, health (physical or mental)
Co-operation with police
Evidence of genuine remorse
Voluntary compensation

CONSIDER YOUR SENTENCE

Compare it with the suggested guideline level of sentence and reconsider
your reasons carefully if you have chosen a sentence at a different level.
Consider a reduction for a timely guilty plea.

DECIDE YOUR SENTENCE
NB. COMPENSATION – Give reasons if not awarding compensation

Theft Act 1968 s.1 Triable either way – see Mode of Trial Guidelines Penalty: Level 5 and/or 6 months	**Theft in breach of trust**

CONSIDER THE SERIOUSNESS OF THE OFFENCE
(INCLUDING THE IMPACT ON THE VICTIM)

IS DISCHARGE OR FINE APPROPRIATE?
IS IT SERIOUS ENOUGH FOR A COMMUNITY PENALTY?
GUIDELINE: → *IS IT SO SERIOUS THAT ONLY CUSTODY IS APPROPRIATE?*
ARE YOUR SENTENCING POWERS SUFFICIENT?

THIS IS A GUIDELINE FOR A FIRST-TIME OFFENDER PLEADING NOT GUILTY

➕ CONSIDER AGGRAVATING AND MITIGATING FACTORS ➖
AND THE WEIGHT TO ATTACH TO EACH

for example	for example
Casting suspicion on others	Impulsive action
Committed over a period	Low value
High value	Previous inconsistent attitude by employer
Organised team	Single item
Planned	Unsupported junior
Senior employee	*This list is not exhaustive*
Sophisticated	
Vulnerable victim	
This list is not exhaustive	

If racially or religiously aggravated, or offender is on bail, this offence is more serious
If offender has previous convictions, their relevance and any failure to respond to previous
sentences should be considered – they may increase the seriousness. The court should make
it clear, when passing sentence, that this was the approach adopted.

TAKE A PRELIMINARY VIEW OF SERIOUSNESS,
THEN CONSIDER OFFENDER MITIGATION

for example
    Age, health (physical or mental)
    Co-operation with police
    Evidence of genuine remorse
    Voluntary compensation

CONSIDER YOUR SENTENCE

Compare it with the suggested guideline level of sentence and reconsider
your reasons carefully if you have chosen a sentence at a different level.
Consider a reduction for a timely guilty plea.

DECIDE YOUR SENTENCE
NB. COMPENSATION – Give reasons if not awarding compensation

Threatening behaviour	Public Order Act 1986 s.4 Triable only summarily Penalty: Level 5 and/or 6 months

CONSIDER THE SERIOUSNESS OF THE OFFENCE
(INCLUDING THE IMPACT ON THE VICTIM)

IS DISCHARGE OR FINE APPROPRIATE?
GUIDELINE: → IS IT SERIOUS ENOUGH FOR A COMMUNITY PENALTY?
IS IT SO SERIOUS THAT ONLY CUSTODY IS APPROPRIATE?

THIS IS A GUIDELINE FOR A FIRST-TIME OFFENDER PLEADING NOT GUILTY

➕ CONSIDER AGGRAVATING AND MITIGATING FACTORS ➖
AND THE WEIGHT TO ATTACH TO EACH

for example	for example
Football related	Minor matter
Group action	Short duration
On hospital/medical or school premises	*This list is not exhaustive*
People put in fear	
Victim serving the public	
Vulnerable victim	
This list is not exhaustive	

If offender is on bail, this offence is more serious
If offender has previous convictions, their relevance and any failure to respond to previous sentences should be considered – they may increase the seriousness. The court should make it clear, when passing sentence, that this was the approach adopted.

TAKE A PRELIMINARY VIEW OF SERIOUSNESS, THEN
CONSIDER OFFENDER MITIGATION

for example
Age, health (physical or mental)
Co-operation with police
Evidence of genuine remorse
Voluntary compensation

CONSIDER YOUR SENTENCE

Compare it with the suggested guideline level of sentence and reconsider your reasons carefully if you have chosen a sentence at a different level. Consider a reduction for a timely guilty plea.

DECIDE YOUR SENTENCE
NB. COMPENSATION – Give reasons if not awarding compensation

Wireless Telegraphy Act 1949 s.1 Triable only summarily Penalty: Level 3	**TV licence payment evasion**

CONSIDER THE SERIOUSNESS OF THE OFFENCE

GUIDELINE: → IS DISCHARGE OR FINE APPROPRIATE?
IS IT SERIOUS ENOUGH FOR A COMMUNITY PENALTY?
(COMMUNITY REHABILITATION AND CURFEW ORDERS ARE THE ONLY
AVAILABLE COMMUNITY PENALTIES FOR THIS OFFENCE)

THIS IS A GUIDELINE FOR A FIRST-TIME OFFENDER PLEADING NOT GUILTY

GUIDELINE FINE – STARTING POINT A

➕	**CONSIDER AGGRAVATING AND MITIGATING FACTORS AND THE WEIGHT TO ATTACH TO EACH**	➖

for example	for example
Failure to respond to payment opportunities *This list is not exhaustive*	Accidental oversight Confusion of responsibility Licence immediately obtained Very short unlicensed use *This list is not exhaustive*

If offender is on bail, this offence is more serious
If offender has previous convictions, their relevance and any failure to respond to previous sentences should be considered – they may increase the seriousness. The court should make it clear, when passing sentence, that this was the approach adopted.

TAKE A PRELIMINARY VIEW OF SERIOUSNESS, THEN CONSIDER OFFENDER MITIGATION

for example
    Age, health (physical or mental)

CONSIDER YOUR SENTENCE

Compare it with the suggested guideline level of sentence and reconsider
your reasons carefully if you have chosen a sentence at a different level.
Consider a reduction for a timely guilty plea. Consider forfeiture and destruction.

DECIDE YOUR SENTENCE

Vehicle interference	Criminal Attempts Act 1981 s.9 Triable only summarily Penalty: Level 4 and/or 3 months

CONSIDER THE SERIOUSNESS OF THE OFFENCE
(INCLUDING THE IMPACT ON THE VICTIM)

IS DISCHARGE OR FINE APPROPRIATE?
GUIDELINE: → IS IT SERIOUS ENOUGH FOR A COMMUNITY PENALTY?
IS IT SO SERIOUS THAT ONLY CUSTODY IS APPROPRIATE?

THIS IS A GUIDELINE FOR A FIRST-TIME OFFENDER PLEADING NOT GUILTY

➕   **CONSIDER AGGRAVATING AND MITIGATING FACTORS**   **➖**
                AND THE WEIGHT TO ATTACH TO EACH

for example	for example
Disabled passenger vehicle	Impulsive action
Emergency service vehicle	*This list is not exhaustive*
Group action	
Planned	
Related damage	
This list is not exhaustive	

If racially or religiously aggravated, or offender is on bail, this offence is more serious
If offender has previous convictions, their relevance and any failure to respond to previous
sentences should be considered – they may increase the seriousness. The court should make
it clear, when passing sentence, that this was the approach adopted.

TAKE A PRELIMINARY VIEW OF SERIOUSNESS, THEN
CONSIDER OFFENDER MITIGATION

for example
    Age, health (physical or mental)
    Co-operation with police
    Evidence of genuine remorse
    Voluntary compensation

CONSIDER YOUR SENTENCE

Compare it with the suggested guideline level of sentence and reconsider
your reasons carefully if you have chosen a sentence at a different level.
Consider a reduction for a timely guilty plea.

DECIDE YOUR SENTENCE
NB. COMPENSATION – Give reasons if not awarding compensation

Public Order Act 1986 s.2 Triable either way – see Mode of Trial Guidelines Penalty: Level 5 and/or 6 months	**Violent disorder**

CONSIDER THE SERIOUSNESS OF THE OFFENCE
(INCLUDING THE IMPACT ON THE VICTIM)

IS DISCHARGE OR FINE APPROPRIATE?
IS IT SERIOUS ENOUGH FOR A COMMUNITY PENALTY?
IS IT SO SERIOUS THAT ONLY CUSTODY IS APPROPRIATE?
GUIDELINE: → ARE YOUR SENTENCING POWERS SUFFICIENT?

THIS IS A GUIDELINE FOR A FIRST-TIME OFFENDER PLEADING NOT GUILTY

➕ CONSIDER AGGRAVATING AND MITIGATING FACTORS ➖
AND THE WEIGHT TO ATTACH TO EACH

for example	for example
Busy public place	Impulsive
Fighting between rival groups	Provocation
Large group	*This list is not exhaustive*
People in fear	
Planned	
Vulnerable victims	
Weapon	
This list is not exhaustive	

If racially or religiously aggravated, or offender is on bail, this offence is more serious
If offender has previous convictions, their relevance and any failure to respond to previous
sentences should be considered – they may increase the seriousness. The court should make
it clear, when passing sentence, that this was the approach adopted.

TAKE A PRELIMINARY VIEW OF SERIOUSNESS, THEN CONSIDER
WHETHER THE CASE SHOULD BE COMMITTED FOR SENTENCE,
THEN CONSIDER OFFENDER MITIGATION

for example
  Age, health (physical or mental)
  Co-operation with police
  Evidence of genuine remorse
  Voluntary compensation

CONSIDER COMMITTAL OR YOUR SENTENCE

Compare it with the suggested guideline level of sentence and reconsider
your reasons carefully if you have chosen a sentence at a different level.
Consider a reduction for a timely guilty plea.

DECIDE YOUR SENTENCE
NB. COMPENSATION – Give reasons if not awarding compensation

Wounding – grievous bodily harm	Offences Against the Person Act 1861 s.20 Triable either way – see Mode of Trial Guidelines Penalty: Level 5 and/or 6 months

CONSIDER THE SERIOUSNESS OF THE OFFENCE
(INCLUDING THE IMPACT ON THE VICTIM)

IS DISCHARGE OR FINE APPROPRIATE?
IS IT SERIOUS ENOUGH FOR A COMMUNITY PENALTY?
IS IT SO SERIOUS THAT ONLY CUSTODY IS APPROPRIATE?
GUIDELINE: → ARE YOUR SENTENCING POWERS SUFFICIENT?

THIS IS A GUIDELINE FOR A FIRST-TIME OFFENDER PLEADING NOT GUILTY

➕ CONSIDER AGGRAVATING AND MITIGATING FACTORS ➖
AND THE WEIGHT TO ATTACH TO EACH

for example	for example
Abuse of trust (domestic setting)	Minor wound
Deliberate kicking/biting	Provocation
Extensive injuries	*This list is not exhaustive*
Group action	
Offender in position of authority	
On hospital/medical or school premises	
Premeditated	
Prolonged assault	
Victim particularly vulnerable	
Victim serving the public	
Weapon	
This list is not exhaustive	

If offender is on bail, this offence is more serious
If offender has previous convictions, their relevance and any failure to respond to previous sentences should be considered – they may increase the seriousness. The court should make it clear, when passing sentence, that this was the approach adopted.

TAKE A PRELIMINARY VIEW OF SERIOUSNESS, THEN CONSIDER WHETHER THE CASE SHOULD BE COMMITTED FOR SENTENCE, THEN CONSIDER OFFENDER MITIGATION

for example
  Age, health (physical or mental)
  Co-operation with police
  Evidence of genuine remorse
  Voluntary compensation

CONSIDER YOUR SENTENCE

Compare it with the suggested guideline level of sentence and reconsider your reasons carefully if you have chosen a sentence at a different level. Consider a reduction for a timely guilty plea.

DECIDE YOUR SENTENCE
NB. COMPENSATION – Give reasons if not awarding compensation

| Road Traffic Act 1988 s.3
Triable only summarily
Penalty: Level 4
Must endorse (3–9 points OR may disqualify) | **Careless driving** |

CONSIDER THE SERIOUSNESS OF THE OFFENCE

GUIDELINE: → IS DISCHARGE OR FINE APPROPRIATE?
IS IT SERIOUS ENOUGH FOR A COMMUNITY PENALTY?
(COMMUNITY REHABILITATION AND CURFEW ORDERS ARE THE ONLY
AVAILABLE COMMUNITY PENALTIES FOR THIS OFFENCE)

THIS IS A GUIDELINE FOR A FIRST-TIME OFFENDER PLEADING NOT GUILTY

GUIDELINE FINE – STARTING POINT B

➕ CONSIDER AGGRAVATING AND MITIGATING FACTORS ➖
AND THE WEIGHT TO ATTACH TO EACH

for example	for example
Excessive speed	Minor risk
High degree of carelessness	Momentary lapse
Serious risk	Negligible/parking damage
Using a hand-held mobile telephone	Sudden change in weather conditions
This list is not exhaustive	*This list is not exhaustive*

Death, serious injury or damage is capable of being aggravation

If offender is on bail, this offence is more serious
If offender has previous convictions, their relevance and any failure to respond to previous sentences should be considered – they may increase the seriousness. The court should make it clear, when passing sentence, that this was the approach adopted.

TAKE A PRELIMINARY VIEW OF SERIOUSNESS, THEN
CONSIDER OFFENDER MITIGATION

for example
   Co-operation with police
   Evidence of genuine remorse
   Voluntary compensation

CONSIDER YOUR SENTENCE

Endorse (3–9 points OR period of disqualification)
Consider other measures (including disqualification until test passed if appropriate –
for example, age, infirmity or medical condition)
Compare it with the suggested guideline level of sentence and reconsider
your reasons carefully if you have chosen a sentence at a different level.
Consider a reduction for a timely guilty plea.

DECIDE YOUR SENTENCE

Dangerous driving	Road Traffic Act 1988 s.2 Triable either way – see Mode of Trial Guidelines Penalty: Level 5 and/or 6 months Must endorse and disqualify at least 12 months Must endorse (3–11 points) if not disqualified **MUST ORDER EXTENDED RE-TEST**

CONSIDER THE SERIOUSNESS OF THE OFFENCE
(INCLUDING THE IMPACT ON THE VICTIM)

IS DISCHARGE OR FINE APPROPRIATE?
IS IT SERIOUS ENOUGH FOR A COMMUNITY PENALTY?
GUIDELINE: → IS IT SO SERIOUS THAT ONLY CUSTODY IS APPROPRIATE?
ARE YOUR SENTENCING POWERS SUFFICIENT?

THIS IS A GUIDELINE FOR A FIRST-TIME OFFENDER PLEADING NOT GUILTY

➕ CONSIDER AGGRAVATING AND MITIGATING FACTORS ➖
AND THE WEIGHT TO ATTACH TO EACH

for example	for example

Avoiding detection or apprehension
Competitive driving, racing, showing off
Disregard of warnings, eg from passengers
  or others in vicinity
Evidence of alcohol or drugs
Excessive speed
Police pursuit
Prolonged, persistent, deliberate bad
  driving
Serious risk
Using a mobile telephone
This list is not exhaustive
	Emergency
	Speed not excessive
	This list is not exhaustive

Serious injury or damage is capable of being aggravation

If offender is on bail, this offence is more serious
If offender has previous convictions, their relevance and any failure to respond to previous sentences should be considered – they may increase the seriousness. The court should make it clear, when passing sentence, that this was the approach adopted.

TAKE A PRELIMINARY VIEW OF SERIOUSNESS,
THEN CONSIDER OFFENDER MITIGATION

for example	
Co-operation with police Evidence of genuine remorse	Voluntary compensation

CONSIDER YOUR SENTENCE

Endorse licence and disqualify at least 12 months unless special reasons apply.
MUST ORDER EXTENDED RE-TEST.
Compare it with the suggested guideline level of sentence and reconsider your reasons carefully if you have chosen a sentence at a different level.
Consider a reduction for a timely guilty plea.

DECIDE YOUR SENTENCE

Road Traffic Act 1988 s.103 Triable only summarily Penalty: Level 5 and/or 6 months Must endorse: (6 points OR may disqualify again)	**Driving whilst disqualified**

CONSIDER THE SERIOUSNESS OF THE OFFENCE

IS DISCHARGE OR FINE APPROPRIATE?
GUIDELINE: → *IS IT SERIOUS ENOUGH FOR A COMMUNITY PENALTY?*
IS IT SO SERIOUS THAT ONLY CUSTODY IS APPROPRIATE?

THIS IS A GUIDELINE FOR A FIRST-TIME OFFENDER PLEADING NOT GUILTY

➕ CONSIDER AGGRAVATING AND MITIGATING FACTORS ➖
AND THE WEIGHT TO ATTACH TO EACH

for example	for example
Driver has never past a test	Emergency established
Driving for remuneration	Full period expired but test not re-taken
Efforts to avoid detection	Short distance driven
Long distance driven	*This list is not exhaustive*
Planned, long term evasion	
Recent disqualification	
This list is not exhaustive	

If offender is on bail, this offence is more serious
If offender has previous convictions, their relevance and any failure to respond to previous sentences should be considered – they may increase the seriousness. The court should make it clear, when passing sentence, that this was the approach adopted.

TAKE A PRELIMINARY VIEW OF SERIOUSNESS, THEN
CONSIDER OFFENDER MITIGATION

for example
   Co-operation with police
   Evidence of genuine remorse

CONSIDER YOUR SENTENCE

Endorse (6 points OR period of disqualification)
Compare it with the suggested guideline level of sentence and reconsider your reasons carefully if you have chosen a sentence at a different level.
Consider a reduction for a timely guilty plea.

DECIDE YOUR SENTENCE

Excess alcohol (drive or attempt to drive)	Road Traffic Act 1988 s.5(1)(a) Penalty: Level 5 and/or 6 months Triable only summarily Must endorse and disqualify *at least* 12 months: disqualify at least 36 months for a further offence within 10 years

CONSIDER THE SERIOUSNESS OF THE OFFENCE
THE LEVEL OF SERIOUSNESS AND GUIDELINE SENTENCE ARE RELATED TO THE BREATH/BLOOD/URINE LEVEL

➕ CONSIDER AGGRAVATING AND MITIGATING FACTORS AND THE WEIGHT TO ATTACH TO EACH ➖

for example
- Ability to drive seriously impaired
- Caused injury/fear/damage
- Police pursuit
- Evidence of nature of the driving
- Type of vehicle, eg carrying passengers for reward/large goods vehicle
- High reading (and in combination with above)

This list is not exhaustive

for example
- Emergency
- Moving a vehicle a very short distance
- Spiked drinks

This list is not exhaustive

If offender is on bail, this offence is more serious
If offender has previous convictions, their relevance and any failure to respond to previous sentences should be considered – they may increase the seriousness. The court should make it clear, when passing sentence, that this was the approach adopted.

TAKE A PRELIMINARY VIEW OF SERIOUSNESS, THEN CONSIDER OFFENDER MITIGATION

for example
- Co-operation with police

CONSIDER YOUR SENTENCE

Offer a rehabilitation course.
Compare your decision with the suggested guideline level of sentence and reconsider your reasons carefully if you have chosen a sentence at a different level.
Consider a reduction for a timely guilty plea.

DECIDE YOUR SENTENCE

BREATH	BLOOD	URINE	DISQUALIFY NOT LESS THAN	GUIDELINE
36–55	80–125	107–170	12 months	B
56–70	126–160	171–214	16 months	C
71–85	161–195	215–260	20 months	C
86–100	196–229	261–308	24 months	CONSIDER COMMUNITY PENALTY
101–115	230–264	309–354	28 months	
116–130	265–300	355–400	32 months	CONSIDER CUSTODY
131+	301+	401+	36 months	

Road Traffic Act 1988 s.170(4) Triable only summarily Penalty: Level 5 and/or 6 months Must endorse: (5–10 points OR disqualify)	**Failing to stop** **Failing to report**

CONSIDER THE SERIOUSNESS OF THE OFFENCE

GUIDELINE: → IS DISCHARGE OR FINE APPROPRIATE?
IS IT SERIOUS ENOUGH FOR A COMMUNITY PENALTY?
IS IT SO SERIOUS THAT ONLY CUSTODY IS APPROPRIATE?

THIS IS A GUIDELINE FOR A FIRST-TIME OFFENDER PLEADING NOT GUILTY

GUIDELINE FINE – STARTING POINT C

➕ CONSIDER AGGRAVATING AND MITIGATING FACTORS ➖
AND THE WEIGHT TO ATTACH TO EACH

for example	for example
Evidence of drinking or drugs	Believed identity to be known
Serious injury	Failed to stop but reported
Serious damage	Genuine fear of retaliation
This list is not exhaustive	Negligible damage
	No one at scene but failed to report
	Stayed at scene but failed to give/left before
	giving full particulars
	This list is not exhaustive

If offender is on bail, this offence is more serious
If offender has previous convictions, their relevance and any failure to respond to previous sentences should be considered – they may increase the seriousness. The court should make it clear, when passing sentence, that this was the approach adopted.

TAKE A PRELIMINARY VIEW OF SERIOUSNESS, THEN
CONSIDER OFFENDER MITIGATION

for example
  Co-operation with police
  Evidence of genuine remorse
  Voluntary compensation

CONSIDER YOUR SENTENCE

Endorse (5–10 points OR period of disqualification)
Compare it with the suggested guideline level of sentence and reconsider
your reasons carefully if you have chosen a sentence at a different level.
Consider a reduction for a timely guilty plea.

DECIDE YOUR SENTENCE

Fraudulent use etc.
Vehicle excise licence etc.

Vehicle Excise and Registration Act 1994 s.44
Triable either way – see Mode of Trial Guidelines
Penalty: Level 5

CONSIDER THE SERIOUSNESS OF THE OFFENCE

GUIDELINE: → IS DISCHARGE OR FINE APPROPRIATE?
IS IT SERIOUS ENOUGH FOR A COMMUNITY PENALTY?
(COMMUNITY REHABILITATION AND CURFEW ORDERS ARE THE ONLY
AVAILABLE COMMUNITY PENALTIES FOR THIS OFFENCE)
ARE YOUR SENTENCING POWERS SUFFICIENT?

THIS IS A GUIDELINE FOR A FIRST-TIME OFFENDER PLEADING NOT GUILTY

GUIDELINE FINE – STARTING POINT B

⊕ CONSIDER AGGRAVATING AND MITIGATING FACTORS ⊖
AND THE WEIGHT TO ATTACH TO EACH

for example
    Bought fraudulently
    Deliberately planned
    Disc forged or altered
    Long term defrauding
    LGV, HGV, PCV, PSV, taxi or private hire
      vehicle
    This list is not exhaustive

If offender is on bail, this offence is more serious
If offender has previous convictions, their relevance and any failure to respond to previous sentences should be considered – they may increase the seriousness. The court should make it clear, when passing sentence, that this was the approach adopted.

TAKE A PRELIMINARY VIEW OF SERIOUSNESS, THEN
CONSIDER OFFENDER MITIGATION

for example
    Co-operation with police
    Evidence of genuine remorse

CONSIDER YOUR SENTENCE

Compare it with the suggested guideline level of sentence and reconsider your reasons carefully if you have chosen a sentence at a different level. Consider a reduction for a timely guilty plea.

DECIDE YOUR SENTENCE

Road Traffic Act 1988 s.143 Triable only summarily Penalty: Level 5 Must endorse (6–8 points OR may disqualify)	No insurance

CONSIDER THE SERIOUSNESS OF THE OFFENCE

GUIDELINE: → IS DISCHARGE OR FINE APPROPRIATE?
IS IT SERIOUS ENOUGH FOR A COMMUNITY PENALTY?
(COMMUNITY REHABILITATION AND CURFEW ORDERS ARE THE ONLY
AVAILABLE COMMUNITY PENALTIES FOR THIS OFFENCE)

THIS IS A GUIDELINE FOR A FIRST-TIME OFFENDER PLEADING NOT GUILTY

GUIDELINE FINE – STARTING POINT B

➕ CONSIDER AGGRAVATING AND MITIGATING FACTORS ➖
AND THE WEIGHT TO ATTACH TO EACH

for example	for example
Defective vehicle	Accidental oversight
Deliberate driving without insurance	Genuine mistake
Driver has never passed a test	Responsibility for providing insurance
Gave false details	resting with another
LGV, HGV, PCV, PSV or taxi or private hire	– the parent/owner/lender/hirer
vehicle	Smaller vehicle, eg moped
No reference to insurance ever having been	*This list is not exhaustive*
held	
This list is not exhaustive	

If offender is on bail, this offence is more serious
If offender has previous convictions, their relevance and any failure to respond to previous
sentences should be considered – they may increase the seriousness. The court should make
it clear, when passing sentence, that this was the approach adopted.

TAKE A PRELIMINARY VIEW OF SERIOUSNESS, THEN
CONSIDER OFFENDER MITIGATION

for example
Difficult domestic circumstances
Evidence of genuine remorse

CONSIDER YOUR SENTENCE

Endorse licence.
Consider the option of a short period of disqualification
where there are aggravating factors.
Compare your decision with the suggested guideline level of sentence and reconsider
your reasons carefully if you have chosen a sentence at a different level.
Consider a reduction for a timely guilty plea.

DECIDE YOUR SENTENCE

Refuse evidential specimen (Drive or attempt to drive)

Road Traffic Act 1988 s.7(6)
Penalty: Level 5 and/or 6 months:
Triable only summarily
Must endorse and disqualify at least 12 months:
disqualify at least 36 months for a further
offence within 10 years

CONSIDER THE SERIOUSNESS OF THE OFFENCE

IS DISCHARGE OR FINE APPROPRIATE?
GUIDELINE: → IS IT SERIOUS ENOUGH FOR A COMMUNITY PENALTY?
IS IT SO SERIOUS THAT ONLY CUSTODY IS APPROPRIATE?

THIS IS A GUIDELINE FOR A FIRST-TIME OFFENDER PLEADING NOT GUILTY

➕ CONSIDER AGGRAVATING AND MITIGATING FACTORS AND THE WEIGHT TO ATTACH TO EACH ➖

for example	for example
Ability to drive seriously impaired	Not the driver
Caused injury/fear/damage	
Evidence of nature of the driving	
Police pursuit	
Type of vehicle, eg carrying passengers for reward/large goods vehicle	
This list is not exhaustive	

If offender is on bail, this offence is more serious
If offender has previous convictions, their relevance and any failure to respond to previous sentences should be considered – they may increase the seriousness. The court should make it clear, when passing sentence, that this was the approach adopted.

TAKE A PRELIMINARY VIEW OF SERIOUSNESS, THEN CONSIDER OFFENDER MITIGATION

for example
Evidence of genuine remorse
Voluntary completion of alcohol impaired driver course (if available)

CONSIDER YOUR SENTENCE

Offer a rehabilitation course.
Endorse licence. DISQUALIFY – a minimum period of 24 months is suggested.
Examine carefully aggravating/mitigating factors disclosed – do these justify any variation in period of disqualification suggested? If substantial aggravating factors, consider higher fine/community penalty/custody
Compare it with the suggested guideline level of sentence and reconsider your reasons carefully if you have chosen a sentence at a different level.
Consider a reduction for a timely guilty plea.

DECIDE YOUR SENTENCE

| Road Traffic Act 1984 s.89(10)
Triable only summarily
Penalty: Level 3 (Level 4 if motorway)
Must endorse (3–6 points OR may disqualify) | **Speeding** |

CONSIDER THE SERIOUSNESS OF THE OFFENCE

GUIDELINE: → IS DISCHARGE OR FINE APPROPRIATE?
(COMMUNITY REHABILITATION AND CURFEW ORDERS ARE THE ONLY
AVAILABLE COMMUNITY PENALTIES FOR THIS OFFENCE)

THIS IS A GUIDELINE FOR A FIRST-TIME OFFENDER PLEADING NOT GUILTY

➕ CONSIDER AGGRAVATING AND MITIGATING FACTORS AND THE WEIGHT TO ATTACH TO EACH ➖

for example	for example
LGV, HGV, PCV or taxi or private-hire vehicles Location/time of day/visibility Serious risk Towing caravan/trailer *This list is not exhaustive*	Emergency established *This list is not exhaustive*

If offender is on bail, this offence is more serious
If offender has previous convictions, their relevance and any failure to respond to previous sentences should be considered – they may increase the seriousness. The court should make it clear, when passing sentence, that this was the approach adopted.

GUIDELINE PENALTY POINTS	LEGAL SPEED LIMITS	EXCESS SPEED – MPH	FINE
3	20–30 mph 40–50 mph 60–70 mph	Up to 10 mph Up to 15 mph Up to 20 mph	A
4 or 5 OR disqualify up to 42 days	20–30 mph 40–50 mph 60–70 mph	From 11–20 mph From 16–25 mph From 21–30 mph	B
6 OR disqualify up to 56 days	20–30 mph 40–50 mph 60–70 mph	From 21–30 mph From 26–35 mph From 31–40 mph	B

TAKE A PRELIMINARY VIEW OF SERIOUSNESS, THEN CONSIDER OFFENDER MITIGATION

for example
Co-operation with police
Fixed penalty not taken up for valid reason

CONSIDER YOUR SENTENCE

Endorse (3–6 points OR period of disqualification. If a new driver accumulates 6 points this will result in automatic revocation of the licence by the DVLA.)
Consider other measures (including disqualification until test passed if appropriate).
Compare it with the suggested guideline level of sentence and reconsider your reasons carefully if you have chosen a sentence at a different level.
Consider a reduction for a timely guilty plea.

DECIDE YOUR SENTENCE

Offences considered appropriate for guideline of discharge or fine, other than in exceptional circumstances

	PENALTY POINTS	MAXIMUM PENALTY	GUIDELINE FINE
ALCOHOL/DRUGS			
In charge over excess alcohol limit OR in charge whilst unfit through drink/drugs or refusing evidential specimen *Consider disqualification.*	10*	Level 4 and/or 3 months E	C
Refusing roadside breath test	4	Level 3 E	A
DRIVER			
Not supplying details *If company-owned, use higher fine when unable to apply endorsement as a minimum*	3*	Level 3 E	C
LICENCE OFFENCES			
† No driving licence, where could be covered, eg if licence not renewed, but would have covered class of vehicle driven, or holder of full licence has lost or misplaced it	–	Level 3	A
† Driving not in accordance with provisional licence (includes where no licence ever held)	3–6	Level 3 E	A
† No excise licence	–	Level 3 or 5 times annual duty (whichever greater)	Actual duty lost plus penalty of Guideline Fine – Starting Point A (1–3 months unpaid duty), B (4–6 months), C (7–12 months) consider a maximum of twice the annual duty
LIGHTS – Driving without	–	Level 3	A
OWNERSHIP – Not notifying DVLA of change etc.		Level 3	A
PARKING OFFENCES			
† Dangerous position	3	Level 3 E	A
† Pelican/zebra crossing	3	Level 3 E	A
TEST CERTIFICATE – Not held	–	Level 3	A
TRAFFIC DIRECTION OFFENCES			
† Fail to comply with height restriction	3	Level 3 E	A
† Fail to comply with red traffic light	3	Level 3 E	A
† Fail to comply with no entry sign	3	Level 3 E	A
† Fail to comply with stop sign/double white lines	3	Level 3 E	A
† Fail to give precedence – pelican/zebra crossing	3	Level 3 E	A

E: Must ENDORSE (unless special reasons) and may disqualify

Offences considered appropriate for guideline of discharge or fine, other than in exceptional circumstances – contd.			
	PENALTY POINTS	**MAXIMUM PENALTY**	**GUIDELINE FINE**
TRAFFIC OR POLICE SIGNS (non endorsable)			
† Fail to comply	–	3	A

† *These offences are eligible for fixed penalty offer. Where there is a valid reason why the case could not be dealt with by fixed penalty (eg holder of a non-uk driving licence, licence at DVLA for change of details etc), impose a fine equivalent to fixed penalty, endorse licence as appropriate and do not order costs.*

In all cases, **consider the safety factor, damage to roads, commercial gain** *and, if driver is not the owner, with whom prime responsibility should lie.*

VEHICLE DEFECTS UP TO AND INCLUDING 3.5 TONNES GROSS VEHICLE WEIGHT			
DEFECTS			
† Brakes/Steering/Tyres (each)	3	Level 4 E	A
† Loss of wheel	3	Level 4 E	A
† Exhaust emission	–	Level 3	A
† Other offences	–	Level 3	A
LOADS			
† Condition of vehicle/accessories/equipment	3	Level 4 E	A
† Purpose of use/passenger numbers/how carried	3	Level 4 E	A
† Weight, position or distribution of load	3	Level 4 E	A
† Insecure load	3	Level 3	A
† Overloading or exceeding maximum axle weight	–	Level 5	A* Plus increase in proportion to percentage of overloading
* Examine carefully evidence of responsibility for overload and, if commercial gain relates to owner, increase the fine.			

† *These offences are eligible for fixed penalty offer. Where there is a valid reason why the case could not be dealt with by fixed penalty (eg holder of a non-uk driving licence, licence at DVLA for change of details etc), impose a fine equivalent to fixed penalty, endorse licence as appropriate and do not order costs.*

In all cases, **consider the safety factor, damage to roads, commercial gain** *and, if driver is not the owner, with whom prime responsibility should lie.*

E: Must ENDORSE (unless special reasons) and may disqualify

Motorway Offences			
	PENALTY POINTS	MAXIMUM PENALTY	GUIDELINE FINE
DRIVING (Consider disqualification)			
† Driving in reverse on motorway	3	Level 4 E	B
† Driving in reverse on sliproad	3	Level 4 E	A
† Driving in wrong direction on motorway	3	Level 4 E	B
† Driving in wrong direction on sliproad	3	Level 4 E	A
† Driving off carriageway – central reservation	3	Level 4 E	A
† Driving off carriageway – hard shoulder	3	Level 4 E	A
† Driving on sliproad against no entry sign	3	Level 4 E	A
† Making U-Turn	3	Level 4 E	A
LEARNERS			
† Learner driver or excluded vehicle	3	Level 4 E	A
STOPPING			
† Stopping on hard shoulder of motorway	–	Level 4	A
† Stopping on hard shoulder of sliproad	–	Level 4	A
PROHIBITED LANE			
† Vehicle over 7.5 tonnes or drawing trailer, or prohibited PSV	3	Level 4 E	A
WALKING			
† Walking on motorway or sliproad	–	Level 4	A
† Walking on hard shoulder or verge	–	Level 4	A

† *These offences are eligible for fixed penalty offer. Where there is a valid reason why the case could not be dealt with by fixed penalty (eg holder of a non-uk driving licence, licence at DVLA for change of details etc), impose a fine equivalent to fixed penalty, endorse licence as appropriate and do not order costs.*

*In all cases, **consider the safety factor, damage to roads, commercial gain** and, if driver is not the owner, with whom prime responsibility should lie.*

Offences relating to buses and goods vehicles over 3.5 tonnes gross vehicle weight (GVW)				
	PENALTY POINTS	**MAXIMUM PENALTY**	**OWNER/ OPERATOR****	**DRIVER**
DEFECTS				
Brakes	3	Level 5 E	C	B
Steering	3	Level 5 E	C	B
Tyres (per tyre)	3	Level 5 E	C	B
Loss of wheel	3	Level 5 E	C	B
Exhaust emission	–	Level 4	C	B
Other offences	–	Level 4	C	B
LOADS				
Condition of vehicle/accessories/equipment	3	Level 5 E	C	B
Purpose of use/number of passengers/how carried	3	Level 5 E	C	B
Weight position or distribution of load	3	Level 5 E	C	B
Insecure load	3	Level 4	C	B
Overloading or exceeding maximum axle weight	–	Level 5	C* *Plus increase in proportion to percentage of overloading	B*
OPERATORS LICENCE				
Not held	–	Level 4	C	B
TACHOGRAPH				
Not properly used	–	Level 5	C	B
Falsification/fraudulent use	–	Level 5	C	B
SPEED LIMITERS – WHERE APPLICABLE				
Not being used or incorrectly calibrated	–	Level 5	C	B
** For an owner/operator, take net turnover into account as appropriate				

E: Must ENDORSE (unless special reasons) and may disqualify

INDEX

Printed in the United Kingdom
by Lightning Source UK Ltd.
114205UKS00001B/19

9 781858 113166